AMERICA's RENEWABLE RESOURCES

Historical Trends and Current Challenges

AMERICA's RENEWABLE RESOURCES

Historical Trends and Current Challenges

Kenneth D. Frederick and Roger A. Sedjo, editors

Resources for the Future
Washington, D.C.

Cloth: 0-915707-60-8/91 $1.00 + .10
Paper: 0-915707-61-6/91 $1.00 + .10

Printed in the United States of America

Published by Resources for the Future
1616 P Street, N.W., Washington, D.C. 20036

Excerpts in chapter 2, unless otherwise attributed, are from CADILLAC DESERT by Marc P. Reisner. Copyright © 1986 by Marc P. Reisner. Used by permission of Viking Penguin, a division of Penguin Books USA Inc.

Library of Congress Cataloging-in-Publication Data

America's renewable resources : historical trends and current
　　challenges / Kenneth D. Frederick and Roger A. Sedjo, editors.
　　　　p.　　cm.
　　Includes bibliographical references and index.
　　ISBN 0-915707-60-8 (cloth). — ISBN 0-915707-61-6 (paper).
　　1. Renewable natural resources—United States—Management.
　　2. Renewable natural resources—Government policy—United States.
　　I. Frederick. Kenneth D.   II. Sedjo, Roger A.
　　HC103.7.A77　　1991
　　333.7'0973—dc20　　　　　　　　　　　　　　　　　91-23102
　　　　　　　　　　　　　　　　　　　　　　　　　　　　CIP

This book is the product of the Energy and Natural Resources Division, Douglas R. Bohi, director, at Resources for the Future. The project editor for the book was Samuel Allen; it was designed by Brigitte Coulton and indexed by Julie Phillips. The cover was designed by Gehle Design Associates.

RESOURCES FOR THE FUTURE (RFF) is an independent nonprofit organization that advances research and public education in the development, conservation, and use of natural resources and in the quality of the environment. Established in 1952 with the cooperation of the Ford Foundation, it is supported by an endowment and by grants from foundations, government agencies, corporations, and individuals. Grants are accepted on the condition that RFF is solely responsible for the conduct of its research and the dissemination of its work to the public. The organization does not perform proprietary research.

RFF research is primarily social scientific, especially economic. It is concerned with the relationship of people to the natural environmental resources of land, water, and air; with the products and services derived from these basic resources; and with the effects of production and consumption on environmental quality and on human health and well-being. Grouped into four units—the Energy and Natural Resources Division, the Quality of the Environment Division, the National Center for Food and Agricultural Policy, and the Center for Risk Management—staff members pursue a wide variety of interests, including forest economics, natural gas policy, multiple use of public lands, mineral economics, air and water pollution, energy and national security, hazardous wastes, the economics of outer space, climate resources, and quantitative risk assessment. Resident staff members conduct most of the organization's work; a few others carry out research elsewhere under grants from RFF.

Resources for the Future takes responsibility for the selection of subjects for study and for the appointment of fellows, as well as for their freedom of inquiry. The views of RFF staff members and the interpretation and conclusions of RFF publications should not be attributed to Resources for the Future, its directors, or its officers. As an organization, RFF does not take positions on laws, policies, or events, nor does it lobby.

Contents

1

Overview: Renewable Resource Trends   **1**

Kenneth D. Frederick and Roger A. Sedjo

2

Water Resources: Increasing Demand and Scarce Supplies   **23**

Kenneth D. Frederick

3

Forest Resources: Resilient and Serviceable   81

Roger A. Sedjo

4

Rangeland Resources: Changing Uses and Productivity   123

B. Delworth Gardner

5

Cropland and Soils: Past Performance and Policy Challenges   **169**

Pierre R. Crosson

6

Wildlife: Severe Decline and Partial Recovery   **205**

Winston Harrington

7

The Growing Role of Outdoor Recreation   **249**

Marion Clawson and Winston Harrington

Tables

Figures

Preface

Sustainability is a popular catchword these days, used in policy debates to focus attention on the question of what will happen to the future quality of the resource base and its ability to support economic growth. Continued growth of the population and of per capita consumption of the world's resources makes the concept of sustainability increasingly attractive as a guide for future development policies, and increasingly contentious as an issue in debates between pro-development and anti-development forces.

Responsibility for understanding the effects of development on the nation's renewable resources falls to the U.S. Department of Agriculture, as provided by the terms of the Renewable Resources Planning Act of 1974 (RPA) and the Resources Conservation Act of 1977 (RCA). The RPA requires "an analysis of the present and anticipated uses, demand for, and supply of the renewable resources of forest, range, and other associated lands" every ten years, while the RCA requires "a continuing appraisal of the soil, water, and related resources of the Nation . . . including fish and wildlife habitat."

In contrast to the future orientation of these acts, this book provides a historical examination of the use and management of the nation's water, forest, rangeland, soil and cropland, and wildlife resources. For each of these renewable resources, the book describes in sweeping terms how the quantity and quality of the resource base has changed over the last century, and how the management of these resources has contributed to the changes. As such, it is a record of one country's experience with the ingredients of sustainability that will be instructive in managing future demands on the resource base, in the United States as well as in other parts of the world.

By limiting its attention to renewable resources, moreover, the book concentrates on that part of the resource base that is most amenable to sustainability. Renewability suggests that the resources under consideration have a natural capacity to replace themselves, although the time frame in some cases can be very long, so that one can naturally think in terms of a balance in the use of these resources that will maintain their continued productivity. Finding that balance is critical to sustainable development, particularly when considering the potential of the resources to provide for multiple uses.

This book also demonstrates the importance of social institutions to the proper management of the nation's resources. Sustainability is not possible without management, and management is not possible without a compatible set of institutions that establish the economic incentives for producing or conserving resources and that impose a set of constraints on these activities. The fact that many of these resources are known as common property resources, which otherwise tend to be available for taking on a first-come-first-served basis, heightens the importance of establishing institutions that will lead to the socially optimal resource development.

The authors are Professor Delworth Gardner of Brigham Young University, an expert on rangeland resources whose participation rounded out the coverage of resources, and five senior researchers on the staff of Resources for the Future (RFF). They are all well-established experts in their respective fields, each with a long history of research and publication on a specific renewable resource. This book is, therefore, a natural outgrowth of their research, and of RFF's research on natural resource management policies and practices and their benefits and costs.

From its beginnings nearly forty years ago, Resources for the Future has recognized that natural resources not only provide raw materials for industrial and agricultural production but also contribute to the quality of life and the environment. Founded as a nonadvocacy organization independent of commercial, government, and conservation interests, RFF has long focused research on the use and abuse of natural resources and the environment. RFF has played a key role in the creation of natural resource economics and in developing methods for assessing the amenity values of those resources. Much of its research has been made available through RFF books; this book joins a long list of titles that also go back to RFF's beginnings.

It is not often enough that researchers get an opportunity to collaborate on a comprehensive study of this kind. This volume owes its origin to George S. Dunlop, then assistant secretary of agriculture for natural resources and environment, and his deputy Douglas MacCleery, who believed that much can be learned about the current status and likely future problems of the nation's renewable resources through a better understanding of past changes in the quality,

use, and management of these resources. Thus RFF gratefully acknowledges the financial and intellectual support of the United States Department of Agriculture (USDA) in the production of this volume. In particular, John Fedkiw of the USDA has been a strong supporter, a source of information, and a constructive critic throughout. In a sense, this volume represents an extension of Fedkiw's historical analysis ("The Evolving Use and Management of the Nation's Forests, Grasslands, Croplands and Related Resources") prepared for the 1989 RPA assessment.

Jeff Sirmon and James McDivitt of the USDA Forest Service facilitated the funding and the department's early review of the manuscript. In addition to that provided by the Forest Service, financial support was provided by the U.S. Department of Agriculture's Economic Research Service, Soil Conservation Service, Extension Service, and Office of Budget and Program Analysis. Further support for this project was provided by The General Service Foundation.

Ken Frederick and Roger Sedjo also wish to thank Resources for the Future for providing an ideal environment for the research and writing, as well as for major financial, administrative, and production support. Bob Fri, former RFF vice president John Ahearne, Paul Portney, and Ted Hand provided administrative support and encouragement. Rich Getrich, Sam Allen, and Brigitte Coulton helped improve the quality and presentation of the manuscript. Debbie Hemphill and Vivian Papsdorf assisted with the typing.

Each of the chapters was reviewed by a number of experts on the particular resource discussed. The valuable contributions of reviewers and others are noted in the acknowledgments at the end of individual chapters. Paul Portney, chairman of the RFF Publications Committee, and three anonymous committee reviewers provided constructive comments on the entire manuscript.

Douglas R. Bohi
Director and Senior Fellow
Energy and Natural Resources Division
April 1991 Resources for the Future

1

Overview:
Renewable Resource Trends

Kenneth D. Frederick and Roger A. Sedjo

This book focuses on understanding the long-term historical trends in the condition and capability of the renewable resources of the United States. The historical approach is based on a belief that much can be learned about the current status and likely future problems of the nation's renewable resources through a better understanding of past changes in the condition, use, and management of the resources. The following chapters examine past trends in the use and management of the nation's water, forest, rangeland, soil and cropland, and wildlife resources, as well as the consequences not only for the resources but for the nation. Current resource conditions are also examined. The final chapter reviews trends in outdoor recreation, an activity that is placing increasing demands on and altering the use of these resources. The capacity to meet the growing demands for outdoor recreation depends in part on the abundance and health of our renewable resources.

Each chapter describes the condition of the resource before any sizable human use or influence, beginning with a look at resource use some two hundred years ago when society's demands on the resources were relatively small. The authors then trace the use and management of the resources and the influence of changing demands, technologies, management systems, policies, and institutions on those resources. Within each chapter the resource study is divided into periods selected to emphasize important historical changes in resource use and management.

This overview briefly reviews past trends in resource use, then examines the renewability of each of the resources focused on in this book, with particular attention being given to the renewability of the resource under natural conditions and its response to human use and abuse. The ability to increase the long-term benefits people have derived from these resources through improved management is considered. Then follow a survey of the six chapters on specific resources and a discussion of common themes and lessons contained in these chapters. Those lessons concern the interdependencies among the resources over time, the role of technology both in contributing to the depletion of and in responding to resource scarcity, and the institutions affecting the use and condition of resources. The overview concludes with thoughts on the adequacy of these resources to meet the demands placed on them over time and the differences between past and future challenges in using and managing renewable resources to respond effectively to society's long-term needs.

Review of Past Trends

The natural resources of the New World must have appeared virtually limitless to European immigrants arriving two hundred or more years ago. The subsistence farming and hunting of the 1 million to 2 million Native Americans then living in the area that now constitutes the contiguous forty-eight states had done little to disrupt the area's rich natural heritage of water, forest, range, and wildlife (Fedkiw, 1989). The area's material resources were still enormous relative to the demands placed on them at the beginning of the nineteenth century. Precipitation was sufficient to support abundant vegetation over about two-thirds of the land;

Well before the end of the nineteenth century people forecast an impending timber famine and expressed concern over the loss of wildlife habitat.

dense forests covered most of the eastern one-third and grasses dominated the vegetation of the middle third. Farther west, precipitation declined and vegetation became more sparse and, except in the Northwest, eventually gave way to desert. The abundant wildlife that populated much of the area provided food and other valued products. These resources were available for the taking and use of those who were determined, clever, and strong enough to capture them. Indeed, the early settlers had no choice but to use the New World's natural resources for food and shelter.

Initially, human influences on and uses of the resources were small and posed little threat to their ability to sustain those uses. Gradually, the small, largely self-sufficient European settlements were replaced by bustling commercial centers that depended on the agricultural and forestry products of the interior. Wildlife provided furs, hides, and meat; timber provided both the most common building material and the principal fuel source during the eighteenth and much of the nineteenth centuries.

With the growth of the population and economy, land-hungry pioneers and entrepreneurs pushed the frontier west. Settlers harvested forests and wildlife for the products they provided, and sometimes cut and burned forests because these were commonly perceived to be obstacles to settlement and agricultural development. Large areas of forest were gradually converted to cropland and pasture for domestic livestock grazing. By 1850, 76 million acres, largely carved out of what had once been part of the vast forest covering the eastern United States, were in crops. The biggest changes were still to come as cropland acreage increased more than fourfold over the next seven decades (Fedkiw, 1989). By 1920, about 384 million acres or 40 percent of the indigenous forest and the attendant wildlife habitat had been cleared. Conversion of the forest was so rapid that well before the end of the nineteenth century people forecast an impending timber famine and expressed concern over the loss of wildlife habitat.

These were only the first of many such forecasts of resource scarcity. The loss of forest cover and native range vegetation, along with farming practices that failed to protect the soil, contributed to widespread erosion. The effects of erosion on the productivity of the nation's cropland became a national concern during the Dust Bowl period of the 1930s. Erosion, together with the loss of cropland to urban and other uses, continues to underlie doubts about the adequacy of the nation's agricultural land to meet long-term demands for food and fiber. Whenever harvests decline and real crop prices rise, concerns about agricultural production capacity reemerge in the headlines.

Much of the western range has little if any cropping potential in the absence of irrigation, and supports only limited grazing on a sustainable basis. Indeed, the capacity of some of this land to support livestock over the long term has been a matter of some concern. By 1890, grazing on western rangeland had exceeded levels that could be supported under drought conditions. Continuing drought and intensification of range use led to a deterioration in the quality of large areas and reports of irreversible degradation around the turn of the twentieth century.

All regions must deal with temporal variations in water supplies, and U.S. history is filled with instances in which drought has produced regional shortages. However, concerns of a national water problem have surfaced only in recent decades. Many of the nation's

Virgin rangeland, Apache National Forest, Arizona

U.S. Forest Service

surface waters became too polluted to support fishing and swimming by the mid-1960s. More recently, widespread droughts, fears of contaminated supplies, and the dependence of some communities on declining groundwater stocks have made the availability of high-quality water one of the nation's principal resource concerns.

Popular perceptions of the adequacy of the nation's natural resources tend to be strongly influenced by relatively short-term events and conditions. Media reports of crop failures, droughts, or other resource problems are likely to be accompanied by forecasts of dire future events. For instance, one widely read and cited book described the 1972 and 1974 crop failures as representing a fundamental shift from a world characterized by surpluses and declining crop prices to one of chronic shortages and sharply rising prices (Brown with Eckholm, 1974). Similarly, the 1980 and 1981 drought that affected large areas of the United States prompted numerous reports that the nation was on the verge of running out of water and had little time for remedies (for examples, see *Newsweek*, February 23, 1981, and *U.S. News and World Report*, June 29, 1981).

Differentiating between long-term trends driven by fundamental conditions and largely ephemeral events that place a nation's food, timber, or water resources under stress is not an easy task. This distinction, however, is important to the formulation of good resource policy. Understanding past trends in the condition and use of the resources and how society has responded to prior resource stress is an important step in making that distinction.

The Renewability of Resources

The resources examined in this book are all renewable to some extent. Renewability suggests a capacity for natural restoration following consumption or use. There are major differences, however, in the time and circumstances under which these resources are renewed. Although most of the resource systems are robust, having withstood disruptions and challenges over eons, they are not indestructible. Renewal may be difficult, slow, and halting. This is more likely

to be the case when the disturbance is severe and unusual, but some natural systems are more fragile than others. In extreme cases, a system may be so disturbed as to preclude near-term renewability.

Important dimensions of renewability are the vulnerability of the resource to deterioration, especially to the point that natural restoration is impossible or unlikely except over long periods; the time over which the resource will naturally be restored after a disruption; and the responsiveness of the resource and its potential for restoration through management. Characterizing resources according to these dimensions is difficult because the renewability of a given resource varies widely depending on a variety of factors. For instance, surface water is generally more readily renewed than groundwater, and the renewability of forests, grassland, and cropland depends greatly on soil and water conditions.

Water is among the more renewable resources: humans have no significant impact on the amount of water in the hydrologic system, the resource can be used and reused indefinitely, and even the impurities are removed through the evaporative process. The next rainfall may be sufficient to renew some supplies. On the other hand, it may take years or decades to restore the quality of a polluted lake and even centuries for natural processes to replenish water withdrawn from confined aquifers.

Soil generation is also a variable process, the rate of renewability depending on the nature of the underlying material, vegetative cover, and other factors. Mineral soils are formed over geologic periods as rock is gradually broken down into small fragments through weathering and the resulting parent material develops into soil horizons through natural processes. Yet, under favorable circumstances, soil conditions can improve from one cropping season to another through the addition of organic matter, which is formed in the soil as plant and animal residues are decomposed by microbial activity. Badly eroded soils on hilly landscapes, on the other hand, may be unable to sustain the vegetation required to prevent further erosion and restore the soil base without special efforts to improve nutrients and stabilize the slopes.

The vegetative systems of forests and grassland have the capacity to reestablish themselves after destruction resulting from fire, pests, logging, or grazing. In fact, forests and grassland are parts of complex ecosystems for which destruction and restoration are components of a continuing natural cycle. Conver-

Increased understanding of the resource systems and improved management practices have tended to increase the productivity of the natural systems to meet the demands of the American people.

sion to cropland has been the principal cause of the reduction of the natural forest or grass cover in the United States. Cropland has varying capacities to revert to its former status when withdrawn from cultivation. Vast areas in the humid East reverted naturally to forests within a few years after they were abandoned for agricultural purposes. In the arid and semiarid West, however, the fate of abandoned cropland can be problematic in the absence of human efforts to provide a vegetative cover to stabilize the soils. Under exceptionally favorable conditions, a cover of grass may be restored within a season or two. Under less favorable conditions, wind and water erosion may further undermine the condition of abandoned cropland.

Wildlife populations generally renew themselves in a seemingly unending cycle, one generation being replaced by the next as long as their habitat remains relatively undisturbed. The ability to adjust to major changes in habitat conditions varies widely among species, and the local loss of some species has been a common result of the conversion of forests, wetlands, and other wildlife habitat to other uses over the past two centuries. In some cases, abrupt changes of habitat have threatened, and occasionally resulted in, global species extinctions, as happened with the dusky seaside sparrow.

Renewable resources have characteristics of both stocks and flows. At any point in time there is a stock that exists as a result of all former flows. Groundwater and surface water reservoirs and the existing forests, grasses, and wildlife populations represent resource stocks that can be consumed, managed, or left entirely to natural processes. The natural processes typically result in resource flows. At any time such processes operate simultaneously to reduce and increase resource stocks. Evaporation reduces and precipitation increases water stocks, and even as tree mortality or soil erosion are occurring, natural processes are simultaneously generating new growth in the forest and new soil formation on the land.

Increasingly over the past two centuries, the stocks and flows of these resources have been determined by the use and the management imposed by a growing human population and a developing economy. On the one hand, this use has sometimes depleted local stocks or adversely altered the natural ability of the resources to renew themselves. In many cases, the user intended to reduce local renewability, as in the conversion of a forest to crops. On the other hand, increased understanding of the resource systems and improved management practices have tended to increase the productivity of the natural systems to meet the demands of the American people.

Resource sustainability requires a long-term balance between renewability and use that ensures the continuing productivity of the resource. Resource systems are often out of balance in the short run. For example, growth tends to exceed mortality in young forests, and old forests ultimately decline as a result of insects, disease, or fire. Only in a mature forest are growth and mortality roughly in balance, and this balance is readily broken by human interference such as logging or natural events such as wildfire. However, it is the long-term relation between growth and loss that determines sustainability.

Sustainable management implies using resource flows from existing stocks without seriously compromising the renewability of the resource for future use. Such management involves, in part, capturing the "losses" and mortality that would otherwise occur naturally. Grazing captures grasses for feed that might otherwise die and decompose as seasons change. Irrigation captures water for use that would otherwise evaporate or flow directly to the sea. Logging captures wood for human consumption that would eventually die and decay.

Prudent management and investments can increase the products that can be extracted from a

resource system on a sustainable basis far beyond naturally occurring resource flows. Management may assist the natural processes in maintaining grasslands through seeding. Water management may involve methods to enhance water collection or to direct or divert water flows to maintain or increase targeted beneficial human uses. Tree planting can accelerate the reestablishment of a forest after a harvest or a fire. In some cases, the productivity of the resource may be stimulated simply by reducing the stock. For instance, a mature forest with no net growth may become a net producer of timber after some of its existing stock is removed, thereby permitting faster growth of the remaining trees. More important, the knowledge and ability to manipulate resource systems, gained largely over the past century, have dramatically increased the capacity to

boost yields well beyond those that would occur naturally. Improved seed varieties and beneficial chemicals combined with proper management can increase nutrient supply and reduce natural pests to enable much higher crop, forest, and range yields. Greater understanding of hydrology, and investments in dams and reservoirs, have increased the capacity to reliably extract water from streams.

Management also can contribute to the recovery of a resource that has been subjected to excessive use or abuse. Logged-over forests and degraded rangeland can be replanted or protected so that recovery can occur naturally, locally extinct wildlife can be reintroduced where suitable habitat is available, and hunting restrictions can be enforced. Cropland fertility can be restored by planting legumes and by introducing chemical or natural nutrients. Numerous examples of the role of management in the recovery of natural systems are presented in this book.

Finally, management can provide protection to the resource from many natural and human-made dangers that reduce or dissipate the actual or potential productivity of the resource. The control of pests, diseases, and fire can protect agricultural and forestry harvests; erosion control systems can protect soils; grazing management can prevent destructive overgrazing; and habitat manipulation and hunting restrictions can encourage the growth of wildlife populations.

As is remarked in subsequent chapters, the balance between the pressures to deplete, protect, and renew the various resources has shifted over time in response to changing demands on the resource by a growing society and changing management practices. Although management is not always wise and beneficial, advances in understanding the underlying natural processes and in the technologies for management have greatly enhanced the potential productivity of our renewable natural resources on a sustainable basis.

Survey of the Chapters

Regional differences in precipitation are a principal determinant of how land has been and can be used practically. Without water, land will not support crops, grazing, forests, or wildlife. In chapter 2, Kenneth Frederick describes how the nation's general economic development during the nineteenth century was shaped largely by the natural (in contrast to the managed) availability of water. Canals, most of which were constructed before 1850, were the principal water projects undertaken during that time. The nation's rivers and harbors helped shape exploration, trade, and the location of major cities; at the same time, precipitation patterns influenced agricultural expansion.

Technological advances early in the twentieth century brought major changes in the uses of and benefits derived from the nation's water resources. Improved water treatment technology virtually eliminated the deadly diseases associated with contaminated water supplies. Advances in water-construction technology, which had changed little from the achievements of the Romans two thousand years earlier and the Dutch several hundred years earlier, facilitated a radical transformation of the nation's plumbing. More than 60,000 dams, with a storage capacity of about 860 million acre-feet (280 trillion gallons), were constructed between 1900 and 1982. Consequently, streams that once were unreliable sources of supply and occasional sources of floods were controlled to provide reliable water supplies for homes, factories, farms, power production, recreation, and other uses. Improvements in pumping technology during the 1930s made it practical to irrigate with water pumped from hundreds of feet below the surface. Water withdrawn from surface and groundwater sources increased more than tenfold in eight decades, to 440 billion gallons per day by 1980.

However, these developments involved important and often unforeseen tradeoffs. Increased control and use of the rivers often have come at the expense of the values provided by free-flowing streams. The combined economic and environmental costs of developing new supplies have increased markedly and continue to rise. Water quality deteriorated badly up through the 1960s as many of the wastes of an expanding and increasingly industrialized economy were ultimately disposed of through the nation's rivers, lakes, and groundwaters. Since then, the nation has spent tens of billions of dollars to improve surface-water quality. Although water quality has generally improved, many pollutants still end up in groundwater and surface-water supplies. Nonpoint sources such as runoff from farms and urban areas are now the principal sources of pollutants in the nation's waters, and these sources are proving difficult to control.

According to Frederick, the good news is that the United States has sufficient water to meet foreseeable demands that are appropriately constrained by price. The bad news is that the institutions required to encourage conservation, protect aquatic ecosystems, and transfer supplies efficiently among uses in response to changing supply conditions and growing demand are still lacking.

Just as water resources influenced the lives of the European settlers, so too did forest resources. The forests that covered most of the eastern United States in 1800 provided settlers with fuelwood, timber, meat, and furs. However, the forests also were an impediment to farming. In chapter 3, Roger Sedjo describes how the demand for agricultural land, fuelwood, and timber led to the clearing of about 384 million acres of forest by 1920, 270 million of which were cleared after 1850. Developments such as the railroad—which consumed large volumes of timber for construction and of fuelwood for steam power—increased the demand for wood, and improvements in logging and in log transportation facilitated the pace of deforestation. Despite the enormous cutting, the real price of lumber rose more than eightfold between 1800 and 1920 as available supplies became farther removed from the population centers. Yet, prices were not high enough to economically justify even minimal forestry management under pre-1920 conditions.

Sedjo argues that 1920 marks the nadir in the condition of the nation's forests. Declining pressure to clear land for agriculture (examined by Pierre Crosson in chapter 5) was the principal cause of the subsequent improvement. Other factors contributing to improvements in the nation's forest inventories include the control of forest fire achieved after 1945, a moderation in the growth of demand for industrial wood, a decline in the demand for fuelwood, technology that allows a more useful product from a given harvest, and a combination of higher timber prices and improved management practices that make forest management profitable. Consequently, the nation's forests, by many criteria, are now in their best condition since the beginning of the twentieth century.

Nevertheless, as the earlier problems diminished new conflicts emerged. The clash between timber and

The harvesting of forests initiates processes that release carbon to the atmosphere, and forest growth captures it. Larger forest inventories constitute larger sinks for carbon.

environmental benefits has intensified in recent years and taken on a new focus: the preservation of old-growth forests and concerns for the viability of threatened and endangered species and for maintaining biodiversity. Although there is potentially considerable economically available timber in the United States, removal of large areas of mature forest from the timber base reduces timber production in some regions. In addition, the emergence of concerns about a global warming induced by rising atmospheric levels of carbon dioxide and other radiatively active gases has focused attention on the role of forests in the global environment. The harvesting of forests initiates processes that release carbon to the atmosphere, and forest growth captures it. Larger forest inventories constitute larger sinks for carbon.

In chapter 4, Delworth Gardner describes the impacts on the nation's rangeland as settlers pushed relentlessly westward in the second half of the nineteenth century. Rangeland declined by 43 million acres during the 1880s as the numbers of cattle and sheep grazing on such land expanded rapidly. Although national policy during this period encouraged the transfer of public land to private ownership, most of the western range remained in the public domain, where open access to the forage contributed to its overuse. A combination of uncontrolled grazing and drought, particularly in the Southwest, resulted in widespread devastation of the ranges and culminated in huge livestock losses during the hard winters in the 1880s. The degradation led to demands for government controls, which began to be realized in the 1890s when restrictions were imposed on grazing on newly created public forest reserves. Federal control over grazing on the public domain was extended to the remaining unreserved rangeland by the Taylor Grazing Act of 1934.

The continued conversion of rangeland to crop production was primarily responsible for a 184-million acre reduction in rangeland between 1890 and 1930. This decline was temporarily reversed during the Great Depression, but resumed again in the 1940s. Rangeland fell steadily from 723 million acres in 1940 to a low of 659 million acres in 1982. The slow decline since 1940 has been largely the result of conversion of range to urban uses. Gardner's assessment of range condition is cautious because the available data are poor. It appears that conditions generally are slowly improving in the absence of extended drought, and that, overall, the range is probably in better shape

Tree planting, Klamath National Forest, California

now than at any time in the twentieth century. Range condition continues to be far below its biological potential, however. Technology exists for improving rangeland, but the economics are questionable.

Moreover, the issue of public versus private ownership of the western range remains contentious even though it was supposedly resolved in favor of the government by the Federal Land Policy and Management Act of 1976. This act formally requires the Bureau of Land Management (BLM) to manage the public domain under the principles of multiple use and sustained yield. Gardner concludes that BLM grazing controls have probably remedied the "common property" problems associated with open access and uncontrolled grazing. He suggests, however, that market allocations of grazing permits are needed to distribute the allowable quantity of forage to the most efficient ranchers. The allocation of the range for grazing as opposed to preserving it for wildlife or recreation has become increasingly contentious in recent years and is likely to remain so for the foreseeable future.

Most of the land that was taken out of forests, pasture, and range from the beginning of the nineteenth century to the 1930s was converted into crop production. In chapter 5, Pierre Crosson shows that the increases in the nation's cropland over this period reflected two underlying factors. One was the growth of demand for crops, spurred by growth in both population and per capita income in the United States and abroad. The other factor was the relatively high cost of labor relative to land, which induced manufacturers to develop and farmers to adopt land-using, labor-saving machinery and equipment for harvesting, threshing, and other farm operations. The gasoline-powered tractor was coming into wide use during the early decades of the twentieth century, boosting labor productivity and freeing tens of millions of acres previously used to grow feed for draft animals for other uses. As a consequence of the emphasis on land-using technologies, almost 98 percent of the increase in crop output from 1880 to 1940 was attributable to the expansion of the land devoted to crop production.

Beginning in the 1930s, crop yields, which had not increased measurably in six decades, began to rise at an unprecedented rate. Yields were still increasing throughout the 1980s. Total factor productivity—a measure of the benefits of improved management and technological change—which was also stagnant before the 1930s, followed the same rising path. The reasons for this abrupt shift from constant to rising yields and total productivity are not entirely clear. Crosson suggests that perhaps by the 1930s most of the land with good potential for crops was already in production, making the land-using mode of expansion no longer economically attractive for farmers. He also emphasizes the importance of the development and adoption of crop varieties responsive to fertilizers, hybrid corn being the prime example. When U.S. and global demand for grains and soybeans began to rise rapidly after World War II, American farmers were ready with a set of land-saving, low-cost technologies that permitted an unprecedented expansion of agricultural production. Crop production more than doubled from the 1939–1941 period to the 1985–1987 period, and cropland harvested declined about 10 percent.

Soil erosion emerged as a major concern in the 1930s. Although the focus was on the effects of erosion on soil productivity, the off-farm benefits of erosion control for improved water quality were recognized. Use of agricultural chemicals was considerably less than current levels and attracted little attention until the 1960s, the beginning of the modern environmental movement. A principal concern of subsequent legislation and regulatory policy has been the effects of pesticides on human health and wildlife. The drainage of wetlands and the effects on water quality of sediment, fertilizers, and animal wastes also are recognized as important.

Current environmental concerns are an integral part of the economic and policy framework in which farmers and agricultural scientists operate. Crosson concludes that a main challenge confronting these groups is to develop new technologies and management practices that will maintain the economic competitiveness of U.S. agriculture while protecting the environmental values at stake in agricultural production.

In chapter 6 Winston Harrington describes the amazement of early European settlers at the abundance and variety of wildlife encountered in the New World, and examines the impact of settlers on wildlife. Conversion of the forests and range to agricul-

Recreational experiences have replaced the commercial production of food and furs as the principal uses of wildlife.

tural and urban uses severely reduced and altered the habitat of the indigenous wildlife. The utilitarian attitudes of the settlers who viewed wildlife as a source of food and clothing, a competitor for resources, and even a source of danger further encouraged the destruction of wildlife and the conversion of its habitat.

The colonies and states enacted some measures to limit the taking of wildlife before and during the nineteenth century. For example, in the colonial period some local limits were placed on hunting. However, these local restrictions were largely ineffective and were overwhelmed by other measures such as the encouragement of control over predator wildlife and the introduction of exotic plant and animal species, which had adverse effects on native wildlife populations. Overexploitation led to declining beaver harvests as early as 1840. By the end of the nineteenth century, the populations of a number of species including elk, bison, black bear, wolf, mule deer, white-tailed deer, and pronghorn antelope, as well as many water fowl species, had been reduced to the point where some believed their survival was in doubt. Commercial landings of some fish species in the Great Lakes and Columbia River peaked in the late nineteenth and early twentieth centuries. A few species such as the passenger pigeon and the heath hen became extinct as a result of heavy hunting and conversion of their habitats to other uses.

Protective measures were largely ineffective until late in the nineteenth century, when the situation regarding a number of valued species had deteriorated sufficiently for a consensus on wildlife protection to develop. Harrington attributes the subsequent improvements in the status of wildlife to three factors: the curbing of excessive killing associated with hunting and predator control, the conservation of habitats, and the restoration of some species to their original ranges. State regulations on hunting became more effective in 1900 when it became a federal crime to cross state lines with wildlife killed in violation of a state law. By 1940, federal and state regulations on hunting had brought overexploitation of wildlife under control. The combined effects of government actions reserving some areas from private development and reduced pressure to convert land to agricultural use slowed, and, in some areas, reversed the decline of suitable habitat. Advances in wildlife science for management of populations and habitats also contributed to improvements in wildlife populations.

Harrington describes three general characteristics of the period since 1940. First, the number and distribution of many species, especially game species requiring forest or rangeland habitat, have improved significantly. Second, rapid development of some of the nation's water resources has affected the wildlife dependent on these waters and their riparian lands. Replacing free-flowing streams with reservoirs has adversely affected some indigenous fish, but has favored species better adapted to the warmer and calmer waters of a reservoir. The draining and filling of wetlands have eliminated some of the most productive wildlife habitat. Third, the uses of and attitudes toward wildlife have become more benign and protective. Recreational experiences have replaced the commercial production of food and furs as the principal uses of wildlife. In addition, the utilitarian attitudes toward wildlife that were dominant before the twentieth century have been supplemented by an enhanced appreciation of the existence of wildlife populations as an end in itself.

One activity that is placing increasing demands on the use of many of these resources is outdoor recreation. Although the emergence of outdoor recreation as an important user of the nation's land and water resources is a twentieth-century phenomenon, government provision of land for such activities in the United States had its origins in the New England village greens. In chapter 7, Marion Clawson and Winston Harrington trace the progression of outdoor recreation in the United States from its original, inconsequential use of natural resources to its current role as one of the most important uses.

Land reservation and custodial management only gradually became national concerns. Creation of Yellowstone National Park in 1872 is often cited as the start of the national park movement. Yet, legislation establishing the concept of a system of managed national parks was not passed until 1916. Large portions of the previously open public domain were reserved for permanent federal ownership by the Forest Reserve Act of 1891. Several states also began to establish parks before the end of the nineteenth century.

Outdoor recreation seldom was pursued far from one's home until the twentieth century. Even today, local community facilities account for more than half of all outdoor recreation. Clawson and Harrington credit the development of the bicycle as a practical and comfortable means of travel with widening the range of recreation early in this century. However, improvements in the automobile and the highway system were the principal factors underlying the rising use of federal recreational facilities. Increases in leisure time and incomes and additions to the park system also contributed to a rapid increase in the use of the federal land for outdoor recreation, especially after World War II. Annual visits to the national park system and the national forests increased from less than 250,000 in 1910 to more than 300 million visits today. The state parks have experienced comparable growth since at least 1940, the first date for which reliable aggregate data are available.

Although the growth in the use of federal recreation sites has been rapid and—except for a brief decline during World War II—sustained, the rate of increase in growth has declined over time. Since 1980, visits to the parks in the national park system have increased no faster than population. Moreover, despite the decades of rapid growth, only about 15 percent of all outdoor recreation activity currently takes place on the federal land; more than half is at community parks and other sites maintained by local governments. The remaining visits are divided about evenly between state parks and private land.

Clawson and Harrington conclude that the United States has the resource capacity to meet expected growth in the demand for future outdoor recreation if its citizens are prepared to pay the costs. Although recreation can often employ resources in a noncompetitive multiple-use manner, tradeoffs among alternative uses are inevitable. The costs associated with allocating additional land and water resources for recreational purposes will rise over time, especially in the absence of improved resource management.

Table 1-1. Major Uses of the Land in the United States, 1982

Land uses	Acreage (millions of acres)	Percentage
Cropland in crops	383	16.9
Idle cropland	21	0.9
Cropland for pasture only	65	2.9
Grassland pasture and range	597	26.3
Forestland grazed	158	7.0
Forestland not grazed	497	21.9
Recreation and wildlife areas[a]	211	9.3
Total area for resource uses	1,932	85.2
Farmsteads, farm roads	8	0.4
Transportation	27	1.2
National defense	24	1.1
Other[b]	274	12.1
Subtotal	333	14.8
Total land area	2,265	100.0

Source: Frey and Hexem (1985).

[a]Includes 83 million acres of forested area.

[b]Includes urban areas, miscellaneous uses not inventoried, and areas of little surface use such as marshes, open swamps, bare rock, desert, and tundra. In 1969 urban areas, roads, and other built-up areas totaled 61 million acres (U.S. Department of Agriculture, 1974).

Lessons and Themes

Interdependencies Among the Resources

Among the themes found in the discussions of resources in this book is that high-value uses tend to attract land and water away from low-value uses. Urban, industrial, and commercial users have almost invariably been able to bid land and water away from users in such sectors as agriculture, forestry, and fish and wildlife. The growth of the nation's population and economy over the past two centuries has led to the expansion of the nation's cities, towns, and highways; this expansion, in turn, has led to a reduction of the land and water available for crops, timber, range, and wildlife.

The direct claims of these high-value uses on the nation's land and water resources remain relatively modest. About 5 percent of the nation's total land base is devoted to urban areas, roads, other built-up areas, and national defense (table 1-1). In addition,

about 32 percent of the nation's total land area remains in forest. Although public, commercial, and industrial activities account for about 58 percent of the nation's water withdrawals, they account for only about 20 percent of the consumptive use (the quantity withdrawn from but not returned to a usable groundwater or surface water source). Moreover, the consumptive use of water for these purposes is less than 2 percent of the average renewable supply in the conterminous forty-eight states (Solley, Merk, and Pierce, 1988).

The indirect effects of these higher-value, more intensive uses on the resources can be much greater than these figures suggest. For instance, although highways occupy only a small percentage of the land, they can modify land parcels and uses by fragmenting wildlife habitats or impeding efficient farming. Moreover, the environmental effects of emissions and effluents from factories, cities, and motor vehicles are not confined to the land and water they use directly; their intensive uses, although providing benefits to some, create pollution that reduces the productivity of the remaining resources for crops, forests, fish and wildlife, and outdoor recreation.

Agriculture generally takes precedence over forestry, range, and wildlife in the use of the remaining land. Indeed, increases in the land devoted to crops that have been necessitated by the growing population and economy have contributed to the reduction of the nation's forests, rangeland, and wildlife habitat. The greatest shifts in land use occurred in the nineteenth and early twentieth centuries when cropland acreage increased from 76 million in 1850 to 319 million in 1900, and to a peak of 413 million in 1930, displacing forests and range in the process.

The earliest agricultural settlements began clearing the eastern forests. Pressures to clear the land for crops, combined with a rapidly growing demand for wood for construction materials and fuel, brought substantial changes in the vegetative cover of the lands. Wildlife was also under pressure in some areas from hunting and losses of habitat. Gradually, the search for additional agricultural land extended to the prairies and rangeland of the West. Even where forests and grassland were not converted to cropland, the ecosystems were often seriously altered by grazing of a variety of domestic animals. These changes in vegetative cover contributed to precipitous reductions in some wildlife populations while also contributing to the expansion of others.

By 1890, the westward expansion within the original forty-eight states was complete. The prairies of the Mississippi Valley had been converted to agriculture and were no longer available for further homesteading. Few areas were left in the West in which to expand dryland agriculture. The former grassland with sufficient precipitation to support crops was already in agriculture and forestland in the West generally was not viable for cropping. Major increases in irrigated agriculture required either large-scale water projects to capture and divert streamflows or improvements in pumping technology to tap groundwater. Although substantial forestland remained in the East, most of it was not well suited to agriculture.

Beginning in the interwar period and accelerating after World War II, agricultural technologies contributed to dramatic increases in crop yields, which greatly relieved pressure on the land base. Even though total agricultural output has much more than doubled, the 1930 level of 413 million acres of cropland use has not been equaled since. Intensive cropping patterns made possible by the use of agricultural chemicals, improved seed varieties, and other managerial and technological improvements made it possible in turn to concentrate crop production on a decreasing amount of land. The higher production that accompanied the improved yields put downward pressure on crop prices, thereby encouraging shifts in production to more productive land and the withdrawal from agriculture—and return to forests and grassland—of marginal land.

The expansion of irrigated agriculture also contributed to higher agricultural yields, thereby reducing pressures to convert other land to crops. In areas of unreliable precipitation, irrigation is essential to the profitable use of many other yield-increasing inputs such as fertilizers and pesticides. Thus irrigation expands the land base suitable for modern agriculture and reduces the pressures on land in the more humid regions. The impact of irrigation on agricultural productivity was reflected in 1982 when about 32 percent of the value of the crops produced was from crops grown on the 13 percent of the acreage that was irrigated (Day and Horner, 1987). Irrigation has also altered the regional distribution of the nation's agriculture and has placed heavy pressures on water resources in some of the nation's most water-scarce regions. For instance, irrigation accounts for nearly 80 percent of the withdrawals and 90 percent of the consumptive use of water in the seventeen western states. The expansion of irrigation in the West was seldom based on economic efficiency criteria or undertaken with full consideration of the environmental implications. Generous subsidies for irrigation projects, low and often subsidized energy costs, and in-

Increases in the land devoted to crops that have been necessitated by the growing population and economy have contributed to the reduction of the nation's forests, rangeland, and wildlife habitat.

stitutions encouraging water withdrawals have encouraged the growth of irrigated agriculture and related rural and urban developments in the West. This growth has come at the expense of the national treasury, groundwater stocks, instream flows, and riparian habitat.

The shift from a land-extensive to a yield-increasing agricultural development path was generally good news for the nation's forests, rangeland, and some of the wildlife habitats and populations that had continuously declined through the nineteenth century and into the twentieth century. Reduced pressures for cropland expansion helped to reverse the decline of forests in many areas. The low level of economic activity during the 1930s led to accelerated abandonment of marginal agricultural land and subsequently the reversion of much of this land to naturally regenerated forests. Government programs also promoted reforestation and restoration of some land.

The expansion and regrowth of forests on former crop and pasture lands, and improvements in range conditions since the 1920s, have contributed to improved habitats for various forms of wildlife. With the strengthening of hunting controls and species reintroduction programs, many wildlife species, particularly game animals, have flourished in recent decades. Some wildlife populations have recently approached or exceeded precolonial levels. However, continuing losses of the nation's wetlands to agricultural uses have contributed to sharp reductions in some waterfowl populations. Moreover, yield-increasing agricultural technologies have been a mixed blessing for wildlife. Agricultural chemicals used as an integral part of these technologies may end up in water supplies, with possible adverse effects on aquatic life. The expansion of irrigation in parts of the West has increased salinity levels of many western streams, and

Yield-increasing agricultural technologies have been a mixed blessing for wildlife.

irrigation drainage in California's San Joaquin Valley has raised selenium concentrations to levels that are toxic to refuge waterfowl.

The introduction and wide acceptance of less erosive farming practices probably have reduced the high rates of soil loss experienced during the Dust Bowl years. Although current erosion is a minor threat to the overall productivity of the nation's cropland, sediment and agricultural chemicals carried in runoff from farmers' fields contribute to water-quality problems in some places. In fact, in chapter 5 Crosson suggests that the off-farm damages of sediment and chemical pollutants may be much greater than the damages to soil productivity.

Demands for outdoor recreation—which might serve as a proxy indicator of the overall demands for those services of the nation's land and water that contribute to the quality of life in ways other than through the production of material goods—have had an increasingly important impact on the use of these resources. These demands have also resulted in policies that have removed large land areas and water supplies from any commercial development and, more recently, have restricted how federal land and water resources in general can be used and managed legally.

Technological Change and Resource Scarcity

Technological changes have influenced the management and general development of natural resource use in a variety of ways. Many of the earliest technological developments encouraged resource use, whereas more recent developments have tended to encourage conservation of resources.

Early technological advances in agriculture facilitated the clearing and preparation of land for crops and greatly increased the amount of land that could be farmed by a single worker. The single-piece cast-iron plow patented in 1797 and the wrought-iron plow with a steel cutting edge developed in 1837 were among the advances that enabled a worker to farm increasingly larger plots as the nineteenth century advanced. The gasoline-engined tractor, first developed in the 1880s and improved in succeeding decades, enabled much greater increases in labor productivity. Greater labor productivity, in the face of an ever-expanding market for agricultural products, provided incentives to obtain and cultivate more agricultural land. A countervailing influence was the

Over the years, technology has been induced in a manner that substitutes cheap, plentiful resources for expensive, scarce ones.

substitution of mechanical for animal power, which eased pressures on the land by reducing the area required for feeding farm animals.

Mechanization of earth moving and development of better concrete early in the twentieth century made it possible to build much larger water projects, and improved pumps in the 1930s facilitated the development of groundwater supplies to increase agricultural production and efficiency. Other innovations stimulated the demand for water and water projects. For instance, the development of electricity and transmission technologies made water power much more versatile, thereby encouraging dam and reservoir construction. Moreover, the acreage that could be practicably irrigated grew as a result of technologies such as sprinkler systems that made it possible to irrigate hilly terrain.

Technological changes in forestry allowed more rapid logging and transport of timber. These changes not only provided more timber, but also facilitated the conversion of timberland to agriculture. The advent of steam power and the railroad also encouraged logging and enabled previously inaccessible stands to be cleared. During the latter part of the nineteenth century, the development of new products increased the demand for wood and wood fiber. For example, wood fiber was increasingly replacing rags as the basic raw material in papermaking by the end of the century.

When technologies using large amounts of resources were developed and adopted, the resources themselves were not regarded, at least by their users, as expensive. The resources appeared to be abundant and the U.S. population was small, especially in the West. Amenity opportunities were readily available

and did not appear to conflict with resource use for commodity production. For example, during the nineteenth century people generally did not regard forests and the wildlife habitat that forests provided as scarce in the eastern United States when they cleared land for crops and timber. Little, if any, value was attributed to the amenity and other instream uses of natural streamflows when people altered and diverted them for irrigation in the late nineteenth and first half of the twentieth centuries.

Gradually, the situation changed. Population and economic growth contributed to the pressures for the conversion of large forest and range areas. The decline of the availability of wildlife, range, and water resources led to a growing realization that these resources were indeed valuable and limited. Technological developments reflected these changes; over the years, technology has been induced in a manner that substitutes cheap, plentiful resources for expensive, scarce ones.

By the 1930s, much of the technological innovation in agriculture was of a yield-increasing nature. Significant increases in crop yields were being realized through the introduction of genetically improved seeds, more effective pest controls, and intensive agricultural management. Continued increases in national agricultural production became much more dependent on improvements in seeds and associated intensive cultivation, and the demand to expand the agricultural cropland acreage declined substantially. Output per acre of arable land, which had declined from 1880 to 1920, increased 180 percent from 1920 to 1980 (Ruttan and Hayami, 1988).

Similar patterns of technological development and resource use emerged for timber and water resources. Following the unprecedented growth in the demand for wood for construction and fuel toward the end of the nineteenth century, total wood consumption actually declined after the turn of the century. In the face of rising relative wood prices, technology responded by providing preferred substitutes, extending the useful life of wood products, and enabling more complete use of the wood resource through more efficient sawing techniques and new uses for low-quality wood species. New methods of construction allowed iron, steel, and concrete to replace wood in many uses, and the growing use of coal, oil, and natural gas dramatically reduced the pressures to harvest timber for fuelwood. Wood preservatives extended the useful life of wood products such as railroad ties and poles, and new milling techniques provided more product from a given log. The increasing use of short-fiber woods for pulping and the development of waferboard panel products are recent examples of technological changes that substitute inexpensive, "low-quality" wood resources for more expensive, "high-quality" wood.

Technology also contributed directly to the regrowth of the forest as more efficient tree-planting techniques were developed and improved tree seedlings were introduced through the development of genetically superior seed stocks. Technological innovations in fire prevention and fire-fighting equipment helped reduce the risk of losses from fire and thereby contributed to the willingness of the forest industry and private landowners to plant trees.

It has been only within the past several decades that users have come to view water as scarce and that irrigators and industrial users have had to deal with rising water prices. Higher water prices have prompted large savings in the water used for industrial cooling because firms have abandoned once-through cooling systems in favor of recycling. Many irrigators dependent on groundwater were forced to adapt to much higher pumping costs as a result of the energy price increases in the 1970s. Farmers who continued to irrigate successfully in the face of much higher water costs adopted a variety of water-conserving techniques, including more efficient water-management practices and less water-intensive crops and seed varieties.

The U.S. experience indicates that the development and adoption of new technologies are induced and encouraged by increases in resource scarcity as perceived by users of the resources. The perceptions of scarcity on the part of an individual farmer, firm, or consumer, however, may differ greatly from the perceptions of society as a whole. Individual perceptions are strongly influenced by institutional and policy considerations that, in turn, have a powerful influence on the development and use of the nation's resources generally—as the next section indicates.

Institutional Factors Affecting the Use and Condition of Resources

Institutional factors such as the laws, policies, programs, and administrative arrangements directed to managing resource use have had major influences on the changing status of the resources. The institutions themselves have evolved over time as resource demands and conditions have changed. Major institutional shifts, however, have generally come only after resource conditions had deteriorated to a state that attracted widespread attention and concern. Frequently, the institutions encouraged use, tolerated questionable practices, and, as with water rights, limited the incentives and opportunities for adjusting resource use and management efficiently to changes in the underlying condition and availability of the resources.

The nature of the resources considered in this book present special challenges to managerial institutions that have responsibility for their effective and efficient use. It is difficult to establish clear property rights over some resources. Rivers, streams, and groundwater resources that flow from one property to another, as well as wildlife that moves over large areas, are common property resources. In the absence of property rights, they are unowned until captured for use. In the absence of effective managerial institutions, this situation often results in the problem of the "tragedy of the commons," in which a common resource is overused because it is available for the taking on a first-come, first-served basis without responsible managerial constraint. The inability to capture the rewards of any protective or enhancing management actions offers individual users little incentive to manage or conserve the commonly owned and used resource.

The depletion of American wildlife stocks during the nineteenth century is a classic example of the overuse and decline of an open-access, common property resource. During that period, people commonly viewed wildlife as available to all until it became the property of the successful hunter; hence, individuals had little incentive to preserve wildlife habitat. Moreover, because people generally viewed wildlife as abundant, there was little pressure for government to provide serious protection. Wood for fuel and materials and grazing on the open range were also typically available for the taking, reflecting the lack of clear ownership and the inability of the government

to exercise management or control, even in cases where these responsibilities had been assigned to the public sector. Water resources also were often withdrawn and polluted with little concern for the impacts on downstream users.

The United States has adopted various approaches to resolve or mitigate the common property problems that contributed to the former depletion and degradation of its resources. The provision of secure private property rights has contributed to improved resource protection and management. Where the open range came under secure private ownership, careful management replaced the myopic treatment given resources held in common (Anderson and Hill, 1975). Similarly, private owners of cropland with secure tenure had market incentives to limit erosion losses that affected productivity. In addition, water-use efficiency has been encouraged where rights have been made secure and transferable, permitting owners to benefit from their own conservation measures or to reallocate supplies through markets from lower- to higher-value uses.

The private sector is also contributing to the preservation of wildlife and its habitat. In some cases, such preservation is a joint product of maintaining the forest for timber production purposes. At other times, it is by design, as in the case of industry efforts to maintain wildlife habitat for hunting or bird watching in order to promote harmonious public relations, or through private sector activities undertaken to pro-

Major institutional shifts have generally come only after resource conditions had deteriorated to a state that attracted widespread attention and concern.

The control of wildfire and animal browsing has provided tree seedlings with an opportunity to mature, [but] ... it alters the natural cycle of the forest and the nature of the wildlife habitat it provides.

vide habitat for hunting for which fees are charged (Lassiter, 1980). Finally, secure land tenure allows independent conservation groups such as the National Audubon Society and The Nature Conservancy to purchase and preserve land containing unique habitat.

On balance, privatization has probably only been a secondary factor in the recovery of the nation's wildlife and the land and water resources upon which it depends. Federal programs aimed at protecting and preserving important portions of the U.S. natural resource base, changes in federal land management practices, and environmental legislation have all been important in this recovery. The first somewhat effective efforts to protect wildlife date back to the creation of the national park and forest systems in the latter part of the nineteenth and early twentieth centuries. In recent decades the federal government has adopted a number of important measures designed to protect the quantity and quality of the nation's land and water resources and assure more effective environmental control in their use for commercial forestry, grazing, or other activities. Laws such as the Wild and Scenic Rivers Act of 1968, the Clean Water Act of 1972, the Endangered Species Act of 1973, the National Forest Management Act of 1976, several acts designating national recreation areas as well as wilderness and roadless areas, and, finally, a pledge by President George Bush to prevent any additional net

loss in wetlands reflect both the growing importance attached to outdoor recreational opportunities and environments and a willingness to protect more of the remaining wildlife habitat from the pressures of future economic development.

Land has considerable capacity to return to its original condition once extreme pressures are removed or sharply curtailed. In some instances, government programs have been used to encourage the recovery of the forests and range by providing management expertise that facilitates the recovery. Although the merits of the Taylor Grazing Act of 1934 are debated, many believe it has contributed to a recovery of the public range and that overall range conditions have improved since 1920. New Deal programs put unemployed people to work reforesting and restoring eroded land and constructing and improving federal and state parks. Programs to prevent and control forest wildfires, together with tax and other incentives, have contributed to the reestablishment of forest on abandoned cropland in the East and to continual increases in the timber stocking on U.S. forests since World War II. The control of wildfire and animal browsing has provided tree seedlings with an opportunity to mature, thereby displacing brush and grasses in areas naturally suited to forest. The control of wildfire, however, is now controversial because it alters the natural cycle of the forest and the nature of the wildlife habitat it provides.

In some cases the unique circumstances of the American experience have resulted in the creation of innovative institutions. In the East, where water was plentiful, the English system of riparian rights (which gives owners of land adjacent to a water body the right to use the water) was adopted. In the West, however, the riparian system was soon deemed inadequate and a system of appropriative rights (which gives priority to the earliest users) evolved and was enacted into law. The appropriation system was well suited to conditions in the West during the nineteenth and early twentieth centuries. It encouraged settlement by providing miners, irrigators, and towns with greater security over water than they would have had under riparian law. It also encouraged off-stream use at the expense of instream flows, which had no status in western water law until recently. Although the resulting decline of streamflows was of little consequence in 1900, it has become one of the most influential factors underlying recent changes in western water institutions. Western water law has been evolving, particularly during the past two decades, to protect instream flows and to facilitate transfers of water rights. Virtually all western states now have some provision for instream water rights, and many have passed laws or made administrative changes designed to facilitate the transfer of water among uses and places. The evolution of these institutions is sure to continue because they still are generally inefficient in responding to changes in the supply and demand for the increasingly scarce water resources in the West.

The Adequacy of Resources

The chapters in this book suggest that the renewable resources of the United States have served the American people well from colonial times to the present. In the early periods, people simply used the abundant resources as needed, giving little thought to the future. Renewable resources provided the substances that allowed the early European settlements to survive, the colonies to grow, and colonial America to prosper. Development was achieved not only through the sweat of the early settlers, but also by using the abundant resources that covered the land. The sheer size of the resource endowment relative to the demands placed upon them precluded most conflicts over alternative resource uses for much of early U.S. history. By the latter part of the nineteenth century, however, the country had expanded from a few settlements on the eastern seaboard to one of continental proportions. At various times over the past one hundred years, many observers have concluded that the demands on the resources have overwhelmed the capacity of those resources to respond.

Experience has shown that the long-term productive potential of these resources is vulnerable; it is renewable only within limits and under wise management. Some valuable soil and water resources have for practical purposes been permanently depleted or degraded, and wetlands continue to be lost. In some cases, the introduction of new technologies has contributed to the decline and degradation of the resources. Nevertheless, many of the earlier concerns over the demise of our renewable resources have

faded. Threats of an impending timber famine are now seldom heard. Typhoid epidemics from contaminated water supplies are a distant memory. In addition, many wildlife populations have recovered from the depths reached early in this century. Aquatic systems, forests, wildlife, rangeland, and cropland have demonstrated a remarkable capacity to restore themselves either naturally or in combination with sound management, once abusive and exploitative uses are reduced. Moreover, technological advances have greatly increased some of the products that can be produced with a given resource base. In some instances, the combination of government programs and market-induced initiatives of the private sector has provided an environment conducive to improved management and protection of threatened resources.

Resource uses have also changed. The nation's economic development has become much less dependent on the conversion of inventory stocks of renewable resources to consumptive purposes even though the consumptive use of many of their products continues to grow. The early European settlers depended on clearing and farming the land, capturing wildlife for their furs and meat, and using timber for construction and fuel. Water provided the principal avenues for commerce and a source of power for industry. Currently, agriculture, forestry, and fisheries combined account for only about 2 percent of the nation's gross domestic product; wildlife is used largely for sport rather than for its commercial value; timber competes with many alternative construction and fuel

Renewable resources provided the substances that allowed the early European settlements to survive, the colonies to grow, and colonial America to prosper.

Ironically, the technologies and industries that have made the economy less dependent on renewable resources often pose the greatest risk to their quality and the health of the ecosystems on which they depend.

products; water is the source of only a small part of the nation's industrial power; and highways, railroads, and airways are usually preferred to water transport.

Although the renewable resources have become relatively less important to the overall economy, their availability and quality increasingly are perceived as important for the quality of life. The resulting changes in perceptions and values attached to the resources by a large portion of the U.S. population are placing new pressures on and posing new problems and challenges for allocating and managing the resources. To ensure human health, the nation is committing billions of dollars to improve the quality of air and water resources that people once took for granted. Wetlands and wild and scenic areas that people once viewed as open territory for developers and water projects are increasingly being protected from these pressures. Forests are now viewed as important repositories for biodiversity and as providers of other environmental services, as well as a source of wood products.

Furthermore, improved scientific understanding of ecosystems as well as an increased ability to detect and monitor changes in the physical and biological world underlie some new resource concerns. The ability to detect the presence of contaminants in water supplies has contributed to the heightened concerns about water quality and increased awareness that

quality can even be affected by activities making no ostensible use of the resource. Until recently, many viewed wetlands as areas to be drained so they could be put to productive use. Given the current understanding of the role of wetlands in providing wildlife habitat, controlling floods, and restoring water quality, the loss of wetlands has become a national concern. However, contradictions and tradeoffs abound, because wetlands are important sources of atmospheric methane, one of the more powerful greenhouse gases. Increased, but still relatively primitive, understanding of the interrelations among the biosphere, geosphere, and atmosphere have led to a host of new resource concerns, including the impacts of stratospheric ozone depletion and tropospheric ozone increases on crop and forest yields, the impacts of acid precipitation on forests and lakes, the overall impacts of humans on endangered species and biodiversity, and the likelihood and implications of a global greenhouse warming.

Ironically, the technologies and industries that have made the economy less dependent on renewable resources often pose the greatest risk to their quality and the health of the ecosystems on which they depend. The chemicals underlying high-yield agriculture sometimes end up contaminating water supplies. The chemical, energy, steel, and other industries that produce the agricultural inputs, and the fuel and construction products that have substituted for forest products, are major polluters of the nation's water and air. Acid rain, and the prospect of global warming stemming largely from industrial growth and development, pose highly uncertain but widely feared longer-term threats to the health of many of the nation's renewable resources.

Challenges

As the nation's ability to provide the material goods considered important to a comfortable life has grown, the accessibility and quality of its recreational and environmental resources have become increasingly important to the quality of life. Protecting, enhancing, and in some cases restoring the quality of the nation's renewable resources to meet the changing demands of both an environmentally conscious population and a huge growing economy is an enormous challenge. The interdependencies among the resource systems and the demands placed upon them are complex. Some problems and solutions are local in nature. Other problems are regional or global and will require a breadth of cooperation that has rarely been achieved in the past. For instance, local concerns such as toxic waste disposal and ambient levels of air pollution are now interspersed with regional concerns such as the effects of acid rain on lakes and forests and global issues such as climate change and loss of biological diversity. Incomplete scientific understanding of the nature and implications of these problems, international externalities that arise when pollutants are transmitted across political borders, and the absence of institutions for resolving international resource disputes greatly complicate the task of successfully meeting future resource challenges.

In a United States with a quarter of a billion people, an annual economy of $5 trillion, and constant technological changes, the nature as well as the magnitude of the nation's resource demands have changed dramatically from those of one to two centuries earlier.

Although the variety of commodity outputs produced from U.S. renewable resources is still much in demand, the demand for their recreational and environmental outputs appears to have increased even more rapidly. Less relative emphasis is now placed on the direct economic benefits of putting the resources to productive uses; greater weight is being given to protecting free-flowing streams, wetlands, forests, wilderness, and wildlife because of their perceived contribution to the quality of life. The growth of discretionary income and leisure has contributed to an increase in the demand for outdoor recreation, which now is a major claimant on the nation's renewable natural resources. Resources once viewed as obstacles to economic progress until they were tamed or replaced are now recognized as essential to the diversity and quality of the environment and our recreational opportunities.

The challenge, then, is to balance potentially competitive and changing relative demands, both commodity and noncommodity, on our renewable resources, while ensuring that they are managed on a long-term sustainable basis.

References

Anderson, Terry L., and P. J. Hill. 1975. "The Evolution of Property Rights." *Journal of Law and Economics* 18 (April): 163–179.

Brown, Lester R., with Erik P. Eckholm. 1974. *By Bread Alone*. New York: Praeger Publishers for the Overseas Development Council.

Day, John C., and Gerald L. Horner. 1987. *U.S. Irrigation: Extent and Importance*. Agricultural Information Bulletin no. 523, Economic Research Service. Washington, D.C.: U.S. Department of Agriculture.

Fedkiw, John. 1989. *The Evolving Use and Management of the Nation's Forests, Grasslands, Croplands, and Related Resources. A Technical Document Supporting the 1989 USDA Forest Service Assessment*. Fort Collins, Colo.: U.S. Department of Agriculture, Forest Service, Rocky Mountain Forest and Range Experiment Station.

Frey, H. Thomas, and Roger W. Hexem. 1985. *Major Uses of Land in the United States: 1982*. Agricultural Economic Report no. 535, Economic Research Service.

Washington, D.C.: U.S. Department of Agriculture.

Lassiter, Roy L., Jr. 1980. "Access to and Management of the Wildlife Resources on Large Private Timberland Holdings in the Southeastern United States." College of Business Administration Monograph Series, no 1. Cookeville, Tenn.: Tennessee Technical University.

Ruttan, Vernon W., and Yujiro Hayami. 1988. "Induced Technical Change in Agriculture." In *Agricultural Productivity: Measurement and Explanation*, edited by Susan M. Capalbo and John M. Antle. Washington, D.C.: Resources for the Future.

Solley, Wayne B., Charles F. Merk, and Robert R. Pierce. 1988. "Estimated Use of Water in the United States in 1985." U.S. Geological Survey Circular no. 1004. Washington, D.C.: GPO.

U.S. Department of Agriculture, Economic Research Service. 1974. *Our Land and Water Resources: Current and Prospective Supplies and Uses*. Washington, D.C.: GPO.

Spring used by pioneers at Logan Canyon, Utah, still in use today

2

Water Resources: Increasing Demand and Scarce Supplies

Kenneth D. Frederick

Water is one of the most readily renewable of the earth's natural resources. Globally, the total quantity of water is essentially constant and is unaffected by human activities; water can be used and reused virtually indefinitely. Evaporation removes the impurities in water picked up from natural and human sources. On the other hand, water is one of the least predictable resources. The hydrologic cycle continuously circulates water from lakes, streams, and oceans through evaporation and from plants through transpiration to the atmosphere, from where it eventually precipitates back to the earth. Water is commonly characterized as a fugitive resource because it naturally flows from one location and one state (liquid, gas, or solid) to another. These characteristics present challenges in managing, controlling, and allocating the resource.

Water also is a vital and versatile resource. It is essential to all life, and a secure supply is required for successful economic activity. Drinking remains the most critical use for human life, but much larger quantities are used for economic and recreational

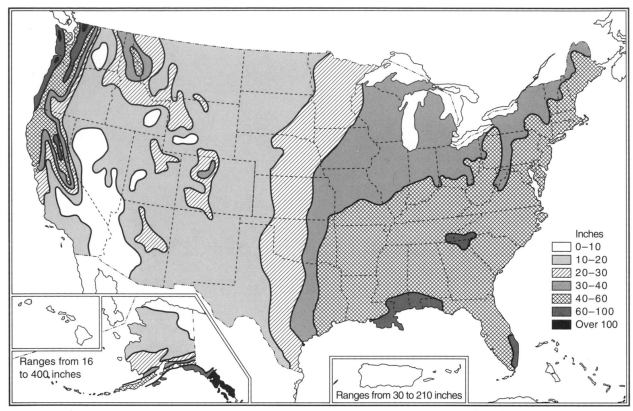

Figure 2-1. Average annual precipitation in the United States and Puerto Rico

Source: U.S. Water Resources Council (1978, vol. 1).

purposes and as an amenity. Water is the resource most widely used by industry, a necessary input for productive agriculture, a medium of transportation, a source of energy, and a vehicle for waste disposition. In addition, water is vital for fish and wildlife habitat and much outdoor recreation.

This chapter reviews the nature, use, development, and management of water resources in the United States since about 1800. The natural supply, which is described in the following section, approximates the water supply around 1800. After 1800, a rapidly growing and expanding nation subjected water to intensive use and management. The historical presentation below highlights important changes in the use and management of water resources. The chapter also considers the current status of water resources and the management practices and policies needed to ensure the availability of supplies to meet Americans' increasing demand for water.

The Nature of Water Resources

Water Supplies

Long-term national averages indicate that the United States is well endowed with water. Annual precipitation averages nearly 30 inches throughout the conterminous United States, and enormous quantities of freshwater are stored in surface and underground aquifers. Although two-thirds of the precipitation is evaporated and transpired quickly back to the atmosphere, the remaining one-third provides a potential renewable supply of 1,400 billion gallons per day (bgd) (U.S. Water Resources Council, 1978, vol. 1). This quantity is fourteen times current U.S. consumptive water use, which is the amount of water withdrawn from but not returned to a usable surface or groundwater source. In addition, freshwater stocks stored on and within 2,500 feet of the earth's surface are equivalent to more than fifty years' cumulative renewable supply.

Surface Water Resources

Long-term national averages of surface water resources are deceptive because large spatial and temporal variations underlie these averages. Regionally, average annual precipitation ranges from less than 1 inch in desert areas of the Southwest to more than 60 inches in parts of the humid Southeast (figure 2-1). One-third of the nation averages less than 20 inches of precipitation annually; much of this precipitation is quickly lost to evapotranspiration. Average annual precipitation for the conterminous United States ranges from more than 54 inches in the Gulf Coast states of Mississippi, Louisiana, and Alabama to 9 inches in Nevada (table 2-1).

Precipitation that is not quickly evapotranspired back to the atmosphere either forms runoff or adds to the water stored in the soil, ground, ice, and snow. Large seasonal variations in storage are common, especially where much of the precipitation is in the form of snow. Interannual changes in storage are associated with fluctuations in the climate. However, in the absence of long-term climate change, interannual changes in storage tend to cancel out over a decade or so. Thus, average annual runoff, which is essentially the difference between precipitation and evapotranspiration, is a better measure of a region's renewable water supply than is precipitation. The potential rate of evapotranspiration rises as the climate becomes hotter and can exceed 70 inches annually in some arid and semiarid areas of the West, where only large rain storms contribute significantly to runoff. Runoff is greater and evaporation is less where the topography is steeper and the precipitation is concentrated in fewer, larger storms. Although potential evapotranspiration is much less in the East, the actual amount of evapotranspiration is much greater because evapotranspiration is less constrained by lack of water in a humid climate (Foxworthy and Moody, 1986). Streamflows are much higher in the East and Northwest; average annual runoff ranges from more than 25 inches in the state of Washington and more

Table 2-1. Average Annual Precipitation and Runoff, by State

Region	Precipitation (inches)	Runoff (inches)
Eastern 31 states		
Alabama	54.8	21.9
Arkansas	48.9	17.0
Connecticut	46.8	23.2
Delaware	41.0	16.4
Florida	53.6	15.4
Georgia	49.9	15.2
Illinois	37.6	10.1
Indiana	39.6	12.7
Iowa	31.9	7.7
Kentucky	46.2	13.1
Louisiana	55.8	19.8
Maine	42.0	24.0
Maryland	42.6	13.6
Massachusetts	43.0	20.3
Michigan	31.0	12.2
Minnesota	25.8	5.1
Mississippi	55.9	21.2
Missouri	38.8	8.4
New Hampshire	41.8	23.1
New Jersey	47.7	21.6
New York	39.2	20.4
North Carolina	49.4	16.2
Ohio	37.9	11.0
Pennsylvania	41.9	22.0
Rhode Island	45.3	24.4
South Carolina	48.8	14.2
Tennessee	50.3	24.4
Vermont	39.9	22.9
Virginia	41.1	14.0
West Virginia	44.1	21.6
Wisconsin	30.7	10.4
Western 17 states		
Arizona	12.6	0.2
California	22.7	8.5
Colorado	17.0	3.0
Idaho	22.0	10.6
Kansas	27.0	3.8
Montana	14.1	3.9
Nebraska	22.6	2.8
Nevada	9.1	0.3
New Mexico	13.1	0.4
North Dakota	17.3	0.6
Oklahoma	33.3	4.7
Oregon	26.8	17.2
South Dakota	17.6	0.7
Texas	28.1	7.2
Utah	13.0	1.2
Washington	39.7	25.9
Wyoming	14.0	3.4

Source: U.S. Geological Survey (1990).

than 20 inches in most of the northeastern states to less than 1 inch in Arizona, Nevada, New Mexico, North Dakota, and South Dakota (see table 2-1).

Except in the Pacific Northwest, water supplies tend to decline from the east toward the west in the United States. For the thirty-one eastern states, precipitation averages 42.5 inches and runoff averages 15.0 inches. In the plains states (that is, Kansas, Nebraska, North Dakota, Oklahoma, South Dakota, and Texas), precipitation averages 25.4 inches and runoff averages 4.5 inches. In the western states of Arizona, Colorado, Montana, Nevada, New Mexico, Utah, and Wyoming, the averages decline to 13.3 inches of precipitation and 1.8 inches of runoff. Water supplies in parts of the Northwest are even more abundant than in the East. Precipitation for the states of Washington and Oregon averages 32.1 inches, well below the average for the East, but runoff averages 20.8 inches, approximately 39 percent above the average for the East. California and Idaho are divided hydrologically; sizable parts of each state are arid and other parts are more characteristic of the relatively well-watered Northwest. Precipitation in these states averages 22.7 and 22.0 inches, respectively, and runoff averages 8.5 and 10.6 inches, respectively (U.S. Geological Survey, 1990).

These long-term regional averages mask intertemporal variations—both seasonal and annual—that can range from droughts to floods. Seasonal variations in runoff can be large. Indeed, in the absence of flow regulation from reservoirs and dams, some streams regularly dry up during some months and flood their banks during others. Where temperatures remain above freezing, runoff corresponds closely to precipitation. In Florida, heavy flows occur in the summer and early fall when rainfall is the heaviest; in the southwestern Pacific coastal area, the heaviest flows occur in winter when rainfall is heaviest. In the northern latitudes and higher altitudes seasonal runoff differs significantly from precipitation because much of the winter precipitation is temporarily stored as ice and snow. In northern California, for instance, much of the precipitation is snow in the mountains and the heaviest runoff is from spring snowmelt. In the Missouri River basin where there is relatively little difference in elevation and ground temperatures over wide areas, melting is concentrated in a relatively brief period and widespread spring flooding is common (Foxworthy and Moody, 1986). In such a basin with large

Table 2-2. Variability of Annual Streamflow: Low and High Flows as a Percentage of Mean Annual Flow for Eighteen Water Resource Regions

Water resource region	Percentage of mean annual flow	
	Low flows	High flows
New England	62	138
Mid-Atlantic	61	145
South Atlantic–Gulf	53	156
Great Lakes	62	143
Ohio	59	143
Tennessee	77	142
Upper Mississippi	54	156
Lower Mississippi	47	175
Souris–Red–Rainy	30	190
Missouri	40	168
Arkansas–White–Red	35	193
Texas–Gulf	22	220
Rio Grande	17	367
Upper Colorado	39	156
Lower Colorado	75	106
Great Basin	46	181
Pacific Northwest	70	135
California	41	184
Total	55	159

Source: U.S. Water Resources Council (1978).

seasonal variability in runoff, reservoirs are essential for expanding the reliable supply of water.

Changing weather patterns also produce year-to-year fluctuations in supplies. Runoff varies more than precipitation, especially in arid and semiarid areas where relatively small changes in precipitation can produce large changes in streamflow. For example, precipitation 20 percent above the mean will increase runoff approximately 150 percent in a semiarid area that averages 20 inches of precipitation, and approximately 30 percent in a humid area that averages 50 inches of precipitation (Foxworthy and Moody, 1986).

The variability in annual streamflow for eighteen water resource regions (table 2-2) reflects low flows (those exceeded in 95 of every 100 years) and high flows (those exceeded in only 5 of every 100 years) as a percentage of a basin's mean annual flow. Flows vary from year to year in all water resource regions but the variations tend to be greater in arid and semiarid regions. For instance, 90 percent of the annual flows in the Northwest and much of the East fall within 60 to 145 percent of the mean. In the arid and semiarid West, however, a range of 40 to 168 percent of the mean is needed to include 90 percent of the annual flows. Although the Lower Colorado River basin stands out as a striking exception to this pattern, this basin produces little water even in the best of years. For instance, a high flow rate in the lower basin is only 17 percent of the mean flow in the Upper Colorado River basin and only about one tenth of 1 percent of the flow in the eighteen water resource regions.

Precipitation that is quickly transpired by trees and plants is often overlooked when considering the adequacy of water supplies. This water is unavailable for either instream or offstream uses, and it is not considered part of the potential renewable supply. Nevertheless, this water is an important part of a region's climate. The quantity and reliability of this water is vital to the health of crops and forests, and it influences a region's development prospects as well as whether irrigation is necessary for agriculture. Much of the water that is evapotranspired is essential to the photosynthesis and, therefore, to the productivity of eastern forests and dryland agriculture.

Groundwater Resources

In addition to the surface water resources, water is naturally available from groundwater resources. Enormous quantities of water are stored in aquifers—subterranean bodies of unconsolidated materials such as sand, gravel, and soil that are saturated with water and are sufficiently permeable to store and release water in useful quantities. Aquifers are recharged by the downward percolation of precipitation or by water from snowmelt, streams, canals, and reservoirs. Seepage from aquifers supplies approximately 30 percent of the nation's streamflow (U.S. Water Resources Council, 1978).

Aquifers can be classified according to how readily they are recharged. Confined aquifers are overlain by relatively impermeable materials, so they contain water under pressure and are recharged only at low rates. Unconfined aquifers are usually closer to the surface and are more readily recharged by percolation from surface waters, which makes them more susceptible to contamination from surface activities. Aquifer recharge and discharge rates vary with changes in precipitation and runoff, but under natural conditions a long-term equilibrium is established where discharge equals recharge.

Pumping disrupts the natural equilibrium of aquifers. Groundwater levels decline as water is withdrawn, resulting in a decrease in an aquifer's rate of discharge and perhaps a rise in the rate of recharge. These adjustments tend to produce a new equilibrium. However, if the rate of pumping exceeds the ability of the aquifer system to adjust discharge and recharge rates to match pumping, groundwater levels fall until economic or other factors reduce pumping. As the quantity of freshwater stored in an aquifer decreases, groundwater levels decline, pumping lifts rise, and well yields decrease; economic factors will reduce and then eliminate groundwater mining long before the water in an aquifer is exhausted. In coastal as well as some inland areas, an aquifer may become unfit for use if freshwater is replaced by saline water. In other areas, the storage capacity of the aquifer itself may be lost if dewatering by pumping results in the compaction of the materials composing the aquifer.

Water Uses

Differences in natural water supplies present opportunities and challenges in the various regions of the country. Water can be transported from one region to another. However, transporting water from its natural channels over long distances is expensive relative to its value in most uses. Within a given region, the usable supply can be augmented through the construction and operation of facilities such as dams, reservoirs, wells, canals, and treatment plants. Where water is scarce, damming, storing, diverting, and protecting water for one use alters its availability for other uses. Beyond that, the usable supply can be diminished through contamination and use.

Consequently, the status of the resource should not be assessed simply in terms of its capacity to provide for a single use such as drinking or irrigation, or even in terms of all offstream uses. Ideally, the status should be valued in terms of all uses (withdrawal and instream), including uses for economic, social, and environmental purposes.

Uses are differentiated as to whether or not water is withdrawn from a natural channel (such as a stream) or a reservoir. People withdraw water for domestic, public, commercial, irrigation, livestock, industrial, mining, and thermoelectric uses. Although water planners often refer to these offstream uses as requirements, the only true requirements are the small quantities individuals need to survive. Where water is scarce, withdrawal uses compete among themselves as well as with instream uses. Except for the portion that is used consumptively, the water withdrawn is returned to a location where it can be used again. Although returnflows are available for reuse, withdrawal of the water usually adversely affects the quality, location, and quantity of the water for alternative uses.

Instream uses include navigation, waste disposal, recreation, fish and wildlife habitat, hydroelectric generation, and amenities. Although these uses can be complementary (as when the provision of water for fish also provides sufficient water for navigation), the demands of each use differ in terms of the timing, quality, and quantity of the desired flow. Consequently, there are likely to be tradeoffs in managing water facilities and in allocating supplies to alternative instream uses. For instance, managing a reservoir and dam for maximum hydropower benefits is likely to reduce the value of the reservoir for recreation and wildlife. Similarly, using a stream for waste disposal diminishes its value for any uses sensitive to the quality of the water.

Quality is an important dimension of the resource. Water is rarely pure outside of a laboratory. It picks up impurities from the atmosphere as it precipitates to earth and also picks up dissolved minerals (commonly referred to as salts) as it comes in contact with soils and rocks. When the salt concentrations become high, as they are in the oceans and in lakes in closed basins, the water is of little value for withdrawal uses. The natural concentrations of salts in the nation's lakes, streams, and aquifers are generally acceptable for most uses. However, anthropogenic activities such as farming and construction can increase the concentrations of these minerals and can contribute other contaminants such as toxic substances, bacteria, nutrients, and sediment that diminish the ability of water bodies to meet both instream and withdrawal uses.

Water Resource Use and Management in the Nineteenth Century

The natural availability of water resources was an important factor in shaping the exploration, settlement, and development of the nation during the nineteenth century, a period of extraordinary expansion for the United States. The nation's borders expanded from the original thirteen states and the territories claimed by these states to the land now encompassed by all fifty states. Population grew from about 4 million in 1790 to more than 75 million by 1900. Rivers provided the principal paths for exploring and trading with the nation's interior, cities grew up around the best harbors and major rivers, mills and factories were located alongside streams to harness the power of flowing water, and agriculture was located where rainfall was adequate or a stream could easily be diverted to irrigate neighboring lands.

Water Transportation

Improved navigation was the objective of the earliest major water projects. Major undertakings involved canal construction by states or private interests to facilitate trade between the interior and the coastal cities. The Erie Canal, which linked the Hudson River with the Great Lakes in 1825, was the most successful of these projects. The financial success of this canal encouraged other projects, most of which were financial disasters. By 1830, 1,300 miles of canals were in use; within a decade, states and private interests had added another 2,000 miles to the U.S. canal network (Fedkiw, 1989). The federal role was limited to Corps of Engineers (COE) activities to improve harbors and clear channels on major rivers.

Dependence on inland water transportation declined with the development of the railroad. Although canals went into decline after 1840 when they faced direct competition with a railroad, the nation's most extensive canal system, the New York State system, remained active throughout the nineteenth century. Traffic on the New York State system peaked between 1868 and 1874, when it averaged more than 6 million tons per year (Martin, 1960). Steamboat traffic on the Mississippi and Ohio rivers continued to flourish until the Civil War, but the disruptions caused by the war prevented the steamboat from regaining its prior preeminence. The railroad emerged as the preeminent mode of transportation from 1860 to 1920 (Howe and coauthors, 1969).

Water and Settlement of the West

By 1802, most of the land beyond the borders of the original thirteen states belonged to the federal government. Over the next sixty-five years, purchases, treaties with foreign governments, and expropriation of Native American land added vast, largely uninhabited areas to the public domain. Revenue enhancement was the principal objective in the early sales of these lands. Gradually this objective gave way to the desire to expand and settle the frontier, which was being pushed westward by squatters. However, water, either too much or too little, was an obstacle to settlement of more than one-third of the original forty-eight states.

The Swamp Lands acts of 1849 and of 1850 encouraged development of floodprone areas in the lower Mississippi River basin. Arkansas, Louisiana, Mississippi, and Missouri received free federal land within their borders under the condition that the receipts from selling the land would be used for flood control and drainage. The resulting uncoordinated construction of local levees was ineffective in protecting the region as a whole from floods (Holmes, 1972).

The Homestead Act of 1862 gave settlers free title to 160 acres after five years of residence and cultivation. For several decades following passage of this act settlers in search of their own land moved westward into increasingly arid areas.

The breaking wave of settlement was eating up half a meridian a year; from one season to the next, settlements were thirty miles farther out. By the late 1870s, the hundredth meridian had been fatefully crossed. There were homes sprouting in central Nebraska, miles from water, trees, and neighbors, their occupants living in sod dugouts suggestive of termite mounds. (Reisner, 1986, p. 36)

In addition to the prospect of free land, settlers were encouraged by the lure of flat, treeless, rich soils; by what proved to be a period of above average rainfall in the semiarid plains; and by a melange of promoters (especially from the railroads and local newspapers) who sought to profit from the settlers. A new school of meteorology emerged with the motto, "Rain follows the plow." Congress provided further fuel for the push westward when it relaxed the requirements for establishing ownership in arid and semiarid areas. The Timber Culture Law of 1873 added congressional legitimacy to the belief that trees would bring rain in the semiarid plains. Under this legislation, anyone who

could keep trees healthy and growing on 40 acres for ten years was granted title to 160 acres of semiarid land. The ownership requirements subsequently were reduced to 10 acres and eight years (Muhn and Stuart, 1988).

John Wesley Powell, however, warned that the water resources of the semiarid plains would not sustain a large influx of farmers. Failure to heed this advice resulted in enormous human tragedy when the climate turned less benign in the late 1880s. The unfortunate settlers who moved into the northern plains experienced a lengthy drought:

> By 1890, the third year of the drought, it was obvious that the theory that rain follows the plow was a preposterous fraud. The people of the plains states, still shell-shocked by the great white winter, began to turn back east. The populations of Kansas and Nebraska declined by between one-quarter and one-half. Tens of thousands went to the wetter Oklahoma territory, which the federal government usurped from the five Indian tribes to whom it had been promised in perpetuity and offered to anyone who got there first. Meanwhile, the windmills of the farmers who remained north were

pumping up sand instead of water, and the huge dark clouds on the horizon were not rain but dust.... When statistics were collected a few years later, only 400,000 homesteading families had managed to persevere on the plains, of more than a million who tried. The Homestead Acts had been a relative success in the East; west of the hundredth meridian, however, they were for the most part a failure, even a catastrophic failure.... (Reisner, 1986, p. 111)

West of the one-hundredth meridian rainfall generally is insufficient for dryland farming; either irrigation or farms much larger than 160 acres are necessary to support a family in the arid West. The region's rugged topography and the paucity of its streams meant that only a tiny fraction of the lands could be irrigated simply by diverting streamflows to riparian lands through gravity flows. Storing and transporting water to nonriparian lands required organization and resources that were in scarce supply in the nineteenth century.

The riparian system of water rights, which was transferred to the West from England and the eastern states, also discouraged investments in nonriparian arid lands. The riparian doctrine gave the owners of the land bordering a stream correlative rights to use of the water. This doctrine posed major problems for development in the West where the streams were few and their flows were unreliable. Even downstream, riparian lands (which often are better suited for irrigation than the high mountainous lands in the headwaters) could be deprived of water by upstream diversions. Consequently, during the second half of the nineteenth century, the western states either supplemented the riparian system of rights or abandoned it for the doctrine of prior appropriation, which had been developed by the area's early gold and silver miners. The doctrine of prior appropriation granted a priority claim to the first person to withdraw water from a stream or lake for a beneficial use over all future claimants. The doctrine worked well in clarifying and protecting the rights of withdrawal users. Indeed, it encouraged withdrawals at the expense of instream flows (Radosevich, 1978). Only recently have the western states passed legislation providing water rights for instream flows. As of 1988, New Mexico was the only western state that had not taken some measures, either legislatively or administratively, to protect instream flows (Shupe, 1989).

The Mormons were the first settlers to successfully establish irrigation in the arid West, in Utah. The Mormons irrigated several thousand acres by 1850, just three years after their arrival. Three decades later, nearly 1 million acres were under irrigation throughout the West, and by the end of the nineteenth century, the total had increased to 7.5 million acres (U. S. General Accounting Office, 1981). Two federal acts provided some, but not significant, encouragement for this expansion. The Desert Land Law of 1877 offered 640 acres of arid lands at a cost of $1.25 per acre to individuals establishing irrigation within three years, and the Carey Land Act of 1894 provided arid land to states or territories to promote reclamation (Muhn and Stuart, 1988).

Drinking Water and Health

Although in the nineteenth century water quantity was rarely a problem for the nation's cities and factories, which generally were located near major water bodies, water quality became an increasingly important health and environmental concern. Water sources used for drinking also served as the principal medium for disposing of municipal and industrial wastes. Consequently, drinking water was a major source of debilitating and deadly disease in the nineteenth century.

Cholera related to contaminated drinking water was common during the early part of the century. Following John Snow's classic study that demonstrated the role of fecal pollution of drinking water in the 1848–1849 cholera epidemic—which killed more than 14,000 people in London—precautions were taken to eliminate this disease (Johnson, 1988). Following the mid-1800s, typhoid became the waterborne disease of particular concern. Initially, the local communities responsible for municipal water supplies lacked the resources as well as the knowledge to treat supplies adequately to eliminate the disease. It was not until the late nineteenth century that experiments showed that slow sand filtration of drinking water supplies could substantially reduce death rates from typhoid fever and other diseases. Soon thereafter, further experiments demonstrated that a combination of rapid sand filtration and coagulation could remove the turbidity, color, and approximately 99 percent of the bacteria from even the most turbid waters. Adoption of this technology spread rapidly during the last decade of the century (Johnson, 1988; Spofford, 1986).

Hydroelectric Power

The first hydroelectric generating plants went into operation in 1882 at Niagara Falls in New York and at St. Anthony Falls in Minnesota. Hydroelectric power use grew rapidly in the following decades, and by the end of the nineteenth century it accounted for a large portion of the total electricity produced in the United States (Payne, 1983). Much greater advances in the production, transmission, and use of electricity awaited the technological discoveries of the twentieth century.

Offstream Water Use

By the end of the nineteenth century, an estimated 40 bgd were being withdrawn from groundwater and surface water supplies to support various water uses. More than 80 percent of the water was taken from surface supplies; relatively shallow and artesian aquifers supplied most of the rest. About 50 percent of all withdrawals went to irrigate an estimated 7.7 million acres; steam electric utilities accounted for 12 percent; public water utilities, about 7 percent; and rural domestic users, 5 percent. The remaining withdrawals—about 25 percent—were accounted for by industrial, mining, rural commercial, military, and several small miscellaneous uses (see appendix 2, table 2-A1).

These levels of use placed little pressure on aggregate supplies; total withdrawals were equivalent to approximately 3 percent of the mean annual surface flow in the forty-eight states. Nevertheless, water rights already were being strongly contested in parts of the West. The variability and generally low flow of most western streams provided little reliable supply, and large quantities of irrigation water were needed to grow crops successfully. Consequently, storage, which required large investments to build dams and reser-voirs, was needed to increase reliable water supplies in the West.

Changes by 1900

Use and development of the nation's water resources underwent major changes during the nineteenth century in response to the growing and changing demands of a population that increased nearly twentyfold. By the end of the century, this growing population was withdrawing 40 bgd from surface water and groundwater sources for a wide variety of uses (see table 2-A1). Recreational opportunities, flood control, and more reliable supplies for municipal and irrigation uses were provided by 2,661 dams constructed by 1900 (U.S. Army Corps of Engineers, 1982; see also appendix 2, tables 2-A2 and 2-A3). Trans-

Early irrigation dam, Utah

portation was facilitated by an extensive system of navigable rivers, canals, and harbors. Water flows provided much of the electricity that was beginning to transform the economy and lives of the populace.

However, major problems and challenges remained. Urban water supplies were still a major source of disease; the capacity of some lakes and streams to assimilate wastes had been exceeded; the welfare and even the survival of countless people living in arid, semiarid, or floodprone areas depended on an unpredictable continuation of benign precipitation patterns; many irrigators and irrigation projects were hopelessly in debt; and the Jeffersonian ideal of creating a large number of self-sufficient, small farmers had been tarnished by oversettlement of marginal arid lands and the fraudulent acquisition of huge private land holdings. With the more easily irrigable lands in the West already developed and the growing need for storage, many people believed greater federal support would be required to promote irrigation and settlement of the arid West. There also was strong sentiment for government support of hydroelectric power development (U.S. General Accounting Office, 1981). These conditions helped set the stage for the conservation period.

The Conservation Period: 1900–1920

The resource problems and abuses that emerged during the nineteenth century contributed to a growing disenchantment with the government policies and private actions that had dominated the development and use of the nation's water, land, and forest resources. The challenges of developing hydroelectric power, irrigation, and safer water supplies, as well as a perceived need for improved understanding of the underlying hydrology of the nation's water resources and the possibilities for putting those resources to better use, also contributed to demands for change. Conservationists believed the solutions lay in an activist federal government that would introduce benevolent, farsighted, scientific management. They believed it was wasteful to leave water resources un-

used if they were capable of producing crops, power, or other valued outputs. Conservationists argued the government should assume responsibility for planning, constructing, and operating the facilities needed to gain control over the natural resources and to put them to "wise use." The views of the conservationists, the origins of which date back to the 1870s in the United States, became ascendant in 1901 when Theodore Roosevelt became president.

The Growing Federal Role

Putting water to use to encourage settlement and development of the West was a major concern of the conservationists. The West was still relatively unsettled in 1900 and those settlers who had attempted to establish farms in the area were in a precarious situation. Precipitation was too sparse and unreliable for highly productive dryland agriculture, and irrigation, which was expensive, had left many irrigators heavily in debt. Thus the conservationists believed the federal government would have to support investments both in storage to increase the safe yield of western streams and in canals to deliver water to irrigable lands.

The Reclamation Act of 1902 reflected those views. Through this legislation, Congress established the Reclamation Service (renamed the Bureau of Reclamation in 1923) to assist in developing the arid West through irrigation. The sale of public lands would produce funding for the irrigation projects. The initial legislation called for irrigators to repay the construction costs without interest over ten years, with the repayments financing additional irrigation projects. However, most farmers were unable to meet the repayment schedule; thus new federal appropriations were required to fund most of the subsequent projects. The Reclamation Extension Act of 1914, which increased the repayment period to twenty years with a five-year grace period, was the first of several increases in the subsidies for federal irrigation projects.

This change in the political environment, as well as technological advances, also fostered the activities of the Corps of Engineers. The 1908 report of the Inland Waterways Commission marked the beginning of a federal effort to systematically improve the nation's waterways to permit the efficient use of improved marine engines, propellers adapted to shallow-draft vessels, and towboats and barges. However, the most effective impetus for renewed interest in inland navigation came during World War I when the railroads were unable to meet the nation's increased transport needs (Howe and coauthors, 1969).

Even though navigation remained the principal concern of the COE during this period, its role in the production of water power increased. Legislation in 1910 mandated that investigations of navigable streams include information on all stream uses affecting navigation. More pointedly, legislation in 1913 directed the COE to include in its reports on watersheds information on developing and using water power. Nevertheless, legislators viewed water power development as a byproduct that might be included in a project that was approved solely on the basis of its navigation benefits. In addition, the Flood Control Act of 1917, which followed two years of disastrous floods in the Mississippi and Sacramento river basins, gave the COE authority for planning and constructing flood control works. Unlike the legislation for navigation projects, this act required states or local communities to pay at least half the costs of constructing levees (Holmes, 1972).

The conservationists sought to establish a national water resources planning agency to coordinate the activities of all federal agencies that were responsible for water resources and to prepare multipurpose plans for the nation's watersheds. The conservationists even succeeded in passing legislation in 1917 to establish a waterways commission to provide planning functions. However, World War I intervened before Congress appointed members to this commission; Congress terminated the commission in 1920 (Holmes, 1972).

Technological Change and Water Development

Technological as well as political factors became conducive to a more concerted effort to control the nation's water resources early in the twentieth century. By the start of the century, water technology had advanced little from the aqueducts constructed about 2,000 years earlier by the Romans and the water control techniques developed several hundred years earlier by the Dutch. Hydraulic construction methods developed during the last half of the nineteenth century had been used to build some dams, but these methods were limited in their applications. Wheel-

barrows and mules were still the principal means of moving earth to construct levees and embankments for controlling water in 1900. Then, early in the twentieth century, several advances combined to greatly increase the economic and technical possibilities for water development. Increased mechanical power started revolutionizing earth moving, improvements in the production of concrete made it possible to build large dams in locations once considered impossible sites, new construction techniques helped lower costs, and improvements in electricity transmission made it easier to match the power potential of large dams with the electricity demands of the cities and factories (Ackerman and Lof, 1959).

These developments contributed to rapid increases in both water use and dam construction. Total water withdrawals more than doubled from 40.2 bgd in 1900 to more than 90 bgd in 1920 (see table 2-A1). Approximately 70 percent of the total increase was for irrigation, which grew 177 percent over the two decades and accounted for more than 60 percent of all withdrawals by 1920. Groundwater use for irrigation increased 2.7 times, but groundwater still accounted for only 15 percent of the irrigation water by 1920. Withdrawals increased for all categories: by 1920, public water utility use doubled from 3.0 bgd to 6.0 bgd, industrial and miscellaneous use rose about 80 percent to 18 bgd, and steam electric utility use increased 84 percent to 9.2 bgd. By 1920, the total installed generating capacity in hydroelectric plants was 4.8 million kilowatts (kW) (Federal Power Commission, 1957).

From 1900 to 1920, 4,734 new dams with a storage capacity of 43 million acre-feet (maf) were completed (table 2-A2). In comparison, during the preceding 200 years, only 2,661 dams with a total storage capacity of 10 maf had been produced. The dominant purposes of these dams were recreation (35 percent), irrigation (25 percent), water supply (18 percent), hydroelectric (9 percent), and flood control (2 percent) (table 2-A3). However, many dams, especially the larger ones, served multiple purposes.

Drinking Water and Public Supplies

Scientists, who recognized the importance of drinking water to good health, introduced methods for treating the water by the turn of the century. High costs limited the adoption of these methods. Consequently, drinking water continued to be a major source of disease until the introduction of chlorination in about 1908. Chlorination provided the nation's approximately 3,000 community water systems with an inexpensive method of ensuring the bacteriological quality of the water. The U.S. Public Health Service issued the first national drinking water standards in 1914, and most communities quickly complied with the standards (Johnson, 1988). Soon thereafter, most Americans took the availability of safe drinking water for granted.

Water quantity was rarely a concern of community supply systems during the conservation period, except in Los Angeles. That city, which is located in a desert with no large neighboring river, doubled in size to about 200,000 people from 1900 to 1904. A severe drought during this period resulted in prohibitions on lawn watering, in the drying up of park ponds, and in a sharp decline in the pressure of the artesian wells used for irrigation in nearby San Fernando Valley. Area leaders recognized that the indigenous water supplies were inadequate to provide for the growth they envisioned, and in 1904 they set out to secure supplemental supplies for Los Angeles. Within a decade, the city was importing water from the Owens Valley through the Los Angeles aqueduct. However, the tactics employed—"chicanery, subterfuge, spies, bribery, a campaign of divide-and-conquer, and a strategy of lies to get the water it needed" (Reisner, 1986, p. 65)—left lasting scars. Memories of the Owens Valley incident would later hamper southern California's efforts near the end of the twentieth century to secure additional water imports. Although Los Angeles was the first, it was certainly not the last area where water use grew to levels far in excess of indigenous, sustainable supplies.

Private Versus Public Water Development: 1921–1932

The political environment for federal water projects shifted following World War I and the election of Warren Harding, the first of three Republican presidents to occupy the White House from 1921 to 1932. Republican conservatives successfully countered most of the conservationists' efforts to establish a more activist federal role in developing and managing the nation's water resources during this period. For instance, on two occasions the conservationists, who remained powerful in Congress, passed legislation to create a government corporation to plan and develop the Tennessee River Valley for power, flood control, navigation, and other purposes; this legislation was vetoed by presidents Coolidge in 1928 and Hoover in 1931 (Holmes, 1972).

The Federal Water Power Act of 1920 established the Federal Power Commission, which began as an interagency cabinet-level committee empowered to sell surplus power generated from federal dams, to license nonfederal power developments on navigable waters and public lands, and to survey water power development opportunities in the United States. These surveys, which were initiated as joint efforts of the U.S. Department of Agriculture, the Department of the Interior, and the Department of War and later undertaken by the Corps of Engineers, established a foundation for subsequent federal water resource investments and efforts to establish basinwide water resource planning (Foster and Rogers, 1988).

The ideological struggle over the proper federal role in water development was particularly evident in the area of hydropower. The Federal Water Power Act of 1920 gave public interests precedence in the use of the power and reserved ultimate ownership rights for the government. Nevertheless, one of Harding's first acts as president was to terminate work on the nearly completed Wilson Dam on the Tennessee River and to try to transfer it to private hands. This dam had been the first of several authorized to provide power for the war effort.

The conflict over private versus public ownership of hydroelectric power, which has yet to be resolved in the United States, did not prevent a rapid expansion of hydropower during this period. Water storage facilities constructed for irrigation, flood control, navigation, and other purposes provided numerous opportunities for power generation that was further bolstered by major technological developments. Electric generating capacity doubled during the 1920s to a total of 9.7 million kW by 1930 (Federal Power Commission, 1957).

By compromising on the issue of federal power, the conservationists did succeed in passing the Boulder Canyon Project Act of 1928, which authorized a huge multipurpose water project on the Colorado

Waters for Economic Development, this accounting method had important implications for western water development.

Water use continued to grow rapidly during the 1920s. Withdrawals increased 21 percent during the decade to a total of 110.5 bgd by 1920 (see table 2-A1). Steam electric utilities, which doubled their water use over the decade, accounted for nearly 50 percent of the total increase. Irrigation use increased only 8 percent, but this sector remained the largest user with 54 percent of the total.

The nation's inventory of dams by 1932 increased by 38 percent from the inventory calculated in 1920; the average annual number of dams completed ($n = 232$) changed little from that of the previous two decades (see table 2-A2). However, storage capacity per dam completed during this period was more than three times that of the earlier period. The nation's total storage capacity increased by 81 maf, an increase of more than 150 percent in twelve years. The relative classification of the dams completed during this period by their primary purpose differed somewhat from that of the 1900–1920 period. Higher percentages of the new dams were intended primarily for recreation (40 percent), water supply (20 percent), hydroelectric power (11 percent), and stock or farm ponds (6 percent) than in the previous period. The percentage of flood control dams (2 percent) remained the same and those for irrigation declined from 25 percent to 16 percent (see table 2-A3).

The Growing Federal Role: 1933–1944

Water projects gained a new rationale in the 1930s as the nation suffered its worst depression and the Great Plains suffered its worst drought in recorded history. Water development projects helped to create desperately needed jobs and to provide greater control over a fickle resource.

Federal Water Projects

As the economy sank into a deep depression and unemployment rates increased, the political climate

River (Holmes, 1972). The centerpiece of the project was Hoover Dam (initially named Boulder Dam), an impressive engineering accomplishment that required major technical innovations. Upon completion in 1935, it became the world's largest dam and an inspiration for countless additional water projects. However, the dam's legacy is not limited to its impressive size and engineering. This project established a precedent for using the revenues from hydroelectric power sales to pay for dams, reservoirs, and power plants. This concept of using power revenues to finance other aspects of a water project was broadened by the Bureau of Reclamation after World War II into a concept of "river-basin accounting." As described in the section on Reshaping the Nation's for direct federal involvement in water projects improved. Franklin Roosevelt's New Deal was welcomed in 1933, and his first 100 days in office brought a rash of new laws to deal with the Great Depression. Two of these laws—the Tennessee Valley Authority Act of 1933 and the National Industrial Recovery Act of 1933 (NIRA) had particular significance for water resource development.

The natural regime of the Tennessee River is characterized by large spring flows that produce destructive floods and low summer flows that inhibit navigation. The intensity and frequency of these events discouraged development and contributed to persistent poverty in the valley. To counter these natural obstacles, the Tennessee Valley Authority Act of 1933 created the Tennessee Valley Authority (TVA)—a public agency with broad powers (including the authority to build and operate dams and reservoirs and to generate and sell hydroelectric power)—to promote development in the region. The TVA is a unique institution in that it brings all the water-related functions of the federal government under a single, independent public body. The TVA used its authority to transform the Tennessee River into one of the most highly regulated rivers in the world within about two decades. The TVA inherited Wilson Dam, and before World War II it had completed six additional multipurpose dams with power plants and locks for navigation. Investments in dams and hydropower facilities within the Tennessee Valley also received high priority during the war.

Title II of the NIRA authorized the creation of the Public Works Administration to create jobs while undertaking public works. The NIRA also gave the U.S. president unprecedented powers to initiate public works, including water projects. The Public Works Administration provided loans and grants to state and local governments and to federal agencies for municipal water works, sewage plants, irrigation, flood control, and water power projects. California's Central Valley Project, the Bonneville and Grand Coulee dams on the Columbia River, and Fort Peck Dam on the Missouri River were among the many major projects authorized under this legislation (Holmes, 1972).

The National Planning Board (created in 1933 under the NIRA) and its successor agencies, the National Resources Board (1934–1935), the National Resources Committee (1935–1939), and the National Resources Planning Board (1939–1943), stimulated and coordinated basinwide resource planning and ranked multiple purpose water projects according to their social importance (Holmes, 1972). Subsequent New Deal legislation further expanded the powers of the executive branch to initiate water studies and projects. The River and Harbor Act of 1935 gave the president authority to initiate navigation improvements, and the Flood Control Act of 1936 initiated a national flood control program and expanded the authority of the Corps of Engineers to develop river basin plans for navigation. Previous federal flood control efforts had been confined largely to the lower Mississippi basin and, to a lesser extent, the Sacramento basin.

Drought and the Dust Bowl

The drought leading to the infamous Dust Bowl extinguished any lingering hopes that "rain would follow the plow." During the 1920s and early 1930s millions of additional acres had been planted to wheat in the Great Plains, a region constituting all or part of ten states extending from Montana and North Dakota in the north to New Mexico and Texas in the south. In 1934 the rains stopped falling and this region entered into its worst drought in more than 300 years (Warrick, 1980). In some areas the drought continued until 1941. Long before that time, however, many harvests had been lost, enormous quantities of soil had eroded with the wind, and, for the second time in fifty years, the region experienced a mass exodus of destitute farmers. Many of these people headed west hoping either to land jobs working on the massive dams being built in California and along the Columbia River or to acquire land with a controlled supply of water.

The U.S. Soil Conservation Services (SCS) was established within the Department of Agriculture in 1935 in part to deal with the farming practices that were believed to have contributed to the Dust Bowl. There was also a growing belief during the 1930s that farming practices were contributing to downstream flooding and that upstream flood protection was needed to complement the downstream levees and dams of the Corps of Engineers. Thus the SCS's early activities focused on assisting farmers in adopting water and soil conservation practices. This mission was broadened by the Water Facilities Act of 1937, which authorized the U.S. Department of Agriculture (USDA) to plan and construct upstream agricultural water-storage facilities on private or public lands. Specific authority to construct such facilities did not come until the 1950s, when the Soil Conservation Service started planning and assisting in the construction of small watershed reservoirs. Initially, the reservoirs were supposed to be designed only for flood protection and agricultural purposes. This restriction was relaxed in 1956 to include municipal and industrial water supplies, recreation, and fish and wildlife habitat as allowable functions of SCS reservoirs (Holmes, 1972; Sampson, 1985).

The intensity and broad geographic extent of the 1934 drought raised concerns about the ability of many public water-supply systems to meet demand. White's (1935) study suggested that these systems performed well overall. Only about 2 percent of the population served by public water supplies were adversely affected by the drought. Most of the shortages were experienced by small communities of fewer than 5,000 people where there was either a failure to build and maintain adequate supply capacity or extreme aridity that made the provision of adequate supplies difficult even in nondrought times.

Water Development and Use

The favorable environment for water development is reflected in the number and size of the dams, public and private, completed during the New Deal era. More than 5,000 dams, or nearly 1.2 per day, were constructed, and reservoir storage capacity was more than doubled during the twelve years (table 2-A2). Recreation (37 percent), stock or farm ponds (21 percent), water supply (17 percent), and irrigation (12 percent) were the major purposes of the dams completed during this period (table 2-A3).

Although hydroelectric power production was the principal purpose of only 3 percent of the dams constructed during this period, power was a product of many of the other dams. In 1935, hydroelectric power provided an estimated 30 percent of the nation's electricity. Although hydroelectric power continued to grow, its role in the overall national power supply declined after the mid-1930s, as cheap fossil fuels were used in central generating plants (Payne, 1983; Holmes, 1972). Federally owned facilities accounted for only a small part (approximately 14 percent as of 1940) of the total hydroelectric capacity. Investor-owned utilities constituted more than two-thirds of the total, and industrial and nonfederal public utilities each contributed nearly 9 percent of the total capacity in the 1940s (U.S. Department of Energy, 1979).

Total water withdrawals increased 54 percent to nearly 170 bgd between 1930 and 1945 (table 2-A1). Nearly 17 percent of the total was from groundwater. Irrigation withdrawals increased 40 percent and ac-

counted for just under 50 percent of the total in 1945. The fastest growth was in industrial and miscellaneous withdrawals, which increased 95 percent to 41 bgd, and steam electric, which increased 70 percent to 31 bgd in 1945. Withdrawals by public water utilities increased 50 percent to a level of 12 bgd.

Reshaping the Nation's Waters for Economic Development: 1945–1969

The rate of dam construction accelerated to a frenetic pace following World War II. More than 35,000 new dams were completed between 1945 and 1969, a rate of nearly 3.9 every day over the twenty-five years (table 2-A2). Although the distribution of ownership of these new dams is unknown, the private sector was undoubtedly an important factor in the number of dams constructed, as less than 5 percent of all dams in the COE's 1982 dam inventory were federally owned. The federal government has been a principal factor in planning and constructing most of the large water projects. The total number of dams increased 230 percent and the total storage capacity increased 170 percent, or by 474 maf, from before 1945 to the end of this period.

Several factors combined to produce a rapid increase in water development and use during the 1933–1944 period. Overall economic growth strengthened as gross private domestic investment increased nearly fourfold in constant dollars within two decades (Council of Economic Advisers, 1989). Some of this investment undoubtedly was directed to developing water supplies. In addition, as the war was drawing to a close federal water projects again were valued as a means of creating jobs. Concerns about the return of mass unemployment contributed to the unprecedented number of water projects authorized by the Flood Control Act of 1944. These concerns proved to be unfounded. Moreover, the importance of hydroelectric power to the war effort quieted some former critics of these projects (Holmes, 1972). Four federal agencies involved in water construction—the Corps of Engineers, the Bureau of Reclamation, the Tennessee Valley Authority, and the Soil Conservation Service—were seeking to expand their activities during this period. Congress, which seemed reluctant to

refuse any water project, regained control over project authorization and funding that had been relinquished with passage of the NIRA. Moreover, technological advances provided new opportunities for private users and suppliers.

The Political Environment: Financing Projects

When Congress abolished the National Resources Planning Board in 1943 and prohibited the transfer of its functions to another agency, the executive branch was left without the capability to prepare overall plans for water resource development or to adequately evaluate those plans produced by construction agencies. This void enabled the congressional committees responsible for each of the construction agencies to gain greater control of the federal water-development agenda (Holmes, 1972). These committees worked closely with construction agencies and local communities in seeking water projects.

The federal government paid all the costs associated with flood control and navigation works and subsidized the costs of providing other project benefits, thus stirring local interest in water projects. The Reclamation Project Act of 1939, for instance, had greatly expanded the subsidies on federally irrigated land. The government gave irrigators a ten-year grace period and as long as fifty years to repay their debts without interest. If this repayment schedule proved too burdensome, the government would reduce further the irrigators' contribution so that it matched their ability to pay (U.S. General Accounting Office, 1981). Thus, regardless of a project's net value to the nation, local communities eagerly sought federal funds and the jobs they provided.

State and local communities had other reasons for seeking water projects. Flood control, improved navigation, more reliable water supplies, and inexpensive hydropower were important benefits to the recipient community even if the net national benefits of a project were negative. Moreover, the "first-in-time, first-in-right" doctrine of water law adopted by the western states provided further incentive for local interests to develop water supplies. Water rights were established by withdrawing the resource from its natural stream and putting it to a beneficial use, and a large-scale water project subsidized by the federal government was one way a community could capture the potential benefits of the resource for its own use.

Before receiving Congress's blessing, a state or community was supposed to justify a water project economically to show that the project would produce positive net national benefits. The Flood Control Act of 1936 established the criteria that flood control projects were to be undertaken only "if the benefits to whomsoever they may accrue are in excess of the estimated costs. . . ." Similarly, the Reclamation Project Act of 1939 required that the total benefits exceed the costs of Bureau of Reclamation projects. Although all federal water development projects have been subject to a benefit-cost criterion since about 1945, there has been little consistency in the analyses carried out by the different agencies.

To reconcile differences in analyses, Congress created a subcommittee of the U.S. Federal Inter-Agency River Basin Committee (which consisted of representatives of federal agencies with water resource responsibilities) in 1946. The 1950 subcommittee report, entitled "Proposed Practices for Economic Analysis of River Basin Projects" (U.S. Federal Inter-Agency River Basin Committee, Subcommittee on Benefits and Costs, 1950)—commonly referred to as the Greenbook—was praised by economists for its sophistication and contribution to understanding public investment issues. The full committee and federal agencies, however, never fully accepted the report (Kneese, 1990). Later several federal documents would attempt to standardize benefit-cost analysis among the water agencies. For example, in 1983, the Reagan administration issued a document known as the *Principles and Guidelines* (U.S. Water Resources Council, 1983). In addition to establishing general standards and procedures, this document provides specific guidance on how federal agencies should calculate benefits and costs.

During the twenty-five years following the end of World War II, federal agencies became adept at producing benefit-cost ratios well in excess of unity for any project that had the support of the senators and representatives who controlled agency budgets. As Marshall (1966, p. 294) noted in the mid-1960s, "the literature is unanimous in alleging that agency practices have the effect of inflating benefits or deflating costs, or both. Moreover, the differences between agency claims and the findings of independent reviewers are not small." For instance, the Missouri Basin Survey Commission could find only one-twelfth the benefits from erosion control and one-third the savings to shippers claimed by the COE. The Bureau of Reclamation commonly distorted costs and benefits by inflating the value of the crops to be produced on project lands and by claiming secondary benefits, often exceeding the primary benefits, that most analysts would not accept as legitimate project benefits. Furthermore, the construction agencies assumed that the value of the water in its preproject use is zero. Thus instream flows were assumed to have no value.

Political considerations replaced objective economic analysis in allocating federal funds to water projects. For instance, Ferejohn's (1974) analysis of the legislation affecting the Corps of Engineers' budgets from 1947 to 1968 demonstrates that the distribution of the COE projects favored the districts represented by the leaders and members of the appropriation and authorization committees and subcommittees in both chambers of Congress who were responsible for COE activities.

The Bureau of Reclamation still might have had problems justifying and funding some of its irrigation projects without the use of "river-basin accounting." This practice and its implications have been described by Reisner:

> With river-basin accounting, one could take all the revenues generated by projects in any river basin—dams, irrigation projects, navigation and recreation features—and toss them into a common "fund." The hydroelectric dams might contribute ninety-five cents of every dollar accruing to the fund, while the irrigation features might contribute only a nickel (and cost three times as much to build and operate as the dams), but it wouldn't matter; as long as revenues came in at a pace that would permit the Reclamation Act's forty-year repayment schedule to be met, the whole package could be considered economically sound. . . . Even if it subverted logic, economics, and simple common sense, it was essential to the Bureau's survival as an institution and to the continued expansion of irrigation in the high, arid West. On the other hand, it was something akin to a blanket death sentence for the free-flowing rivers in sixteen states. (Reisner, 1986, pp. 140–142)

In the absence of a central agency with the capacity and responsibility for overall river-basin planning, the construction agencies had considerable latitude to develop their own plans and projects. The enabling legislation of each agency placed limits on the type of projects each was supposed to consider. These jurisdictional limits suggested a need for interagency cooperation to agree on an overall strategy for developing a basin's resources. No such cooperation materialized, however. To the contrary, the agencies often competed for hegemony to develop a basin in their own image (Holmes, 1979).

Competition between the Corps of Engineers and the Bureau of Reclamation had been particularly keen in the Missouri River basin. The COE (supported by lower basin states) wanted to build low, wide dams that would create a chain of huge reservoirs for navigation and flood control for the lower basin. These projects were incorporated into the Corps of Engineers' Pick plan, named after Lewis Pick, director of the Corps' regional office in Omaha when the plan was formulated and later chief of engineers. The Bureau of Reclamation (supported by upper basin states) wanted to build irrigation projects and high dams to generate power to pay for the irrigation. Ninety dams and several hundred irrigation projects were included in the bureau's Sloan plan, named after bureau engineer Glenn Sloan, who drew up the agency's basin-wide development plan. The two plans seemed irreconcilable until a hasty truce was arranged in 1944 under a threat that the basin might otherwise be placed under a TVA-like regional authority. The resulting Pick-Sloan plan, authorized by the Flood Control Act of 1944, contained almost all of the projects (316 total, including 112 dams) proposed under the COE's Pick plan and the bureau's Sloan plan. Pick-Sloan was designed to gain congressional approval for projects that would keep both agencies busy for decades. It reflected the narrow interests of both agencies; the absence of any concern about how water projects might best contribute to the region's development; and a callous disregard for taxpayers, wildlife, and Native Americans (Reisner, 1986).

Because the Corps of Engineers became much more successful in securing funding for its projects, development of the basin has largely fit the image of that agency. A 300-foot-wide channel on the Missouri River connects Sioux City, Iowa, to the mouth of the Missouri River near St. Louis, Missouri, and six major dams on the mainstem have created an almost continuous chain of reservoirs where the river once flowed freely in North Dakota and South Dakota. From the perspective of the upper basin states, 1.2 million acres of their prime agricultural land have been inundated to provide flood control, navigation, and hydropower largely for the benefit of other states. Few of the irrigation projects authorized under the Pick-Sloan plan were ever built. The economic and environmental costs are so high relative to their benefits that, currently, the projects are controversial within the upper basin states.

Thinking Big About Water Development

The early 1960s were particularly heady times for the Bureau of Reclamation and the Corps of Engineers; their budgets were generally large and their plans often were grandiose. Structural approaches—that is, dams, reservoirs, and canals—supplemented by research to develop new technologies such as desalinization and weather modification were widely accepted as the way to provide for growing water demands.

One of the more grandiose schemes was the Bureau of Reclamation's Pacific Southwest Water Plan, which called for intensive development of the water resources of the nation's driest five-state area. The version the bureau submitted to the president in 1964 recommended seventeen projects and programs, including a plan to pump Colorado River water over the mountains into central Arizona for Phoenix and Tucson, two big dams on the Trinity River in northern California, a tunnel to divert water from the Trinity River to the Sacramento River, a wider California state

From the perspective of the upper basin states, 1.2 million acres of their prime agricultural land have been inundated to provide flood control, navigation, and hydropower largely for the benefit of other states.

aqueduct to deliver more water from the north to the central and southern parts of the state, and two large hydropower projects at Bridge and Marble canyons, located at opposite ends of Grand Canyon National Park on the Colorado River. These two dams would not add to the effective water supply in the basin because of the enormous storage called for in the Colorado River Storage Project approved in 1956. In fact, increased evaporation from the reservoirs might result in a net loss of effective water supply in some years. Nevertheless, the dams at Bridge and Marble canyons were a key component of the project because the power revenues from these dams were needed to give the scheme even a vague pretense of ever generating enough revenue to repay the reimbursable costs. The only sites left in the Colorado basin for "cash register" dams—dams capable of producing such large amounts of power—were in the Colorado River gorge. Although the proposed dams were not supposed to flood the park itself, they would flood Grand Canyon National Monument and several beautiful side streams. Moreover, they would leave the park situated between two large reservoirs backed up behind Marble Gorge Dam just upstream and Bridge Canyon just downstream. The perceived threat that these dams posed to the Grand Canyon was instrumental in rallying opposition to and the demise of most of the Pacific Southwest Water Plan (Holmes, 1979; Reisner, 1986).

Even if this ambitious water plan had been fully implemented, some people anticipated a time when the arid Southwest would need even more water to satisfy the demands of its rapidly growing population and economy. The Bureau of Reclamation apparently shared this view, and thus undertook preliminary studies for an interbasin transfer from the Columbia River (which has a mean annual flow about twenty-two times that of the Colorado) to the arid Southwest. In 1968, however, Congress imposed a ten-year moratorium (which was subsequently extended) on undertaking feasibility studies for such a transfer. Legislators from the Southwest accepted the moratorium as a condition for the authorization of the Central Arizona Project, which, upon completion in the early 1990s, will pump 1.2 maf annually from the Colorado River at Lake Havasu to Phoenix, Tucson, and surrounding areas (Reisner, 1986; Welsh, 1985).

The Senate Select Committee on National Water Resources in its 1961 report emphasized the importance of increasing municipal, industrial, and recre-

ational water supplies, and the role of water quality and pollution abatement in achieving these increases. Although these had not been traditional concerns of the water-development agencies, the Water Supply Act of 1958 had expanded the authority of these agencies to include municipal, industrial, and recreation uses as part of their projects. Moreover, the 1961 report identified streamflow regulation through reservoir construction and watershed management as a principal means of achieving the needs outlined in the report (Holmes, 1979).

The record drought that gripped the Northeast from 1962 to 1965 broadened the base of support for additional water projects. The drought prompted Congress in 1965 to direct the Corps of Engineers to develop plans to meet the long-term water "needs" of the region extending from Maine to southern Virginia and to expand COE authority to permit its participation in the construction, operation, and maintenance of water supply facilities such as reservoirs, major interbasin conveyance facilities, and purification plants (Holmes, 1979). The COE study, which was not completed until more than a decade after the end of the drought, recommended initiating a massive construction program (U.S. Army Corps of Engineers, 1977).

The Tennessee Valley Authority was the only federal water-development agency that was not expanding its construction activities in the early 1960s. But by this time the TVA had gained control of the mainstem of the Tennessee River through the 31 large dams and reservoirs already in place. With almost no free-flowing water left in the mainstem, TVA focused its water-development activities on the tributaries that still were experiencing periodic flooding (Holmes, 1979).

Ambitious water planning during this period was not limited to the federal agencies. In 1959, the California State Water Project authorized construction of a major aqueduct and storage system designed to provide flood protection in northern California and facilities to move large quantities of water from the north to the arid central and southern parts of the state. Even the largest federal and state plans paled in comparison with schemes prepared by private engineering and construction firms. The most ambitious plan of all was the North American Water and Power Alliance, conceived in the 1950s and promoted with considerable zeal in the 1960s; this plan would bring 110 maf of water annually (about eight times the virgin flow of the Colorado River) from Alaska and northern Canada to the western United States and northern Mexico at a cost in the hundreds of billions of dollars (Reisner 1986; Welsh 1985).

Water Pricing and Use

These ambitious plans for more and bigger water projects were at least in part a response to the nation's seemingly insatiable thirst. Water use rose rapidly following World War II. From 1945 to 1970, total withdrawals for offstream uses increased 117 percent to 370 bgd; per capita withdrawals increased 48 percent from about 1,200 to about 1,800 gallons per day (see tables 2-A1 and 2-A4).[1] The largest increases in water withdrawals from 1945 to 1970 were for thermoelectric power production, which displaced irrigation as the nation's largest withdrawer of water by 1965. This sector alone accounted for nearly 70 percent of

the increase in water withdrawals from 1945 to 1970 and 46 percent of all withdrawals by the end of this period. Water use for irrigation increased 56 percent from 1945 to 1970 and accounted for 35 percent of all withdrawals in 1970. Public-supplied water increased 125 percent and other industrial uses increased only 15 percent. Instream uses for hydroelectric power increased 155 percent from 1950 to 1970 (table 2-A4). Installed hydroelectric capacity in millions of kilowatts totalled 12.4 in 1940, 18.7 in 1950, 33.1 in 1960, and 51.9 in 1970. Federally owned capacity accounted for 54 percent of the increase over the twenty-five years 1945–1970 as it increased from 14 percent to 44 percent of the total (U.S. Department of Energy, 1979).

The low price of water to the user contributed to the magnitude of the increase in use. Traditionally, water was—and has been—treated as free. Offstream users paid only the costs associated with transporting and, if necessary, treating the water. There was no charge for the original right to use the water.[2] In many cases, subsidies as well as the pricing policies of water utilities further reduced a user's costs. Moreover, there was no charge for returning water to a stream in degraded condition. The low prices resulting from these practices not only increased water use and abuse; they also increased the demand for projects to provide more water.

The Bureau of Reclamation program provided irrigators with particularly generous federal subsidies. The level of subsidy expanded both legislatively and administratively by bureau decisions that were favorable to irrigators. One estimate suggests that the federal subsidies for irrigation projects ranged from 57 percent to more than 90 percent of the construction costs. The average subsidy was approximately 80 percent of the costs (Wahl, 1989).

Municipal and industrial users generally were expected to pay their own way. The Public Works Administration provided loans and grants that could be used for municipal water works during the New Deal period, but these uses were not even eligible objectives for federal water projects until the Water Supply Act of 1958 made it federal policy to assist the states and local communities by providing water storage for municipal and industrial uses (Holmes, 1972). Even then, the costs of providing municipal and industrial storage were supposed to be fully reimbursable. Nevertheless, all water provided by federal projects received at least an implicit subsidy stemming from the artificially low interest rates used by these agencies coupled with the fifty-year repayment period. Additional municipal and industrial subsidies provided by the act stem from a provision allowing 30 percent of all construction costs to be allocated to future demand, with interest and principal payments on this portion of the project deferred up to ten years. According to one estimate, the subsidy received by municipal and industrial users as a percentage of the combined capital, operation, and maintenance costs amounted to 29 percent for Bureau of Reclamation projects and 46 percent for COE projects (Wahl, 1989).

The planning and pricing policies of the urban water industry also encouraged the growth in municipal water use. Publicly owned municipal systems had traditionally treated water as a necessity to be supplied at the lowest possible cost. Municipal demand had been assumed to grow in line with population and economic growth and to be unresponsive to price. Consequently, rates often had been set just high enough to cover average costs, including a "fair" return to capital and an allowance for future expansion. Average-cost pricing in a rising-cost industry such as water resulted in prices below marginal costs. This in turn encouraged water use to rise to a point where the costs of the additional supply exceeded the benefits of the additional use (Frederick and Kneese, 1990). Also, average-cost pricing often was imposed by regulations on private water suppliers to limit the large profits that might otherwise be earned by these monopolistic suppliers.

The increase in water use for thermoelectric power production reflected the nation's rapid industrial growth during this period as well as the fact that industry was not paying the full costs of its water use. Most industrial water was withdrawn directly from a lake or stream by the using firm. Although there were no direct subsidies involved, these firms did not pay for either the opportunity costs of the water consumptively used or the environmental costs of their return flows. Nearly all of the water withdrawn for thermoelectric power cooling during this period was returned to a surface or groundwater source. Thus, the principal environmental effects may have resulted from the increase in temperature of the receiving water bodies. Higher water temperatures can be detrimental to some aquatic life and tend to accelerate damages inflicted by other pollutants. An increase in water temperature also induces higher evaporation rates.

Irrigation, the other major offstream water use, was by far the largest consumptive use. In 1965, irrigators accounted for one-third of the nation's withdrawals and 6 of every 7 gallons of consumptive use. Within the seventeen western states, these percentages were even higher. More than 90 percent of the consumptive use of western water was attributable to irrigating approximately 33 million acres in the mid-1960s. Thus, in the nation's most water-scarce areas, irrigators were the largest water users.

The Greening of the West

Irrigated acreage grew at approximately 2.6 percent annually in the quarter-century following World War II to a total of 39 million acres in 1969. Five of every six of the additional acres irrigated during this period were in the seventeen western states, which accounted for 89 percent of the national total in 1969 (table 2-A5).

The post–World War II expansion of western irrigation differed considerably in both its location and character from that prevailing in 1945. The Mountain states, as defined by farm production region (figure 2-2), accounted for more than half of the nation's irrigated lands in the mid-1940s (table 2-A5). Much of the irrigation in this region involved flooding riparian fields with gravity flows to grow relatively low-value crops such as pasture and hay (Frederick with Hanson, 1982). In contrast, the expansion over the next twenty-five years depended largely on new pumping technologies and large-scale water development projects. Bureau of Reclamation projects added 4.4 million irrigated acres, one-fourth of the West's total increase over the 1945–1969 period. Most of the rest of the 15.4-million-acre increase in irrigation in the West was based on groundwater. Moreover, 7 of every 8 additional acres irrigated in the West were in the Plains and Pacific states where high-value crops such as grains, fruits, and vegetables dominated.

Groundwater was a largely untapped resource in the mid-1930s. Its use was limited to areas where there was either artesian pressure or low pumping lifts. The maximum distance for lifting water with the suction pump in use at that time was approximately 25 feet. Perfection of the vertical turbine pump in the late 1930s greatly increased the depths from which groundwater could be pumped economically. Although submersible pumps were developed around

1920, their use was limited to the oil industry until 1948, when they became available commercially for general use (Ackerman and Lof, 1959). The combination of these technologies, which increased the effective pumping depth to nearly 300 feet, and the availability of low-cost energy encouraged a rapid development of groundwater irrigation in the West after World War II. Groundwater use for western irrigation rose from 18.2 to 46.2 maf between 1950 and 1970 and from 21 to 35 percent of all water withdrawals by western irrigators (table 2-A6).

The greatest expansion in groundwater pumping occurred in the High Plains, an area covering parts of Texas, New Mexico, Oklahoma, Colorado, Kansas, and Nebraska, where the Ogallala aquifer is the principal source of water. The High Plains alone accounted for nearly 4 of every 10 additional acres irrigated in the West during the first two decades following World War II (Frederick with Hanson, 1982). Irrigation on the High Plains started in Texas south of the Canadian River where the growing season is longer and pumping distances, at least initially, were less. However, the saturated thickness of the aquifer is also generally less in the southern High Plains than it is north of the Canadian River, and the Ogallala aquifer receives little recharge south of the Platte River and the Sandhills of Nebraska. Consequently, groundwater stocks in the southern High Plains were

soon being mined, and by the mid-1960s declining water supplies started to be reflected in a decline in the area's irrigated acreage (Frederick with Hanson, 1982). According to one estimate, the volume of water stored in the Ogallala aquifer south of the Canadian River declined by about 100 maf or more than 40 percent of its original volume by 1972 (U.S. Department of the Interior, 1973).

Irrigation has actually increased at a faster rate in the East than in the West since 1945. Yet, only 4.2 million acres, less than 11 percent of the nation's total, were irrigated in the thirty-one eastern states as of 1969. More than 80 percent of this acreage was in the Southeast and Delta regions (figure 2-2) where growing seasons are long and water supplies relatively abundant. Much of the irrigation was for high-value fruit and vegetable crops and rice, which require large quantities of water. It would be another decade or so before water availability would be viewed as an important constraint on the growth of irrigation in these regions.

Emerging Concerns and Policy Initiatives in the 1960s

The conventional wisdom in the early 1960s seemed to be that any water problem could be solved through

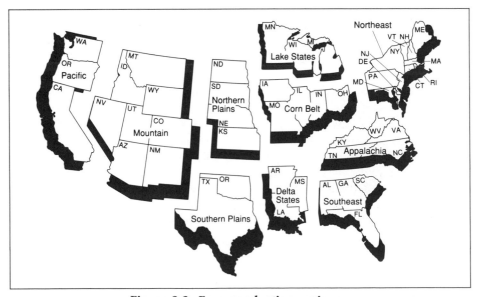

Figure 2-2. Farm production regions

Source: Day and Horner (1987).

technological change or by building another dam, levee, reservoir, canal, or treatment plant. The technical and physical capacity to manipulate water for human needs had increased dramatically during the previous six decades or so, and optimists expected the future to bring more of the same.

Before the 1960s, water planners either ignored the impact on instream values associated with water projects and increased withdrawals or viewed them as minor considerations. Although the construction agencies had been obliged since the late 1940s to consult with the U.S. Fish and Wildlife Service about the impact of their projects on wildlife and with the National Park Service about the impact on scenic and historic sites, these services had little influence on the design and selection of water projects. The construction agencies, on the other hand, attached little importance to recreational and scenic values.

When flows were abundant relative to the demand for instream uses (which was generally true in the United States for much of the first half of the twentieth century), the impacts of projects on streamflows could be ignored without little distortion of an efficient planning strategy. But the tradeoffs associated with the traditional structural approach to solving water problems became increasingly difficult to ignore in the 1960s. The tremendous post-World War II growth in the number of dams constructed and in the quantities of water withdrawn from and the wastes dumped into the nation's streams exacted a heavy toll on the environmental and other instream values provided by the nation's water resources. Many lakes and streams had become too polluted for swimming, fishing, or even boating. Moreover, coincident with the decline in the number of high-quality streams, the nation was placing higher values on their uses.

The lack of coordinated basinwide planning, the substitution of political considerations for economic criteria, and the tendency to overlook environmental impacts in selecting water projects resulted in the construction of many projects of dubious social merit. Reisner (1986) concluded that federal agencies not only competed with each other for authorization and funding to mold a basin in their own images, but sometimes an agency seemed to work at cross purposes with itself. The Corps of Engineers, for instance, built dams to control flooding while its channelization of streams and drainage of wetlands tended to induce more flooding. When the drained wetlands were in-

When the drained wetlands were intensively farmed, the resulting increases in soil erosion meant the COE had to spend more time dredging to keep river channels open for navigation.

tensively farmed, the resulting increases in soil erosion meant the COE had to spend more time dredging to keep river channels open for navigation.

Federal participation based on political criteria also created a bias for larger facilities than economic criteria would justify, suggesting the nation could have benefited more from its enormous investment in water projects. According to Holmes (1972), the Corps of Engineers tended to design the largest flood control structures that could be built with an average benefit-cost ratio of unity or greater, even though smaller facilities might have provided higher expected net returns. Federal subsidies provided through the Soil Conservation Service encouraged the building of facilities in which the federal share of costs was higher, even where there were alternatives offering higher net national returns. Grants to municipalities for wastewater treatment, which were initiated in 1956 through the Public Health Service and subsequently increased, encouraged more capital-intensive solutions to curbing municipal discharges than would have occurred in the absence of subsidies (Congressional Budget Office, 1985).

The social costs of many water uses and some of the environmentally damaging projects pushed by the construction agencies received more scrutiny by the mid-1960s. Public hostility to the development emphasis of the federal agencies was fueled by proposals that threatened some of the nation's greatest natural ecosystems, including the Grand Canyon, the Everglades, and San Francisco Bay. Publication of Rachel Carson's *Silent Spring* in 1962 helped awaken public concerns over water quality. Recommendations in 1962 by the Outdoor Recreation Resources Review Commission for pollution-control investments to protect water recreation further supported transforming federal water policies from a development orientation to a more preservationist–environmentalist orientation (Holmes, 1979).

Two legislative acts—the Water Resources Planning Act of 1965 and the Water Pollution Control Act of 1965—reflected a recognition of the potential benefits of changing federal water planning and project selection and of providing greater protection for water-quality and environmental values. The Water Resources Planning Act established the Water Resources Council (WRC), which had a responsibility to encourage and supervise river-basin planning and prepare comprehensive and consistent water policies for the executive branch. The WRC had some success in encouraging the use of basinwide plans to select water projects and in introducing consideration of alternative ways (including nonstructural approaches) to meet water demands. On the other hand, because the WRC was controlled by the development agencies and its funding depended on normal congressional and executive branch approvals, it failed to provide an in-

dependent, critical perspective (Holmes, 1979). Activities of the WRC ceased in the early 1980s when the Reagan administration terminated its funding.

The Water Pollution Control Act of 1965 gave the federal government a more active role in protecting the quality of interstate waters. Previously, the federal role had been to assist the states in meeting their responsibilities and to encourage solutions to interstate pollution disputes. Under this new legislation, the federal government could set standards for interstate waters and had more authority to deal with polluters. In addition, each state now was required to establish and enforce quality standards for navigable waters within its borders. Funding for sewage treatment plant and interceptor sewer construction grants was increased to $150 million per year, three times the original funding provided in 1956. These grants now were permitted to cover as much as 55 percent of construction costs, compared with the 30-percent ceiling established in 1956. Nevertheless, federal funds still accounted for only a small fraction of the investments in such facilities (Freeman, 1978; Holmes, 1979).

The problems that received increasing attention during the 1960s were not entirely unanticipated. A number of analysts had questioned the traditional assumptions underlying water use and development patterns and the activities of the construction agen-

Wastewater treatment plant, District of Columbia

cies. Gilbert White (1986) demonstrated in the late 1930s that by encouraging development in the floodplains, the Corps of Engineers' exclusive reliance on structural measures for flood protection could increase rather than reduce life and property losses from floods. White also pointed out that more water was not necessarily the panacea for satisfying rising water demands and that economic growth did not necessarily depend on a comparable growth in water use, as was commonly assumed. Industry, for instance, tended to adapt to the availability of water (Kates and Burton, 1986). According to Nathaniel Wollman's studies for the Senate Select Committee on National Water Resources in the early 1960s, water quality rather than quantity was the more serious threat to supplies in many regions of the nation (Wolman and Wolman, 1986).

Encountering Economic and Environmental Limits: 1970–1990

Rising Costs and Shrinking Budgets Curtail New Water Projects

Water-project construction peaked in the mid- to late 1960s. On average, more than 2,000 dams and nearly 29 maf of new storage were completed each year from 1965 to 1969. In contrast, the annual averages dropped to 1,069 dams and less than 10 maf for the 1970–1982 period (U.S. Army Corps of Engineers, 1982).

The most grandiose of the water development schemes proposed in the early 1960s were not authorized to be built, and many authorized projects were not funded as a result of rising costs and tighter budgets. The budgets of the construction agencies came under pressure in the late 1960s as a result of the costs of the Vietnam War, and then again in the 1980s as a result of concerns over the enormous federal budget deficits and the reluctance to raise taxes to finance new projects. Excluding expenditures for domestic water supplies and wastewater treatment facilities, which traditionally have been local responsibilities, public spending to plan, construct, finance,

operate, maintain, and repair water resource facilities peaked in 1968 at $9.1 billion (in 1984 dollars). By 1984, spending on these items had declined 23 percent to $7 billion. Because operating expenditures actually rose over this period, the decline in annual capital expenditures was much greater, from slightly more than $5 billion in the late 1960s to about $2 billion in 1984 (in constant dollars) (Schilling and coauthors, 1987).

Increases in the discount rates that the federal agencies were required to use for water-supply projects made it increasingly difficult to demonstrate favorable economic returns, especially for irrigation and navigation projects for which most of the benefits are delayed many years. The discount rate rose from 2.5 percent in the 1950s, to 3.25 percent in the early and mid-1960s, to 4.625 percent in fiscal year (FY) 1969. Since that time the rate has been reviewed annually, with year-to-year changes limited to 0.25 percent (Holmes, 1979). The highest rate to date has been 8.875 percent in the early 1980s and again in FY 1989 and 1990.

Growing concerns about budget deficits, rising costs, and adverse environmental impacts may have slowed, but they certainly did not end, federal investments in water projects of questionable economic and environmental merit. President Jimmy Carter discovered the strength of the congressional pork-barrel system when he issued a "hit list" of such water projects for termination. Carter's efforts to eliminate these projects, however, probably did more to undermine the effectiveness of his presidency than it did to eliminate the targeted projects. There were no new hit lists under the Reagan administration. Nevertheless, Congress became much more selective in its support of water projects as public concerns about the effects of such projects on the environment as well as concerns about the federal deficit mounted, and as the president threatened to veto public works appropriations that he considered excessive. The biggest threat to the water pork barrel came in 1986 with passage of Public Law 99–662, which required a significant increase in local cost sharing for the Corps of Engineers' water projects.

Cost sharing is a potentially important means of curbing the excesses associated with federal water projects. President Franklin Roosevelt first proposed the idea in 1940, and virtually every president since has made similar proposals (Holmes, 1979). Cost sharing, particularly if the local shares are high, can have a dramatic impact on the demand for water projects. As long as the federal government pays all or most of the costs, a project's economic costs are viewed as benefits in the form of jobs and lucrative contracts to the local communities. Under such conditions, even projects that potentially have strongly negative net national benefits are assured of attracting local supporters. Local support, however, declines sharply as the local share of the costs rises.

The cost-sharing formulas established in 1986 for the COE projects varied with the functions to be served. The local shares were set at 100 percent of the construction and the operation and maintenance costs for hydropower, municipal, and industrial uses; between 25 and 50 percent of the construction costs and 100 percent of the operation and maintenance costs for flood control; and 25 percent of all costs associated with water quality and fish and wildlife purposes. The introduction of cost sharing for COE projects has had an impact. A number of projects have been downsized and are being phased in over longer periods to accommodate local funding priorities. The prospective drain on local finances has sapped much of the local support for some of the larger and more economically and environmentally suspect projects.

The Bureau of Reclamation, which is not covered by Public Law 99–662, has resisted standardized cost-sharing percentages for its irrigation and flood control works. Furthermore, the bureau has historically resisted setting rates for irrigators high enough to recover the local shares called for in the various acts that constitute reclamation law. Because of deferrals and use of power revenues to cover irrigation construction costs, most irrigators have managed to pay only a small fraction of the amount called for in legislation (Wahl, 1989). In the late 1980s, the bureau did move in the direction of reform by negotiating enhanced cost sharing for three projects: the Buffalo Bill Modification Project in Wyoming, the Central Arizona Project Plan 6, and Animas La Plata (N. Starler, personal communications, March 9 and June 12, 1989).

Federal water projects were not the only ones to be impacted by rising economic costs and environmental concerns. The costs of water-supply projects generally are sure to rise even in the absence of any changes in discount rates or subsidies, for three reasons. First, as a river basin is developed, the best reservoir sites for storing water and generating hy-

> *As long as the federal government pays all or most of the costs, a project's economic costs are viewed as benefits in the form of jobs and lucrative contracts to the local communities.*

dropower are developed first. Consequently, subsequent increases in storage and generating capacity require larger investments in dams. A study of changes by decade in reservoir capacity produced per unit volume of dam constructed, for the nation's 100 largest dams, indicated the extent of the diminishing returns. In the 1920s, a cubic yard of dam produced an average of 10.4 acre-feet in reservoir capacity. The average declined in each succeeding decade, and by the 1960s only 0.29 acre-feet of storage was produced per cubic yard of dam (U.S. Geological Survey, 1984).

Second, as Walter Langbein of the U.S. Geological Survey demonstrated, "each successive increment of control (safe yield) requires a larger amount of reservoir storage space than the preceding increment" (U.S. Geological Survey, 1984, p. 30). At some point, the increase in evaporation losses associated with additional surface storage can more than offset any gains in safe yield. A study of the nation's water resource regions suggests that safe yield reaches a maximum when storage is in the range of 160 to 460 percent of a region's average renewable supply (Hardison, 1972). The Colorado River basin, with reservoir capacity equivalent to more than four times the basin's annual renewable supply, is already close to, if not beyond, the point of diminishing net yields.

Third, society's costs of storing and diverting water also increase over time because the value of the forgone instream benefits rises as streamflows are depleted. The increasing emphasis placed on preserving instream flows attests to the growing importance of these opportunity costs. The values attached to natural streamflows are likely to continue increasing as the supply declines due to increased diversions and the demand rises as a result of population and income growth.

In Search of "Fishable and Swimmable" Waters

Despite the adoption of increasingly strict standards and the higher level of federal support for treatment plants, the quality of most of the nation's waters continued to decline during the 1960s. The nation's commitment to reversing this trend and protecting environmental values generally was strengthened by the National Environmental Policy Act of 1969, which required all federal agencies to assess the full environmental impacts of their actions and which created the Environmental Protection Agency (EPA) in 1970. Responsibility for setting and enforcing federal water-quality standards, which initially had resided in the Public Health Service within the U.S. Department of Health, Education, and Welfare and subsequently in the U.S. Department of the Interior, was transferred to the newly created EPA.

A strategy for cleaning up the nation's waters was set forth in the Federal Water Pollution Control Amendments of 1972. This legislation, commonly known as the Clean Water Act of 1972, represented a major policy shift. The act established ambitious goals of restoring all navigable waters to a "fishable and swimmable" condition by July 1, 1983, and eliminating all discharges of pollutants into these waters by 1985. To achieve these goals, EPA was to set technology-based effluent standards. Industry was to adopt the "best practicable control technology" by 1977 and the "best available technology economically achievable" by 1983. New industrial sources had to meet the even stricter standard of "best available demonstrated control technology." Public facilities were to provide "secondary treatment" of all discharges by 1977 and use of the "best practicable waste treatment technology" by 1983 (Freeman, 1978). The maximum grant to a municipality for waste treatment facilities was increased from 55 to 75 percent of construction costs. More important, a sharp increase in funding for this grant program made the federal gov-

ernment the dominant funding source of municipal wastewater treatment plants. Federal expenditures for these facilities increased from less than $2 billion by 1972 to $37 billion from 1972 to 1985 (U.S. General Accounting Office, 1986). In contrast to the requirements for federal involvement in other water projects, the objectives of the Clean Water Act of 1972 (and subsequent water-quality legislation) and federal funding for water-quality improvements were not subjected to any benefit-cost criteria. This asymmetry reflects the great difficulties encountered in attempting to quantify the principal benefits of water-quality improvements. Nevertheless, the various water quality acts mandated enormous investments in improved waste-treatment technologies, which often have been supported by federal funds irrespective of costs and measurable benefits.

The initial focus of the pollution control efforts were on the more conventional pollutants such as biochemical oxygen demand, nuisance-plant growth,

suspended solids, and fecal coliform bacteria that largely were responsible for the unsightly, malodorous state of many streams and reservoirs. Discharges of nutrients such as phosphorus and nitrogen stimulate the growth of algae and other aquatic plants. This plant growth depletes the dissolved oxygen, which contributes to fish mortality. Sedimentation resulting in excess levels of suspended solids can destroy aquatic habitats, damage fish, and result in aesthetic degradation. Moreover, bacterial contamination makes water unsafe for recreation and shellfish harvesting (U.S. Environmental Protection Agency, 1978).

In 1972, the primary threat to the nation's waters was discharge of conventional pollutants from industrial and municipal pipes and ditches into surface waters. The technology-based effluent standards and the construction grants program targeted at these point sources achieved major reductions in pollutants. For instance, although population and inflation-adjusted gross national product were increasing by 11 and 25 percent, respectively, between 1972 and 1982, municipal biochemical oxygen demand (BOD) loads declined 46 percent and industrial BOD loads declined 71 percent. These gains did not come cheap, however. Adding industrial and state and local government expenditures to those of the federal government, the nation spent more than $100 billion to limit and treat industrial and municipal wastes in the fifteen years following passage of the Clean Water Act of 1972 (Smith, Alexander, and Wolman, 1987). The generous federal subsidies of the construction grants program, which was not subjected to any economic feasibility test, encouraged communities to seek more capital-intensive solutions than would have been economically desirable in the absence of federal subsidies.

Despite the sizable investments to control municipal and industrial point sources of pollution, those sources remain significant contributors of BOD, bacteria, nutrients, toxic substances, and other pollutants of the nation's surface waters (U.S. Environmental Protection Agency, 1987). One estimate suggests an additional $118 billion is needed to construct municipal waste treatment plants through the end of the century (Smith, Alexander, and Wolman, 1987). The recent decline in federal financial support makes it unlikely that all these investments will be made. The maximum construction grant subsidy was reduced to 55 percent in 1985, and the Clean Water Act Amendments of 1987 call for phasing out federal construction grants altogether by 1994. The 1987 act authorizes a final $18 billion dollars to construct sewage treatment facilities and to establish a revolving fund to assist in financing future projects. However, current federal budget deficits make it unlikely that this terminal funding will be fully appropriated.

The Threat of Toxic Substances

Concerns about toxic pollutants and their effect on the quality of the nation's waters began to sharpen in the mid-1970s. Heavy metals, pesticides, and other chemical compounds can have adverse effects on humans, wildlife, and natural environments even in extremely low concentrations. Heavy metals such as cadmium, chromium, copper, lead, nickel, mercury, and zinc that are toxic to fish at low concentrations and produce a variety of health problems in humans are widely used in industry. More than 60,000 commercial chemical substances, some known to be highly toxic, are currently used in the production of the nation's food and other products (U.S. Environmental Protection Agency, 1987). For most substances, however, little is known about the long-term impacts of various exposure levels on human and aquatic health.

Toxic substances pose a much more difficult regulatory problem than the other pollutants. Many are invisible, odorless, sometimes highly persistent in the environment, and difficult to detect in the low concentrations that can be harmful. The tasks of identifying whether a particular substance is toxic and determining the health impacts associated with various levels and durations of exposure are daunting, if not impossible. Scientists have incomplete knowledge of the results of exposure to various substances, and even additional investments in detection would leave large gaps in that knowledge. Even if full knowledge of contaminant levels were available, the effects of chronic exposure could only be estimated with great imprecision. Laboratory studies on animals and epidemiological studies are helpful in identifying problems, but they fall short of quantifying the effects on humans of exposure to individual or combinations of substances. The possibility of synergistic and antagonistic effects among the chemicals presents an overwhelming number of combinations of substances that might be detrimental. Because latency periods may involve decades, long-term studies might be needed to understand the impacts of various exposure levels. Yet, when current mortality and morbidity rates are the result of several decades of exposure, postponing action until better evidence is available risks greatly amplifying the problem and having to deal with conditions only marginally related to those that prevailed during the study period. Thus, as Russell (1978, p. 14) observed, "we are left in the uncomfortable situation of having to choose an appropriate insurance policy and premium on the basis of almost no quantitative knowledge of the risk."

A policy dilemma would not exist if toxic substances could be eliminated easily and inexpensively from the environment. However, conventional municipal treatment technologies do not remove many of these substances. Pretreatment of industrial effluent can keep some toxics out of municipal sewage. But if the industrial wastes are then disposed of in landfills or in the atmosphere, they still may show up in groundwater and surface water supplies.

Agricultural pollutants pose an even more daunting problem because their sources are so diffuse. More than 50,000 pesticide products have been registered

---

Burial was considered the best way to eliminate the threat of a toxic substance to human health and the environment in the early 1970s; a decade later, the nation was making commitments to spend tens of billions of dollars to clean up landfills.

---

since 1947, and approximately 3.5 billion pounds of pesticide products are applied each year throughout the United States (U.S. Environmental Protection Agency, 1987). A relatively small but unknown portion of these pesticides ends up in the nation's water supplies. Preliminary results from the EPA National Survey of Pesticides in Drinking Water Wells found some level of pesticides in 6 of the 180 community wells and in 9 of the 115 private wells sampled. The pesticide residues in 3 of these wells exceeded EPA's life-time health advisory level. Nitrate/nitrite residues, which can occur in the environment naturally or be introduced through fertilizers and wastes from farm animals, were found in 79 of the community wells and 66 of the private wells. The drinking water standard of 10 parts per million was exceeded in 8 of the wells (U.S. Environmental Protection Agency, 1989). The EPA has prohibited or restricted use of several highly persistent pesticides with known toxicity, such as DDT. However, policy formulation becomes much more difficult and controversial when there are great uncertainties about the actual (versus the potential or theoretical) health and environmental effects of both the chemical that might be restricted and any alternatives.

A 1974 study that allegedly demonstrated a causal link between the incidence of cancer and use of Mississippi River water (which contains large amounts of chlorinated sewage effluents) as a source of drinking water revived dormant fears that U.S. drinking water is unsafe (Wade Miller Associates, Inc., 1987). Although exposure to toxic substances appears to have adverse health effects, the enormous benefits from industrial, agricultural, and household uses of chemicals precludes policies from banning the production or use of many substances in the absence of strong evidence of actual detrimental impacts. A number of major environmental laws have attempted to balance these concerns by limiting human exposure to these substances without imposing undue costs on the economy. The Safe Drinking Water Act of 1974, which charged the EPA and the states to require water suppliers to limit contaminants in drinking water, was the first of a series of important legislation addressing the problems of toxic substances in water. The Safe Drinking Water Act Amendments of 1986 specified eighty-three contaminants for EPA regulation, and eventually will require filtration of nearly all surface water supplies and treatment of most groundwater supplies (Wade Miller Associates, Inc., 1987).

Other major legislation prompted, at least in part, by water-quality concerns includes the Federal Insecticide, Fungicide, and Rodenticide Act Amendments of 1975, the Toxic Substances Control Act of 1976, the Resource Conservation and Recovery Act of 1976, the Clean Water Act Amendments of 1977, and the Comprehensive Environmental Response, Compensation, and Liability Act of 1980 (commonly known as the Superfund law) (Portney, 1986). This plethora of legislation reflects the importance attached to limiting human exposure to toxics, the uncertainty about how to do it, as well as a growing understanding of the complexity of the problem. For instance, burial was considered the best way to eliminate the threat of a toxic substance to human health and the environment in the early 1970s; a decade later, the nation was making commitments to spend tens of billions of dollars to clean up landfills that were leaching toxics into both groundwater and surface water supplies.

Nonpoint Source Pollutants

Nonpoint sources such as runoff from farms, urban areas, and construction sites and leakage from landfills and septic systems currently are the principal sources of both conventional and toxic pollutants in much of the country (U.S. Environmental Protection Agency, 1987). Yet, only 1 percent of federal water pollution control funding through 1981 had been allocated to nonpoint problems (Copeland and Zinn, 1986). One reason for this lack of funding is that nonpoint pollutants are more difficult to contain; by definition, there is no specific point where they can be intercepted and treated before they enter a water body. The problems as well as the solutions usually involve land-use rather than water-use practices.

The initial federal effort to curb nonpoint water pollution was through the 208 planning process specified in section 208 of the Clean Water Act of 1972. This process required that states develop plans to identify nonpoint sources of pollution and to recommend procedures and methods for controlling them to the extent possible. The 208 planning process was not considered a great success by Congress, and its federal support was terminated in 1980. Federal support for state planning was restored by the Water Quality Act of 1987 after studies showed that nonpoint pollutants had become the primary reason why

many lakes and streams failed to meet their designated uses (Carriker and Boggess, 1988).

Erosion from agricultural land adds sediment and nutrients to water bodies, where they contribute to eutrophication, siltation, and other problems. The Soil Conservation Service is committed to reducing erosion, but its efforts historically have emphasized the productivity rather than the water-quality effects of erosion. Although the productivity emphasis still persists, the federal government has paid greater attention recently to the impact of agriculture on water quality. For example, the SCS conservation program in 1988 made water quality the number two priority after productivity. In addition, President George Bush's water-quality initiative, presented in his 1990 budget proposal to Congress in February 1989, has prompted "a new focus and coordinated commitment to the goal of protecting the Nation's water from contamination by agricultural chemicals and waste products applied on agricultural lands" (U.S. Department of Agriculture and Cooperating State Agencies, 1989). The initiative proposes to increase the USDA's funding for water-quality activities by $41.2 million per year from its current level of $140 million.

In 1980, the USDA and EPA initiated the Rural Clean Water Program, a pilot program designed to demonstrate the impact of best agricultural management practices on water quality. This program provided federal cost sharing to farmers who adopted farming practices that would contribute to better water quality. The program was never well funded, nor was it targeted to areas where it might contribute maximally to alleviating water-quality problems. Thus, evidence suggests that no significant improvements in water quality were achieved by this program. An assessment of the program concluded that "if high economic benefits to the public are desired in future programs, more careful consideration of project selection than that which occurred in RCWP [Rural Clean Water Program] will need to be given to the nature of the impaired water resources, the number of users affected, and the extent to which water quality improvements can be achieved at reasonable costs" (Piper, Magleby, and Young, 1989, p. v). The program indicated that the costs of structural practices such as animal waste storage systems and terraces are high compared with the costs of conservation tillage. The higher costs of the structural alternatives are justified only when the benefits of improved water quality are especially high (as with a heavily used lake or estuary) or when these alternatives are required to bring water quality up to the threshold levels where user benefits are generated.

The Conservation Reserve Program (CRP) established under the Food Security Act of 1985 has been the most ambitious effort to reduce excessive erosion, curb agricultural nonpoint pollution, and reduce crop production. Under this program, farm owners or operators can volunteer during designated sign-up periods to retire highly erodable cropland for ten years. If their land is accepted into the conservation reserve, the farmers receive an annual rent and half the cost of establishing a permanent land cover (such as grass or trees) from the USDA. Under the program, 40 million to 45 million acres of highly erosive land could be withdrawn from crop production for a ten-year contract period by the early 1990s. As of February 1989, 30.6 million acres had been placed in the reserve. Most of the Conservation Reserve Program lands are located in the drier areas of the West where water erosion generally is not great; relatively little of the retired land is located where it could contribute to improved water quality. In the absence of targeting scarce funds to such areas, investments in controlling soil erosion through the CRP are likely to provide low returns in terms of improved water quality (Gianessi and coauthors, 1988). The eligibility requirements for the CRP have been gradually relaxed "to include lands not presently experiencing excessive erosion, and lands having nonexistent or minimal erosion potential but whose cultivation poses water quality problems" (U.S. Department of Agriculture, 1989, pp. 21–24). These changes are one reason why the average erosion rate of Conservation Reserve Program land declined from 25 to 27 tons per acre per year for the first three sign-up periods to only 14 tons per acre per year for the eighth sign-up period, which ended in February 1989. Nevertheless, the water-quality benefits may have increased with the more recent sign-ups because cropland areas 66 to 99 feet wide adjacent to permanent water bodies were now eligible for placement in the reserve as filter strips.

Environmental Challenges to Water Projects

Environmentalists have used several legislative acts— the National Environmental Policy Act of 1969 (NEPA), the Clean Water Act of 1972, the Wild and Scenic Rivers Act of 1968, and the Endangered Species Act of 1973—to delay, alter, or eliminate water projects. The National Environmental Policy Act of 1969 requires all federal agencies to include an environmental impact statement (EIS) as part of a project's analysis. Although this requirement does not in itself restrict water projects, it does force federal water resource agencies to consider the environmental impacts. Moreover, it provides project critics with a legal tool for challenging an agency's analysis of the environmental impacts and for proposing alternative uses of the water resources that would be affected by the project. Just the process of publicly airing the environmental implications can lead to environmentally desirable adjustments in water projects or even to the withdrawal of some project proposals.

The potential impact of the EIS requirement for water resources could be broadened by requiring federal agencies to prepare such studies before entering into new long-term contracts involving water use. Such an extension of the EIS requirement would provide an opportunity to review and perhaps reform some of the policies that provide federally subsidized irrigation water and hydropower and that contribute to large economic inefficiencies and adverse environmental impacts from federal reclamation projects. The first of many long-term contracts between the U.S. Department of the Interior and irrigators in the San Joaquin Valley of California expired in February 1990. The EPA proposed that the department undertake an environmental impact statement before renewing its contract with the Friant Irrigation District. Such a study would likely identify certain gross inefficiencies in the current uses of federally supplied water as well as alternative water-marketing arrangements that might be designed to contribute significant environmental benefits. The Department of the Interior has reluctantly agreed to undertake an EIS of the water-supply contract. However, the potential impact of the study on water resource use and the environment is likely to be negligible in view of the department's decisions to renew the long-term service contracts before the completion of the EIS, and to guarantee water users the same quantities of water regardless of the study outcome (U.S. Department of the Interior, 1989). In light of the existing conditions, the department's proposed approach could dissipate an opportunity to readdress some of the most important federal water policies that currently are rooted

in an era when demands on the resource and environmental concerns were much more modest than they are today.

Another example of the powerful influence of environmental issues on water resources is the 404 permitting process mandated under the Clean Water Act of 1972, which enables the EPA to veto water projects on environmental grounds. In 1989, the EPA initiated such a veto and, at least temporarily, halted the Two Forks dam and reservoir project on the South Platte River in Colorado. In November 1990, EPA administrator William Reilly vetoed the project. Environmentalists had criticized the project, which would have a storage capacity of 1.1 maf and increase Denver's water supply by 98,000 acre-feet, as being destructive, expensive, and unnecessary. These sentiments were echoed in the EPA's veto, which came after nearly a decade of planning; numerous modifications to mitigate adverse environmental impacts; the expenditure of more than $40 million on an EIS; and the issuance of a permit by the Corps of Engineers. The EPA's veto of these permits demonstrated the powerful influence as well as the unpredictability of environmental issues on water products.

The Wild and Scenic Rivers Act of 1968, the Endangered Species Act of 1973, and subsequent amendments provide narrower but potentially more powerful instruments for influencing the design and location of water development projects. As of January 1989, the Wild and Scenic Rivers Act of 1968 had designated 119 rivers and stretches of rivers as wild and scenic, and hundreds more were under review as possible additions to the system ("Plan Would Triple Number of Wild, Scenic Rivers," 1989). Once a river is included in the federal wild and scenic river system, water projects that would excessively damage the area's natural amenities appear to be precluded. Consequently, designation as a wild and scenic river drastically reduces the development prospects for a river. In 1981, thirteen northern California rivers that had been viewed by water developers as large potential sources of supplemental water for the Southwest and had long been priority development targets of both the Corps of Engineers and the Bureau of Reclamation were added to the system. In addition to crimping the development prospects of the federal water resource agencies, this act has contributed to a growing recognition that new supplies are not always forthcoming to meet the unconstrained demands of the rapidly growing West.

The Endangered Species Act of 1973, another powerful piece of legislation, prohibits federal agencies from undertaking actions that threaten the survival or critical habitat of a species officially designated as endangered. Water development agencies must await the results of biological studies of a project's impacts on endangered species before undertaking any actions that might result in irreversible or irretrievable damage. Where a threat is identified, the project must be altered or canceled to remove the threat. Furthermore, any person can file a civil suit against the United States or one of its agencies for violating the act (Harrington and Fisher, 1982). As the TVA and environmentalists discovered in the case of Tellico Dam on the Little Tennessee River, this legislation can be a potentially powerful weapon for delaying or blocking water projects. Environmentalists' claims that Tellico Dam would destroy the only remaining habitat of the snail darter, a 3-inch-long perch, tied the project up in the courts for more than two years. In 1978 the U.S. Supreme Court upheld an injunction halting the dam, which by then was more than 90 percent completed. The Court's decision led to the Endangered Species Act Amendments of 1978, which created the Endangered Species Committee; its members are cabinet officers who resolve cases in which species preservation presents irreconcilable conflicts with economic development objectives. Much to the surprise of Tellico Dam supporters, the committee decided in favor of the snail darter and against completion of the dam, which the committee concluded was a poor economic investment even though it was, by that time, nearly 95 percent completed. Supporters of the dam then resolved to have this decision overturned by Congress. In 1979 they succeeded in passing legislation exempting Tellico Dam from the endangered species laws and providing funding for its completion. Although President Carter disapproved of this circumvention of the endangered species legislation, the act reviving Tellico Dam was virtually veto-proof because it was attached to a continuing resolution to keep the government operating after October 1, 1979. Subsequently, the snail darter was found in other habitats unaffected by Tellico Dam (R. K. Davis, 1988).

The potential powerful influence of the Endangered Species Act of 1973 over water-development projects also was demonstrated in May 1990 when the U.S. Fish and Wildlife Service issued an opinion that the proposed Animas-La Plata Project for the San Juan River system in southwestern Colorado and northwestern New Mexico would threaten the Colorado squawfish. This ruling brought to a halt and eventually could kill one of the few remaining large water projects planned by the Bureau of Reclamation. The project would provide approximately 120,000 acre-feet of water to irrigate more than 70,000 acres of land, another 80,000 acre-feet of water for municipal and industrial use, and would settle some long-standing Native American water claims. Economists have criticized the project for costs well in excess of benefits; environmentalists have criticized it for its adverse impacts on streamflows and fish habitats. At the time of the Fish and Wildlife Service's opinion, President Bush had already included second-year funding for the project in his FY 1991 budget and the Bureau of Reclamation had executed repayment contracts with local groups (Western States Water Council, 1990).

Even when an endangered species apparently is not threatened, groups opposed to a water project for other reasons may seek to establish such a link. For instance, opponents of a plan to divert water from the West Pearl River to the East Pearl River in Mississippi have indicated their intent to come up with an endangered species whose habitat would be threatened by the project ("Search Is On for New Snail Darter," 1988). Environmentalists also have used the Endangered Species legislation to alter management of existing projects. For example, through the legislation they altered releases from dams on the main stem of the Missouri River to protect the nesting

Even when an endangered species apparently is not threatened, groups opposed to a water project for other reasons may seek to establish such a link.

grounds of the least tern and the piping plover, officially designated endangered and threatened species, respectively. Likewise, during the summer of 1989 the Bureau of Reclamation sent 300,000 acre-feet of water around the turbines at Shasta Dam on the Sacramento River in California, at a power loss valued at $3.5 million, to provide colder water for the spawning of winter-run Chinook salmon. The state of California had designated the Chinook salmon as endangered, and the species was subsequently placed on the federal list of threatened species (Western States Water Council, 1990).

Public Trust: A Challenge to Traditional Water Uses

In addition to environmental legislation, another instrument for protecting water resources is the public trust doctrine. This doctrine, which holds that the state as trustee has an obligation to protect instream values, is being used and tested in a number of state courts as an instrument for protecting streamflows. In states where the doctrine is recognized, the courts generally have held that public trust considerations must be integrated with state water laws. Consequently, the public trust doctrine could become the basis for limitations on private diversion rights.

The California Supreme Court supported this interpretation in a decision involving Mono Lake. The Mono Lake case stems from a suit to restore and protect the lake's unique scenic and ecological values by limiting diversions from streams feeding the lake. Los Angeles, under a prior appropriation permit issued by the state, has diverted the flow of four of the lake's five feeder streams. Over five decades, these diversions have lowered the lake level 45 feet and have reduced its volume by half. At current withdrawal rates, some experts believe the lake's ecological system will be destroyed within another twenty to twenty-five years. Los Angeles, on the other hand, receives one-seventh of its water from the region, and the inability of the state to meet its water-delivery obligations under the State Water Plan has raised questions about the ability of the city as well as the rest of southern California's coastal area to meet future water demands (Wahl and Davis, 1986).

The California Supreme Court ruled that the state does have a public trust obligation to protect unique ecosystems. These obligations, however, do not nec-

essarily have a superior status to those of water-diversion rights. A diversion detrimental to instream habitat uses would not violate public trust obligations as long as the trust interests were considered and balanced against the withdrawal benefits (P. N. Davis, 1988). In the spring of 1989, the California Supreme Court upheld a ruling that the state Water Resources Control Board must reconsider Los Angeles's water right because that right does not provide sufficient downstream protection as specified under the state's fish and game code. The board has until September 1993 to issue a ruling. In the meantime, a superior court judge issued an injunction against further diversions from the Mono Lake region by Los Angeles so that the lake level could rise at least 2 feet. This restriction was followed by state legislation that established an Environmental Water Fund, with $36 million earmarked to help Los Angeles develop alternative sources of water and energy to replace losses from Mono Lake ("Calif. High Court Rules Against L.A.," 1989; "Judge Rules for Mono Lake," 1989; "Los Angeles Loses Again . . . ," 1990). Although the legal struggle for the waters of the Mono Lake region clearly has important implications for both Los Angeles and the region, its ramifications are likely to extend well beyond the principals directly involved. The case provides an important precedent for further applications of the public trust doctrine as an instrument for challenging long-standing water withdrawal rights.

States' Initiatives to Protect Their Waters

Since 1980, state legislatures increasingly have acted to protect water quality, preserve instream flows, and limit development of groundwater and surface water. Several states have designated their own wild and scenic rivers to be protected from developers; restricted the use of pesticides and other chemicals; and curtailed development in areas dependent on declining groundwater tables, overlying aquifers sensitive to contamination, or surrounding important and ecologically vulnerable surface waters.

Because the federal government lacks any comprehensive role in protecting groundwater, state actions are particularly important to protect the source of more than half of the nation's drinking water. By 1988, forty-one states had adopted standards beyond those of the federal government for drinking water. The level of the standards adopted by the states and the contaminants covered by those standards vary among the states. The variations among state standards may be more a reflection of uncertainty, lack of knowledge, and chance than of actual differences in the conditions and risks posed by toxic substances. The usefulness of the standards and their effectiveness in protecting groundwater are not quantitatively known (U.S. General Accounting Office, 1988).

Depleting Groundwater Supplies

The Second National Water Assessment, which provides an overview of the nation's water situation as of 1975, is the most recent comprehensive effort to assess the adequacy of the nation's renewable supplies to meet both offstream and instream water uses. The water supply data used in the assessment are based on long-term statistical streamflow frequency curves estimated in the absence of consumptive use. Complementarity was implicitly assumed among instream uses, and desired instream flows were estimated as the higher of the minimum flows required for navigation or fish and wildlife habitat. Fish and wildlife needs, which were higher in all subregions, still may provide a reasonable proxy for all instream uses. Offstream water use was estimated as the amount of water that would have been withdrawn if 1975 had been an average hydrologic year. Nationally, water withdrawals and consumptive use declined slightly between 1975 and 1985 (table 2-A4).

Although the assessment was for 1975, it still provides useful insights on current conditions because long-term renewable supplies as well as aggregate consumptive water use have changed little in the past decade. Total water use, defined as the sum of consumptive use and desired instream flows, was approximately 85 percent of average annual streamflow as of 1975 (U.S. Water Resources Council, 1978). Water use exceeded the average renewable supply in four western water resource regions and in twenty-four water resource subregions. The water-deficit areas included central and southern California, Nevada, most of Arizona, New Mexico, eastern Colorado, and the western sections of Texas, Oklahoma, Kansas, and Nebraska (Frederick with Hanson, 1982). Deficits are made up either by having streamflows fall below desired levels or by groundwater mining—the dewatering of an aquifer over a sustained period.

Groundwater, which accounts for more than one-fifth of all freshwater withdrawals, is being mined in a number of areas throughout the country. The most extensive mining is associated with irrigation, especially in the West and South. In 1983, groundwater levels underlying more than 14 million irrigated acres in eleven states within these regions declined from 6 inches to more than 5 feet. These figures do not include another 2 million acres in the Texas High Plains taken out of irrigation since the mid-1970s largely because of higher pumping costs resulting from declining groundwater tables and rising energy costs. More than three-fourths of the lands with high rates of groundwater mining are in four western states: California, Kansas, Nebraska, and Texas. In the Central Valley of California, the nation's most productive agricultural area, heavy groundwater use is resulting in a mixing of some underlying saline water with the valley's freshwater aquifer. Groundwater levels are even declining 6 inches or more annually under nearly 17 percent of the irrigated acreage in Arkansas and Florida, two of the nation's wettest states. These two states account for almost half of the irrigated acreage in the thirty-one eastern states (Sloggett and Dickason, 1986; Day and Horner, 1987).

Although groundwater mining for urban uses is not as extensive, the costs associated with the loss of urban supplies are likely to be much greater than the agricultural losses. The freshwater aquifers used by suburbs around Chicago and by Long Island, Cape Cod, and other areas are being mined. Saltwater intrusion (see the section entitled Quality of the Nation's Water) poses an immediate threat to some coastal aquifers. Land subsidence associated with groundwater mining is a problem in some locations, including the Central and Santa Clara valleys in California, Las Vegas, and the Houston-Galveston area of Texas (U.S. Geological Survey, 1984). In addition to the permanent loss of water-storage capacity, structural damage to buildings, roads, bridges, and well casings and increased susceptibility to flooding are commonly associated with subsidence. Sinkholes, which result from a sudden collapse of underlying rock that has been dissolved and weakened by circulating water, can result in major property damage and even loss of life when they occur in settled areas. Although sinkholes develop from natural processes, there is evidence that groundwater pumping has accelerated their development in some locations in Alabama, Florida,

Courtesy of Bonneville Power Administration

Georgia, Tennessee, Pennsylvania, and Missouri (U.S. Geological Survey, 1984).

Allocating Supplies Among Alternative Uses

The combination of rising costs, a slowing in the development of new storage, and increasing measures to restore and protect streamflows are reflected in the growth of offstream water uses since 1970. Water withdrawals and consumptive uses increased at a declining rate from 1970 to 1980, and then declined (table 2-A4). On a per capita basis, offstream water use has declined since the mid-1970s.

Underlying these aggregates are important differences in the growth of various uses. Withdrawals for public supplies and rural domestic and livestock uses continued to increase both absolutely and on a per capita basis throughout the period. Nevertheless, these uses still accounted for only about 9 percent and 2 percent, respectively, of total withdrawals in 1985. Irrigation and industry remain the dominant offstream water users; they are also the sectors for which there have been significant reductions in use in response to factors such as rising water costs, problems in se-

curing additional supplies, transfers to other users, and water-quality regulations.

The nation's irrigated acreage increased from about 39 million acres in 1969 to a little more than 50 million in 1978 (table 2-A5). Since 1978 the national total has declined. Eastern irrigation has continued to expand and as of 1982, accounted for more than 15 percent of the national total. However, even in the well-watered East, water supply has become an important constraint within the more intensively irrigated areas, such as central Florida. For most of the East, however, economic factors largely unrelated to the cost of water remain the principal constraints to the expansion of irrigation.

In the West, where irrigation is often essential for productive agriculture, water availability is dictating major changes in irrigated acreage. For the seventeen western states, irrigated acreage increased from 34.8 million in 1969 to 43.1 million in 1978 (table 2-A5); total water withdrawals increased from nearly 134 maf in 1970 to approximately 153 maf in 1980 (table 2-A6), suggesting a reduction of 8 percent in water use per acre. Subsequently, irrigated acreage declined to 41.3 million by 1982 (table 2-A5) and irrigation water withdrawals declined to 140 maf by 1985 (table

2-A6), implying an additional 5-percent decline in the average rate of water use per acre. The differing growth patterns of the West's four farm production regions reflects, in part, differences in the availability and prices of water and energy. In the Pacific and Mountain regions, irrigated acreage has declined since the late 1970s. The combined reduction in irrigated acreage for the two regions was only 3 percent between 1978 and 1982 (table 2-A5), but groundwater use for irrigation in these regions declined by 11.7 maf or 32 percent between 1980 and 1985 (table 2-A6). In the Southern Plains, which depends heavily on declining groundwater supplies, irrigated acreage actually has declined from the level reached in 1969 (table 2-A5). Groundwater use for irrigation in the Southern Plains in 1985 was less than half the level of 1965 (table 2-A6). In the Northern Plains region, irrigated acreage continued to increase, but even here irrigation water withdrawals declined between 1980 and 1985. Irrigation for the plains states as a whole continued to grow until the late 1970s when declining well yields, increasing pumping depths, rising energy costs, and a general decline in the profitability of U.S. agriculture combined to reverse the overall acreage irrigated. Between 1975 and 1988, the index of prices farmers received for their crops increased 19 percent and the index of the prices paid for all production items increased 73 percent (Council of Economic Advisers, 1989).

The decline in industrial freshwater withdrawals between 1980 and 1985 reflects improvements in plant efficiencies as well as increased reuse. Withdrawals for industrial uses other than thermoelectric power declined by more than 30 percent from 1980 to 1985. Thermoelectric power withdrawals declined nearly 10 percent, but even with this reduction, thermoelectric remains the nation's largest withdrawal user of water.

Quality of the Nation's Water

Quality as well as quantity is important in assessing the adequacy of supplies. All groundwater and surface water contains minerals (commonly referred to as salts) dissolved from soil and rock, and even precipitation picks up impurities in the atmosphere. Most withdrawal and instream uses can tolerate wide ranges of impurities without serious loss in utility. Nevertheless, the utility and value of the resource tends to decline as the level of salts or other contaminants such as toxic substances, bacteria, nutrients, biochemical oxygen demand, and sediment increase.

SURFACE-WATER QUALITY

The quality of a water body can be defined in various ways, including the effluents it receives; its chemical, physical, and biological attributes; and the socioeconomic benefits and costs associated with specific uses. The *National Water Quality Inventory: 1986* (U.S. Environmental Protection Agency, 1987) assessment of surface-water quality is based on state reports indicating whether state water resources are capable of fulfilling the uses designated by the states. The results of the inventory suggest that nearly 18 percent of the assessed rivers, lakes, and estuaries were capable of only partially supporting their designated uses, and that 7 percent were too polluted to support any designated uses (table 2-3). These

Table 2-3. Degree to Which the Quality of the Nation's Rivers, Lakes, and Estuaries Support Their Designated Uses

Level of support	Water body (percentage)[a]		
	Rivers	Lakes	Estuaries
Fully supporting	74	73	75
Partially supporting	19	17	18
Not supporting	6	7	7
Unknown	1	2	0.3

Source: U.S. Environmental Protection Agency (1987).

[a]The degree of support was measured as a percentage of the total assessed miles of rivers, acres of lakes, and square miles of estuaries.

Table 2-4. Primary Pollution Sources in the Nation's Water Resources That Failed to Fully Support Their Designated Uses as of 1986 (in percentages)

Water body	Point sources			Nonpoint sources	Natural	Other
	Industrial	Municipal	Combined sewers			
Rivers and streams	9	17	1	65	6	2
Lakes and reservoirs	1	8	0.03	76	12	3[a]
Estuaries and coastal waters	8	22	4	45	3	18

Source: U.S. Environmental Protection Agency (1987).

Note: The percentages are derived from weighted averages based on miles of rivers and areas of lakes and estuaries.

[a]Row does not add to 100 because of rounding.

percentages may overstate the national magnitude of the water-quality problem because the states tend to focus their monitoring resources on the waters most likely to have problems. Only 21 percent of the nation's rivers, 32 percent of the lakes, and 55 percent of the estuaries actually were assessed for the 1986 inventory. If all the water bodies that were not assessed for the 1986 inventory had fully supported their designated uses, then 95 percent of the river miles, 92 percent of the lake acres, and 86 percent of the estuary areas would have supported their designated uses (Fedkiw, 1989). Although this conditional calculation probably understates the extent of the nation's surface-water quality problems, it does help establish a range that suggests from 74 to 92 percent of all surface waters fully supported their designated uses.

Nonpoint source pollutants were the principal source of the nation's surface-water–quality problems in 1986 (table 2-4). Farms, streets, and sites of construction and mining activities were the principal nonpoint sources. Of the water bodies failing to fully support their designated uses, nonpoint sources were the primary culprit on 65 percent of the rivers and streams, 76 percent of the lakes and reservoirs, and 45 percent of the estuaries and coastal waters. Municipal wastewater and industrial discharges, the primary point sources of pollution, were the principal problem on 27 percent of the rivers and streams, 9 percent of the lakes and reservoirs, and 34 percent of the estuaries and coastal waters failing to fully support their designated uses. Natural sources were important polluters of lakes and reservoirs (U.S. Environmental Protection Agency, 1987).

GROUNDWATER QUALITY

Only a small fraction of the nation's vast groundwater resources is known to be contaminated to the extent that those resources fail to meet state and federal drinking-water standards. Groundwater monitoring, however, is infrequent or nonexistent in most areas because effective monitoring is expensive. The task of significantly improving knowledge of groundwater quality is complicated because millions of potential sources of pollutants exist; these pollutants might seep at varying but unknown rates into valued supplies. The problems of overcoming this lack of knowledge are particularly disturbing because groundwater is the source of drinking water for more than half the nation's people. Most of the groundwater used for drinking is treated by the water-supply companies before consumption. Yet, the water consumed by self-supplied households and small community suppliers is likely to go untested and untreated.

In addition, millions of septic and underground storage tanks pose potential threats to the nation's groundwater. Indeed, these were the two most frequently cited sources of groundwater contamination out of sixteen sources listed in the 1986 *National Water Quality Inventory* (U.S. Environmental Protection Agency, 1987). There are nearly 20 million on-site domestic waste disposal systems in the country. All of these systems have the potential for contaminating groundwater with nitrates, phosphates, pathogens, inorganic contaminants, or other toxics that might find their way into household drains. Septic systems are the most common of these, and The Conservation Foundation (1987) has suggested that perhaps one-third of the nation's septic systems were operated in a manner threatening to groundwater quality as of 1980. Moreover, an estimated 1.5 million underground tanks are used to store hazardous substances or petroleum products. Most of these tanks are made of carbon steel and are not protected from corrosion; their life expectancy underground is 15 to 20 years, and an estimated 1 million tanks are at least 16 years old. The number of leaking underground storage tanks has increased rapidly in recent years and is expected to continue to increase. The petroleum industry alone may already have as many as 350,000 leaking tanks (The Conservation Foundation, 1987).

Agriculture was the third most commonly cited source of groundwater pollution in the 1986 water-quality inventory (U.S. Environmental Protection Agency, 1987). Agricultural chemicals are applied to most of the 325 million to 375 million acres typically planted to crops from year to year in the United States. Some of these chemicals reach the nation's groundwater supplies. The East and Gulf coasts and the upper Midwest are particularly susceptible to pesticide contamination; the Great Plains, parts of the Northwest, Southwest, and Corn Belt are susceptible to nitrate contamination; and both problems are common in parts of the Lake States, Corn Belt, and Northeast (Nielsen and Lee, 1987).

The farmers themselves are among those most at risk for existing or potential groundwater contamination stemming from agricultural sources. Risks are greater for the 19 million people who get their drinking water from private wells. These wells tend to be shallower, and thus much more readily contaminated by percolation from septic systems, underground storage tank leakage, and agricultural or other sources than the deeper wells used by public water systems. Yet, private wells are less likely to be monitored and regulated. Just a one-time monitoring, using state-of-the-art methods, of the wells used for drinking water could cost an estimated $1.4 billion (Nielsen and Lee, 1987). The interim results of the EPA's (1989) national survey of pesticides in drinking water found pesticide residues in only 5 percent of the sampled wells, and nitrate or nitrite residues in nearly half of the wells. The pesticide concentration levels exceeded the EPA's lifetime health-advisory levels in 1 percent of the wells, and the nitrate/nitrite levels exceeded drinking water standards in 3 percent.

On-site and municipal landfills, abandoned waste sites, surface impoundments, and oil and gas brine pits account for the fourth through eighth most frequently cited sources of groundwater contamination (U.S. Environmental Protection Agency, 1987). From 42 to 55 percent of the nation's hazardous waste is managed in surface impoundments and landfills, which, until recently, dumped wastes into unlined pits or lagoons with only the soil between the wastes and the groundwater (McCarthy and Reisch, 1987). Since passage of the Hazardous and Solid Waste Amendments of 1984, double liners and leachable collection systems have been required for new land-disposal facilities. This legislation unrealistically called for retrofitting previously existing sites by November 1988. Billions of dollars are expected to be spent by the year 2000 to reduce the potential threats to groundwater from these unlined sites. But even this action will not eliminate the problem entirely. In recognition of the magnitude of the potential sources of contamination and the need to target the limited resources available for resolving the problem efficiently over time and consistent with available funding, the EPA has placed the worst sites on a national priorities list for long-term remedial action. This list of "Superfund" sites that the EPA suggests pose the greatest hazards to human health and the environment totaled nearly 1,200 sites as of July 1988 (*Environment Reporter*, 1988).

Saltwater intrusion ranks ninth on the EPA's list of principal sources of groundwater contamination reported by the states (U.S. Environmental Protection Agency, 1987). Saltwater intrusion associated with the mining of an aquifer's freshwater supplies is reported in thirty-four states, but it is a serious problem in only a few of the nation's most intensively used and highly valued aquifers (U.S. Geological Survey, 1984). Miami, Tampa, and Jacksonville in Florida; seven counties in New Jersey; and the southern and central coasts of California are among the locations where the EPA has identified saltwater intrusion as a problem. The potentially most costly problems are on Long Island and Cape Cod, where existing supplies are threatened by both saltwater intrusion and chemical pollution and where it would be particularly expensive to develop alternative water supplies. In recognition of the nature of these threats, Nassau County on Long Island has imposed major constraints on groundwater use and land use development.

Aquifers differ in their susceptibility to contamination and the prospects for cleaning them up once they are polluted. Confined aquifers are protected by a relatively impermeable confining layer, and thus their quality is less affected by most overlying land-use practices or by surface-water quality. Consequently, land overlying a confined aquifer may be an appropriate site for locating activities, such as feedlots, that could threaten groundwater supplies in other areas. On the other hand, confined as well as unconfined aquifers are susceptible to contamination from drilling activities. Oil and gas exploration and development and the injection of wastes into deep geological strata can contaminate groundwater resources if the design, construction, placement, operation, or abandonment of the wells are flawed. Once such an aquifer is contaminated, the prospects of cleaning it up through either natural or human means are poor. Unconfined aquifers are generally shallow and are likely sources of private water supplies in rural areas. Because water circulates through unconfined aquifers more frequently, they are more readily contaminated and contaminants are flushed out faster. Nevertheless, it can still take decades or centuries for natural forces alone to restore the quality of a contaminated unconfined aquifer.

Overview of the Current Situation

The nation's water infrastructure now includes more than 80,000 dams; 25,000 miles of inland and intracoastal navigation channels supported by over 200 locks and dams; tens of thousands of groundwater pumps; and millions of miles of canals, pipes, and tunnels (Schilling and coauthors, 1987). This constitutes the most extensive and elaborate system of water projects on earth.

The infrastructure has drastically altered the hydrology of the United States over the past century and has made possible an impressive array of benefits. Streams that once were unreliable—flooding their banks at times and drying up at others—have been converted into controlled and dependable sources of supply. Billions of gallons of groundwater are pumped annually, often from hundreds of feet or more, to irrigate fields and provide water for households and other users. Nearly all the country's 240 million people have access to relatively inexpensive tap water. Tens of thousands of recreational reservoirs have been created. Former wetlands and floodprone areas have been developed intensively for urban and agricultural purposes. About 45 million irrigated acres produce nearly one-third of the value of the nation's crop pro-

Removing the salts that tend to accumulate in and threaten the productivity of irrigated lands without damaging downstream water users and ecosystems is a continuing problem.

duction (Day and Horner, 1987). In addition, hydropower generates approximately 11 percent of the nation's electricity and 4 percent of its total energy. The ability to overcome any limits the nation's natural hydrology might once have imposed on economic development is evident from the deserts that have been converted into vast urban areas spotted with lakes and golf courses.

These developments, however, do introduce problems. For example, the rising demands on the nation's waters stemming from the growing population and economy have imposed high environmental costs. Thousands of miles of once free-flowing streams with their attendant fish and wildlife habitat have been forgone. Water-quality problems have impaired the usefulness of about 25 percent of the nation's assessed surface waters (table 2-3). From 30 to 50 percent of the wetlands in the lower forty-eight states have been converted to other uses over the past 200 years (U.S. Office of Technology Assessment, 1984). These losses have been accompanied by a growing realization of and appreciation for the natural ecological services such as floodwater storage, erosion control, fish and wildlife habitat, water-quality improvements, and recreational and esthetic values that often are lost when people drain wetlands for other uses. The change in perceptions regarding wetlands is strikingly evident in the Bush administration's policy of no further net loss in wetlands. This policy has forced some communities to shelve or alter their land and water development plans.

The sustainability of America's current water use patterns is another concern. Current water use depends on nonrenewable supplies in some areas. Declining groundwater levels, saltwater intrusion, and land subsidence are depleting or damaging the quality of water in aquifers underlying millions of acres. Removing the salts that tend to accumulate in and threaten the productivity of irrigated lands without damaging downstream water users and ecosystems is a continuing problem. Sedimentation of reservoirs is resulting in losses in water-storage capacity. The water supplies of tens of millions of people residing in some of the nation's oldest and largest cities depend on antiquated, inefficient delivery systems that are prone to major breakdowns. Furthermore, the prospect of global climate changes induced by a greenhouse warming could produce major and largely unpredictable changes in the nation's hydrology, which would be difficult to handle with the existing institutions and infrastructure.

Investments in new water-supply projects peaked about 1970 and are unlikely to increase again because all the best physical and cost-effective sites (as well as many poor ones) for building dams, ports, navigable waterways, and irrigation projects already have been developed. On the other hand, expenditures for maintaining and rehabilitating the existing infrastructure are increasing. Waterways and ports are dredged almost continuously just to maintain their existing capacity to handle traffic. Dams usually are thought to require little maintenance. Yet, a national inventory of nonfederal dams indicated that 2,925— one-third of those dams inspected—were unsafe (U.S.

Army Corps of Engineers, 1982). Cost estimates to upgrade these dams range from $2 billion to $7 billion (Schilling and coauthors, 1987). Because only about 1 of every 7 nonfederal dams actually was inspected, the costs of upgrading all unsafe dams may be much higher than these figures indicate. The inspection did focus, however, on those dams believed to pose the greatest public safety and economic threats. Moreover, a 1989 report by the inspector general of the U.S. Department of the Interior concluded that 31 of the 54 dams operated by the Bureau of Indian Affairs are unsafe because of inadequate maintenance, and pose a serious threat to life and property ("Interior Report Rates 31 Dams . . . ," 1989).

In terms of flood control, the Corps of Engineers estimates that existing structures have prevented flood damages of about $150 billion (Schilling and coauthors, 1987). Nevertheless, actual flood damages have been increasing over time largely because of three factors: an increase in floodplain development encouraged in part by COE protective structures; an increase in the real value of properties constructed in floodplains; and upstream developments that have increased runoff rates and flood peak frequencies. Moreover, future flood losses are likely to continue increasing in the absence of further preventive measures because urban expansion into the floodplains is rising by 2 percent annually (Schilling and coauthors, 1987). The largest flood-related losses of property and life sometimes are associated with dam failures; upgrading unsafe dams that threaten urban areas assumes greater importance as a floodplain becomes more intensively developed. In addition, nonstructural measures, which often are more cost effective than new dams and levees for reducing flood damages, have received increased support from federal, state, and local government agencies in recent years. These measures include land use and development regulations and advance-warning and evacuation planning to reduce damages in the event of a flood.

Sedimentation of reservoirs is another long-term problem for maintaining the effectiveness of the nation's water-resource infrastructure. The Bureau of Reclamation builds additional storage capacity when the predicted sedimentation accumulations over the economic life of the reservoir exceed 5 percent of the reservoir's capacity. Actual sedimentation rates on federally operated reservoirs are generally at or below predicted levels (Strand, 1989). However, data on the sedimentation rates for the vast majority of

A national inventory of nonfederal dams indicated that 2,925—one-third of those dams inspected—were unsafe.

the nation's dams are poor or nonexistent. One estimate suggests that from 1.4 to 1.5 maf of lake and reservoir storage are lost annually to sediment (Guldin, 1989). Accumulated over a decade, these loss rates imply a reduction of slightly more than 2 percent in the nation's aggregate reservoir capacity (U.S. Geological Survey, 1984). These losses in capacity contributed to a decline in available storage from the equivalence of 216 to 201 days of withdrawals between 1970 to 1980. Relative declines in storage imply increased risk of offstream water-supply deficiencies (U.S. Geological Survey, 1984).

Lost reservoir capacity will be expensive to replace. Dredging sediments generally has been more expensive than raising the height of existing reservoirs or building new reservoirs, and the costs of developing new storage are high and increasing over time. Disposing of the dredge spoil may be an even more serious problem associated with dredging. Attempts to flush sediment from existing reservoirs have been only marginally successful at best. Under certain conditions, the most promising technique may be to empty the reservoir to a minimum elevation in anticipation of a flood runoff capable of transporting high sediment concentrations. This operating scheme requires a low-level outlet from the reservoir, and it entails forgoing the benefits of storing some runoff (Strand, 1989).

Protecting and improving water quality have been the objectives of the largest investments in new water facilities in recent years. About $12 billion annually has been spent recently for the construction, operation, and maintenance of municipal wastewater treatment facilities. In 1986, 16,000 facilities were capable of removing more than 85 percent of the total pollutants produced by 70 percent of the population and 160,000 industrial sources. A 1986 survey undertaken by the Environmental Protection Agency suggested that with no population growth, an additional $60.3 billion (January 1986 dollars) was needed to bring publicly owned wastewater treatment facilities up to the minimum treatment standards of the Clean Water Act of 1972. Assuming no regulatory or technological changes, $15.9 billion more is expected to be needed by 2005 to handle the wastes of the nation's additional population (Apogee Research, Inc., 1987).

Wastewater treatment facilities are only part of the infrastructure needed to provide and maintain the current high-quality, reliable supplies for domestic uses. Estimates of the total capital costs of addressing

some or all of the needs of the nation's water supply systems range from $3.7 billion to $10.7 billion (1982 dollars) annually over the next 20 years (Wade Miller Associates, Inc., 1987). Some of the most urgent and costly investments are needed in the Northeast, where the supply and distribution facilities of many cities have deteriorated to the point where breakdowns are common and large amounts of water are lost through leaks. New York City, for instance, is plagued by an average of nearly two water-main failures every day, and the entire supply for the city depends on two main tunnels linking the city with eighteen reservoirs located in three watersheds. These tunnels have been in continuous service since 1917 and 1936, and on peak days, they handle flows 60 percent above their design levels. They have never been repaired or even inspected, and there is no way of doing so until the third tunnel now being constructed is completed sometime in the 1990s. Upgrading the distribution system will be expensive. The third tunnel alone will cost in excess of $5 billion, and replacing antiquated feeder pipes would cost millions more. The costs of not making these investments, however, may be even higher. Disruptions in service are already common and cost millions of dollars annually. In the absence of major rehabilitation investments, these costs will rise and the system will become less efficient and more vulnerable to major breakdowns. One possible scenario for a real water crisis would be to have one of New York City's two main tunnels fail before the third is completed (Frederick, 1986).

Meeting Future Water Demands

Supply and Demand Changes

Increasing affluence, leisure time, and population tend to increase the demand for water and water services. Development and adoption of more water-efficient technologies can temper or even reverse the growth in demand for agricultural, domestic, commercial, industrial, and other withdrawal uses. Indeed, the decline in the quantities of water withdrawn for irrigation and thermoelectric uses from 1980 to 1985 (table 2-A4) probably is attributable in part to improvements in water-use efficiency. But technology is not likely to offer any suitable and comparable substitutes for such instream services as fish and wildlife habitat, water-based recreation, and the amenities of natural waterways. As the search for clean sources of energy intensifies, hydroelectric power becomes more attractive relative to many of the alternative sources of power. Increasing incomes as well as a growing appreciation for the potential values that can be provided by improving streamflows in some areas are likely to increase demands for these instream services faster than the rate of population growth.

Actual water use, of course, will be limited by available supplies and how they are allocated among competing uses. Effective supplies are influenced by investments to control flows, by uses that alter the quality or long-term availability of water, by technological changes, and by management of supply systems. Investments in new dams and reservoirs can increase effective supplies for offstream use, but the costs of these supplies are high relative to the prices people are accustomed to paying for water, and these investments are likely to have adverse effects on instream uses. Interbasin transfers can move water from low-value to high-value uses, but they do not add to total supplies. Moreover, the institutional obstacles to such transfers are increasing as potential exporters become more aware of the environmental and other opportunity costs associated with the loss of water. Groundwater supplies are being mined in a number of areas, and the potential for contamination threatens the utility of both groundwater and surface water in many locations.

Another element that may affect the balance of future water supplies and demand is greenhouse warming, which is associated with increasing atmospheric concentrations of carbon dioxide and other trace gases such as nitrous oxide, methane, chlorofluorocarbons, and tropospheric ozone. If the globe does indeed get warmer, the hydrologic cycle will accelerate. Globally, this will mean increased rates of evaporation and increased precipitation. A warming of 2 to 5 degrees Celsius (the range expected to result from an equivalent doubling of carbon dioxide) is expected to increase average global precipitation and evaporation by 7 to 15 percent (Schneider, Gleick, and Mearns, 1990). Regional impacts are likely to include changes in precipitation and runoff patterns, evapotranspiration rates, and the frequency and intensity of storms. The impact of higher temperatures on annual runoff is likely to be adverse in arid areas; the impact on seasonal streamflow patterns will be greatest in areas such as northern California, where precipitation currently comes largely in the form of winter snowfall and runoff comes largely from spring and summer snowmelt.[3]

The possibility of greenhouse warming adds uncertainty to the future supply and demand for water. The hydrologic impact on any particular region is unknown, but could be severe because of increased hydrologic uncertainty and the fact that the existing infrastructure, management practices, and patterns of use are predicated on the existing climate and will almost certainly be less well adapted to a new hydrologic regime. Additional infrastructure has been the traditional means of responding to water problems, and this approach might help prevent climate-induced flooding or shortages. Such investments would be costly, however, and, in the absence of a clearer idea of the nature of climatic changes, may be of little value.

The high costs of developing additional storage and the large uncertainties regarding regional hydrologic changes suggest the importance of exploring both the technological alternatives for increasing the quantity and quality of available supplies and the opportunities for increased flexibility in managing and allocating limited supplies. Lower-cost sources of supply, improved management of existing supplies, and greater flexibility in the allocation of limited water supplies in response to changing conditions are desirable goals even in the absence of climate change; the uncertainty associated with the possibility of a greenhouse warming gives added weight to these objectives.

Technology as a Means of Increasing Supplies

In the early 1960s, expectations were high that desalinization, weather modification, or icebergs would be potential sources of large quantities of low-cost water. The optimistic expectations that once greeted these technologies have virtually vanished, however.

The technology exists to upgrade the vast amounts of saline water available in the oceans and in some aquifers to any quality desired. The costs of doing so, however, are much too high for most uses with current technologies and prices. Desalinization of sea water to levels suitable for domestic or even most agricultural uses is currently about five to ten times the costs of developing conventional supplies. Barring major declines in energy prices and unanticipated technological developments, desalinization of highly saline water will remain relatively expensive for all but the highest-value uses in the most water-scarce regions. Nevertheless, the economics of upgrading brackish waters with salt concentrations well below those found in the oceans and of recycling municipal and industrial wastewaters are more promising. A variety of technologies already exist to improve water quality, and the economics of using them will improve as water becomes more expensive or difficult to acquire and as environmental regulations force greater treatment of effluent flows. Moreover, new treatment technologies are more likely to emerge if the nation's commitment to improved water quality continues.

Making use of lower-quality supplies may be a practical alternative to more extensive treatment for many water uses. Few uses require water that meets drinking standards, and there is likely to be considerable resistance to using recycled wastewater for drinking even if it does meet all health standards. With less extensive treatment, wastewater can be upgraded to levels suitable for irrigating parks, roadways, golf courses, and perhaps crops. Indeed, some industrial users are finding it profitable to use lower-quality but more readily available water supplies. Some irrigators are now growing salt-tolerant crops with saline water that would be toxic to most plants.

Like desalinization, purposeful weather modification once was viewed as a promising way to provide low-cost water to some of the nation's more arid regions. Cloud seeding is done occasionally, especially during the winter in ski-resort areas. However, more than forty years of largely disappointing research results have tarnished the prospects of gaining large new water supplies through cloud seeding. Congress's withdrawal of funding for the Bureau of Reclamation's weather modification program for FY 1989 reflects this pessimism. Yet, even if the technology were well developed and the economics were favorable, legal objections from groups that might be adversely affected would likely limit the use of cloud seeding for enhancement of precipitation. For instance, downwind residents who believe they would be deprived of precipitation that otherwise would fall on their own lands might object, as might downstream residents who could suffer increased flooding and town officials who would incur higher snow-removal costs.

Towing icebergs from Antarctica for use by arid coastal cities was one of the more unusual proposals for increasing water supplies. Enormous quantities of freshwater are stored as polar ice. A study done in the early 1970s (Hult and Ostrander, 1973) presented an optimistic picture of the possibilities for using icebergs for supplementing supplies in southern California. More recent assessments focusing on the technical, legal, economic, and environmental problems are much more pessimistic. There is little reason to expect that icebergs will significantly augment the water supplies of any region in the United States within the foreseeable future (Frederick with Hanson, 1982).

Less exotic but seldom used opportunities for increasing water supplies involve water harvesting—the diversion of runoff to fields or cisterns—and the

Removal of high-water-using plants that thrive along streams and have little direct value to humans may increase streamflows. Elimination of these phreatophytes, however, is likely to reduce wildlife habitat.

management of vegetation to reduce evapotranspiration and to increase runoff. Water harvesting is an ancient technology that has seldom been used in the United States. Harvesting might help some western farmers and small towns make better use of rainfall. The supply benefits, however, would likely be limited. Forests can be managed to produce more runoff. Managing a forest for improved water yields is likely to introduce conflicts with the more traditional forest resource objectives, such as timber production or recreational opportunities (Bowes and Krutilla, 1989). Removal of high-water-using plants that thrive along streams and have little direct value to humans may increase streamflows. Elimination of these phreatophytes, however, is likely to reduce wildlife habitat.

Water-conserving technologies can increase the effective supply of water by reducing water use. For instance, seed varieties that make more efficient use of moisture can increase the effective supply of irrigation water. However, the development and adoption of such technologies has been discouraged because of the absence of adequate incentives to conserve irrigation water.

Improved Management of Existing Supplies

The nation's reservoirs and water-supply systems have traditionally been managed independently of each other under their own sets of operating rules and objectives. Studies of coordinated system management approaches, as well as at least one actual application, suggest that integrated management of reservoirs and supply systems offers a low-cost, environmentally benign means of increasing safe water yields under some conditions.

Joint operation of the storage and distribution facilities of the three principal water-supply agencies servicing the Washington, D.C., metropolitan area was initiated in 1982. With relatively little new investment in infrastructure, the new institutional arrangements increased drought-condition water yields in the region by nearly one-third. This represents between $200 million and $1 billion of savings compared with the costs of achieving comparable increases in yields under separate management. These savings were achieved primarily through more effective use of existing storage for water supplies by using Potomac River water whenever flows were high, and saving water stored in the reservoirs for periods of low flow (Sheer, 1986). However, this strategy increases effective water supplies by sacrificing flood-control storage in the basin.

The potential gains from integrated management of water-supply systems in other areas of the country are largely unexplored. However, two studies by Sheer (1986) suggest that major benefits also may be possible under conditions different from those in Washington, D.C. Sheer's analyses indicate that a 20-percent increase in the supplies of the Houston, Texas, system could be achieved through conjunctive management of groundwater and surface water, and water shortages in the North Platte River basin could be reduced by about 30 percent through joint management of supplies. Sheer concludes that "expenditures on improved management probably will be the most cost-effective water-supply investment possible over the next decade" (Sheer, 1986, p. 112).

Demonstrating opportunities for improved management may be easier than making the changes required to take advantage of the opportunities. Water-supply systems seldom are operated as integrated systems despite a substantial literature proclaiming the potential benefits of doing so. The obstacles to integrated management are largely institutional—separate ownership of facilities, multistate jurisdictions, and state water laws.

Demand Management

Water will become more scarce in the coming decades as demand increases faster than supply in most areas. Scarcity per se is no cause for alarm; all economic goods and resources are scarce. Scarcity becomes a problem in the absence of an efficient means for allocating scarce goods and resources among competing uses as supply and demand conditions change over time.

Allocating productive resources among producers and goods and services among consumers is the primary function of an economic system. The United States has a mixed economy that relies on a combination of public regulations and free markets. The national policy preference is to rely on markets and prices wherever appropriate. In a competitive market economy, prices provide signals and incentives to encourage efficient use and the development of new supplies and to allocate limited supplies to their most valued uses. With water resources, however, the tendency has been to rely on government regulations that inhibit the development of markets and private market incentives.

The nature of water resources makes it difficult and, in many cases, perhaps impossible to develop efficient markets. Public regulations often add additional obstacles to the development of market approaches. Efficient markets must satisfy two conditions. First, there must be well-defined, transferable property rights in the commodity being traded. It is difficult to establish clear property rights in a resource such as water that naturally moves among the atmosphere, surface-water reservoirs, and groundwater reservoirs. Second, a market transfer is efficient only if the full costs are borne by the buyers and sellers. However, transferring water from one use or location to another commonly affects third parties by altering the timing, location, quality, and quantity of water available for others. Another problem is that some of the services provided by water, such as the amenities provided by free-flowing streams, usually are not marketed and are inadequately provided for when left only to market forces. Moreover, because it is generally impractical to have more than one supplier, water prices for domestic and commercial users are set by utility managers and regulatory agencies rather than by the interaction of supply and demand (Frederick and Kneese, 1990).

Despite these shortcomings, water marketing does occur in the West where water scarcity is most prominent. With appropriate state and federal policies, water marketing could play a much greater role in allocating water resources and in providing incentives for con-

serving and preserving them. Reducing transactions costs that often are unnecessarily high because of long delays, uncertainties, and legal fees would improve the use of markets for transferring water on a timely basis. The eastern states are beginning to move away from the riparian doctrine of water law as permits are introduced for allocating supplies. Market incentives could be introduced by establishing transferable property rights in these permits. Moreover, the introduction of marginal-cost pricing by water utilities would provide consumers with greater incentive to conserve and utilities with increased revenues to repair antiquated, inefficient water-supply infrastructure. The costs of adding to water supplies are rising sharply; thus marginal costs tend to be much higher than average costs, the usual base for setting consumers' prices. Average cost-pricing undermines or reduces the economic incentive to conserve.

Another means for managing demand is through regulations. Regulations are almost always adopted to limit use during periods of extreme drought and to control the disposal of wastes into water bodies. Relying exclusively on markets to respond to the changes in supplies resulting from droughts is likely to be disruptive. Large and politically unacceptable price increases are apt to be needed to bring demand voluntarily into line with drought-reduced supplies. Currently, responses to drought are likely to start with appeals for voluntary conservation and, if conditions deteriorate, move on to restrictions on use. Nonessential outdoor uses such as watering lawns and washing cars and sidewalks are usually the first uses to be curbed; businesses also may be required to reduce use by specified amounts.

Regulations also are being adopted to curb the long-term growth of water demand, and not just to deal with the temporary disruptions of extreme events. Groundwater pumping is restricted in many states. For example, New Mexico has long imposed limits on groundwater pumping, and Arizona's Groundwater Management Act of 1980 represents the nation's most comprehensive plan to curb and eventually eliminate groundwater mining. In addition, communities facing problems in developing additional supplies are looking to reduce demand by imposing water-conserving standards for items such as showerheads, toilets, and appliances that use large amounts of water. Massachusetts already has passed legislation that will require all new construction and remodeling to install toilets that use no more than 1.6 gallons per flush.

Other localities are expected to follow this precedent. To assist in this effort, legislation to establish national standards for the manufacture and labeling of certain plumbing products has been introduced into both houses of Congress. Proponents of the legislation argue that manufacturers would not produce water-conserving products in large enough quantities to achieve economies of scale in the absence of requirements to meet water-conserving standards. Or, if these items were produced and marketed, consumers would not buy them because they pay so little for their water under the average-cost pricing policies normally used by the water industry.

Technology-based effluent standards have been the principal tool employed for achieving water-quality objectives. The high costs of past water-quality measures combined with the problems encountered in trying to meet the legislatively established water-quality objectives are reasons for exploring whether economic incentives could be used to improve water quality at less cost. Effluent charges approximating damages or marketable discharge permits could be used to provide incentives for developing and adopting more cost-effective technologies for reducing pollution discharges. If irrigators paid water prices that more nearly reflected the full costs of their use, there would be greater incentive to adopt water-management practices that would reduce the loadings of salts, agricultural chemicals, and other pollutants currently attributable to irrigation (Frederick, 1987).

With appropriate state and federal policies, water marketing could play a much greater role in allocating water resources and in providing incentives for conserving and preserving them.

Adapting to Changing Supply and Demand

The United States continues to enjoy relatively abundant water resources. Control over these resources grew enormously over the past century. However, the water demands to support a $5-trillion economy and nearly one-quarter of a billion people, most of whom expect virtually unlimited quantities of high-quality water to be available at a nominal price, have grown even more. Although the nation has achieved considerable success (albeit at a high cost) in cleaning up its waters, protecting and restoring water quality will be a continuing challenge. In particular, reducing nonpoint source pollutants and protecting drinking water supplies from toxic substances are problems currently lacking effective solutions. An effective strategy for meeting water-quality objectives will need to target the resources designated for achieving these ends to the areas where they will produce the greatest net benefits.

The costs of using water will rise in the future; only the nature of the costs is in doubt. When water is underpriced for uses such as irrigation and waste disposal, more of society's costs take the form of deteriorating aquatic ecosystems, loss of instream values, restrictions on development resulting from the inability to secure adequate water supplies, and perhaps more frequent interruptions in service. On the other hand, when the costs are borne by users who have incentives to conserve and opportunities to sell water rights, then the resource is used more efficiently, the highest-value uses are assured of an adequate supply, and the nation derives greater net benefits from its resources. By facilitating and reducing the costs of adapting to changing supply and demand conditions, this approach also would provide a renewed realization that there is plenty of water to meet everyone's demands.

Notes

The author is indebted to John Fedkiw for providing numerous source materials as well as insightful and detailed comments on several drafts of this chapter, and to Emery Castle, Larry Mac-Donnell, David Moody, Paul Portney, Kyle Schilling, John Schefter, Norm Starler, Clive Walker, Richard Wahl, and three anonymous reviewers for their constructive comments.

1. The 1945 and 1970 water use data are from different sources that, based on their estimates for 1950 and 1955, are not completely consistent. Nevertheless, because the differences among the sources are not major, the two sources do appear to provide a good indication of changes in use from 1945 to 1970.

2. Then as now, however, when water rights or land with appurtenant water rights were sold, the water was no longer viewed as free. If the rights to water were clearly defined and transferable, there were costs associated with using water for one purpose if that water could be put to alternative uses.

3. For a more extensive discussion of the potential hydrologic implications of a greenhouse warming, see Frederick and Gleick (1989).

Appendix 2

Table 2-A1. Estimated Water Use in the United States, 1900–1958

Purpose	Water use (billions of gallons per day)							
	1900	1910	1920	1930	1940	1945	1950	1958
Irrigation[a]	20.2	39.0	55.9	60.2	71.0	83.1	100.0	127.5
Public supply	3.0	4.7	6.0	8.0	10.1	12.0	14.1	19.7
Rural domestic and livestock	2.0	2.2	2.4	2.9	3.1	3.1	4.6	5.8
Other industrial[b]	10.0	14.0	18.0	21.0	29.0	41.0	38.1	56.4
Thermoelectric power	5.0	6.5	9.2	18.4	23.2	31.2	45.9	89.9
Total offstream water use	40.2	66.4	91.5	110.5	136.4	170.4	202.7	299.3
Source of water								
Ground	7.3	11.7	15.8	18.2	22.6	28.3	35.2	54.0
Surface	32.9	54.7	75.7	92.3	113.8	142.2	167.5	245.3

Source: Picton (1960).
[a]Total withdrawals including delivery losses.

[b]Manufacturing and mineral industries, rural commercial, air conditioning, resorts, hotels, military and other state and federal agencies, and other miscellaneous uses.

Table 2-A2. Dams Completed in the United States, 1700–1982

Period	Number of dams	Storage capacity of dams (maf)	Average increases		Cumulative total by end of period	
			Dams per year	Storage capacity per dam (1,000 acre-feet)	Dams	Storage capacity (maf)
1700–1899	2,661	10	—	4	2,661	10
1900–1920	4,734	43	225	9	7,395	52
1921–1932	2,786	81	232	29	10,181	133
1933–1944	5,135	146	428	28	15,316	279
1945–1969	35,273	474	1,411	13	50,589	753
1970–1982[a]	12,830	117	1,069	9	63,419	869

Source: U.S. Army Corps of Engineers (1982).
Note: Table represents only dams at least 6 feet high with at least 25 acre-feet of storage, or at least 25 feet in height with at least 15 acre-feet of storage. Rows may not add because of rounding.

[a]The 1982 numbers include only one dam with a storage of 85 acre-feet. Consequently, the annual averages for the 1970–1982 period are based on 12 years.

Table 2-A3. Major Purposes of Dams Constructed, Before 1900 to 1982

Period	Total number of dams constructed	Major purpose of dams (percentage of total)						
		Irrigation	Hydroelectric	Flood control	Water supply	Recreation[a]	Navigation	Stock or farm pond
Before 1900	2,661	11	5	2	19	48	1	3
1900–1920	4,734	25	9	2	18	35	1	3
1921–1932	2,786	16	11	2	20	40	[b]	6
1933–1944	5,135	12	3	3	17	37	1	21
1945–1969	35,273	9	1	18	11	34	—[b]	20
1970–1982	12,830	8	—[b]	22	6	30	—[b]	22
Total 1700–1982	63,419	11	2	15	12	35	—[b]	18

Source: U.S. Army Corps of Engineers (1982).
Note: Table includes only dams at least 6 feet high with at least 25 acre-feet of storage, or at least 25 feet high with at least 15 acre-feet of storage.

[a]The relative importance of recreational dams is overstated by the percentages of dams because most of these dams are relatively small.
[b]Denotes less than 0.5 percent.

Table 2-A4. Estimated Water Use in the United States, 1950–1985

Purpose	Water use (billions of gallons per day)							
	1950[a]	1955[a]	1960[b]	1965[c]	1970[d]	1975[e]	1980[e]	1985[e]
Offstream water use								
Irrigation	89	110	110	120	130	140	150	140
Public supply	14	17	21	24	27	29	34	37
Rural domestic and livestock	4	4	4	4	5	5	6	8
Thermoelectric power	40	72	100	130	170	200	210	190
Other industrial	37	39	38	46	47	45	45	31
Total[c]	100	240	270	310	370	420	440	400
Consumptive use	NA[f]	NA[f]	61	77	87[g]	96[g]	100[g]	92[g]
Source of water								
Ground	34	47	50	60	68	82	83	73
Surface	140	180	190	210	250	260	290	260
Instream use								
Hydroelectric power	1,100	1,500	2,000	2,300	2,800	3,300	3,300	3,100

Source: Solley, Merk, and Pierce (1988).

[a]Forty-eight states and the District of Columbia.

[b]Fifty states and the District of Columbia.

[c]The itemized withdrawals do not add to the total because of the rounding used in U.S. Geological Survey Circular no. 1004 (Solley, Merk, and Pierce, 1988). The data are generally rounded to two significant figures.

[d]Fifty states, the District of Columbia, and Puerto Rico.

[e]Fifty states, the District of Columbia, Puerto Rico, and the Virgin Islands.

[f]Not available.

[g]Freshwater only.

Table 2-A5. Irrigated Land in Farms by Farm Production Region, 1939–1982 (millions of acres)

Region	1939	1945	1949	1954	1959	1964	1969	1974	1978	1982
Southern Plains	0.9	1.3	3.2	4.8	5.9	6.7	7.4	6.9	7.5	6.1
Northern Plains	0.6	0.8	1.1	1.6	3.0	3.4	4.6	6.2	8.8	9.3
Mountain states	9.9	10.7	11.6	11.2	12.1	12.8	12.8	12.3	14.8	14.1
Pacific states	5.8	6.6	8.3	9.3	9.8	10.4	10.0	10.6	12.0	11.9
17 western states	17.2	19.4	24.3	27.0	30.7	33.2	34.8	36.0	43.2	41.3
Delta states	0.6	0.8	1.0	1.7	1.3	1.7	1.9	1.8	2.7	3.1
Southeast	0.1	0.2	0.4	0.5	0.5	1.3	1.5	1.6	2.5	2.3
31 eastern states[a]	0.7	1.1	1.5	2.6	2.3	3.7	4.2	4.3	7.0	7.6
48 states	18.0	20.5	25.8	29.6	33.0	36.9	39.0	40.3	50.2	48.9

Sources: Zinn and Turner (1986); Day and Horner (1987).

Note: Numbers may not add because of rounding.

[a]Also includes the Northeast, Lake states, Corn Belt, and Appalachia.

(continued)

Table 2-A6. Groundwater and Surface Water Withdrawn for Western Irrigation, 1950–1985 (millions of acre-feet)

Region and source	1950	1955	1960	1965	1970	1975	1980	1985
Northern Plains								
Groundwater	0.8	1.6	2.8	4.1	6.2	11.2	13.5	11.0
Surface	2.2	2.3	3.7	2.9	3.0	3.1	4.0	3.1
Total	3.0	3.9	6.5	7.0	9.2	14.3	17.5	14.1
Groundwater as percentage of total	26	42	43	58	68	78	77	78
Southern Plains								
Groundwater	1.9	7.5	9.3	13.3	9.6	11.1	8.1	6.5
Surface	3.1	4.2	3.6	2.9	2.9	2.8	2.3	3.1
Total	5.0	11.7	12.9	16.2	12.5	13.9	10.4	9.6
Groundwater as percentage of total	37	64	72	82	77	80	78	68
Mountain states								
Groundwater	5.3	9.9	12.2	11.4	11.3	14.5	15.1	11.9
Surface	42.3	53.9	45.4	47.2	52.2	50.8	53.9	57.9
Total	47.6	63.8	57.6	58.6	63.5	65.3	69.0	69.8
Groundwater as percentage of total	11	16	21	20	18	22	22	21
Pacific states								
Groundwater	10.3	12.0	11.6	12.8	19.1	19.3	21.3	12.8
Surface	18.9	29.7	25.4	26.5	29.6	31.6	34.6	33.4
Total	29.2	31.7	37.0	39.3	48.7	50.9	55.9	46.2
Groundwater as percentage of total	35	30	31	33	39	38	38	28
17 western states								
Groundwater	18.2	31.0	35.9	41.6	46.2	56.0	58.0	42.3
Surface	66.6	88.0	78.0	79.5	87.7	88.4	94.7	97.5
Total	84.8	119.0	113.9	121.1	133.9	144.4	152.7	139.8
Groundwater as percentage of total	21	26	32	34	35	39	38	30

Sources: MacKichan (1951, 1957); MacKichan and Kammerer (1961); Murray (1968); Murray and Reeves (1974, 1977); Solley, Chase, and Mann (1983); Solley, Merk, and Pierce (1988).

References

Ackerman, Edward A., and George O. G. Lof. 1959. *Technology in American Water Development*. Baltimore, Md.: The Johns Hopkins University Press for Resources for the Future.

Apogee Research, Inc. 1987. *Wastewater Management: Current Policies and Future Options*. Final report prepared for the National Council on Public Works Improvement. Washington, D.C., May.

Bowes, Michael D., and John V. Krutilla. 1989. *Multiple-Use Management: The Economics of Public Forestlands*. Washington, D.C.: Resources for the Future.

"Calif. High Court Rules Against L.A. in Diversion of Mono Lake." *U.S. Water News* 5 (June 1989): 8.

Carriker, Roy R., and William G. Boggess. 1988. "Agricultural Nonpoint Pollution: A Regulatory Dilemma." In *Forum for Applied Research and Public Policy*, vol. 3, no. 2. Knoxville, Tenn.: Tennessee Valley Authority.

Carson, Rachel. 1962. *Silent Spring*. New York: Houghton Mifflin.

Congressional Budget Office. 1985. *Efficient Investments in Wastewater Treatment Plants*. Washington, D.C.: GPO.

Conservation Foundation. 1987. *Groundwater Protection—Groundwater: Saving the Unseen Resource and a Guide to Groundwater Pollution: Problems, Causes, and Government Responses*. Washington, D.C.: The Conservation Foundation.

Copeland, Claudia, and Jeffrey A. Zinn. 1986. *Agricultural Nonpoint Pollution Policy: A Federal Perspective*. Congressional Research Service Report no. 86-191 ENR, TD 420 U.S. B. Washington, D.C.

Council of Economic Advisers. 1989. *Economic Report of the President*. Washington, D.C.: GPO.

Davis, Peter N. 1988. "Protecting Waste Assimilation Streamflows by the Law of Water Allocation, Nuisance, and Public Trust, and by Environmental Statutes." *Natural Resources Journal* 28 (Spring): 357–391.

Davis, Robert K. 1988. "Lessons in Politics and Economics from the Snail Darter." In *Environmental Resources and Applied Welfare Economics: Essays in Honor of John V. Krutilla*, edited by V. Kerry Smith, 211–236. Washington, D.C.: Resources for the Future.

Day, John C., and Gerald L. Horner. 1987. *U.S. Irrigation: Extent and Economic Importance*. Economic Research Service, Agriculture Information Bulletin no. 523. Washington, D.C.: U.S. Department of Agriculture.

Environment Reporter. 1988. Vol. 19, no. 9: 310.

Federal Power Commission. 1957. *Hydroelectric Power Resources of the United States: Developed and Undeveloped 1957*. Washington, D.C.: Federal Power Commission.

Fedkiw, John. 1989. *The Evolving Use and Management of the Nations' Forests, Grasslands, Croplands, and Related Resources. A Technical Document Supporting the 1989 USDA Forest Service RPA Assessment*. Fort Collins, Colo.: U.S. Department of Agriculture, Forest Service, Rocky Mountain Forest and Range Experiment Station.

Ferejohn, John A. 1974. *Pork Barrel Politics: Rivers and Harbors Legislation, 1947–68*. Stanford, Calif.: Stanford University Press.

Foster, Charles H. W., and Peter P. Rogers. 1988. *Federal Water Policy: Toward an Agenda for Action*. Energy and Environmental Policy Center Discussion Paper no. E-88-05. Cambridge, Mass.: Harvard University.

Foxworthy, Bruce L., and David W. Moody. 1986. "National Perspective on Surface-Water Resources." In *National Water Summary 1985—Hydrologic Events and Surface-Water Resources*, Water-Supply Paper no. 2300, prepared for the U.S. Geological Survey. Washington, D.C.: GPO.

Frederick, Kenneth D. 1986. "Watering the Big Apple." *Resources* 82 (Winter): 2–4.

———. 1987. "Discussion of the Mineral Water Quality Problem from Irrigated Agriculture." In *Annual Policy Review 1986: Agriculture and the Environment*, edited by Tim T. Phipps, Pierre R. Crosson, and Kent A. Price, 117–122. Washington, D.C.: Resources for the Future.

Frederick, Kenneth D., and Peter H. Gleick. 1989. "Water Resources and Climate Change." In *Greenhouse Warming: Abatement and Adaptation*, edited by Norman J. Rosenberg, William E. Easterling III, Pierre R. Crosson, and Joel Darmstadter, 133–143. Washington, D.C.: Resources for the Future.

Frederick, Kenneth D., with James C. Hanson. 1982. *Water for Western Agriculture*. Washington, D.C.: Resources for the Future.

Frederick, Kenneth D., and Allen V. Kneese. 1990. "Reallocation by Markets and Prices." In *Climate Change and U.S. Water Resources*, edited by Paul E. Waggoner, 395–419. New York: John Wiley & Sons.

Freeman, A. Myrick III. 1978. "Air and Water Pollution Policy." In *Current Issues in U.S. Environmental Policy*, edited by Paul R. Portney, 12–67. Baltimore, Md.: The Johns Hopkins University Press for Resources for the Future.

Gianessi, Leonard P., Henry M. Peskin, Tim T. Phipps, Cynthia A. Puffer, and Pierre R. Crosson. 1988. "Analysis of the Effects of the Conservation Reserve Program on the Quality of the Nation's Waters." Resources for the Future. Typescript.

Guldin, Richard W. 1989. *An Analysis of the Water Situation in the United States: 1989–2040: A Technical Document Supporting the 1989 USDA Forest Service RPA Assessment*. General Technical Report RM-177. Fort Collins, Colo.: U.S. Department of Agriculture, Forest Service, Rocky Mountain Forest and Range Experiment Station.

Hardison, C. H. 1972. "Potential United States Water-Supply

Development." *Irrigation and Drainage Division Journal* 98: 479–492.

Harrington, Winston, and Anthony C. Fisher. 1982. "Endangered Species." In *Current Issues in Natural Resource Policy*, edited by Paul R. Portney, 117–148. Washington, D.C.: Resources for the Future.

Holmes, Beatrice Hort. 1972. *A History of Federal Water Resources Programs, 1800–1960*. Miscellaneous Publication no. 1233, Economic Research Service. Washington, D.C.: U.S. Department of Agriculture.

———. 1979. *History of Federal Water Resources Programs and Policies, 1961–70*. Miscellaneous Publication no. 1379, Economics, Statistics, and Cooperative Service. Washington, D.C.: GPO.

Howe, Charles W., Joseph L. Carroll, Arthur P. Hurter, Jr., William J. Leininger, Steven G. Ramsey, Nancy L. Schwartz, Eugene Silberberg, and Robert M. Steinberg. 1969. *Inland Waterway Transportation: Studies in Public and Private Management and Investment Decisions*. Washington, D.C.: Resources for the Future.

Hult, J. L., and N. C. Ostrander. 1973. *Antarctic Icebergs as a Global Fresh Water Resource*. A report prepared for the National Science Foundation, no. R-1255-NSF. Los Angeles, Calif.: The Rand Corporation.

"Interior Report Rates 31 Dams as Unable to Stand a Flood." 1989. *U.S. Water News* 6 (November): 13.

Johnson, Charles C., Jr. 1988. "Historical Review of Drinking Water." In *Perspectives on Water*, edited by David H. Speidel, Lon C. Ruedisili, and Allen F. Agnew, 136–139. New York: Oxford University Press. (Originally published as *Drinking Water and Human Health* [Chicago, Ill.: American Medical Association, 1984]).

"Judge Rules for Mono Lake." 1989. *U.S. Water News* 6 (August): 9.

Kates, Robert W., and Ian Burton, eds. 1986. *Geography, Resources, and Environment: Selected Writings of Gilbert F. White*, vol. 1. Chicago, Ill.: University of Chicago Press.

Kneese, Allen V. 1990. "Benefit-Cost Analysis: The Historical Context." Resources for the Future. Typescript.

"Los Angeles Loses Again in Mono Lake Case." 1990. *U.S. Water News* 6 (February): 15.

MacKichan, Kenneth A. 1951. "Estimated Use of Water in the United States in 1950." Circular no. 115. Washington, D.C.: U.S. Geological Survey, May.

———. 1957. "Estimated Use of Water in the United States in 1955." Circular no. 398. Washington, D.C.: U.S. Geological Survey.

MacKichan, Kenneth A., and J. C. Kammerer. 1961. "Estimated Use of Water in the United States in 1960." Circular no. 456. Washington, D.C.: U.S. Geological Survey.

Marshall, Hubert. 1966. "Politics and Efficiency in Water Development." In *Water Research*, edited by Allen V. Kneese and Stephen C. Smith, 291–310. Baltimore, Md.: The Johns Hopkins University Press for Resources for the Future.

Martin, Roscoe C. 1960. *Water for New York: A Study in State Administration of Water Resources*. Syracuse, N.Y.: Syracuse University Press.

McCarthy, James E., and Mark E. Anthony Reisch. 1987. *Hazardous Waste Fact Book*. Congressional Research Service Report no. 87-56 ENR. Washington, D.C.

Muhn, James, and Hanson R. Stuart. 1988. *Opportunity and Challenge: The Story of BLM*. Washington, D.C.: GPO.

Murray, C. Richard. 1968. "Estimated Use of Water in the United States in 1965." Circular no. 556. Washington, D.C.: U.S. Geological Survey.

Murray, C. Richard, and E. Bodette Reeves. 1974. "Estimated Use of Water in the United States in 1970." Circular no. 676. Washington, D.C.: U.S. Geological Survey.

———. 1977. "Estimated Use of Water in the United States in 1975." Circular no. 765. Arlington, Va.: U.S. Geological Survey.

Nielsen, Elizabeth G., and Linda K. Lee. 1987. *The Magnitude and Costs of Groundwater Contamination from Agricultural Chemicals: A National Perspective*. Economic Research Service, Natural Resource Economics Division, Staff Report no. AGES870318. Washington, D.C., June.

Payne, Charles M. 1983. "Harnessing Water for Electricity—One More Time." In *Using Our Resources, 1983 Yearbook of Agriculture*, edited by Jack Hayes, 354–360. Washington, D.C.: U.S. Department of Agriculture. Reprinted in *Perspectives on Water: Uses and Abuses*, edited by David H. Speidel, Lon C. Ruedisili, and Allen F. Agnew, 158–160. New York: Oxford University Press, 1988.

Picton, Walter L. 1960. "Water Use in the United States, 1900–1980." Prepared for the Business and Defense Services Administration, U.S. Department of Commerce. Washington, D.C.: GPO.

Piper, Steven, Richard S. Magleby, and C. Edwin Young. 1989. *Economic Benefit Considerations in Selecting Water Quality Projects: Insights from the Rural Clean Water Program*. Economic Research Service, Staff Report no. 89-18. Washington, D.C.: U.S. Department of Agriculture.

"Plan Would Triple Number of Wild, Scenic Rivers." 1989. *U.S. Water News* 5 (January): 8.

Portney, Paul R. 1986. "Environmental Evolution." *Resources* 85 (Fall): 1–4.

Radosevich, George E. 1978. *Western Water Laws and Irrigation Return Flow*. Report no. EPA-600/2-78-180. Ada, Okla.: Environmental Protection Agency, August.

Reisner, Marc. 1986. *Cadillac Desert: The American West and Its Disappearing Water*. New York: Viking Press.

Russell, Clifford S. 1978. *Safe Drinking Water: Current and Future Problems*. Preliminary report of a national conference in Washington, D.C., March 1978. Washington, D.C.: Resources for the Future.

Sampson, R. Neil. 1985. *For Love of the Land: A History of the National Association of Conservation Districts.* League City, Tex.: National Association of Conservation Districts.

Schilling, Kyle E., C. Copeland, J. Dixon, J. Smythe, M. Vincent, and T. Peterson. 1987. *Water Resources: The State of the Infrastructure.* Report to the National Council on Public Works Improvement. Washington, D.C.: National Council on Public Works Improvement.

Schneider, S. H., P. H. Gleick, and L. O. Mearns. 1990. "Prospects for Climate Change." In *Climate Change and U.S. Water Resources,* edited by P. E. Waggoner, 41–73. New York: John Wiley & Sons.

"Search Is On for New Snail Darter." 1988. *U.S. Water News* 5 (December): 13.

Sheer, Daniel P. 1986. "Managing Water Supplies to Increase Water Availability." In *National Water Summary 1983—Hydrologic Events and Issues,* Water-Supply Paper no. 2300, prepared for the U.S. Geological Survey. Washington, D.C.: GPO.

Shupe, Steven J. 1989. "Keeping the Water Flowing: Stream Flow Protection Programs, Strategies and Issues in the West." In *Instream Flow Protection in the West,* edited by Lawrence J. MacDonnell, Teresa A. Rice, and Steven J. Shupe, 1–21. Boulder, Colo.: Natural Resources Law Center, University of Colorado School of Law.

Sloggett, Gordon, and Clifford Dickason. 1986. *Ground-Water Mining in the United States.* Natural Resources Economics Division, Economic Research Service, Agricultural Economic Report no. 555. Washington, D.C.: U.S. Department of Agriculture, August.

Smith, Richard A., Richard B. Alexander, and M. Gordon Wolman. 1987. "Water-Quality Trends in the Nation's Rivers." *Science* 235 (March 27): 1607–1615.

Solley, Wayne B., Edith B. Chase, and William B. Mann IV. 1983. "Estimated Use of Water in the United States in 1980." U.S. Geological Survey Circular no. 1001. Alexandria, Va.: U.S. Geological Survey.

Solley, Wayne B., Charles F. Merk, and Robert R. Pierce. 1988. "Estimated Use of Water in the United States in 1985." U.S. Geological Survey Circular no. 1004. Washington, D.C.: GPO.

Spofford, Walter O., Jr. 1986. "Giardiasis: A Return of Waterborne Disease?" *Resources* 83 (Spring): 5–9.

Strand, Robert I. 1989. "Reliability of Reservoir Sedimentation Predictions." Paper prepared for the proceedings of the workshop Water Science and Engineering in River Impoundments—Status, Information Groups and Research Priorities, held at Barkley Lake, Ky., April 8–11.

U.S. Army Corps of Engineers. 1977. *Northeastern United States Water Supply Study: Summary Report.* Washington, D.C.: North Atlantic Division, U.S. Army Corps of Engineers.

———. 1982. *National Program of Inspection of Non-Federal Dams: Final Report to Congress.* Washington, D.C.: Department of the Army.

U.S. Department of Agriculture. 1989. *Agricultural Resources: Cropland, Water, and Conservation Situation and Outlook.* Economic Research Service, Report no. AR-16. Washington, D.C., September.

U.S. Department of Agriculture and Cooperating State Agencies. 1989. *Water Quality Program Plan to Support the President's Water Quality Initiative.* Washington, D.C., July.

U.S. Department of Energy. 1979. *Hydroelectric Power Evaluation.* Report no. DOE/FERC-0031. Washington, D.C.: GPO, August.

U.S. Department of the Interior. 1973. *West Texas and Eastern New Mexico Import Project.* Washington, D.C.: Bureau of Reclamation.

———. 1989. "Interior Secretary Lujan Announces Environmental Impact Statement to Be Prepared for California's San Joaquin River Basin." News release, Office of the Secretary. Washington, D.C., November 29.

U.S. Environmental Protection Agency. 1978. *National Water Quality Inventory: 1977 Report to Congress.* No. EPA-440/4-78-001. Washington, D.C., October.

———. 1987. *National Water Quality Inventory: 1986 Report to Congress.* No. EPA-440/4-87-008. Washington, D.C., November.

———. 1989. "National Survey of Pesticides in Drinking Water Wells." Press advisory, Office of Public Affairs, Washington, D.C., September 1.

U.S. Federal Inter-Agency River Basin Committee, Subcommittee on Benefits and Costs. 1950. "Proposed Priorities for Economic Analysis of River Basin Projects." Washington, D.C., May.

U.S. General Accounting Office. 1981. *Federal Charges for Irrigation Projects Reviewed Do Not Cover Costs.* Report no. PAD-81-07. Washington, D.C., March 3.

———. 1986. *Water Quality: An Evaluation Method for the Construction Grants Program—Methodology.* Report no. PEMD-87-4A, vol. 1. Washington, D.C., December.

———. 1988. *Groundwater Quality: State Activities to Guard Against Contaminants.* Report no. GAO/PEMD-88-5. Washington, D.C., February.

U.S. Geological Survey. 1984. *National Water Summary 1983—Hydrologic Events and Issues.* Water-Supply Paper no. 2250. Washington, D.C.: GPO.

———. 1990. *National Water Summary 1987—Hydrologic Events and Water Supply and Use.* Water-Supply Paper no. 2350. Washington, D.C.: GPO.

U.S. Office of Technology Assessment. 1984. *Wetlands: Their Use and Regulation.* Report no. OTA-O-206. Washington, D.C., March.

U.S. Water Resources Council. 1978. *The Nation's Water*

Resources 1975–2000. Vols. 1 and 3. Washington, D.C.: GPO.

———. 1983. *Economic and Environmental Principles and Guidelines for Water and Related Land Resources Implementation Studies*. Washington, D.C.: GPO, March 10.

Wade Miller Associates, Inc. 1987. *Infrastructure Policy Issues in Water Supply*. Final report to The National Council on Public Works Improvement. Arlington, Va., May 8.

Wahl, Richard W. 1989. *Markets for Federal Water: Subsidies, Property Rights, and the Bureau of Reclamation*. Washington, D.C.: Resources for the Future.

Wahl, Richard W., and Robert K. Davis. 1986. "Satisfying Southern California's Thirst for Water Efficient Alternatives." In *Scarce Water and Institutional Change*, edited by Kenneth D. Frederick with Diana C. Gibbons. Washington, D.C.: Resources for the Future.

Warrick, Richard A. 1980. "Drought in the Great Plains: A Case Study of Research on Climate and Society in the USA." In *Climatic Constraints and Human Activities, IIASA Proceedings Series*, edited by Jesse Ausubel and Asit K. Biswas, 93–123. New York: Pergamon Press.

Welsh, Frank. 1985. *How to Create a Water Crisis*. Boulder, Colo.: Johnson Books.

Western States Water Council. 1990. "Western States Water" (Weekly Report). Midvale, Utah, May 18.

White, Gilbert F. 1935. "Shortages of Public Water Supplies in the United States During 1934." *Journal of the American Water Works Association* 27 (July): 841–854. Condensed version reprinted in *Geography, Resources, and Environment: Selected Writings of Gilbert F. White*. Vol. 1, edited by Robert W. Kates and Ian Burton. Chicago, Ill.: University of Chicago Press, 1986.

———. 1986. "Evaluating the Consequences of Water Management Projects." Excerpts from an unpublished paper of March 21, 1971, reprinted in *Geography, Resources, and Environment: Selected Writings of Gilbert F. White*. Vol. 1, edited by Robert W. Kates and Ian Burton. Chicago, Ill.: University of Chicago Press.

Wolman, M. Gordon, and Abel Wolman. 1986. "Water Supply: Persistent Myths and Recurring Issues." In *Geography, Resources, and Environment: Themes from the Work of Gilbert F. White*. Vol. 2, edited by Robert W. Kates and Ian Burton, 1–27. Chicago, Ill.: University of Chicago Press.

Zinn, Jeffrey, and Elizabeth Turner. 1986. "Western Irrigation: Background Data on Current Issues." Report no. 86-696 ENR. Washington, D.C.: Congressional Research Service, May 1.

3

Forest Resources: Resilient and Serviceable

Roger A. Sedjo

The favorable condition of American forests today is remarkable considering the tremendous pressures that people historically have placed on the forests. From the relatively undisturbed condition of forests in precolonial days to the rapid conversion of forest to agricultural land during the mid-1800s to early 1900s and to the recovery of forest stocks since then, U.S. forests have demonstrated their serviceability and resiliency.

This chapter traces the history of U.S. forests and forestland—that is, land at least 10 percent stocked by forest trees of any size, including land that formerly had tree cover and will be naturally or artificially regenerated—and examines both how Euro–Americans used the forests and the factors influencing this use. The chapter focuses on the forest as a source of wood resources in the form of industrial wood (wood that is processed into products such as lumber, paper, and wood panels) and on forestland as a source of land that can be converted to nonforest uses, particularly agriculture. Only limited attention is given to the multiple uses of forest other than timber because other chapters in this volume focus on forest outputs such as watershed protection, erosion control, wildlife habitat, and recreation. Special attention, however, is given to forestland clearing, which allowed the introduction of other land uses, especially agricultural uses, as well as to the land area in forest; to timberland—forestland that is producing or is capable of producing crops of industrial wood and that is not withdrawn from timber use by statute or administrative regulation; and to the inventory (stock) of timber and the quality of the forest. Moreover, the chapter analyzes the major forces operating on the forest and how these forces and the forests have changed across four periods: 1600 to 1849, 1850 to 1920, 1921 to the end of World War II, and the postwar period—1945 to the present. A retrospective view summarizes the historic trends, details the ways in which the forests have served the society, and describes the state of American forests today.

Abundant Forests and the Conversion to Agriculture: 1600–1849

In precolonial America, the forest landscape consisted of a diverse mosaic of forests of different ages and species composition. Although individual forests experienced continuing change, net growth for the aggregate forest was negligible because the growth and decline of individual trees and forests effected little change on total forest volume. In mature forests, growth was matched by mortality.

Forest fires were a common feature of American forests, both before and after European settlement. An old forest would be weakened by infestation and disease and ultimately would succumb to fire, which is part of the natural ecosystem of most American forests. The ashes, unburned residue, and soils exposed by the fire would provide the bed for the birth of a new forest. Many species, especially the shade-intolerant conifer, require fire to eliminate existing vegetation to allow in the direct sunlight needed for a stand to develop. On previously burned land, forest stands underwent a predictable succession of changes. The new forest usually consisted of shade-intolerant, fast-growing species. As these "pioneer" species ma-

tured, seedlings and saplings of different species, predominantly hardwoods, began to appear in the understory. These species grew more slowly and were more shade tolerant.

Ultimately, the more slowly growing species achieved and retained dominance, displacing the pioneer species. The forest would move through a natural succession of forest types, ultimately converging on a "climax" forest. Eventually, however, these forests, too, would age, become overmature, and ultimately succumb to disease, insects, and fire, and a new cycle would begin with the return of the pioneer species. In some cases the disturbances were small and highly localized; in others the disturbances involved large forest areas. As was common in the pine forests of the South, periodically recurring disturbances, such as fire in pine stands, frequently interrupted the cycle. Thus the succession cycle in which the slower-growing, shade-tolerant hardwood gradually displaced the pine was bypassed and the burned-over pine forest would begin again on the exposed mineral soils with a new, young, naturally regenerated pine forest.

Human effects on precolonial forests were minimal. In some places, Native Americans used fire to clear away trees to allow cropping, grazing, and ease of transportation. Generally, though, the forest was left to follow its natural life cycle, undisturbed by human activities.

European Settlers Arrive

Then European settlers arrived at an America that they characterized as different from Europe in its abundance of wood, countless fast-running streams, and limitless vacant land (Hawke, 1988). Although vacant, the land was not empty. European settlers on the East Coast of North America found the area predominantly occupied by dense forests. New England, for example, had an almost unbroken forest covering an estimated 90 to 95 percent of the land area (Barrett, 1980). Approximately 950 million acres of forest existed in precolonial America in the area currently known as the United States (Clawson, 1979). Many of the early settlers' immediate needs involved use of the forest, which provided a variety of products and services, including wildlife for food and pure water, and wood for building and for fuel. A sawmill reportedly was established in Jamestown in colonial

Virginia in 1607; and the first documented construction of a sawmill was in Berwick in what is now Maine in 1631 (Brown, 1919). Shelters, fortifications, fences, wagons, ships, and other structures all required large amounts of wood from the omnipresent forest. The settlers also produced naval stores, such as gum and pitch, from the forest. The British Crown declared many of New England's tall white pines to be its property so that shipbuilders could make them into masts for the Royal Navy. In addition, the forest satisfied fuel needs from the colonial period until into the twentieth century.

Clearing the Forest for Agriculture

As important as the use of forest outputs was to the early settlers, of equal importance was the need to convert land to agricultural uses. The early settlers required land for cropping and pasture, and once settlement moved beyond the few sites that Native Americans had planted, the settlers had to wrest land from the forest. The forests also were an impediment to the construction of towns and roads. However, with the implements of the day, land clearing was a slow, arduous task. It took about half a century to carve out of the wilderness a farm with cleared fields. People often began clearing by girdling the trees—that is, removing a strip of bark around the entire trunk and thereby killing the tree, a technique known in England. As soon as sunlight filtered through the withered branches, planting could begin. Slowly the trunks of the trees were removed while the stumps were left to rot in the fields (Hawke, 1988).

Clearing of the eastern seaboard for agriculture began before 1650 in New England and the mid-Atlantic states and 100 years later in the South (Walker, 1980). Initially, the land clearing by the settlers was small, barely rivaling the land clearing done by Native Americans to allow them to practice their limited cropping. Colonial settlers adopted the Native American use of fire to improve grazing, remove unwanted vegetation, and control pests (Pyne, 1981; U.S. Department of Agriculture, 1988b). (This technique would later develop into a common pattern to control forest vegetation.) Large forest fires probably occurred both before and after settlement. As early as 1825 the Miramichi and Piscataquis fires were recorded to have burned 3 million acres in Maine and in New Brunswick, Canada.

Gradually, as the European population grew and moved inland away from the coastal settlements, more land had to be cleared. Before the mid-1800s, most of the decrease in American forestlands resulted from the conversion to other, predominantly agricultural, uses. Farm woodlands were used for grazing; acorns and other browse in hardwood forests provided forage for hogs, which became the leading domestic meat staple in the early American diet. Sheep and cattle also grazed in forest pastures; and regular burning became a management tool for controlling the forest and encouraging the growth of grassy vegetation.

The abundance of wood the early settlers found resulted in innovations uniquely suited to their new environment. In the Chesapeake Bay region, for example, settlers replaced the early post-and-rail fences with split-rail zigzag fences. Although the Europeans viewed the system as wasteful because it used large quantities of the plentiful wood and tillable land, unskilled workers could build such fencing much more quickly than traditional fencing; in addition, the split-rail zigzag fence was durable and easy to repair (Hawke, 1988).

Although the settlers were clearing the land for agriculture and other uses, Clawson (1979) estimated that the total area cleared before 1800 "was modest" and that even until the mid-nineteenth century "it was comparatively small" (p. 1168); Williams (1988) estimated that the amount of forest cleared by 1850 was only about 114 million acres. During this early period, much of the direct value of the forest to the settlers was in the form of fuelwood, either directly or sometimes in the form of charcoal. It is estimated that during 1800 more than 60 percent of the wood harvested was used for fuel. By 1850 this figure had declined to only 50 percent (Williams, 1987). In 1840, farmers were selling 5 million cords of firewood annually and firewood provided 95 percent of the British thermal units produced in 1850 (Davis, 1983). Gradually, however, industrial uses such as lumber, woodpulp, and plywood would dominate. Neverthe-

less, the conversion to agriculture continued through the nineteenth century.

Nadir of the Forests, and the Provision of Management: 1850–1920

In 1800, the U.S. population was an estimated 5.8 million; by 1850, it was 23.2 million; by 1900, it had tripled to 76.0 million; and by 1920, it was 105.7 million. Given the rapid increase in the population, it is not surprising that the pace of land clearing increased dramatically. People could use much of the land in the east for agriculture if they invested in its "improvement," which generally consisted of logging and land clearing. Settlers in the Lake States initially exploited the forests during the mid-1800s to provide lumber for Ohio Valley farms, and later both to provide timber and to open the region to farming (Hansen, 1980). Before 1860, farmers cleared the hills of the Piedmont in the South for agriculture (Walker, 1980). By 1879, the estimated total area of cleared land was 223 million acres—twice the size in 1850 (Williams, 1987). The pace of land clearing continued and by 1920, the forest had declined to about 600 million acres—the nadir of the forest.

The 1850–1920 period also saw logging increase greatly. The tremendous logging and land-clearing activities that occurred from the mid-1800s into the

Probably most of the industrial wood obtained by the mid-1800s came from farm-owned woodlands that people cleared for farming.

early 1900s were driven by a combination of two forces. The first was the continued desire for agricultural land (Clawson, 1981). Probably most of the industrial wood obtained by the mid-1800s came from farm-owned woodlands that people cleared for farming (Lane, 1959). In the South alone, it is estimated that by 1860, 43 percent of the total land area was farmland, although a substantial part of the farm holding remained in forests (U.S. Department of Agriculture, 1988b). The second force generating logging and land clearing was the increasing requirement of a dynamic American economy for more resources of all types, including wood and timber (see appendix 3, figure 3-A1). The experience of the Lake States is representative of the pressures people put on the forests for both the land and timber during this period of expansion:

> Lumber for the farms of the Ohio River Valley and the interior prairie country of Illinois came largely from Michigan and Wisconsin pineries. In the 10–20 years following the Civil War, considerable logging activity was already going on in Michigan. Following the period of tremendous growth when the prairies of the midwest were settled, the logging of the Lake States forests increased to a fever pitch, moving to Minnesota as the best timber to the east was logged. In 1902, the region led the rest of the country in timber production. This grand era came to an end about 1910, when the bulk of the good white and red pine was gone (Hansen, 1980, p. 78).

In addition, farming played a role on the cutover timberlands:

> Overexpansion of farming in the later years induced the clearing of vast acreages of submarginal soil types and the destruction of the forest regeneration that might have followed the logging. Land clearing fires, and wildfires that were considered good because they got rid of slash that was a hindrance to farming were widespread (Hansen, 1980, p. 79).

As the American frontier moved out of the eastern forests and onto the midwestern prairies and grasslands, the pressure to clear forestland for agricultural use gradually abated.

Even where the pressure to deforest to provide new lands for agriculture lessened, it was replaced by a growing demand for wood for industrial and fuel purposes as the U.S. economy experienced an unprecedented era of population expansion and rapid in-

Technology contributed both to the growing demand for wood and to the enhanced capacity to draw timber from the forest.

dustrial growth. From 1850 until 1920, consumption of industrial wood increased by a factor of five and consumption of fuelwood increased by a factor of three (U.S. Department of Commerce, Bureau of the Census, 1975). Population had increased by more than 75 million between 1850 and 1920, and the economy exhibited an annual growth rate of more than 3 percent. During this seventy-year period, the demand for wood for fuel and industrial uses increased significantly, and wood uses increasingly replaced the desire for new lands as the principal motivation for the logger's activities.

Technology, a major factor leading the economic expansion that was absorbing vast volumes of timber, contributed both to the growing demand for wood and to the enhanced capacity to draw timber from the forest. Railroads, which required large volumes of timber for ties, bridges, and other construction as well as fuelwood for steam power, were replacing canals and other waterborne means as the principal mode of transportation. Wood-fueled, steam-powered equipment began to complement human, animal, and water power in the tasks of logging and transporting the logs to mills and finally to markets. The dramatic improvements in equipment and transportation provided an enhanced capability to efficiently log forests and convert forestland to other uses.

From 1850 to 1920, the center of the lumbering industry was moving continuously to the west and south. New York succeeded Maine as the leading lumbering state in 1839. In 1860, Pennsylvania became the lead producer; in the 1870s, it was Michigan. A decade later, lumber production in the Lake States reached its peak, and by the end of the nineteenth

century lumber output in the South exceeded that of the Lake States, peaking in 1909 but remaining high throughout the 1920s. By the 1920s, West Coast lumber was actively competing in eastern and midwestern markets despite significant transportation costs (Fedkiw, 1989). The westward expansion of logging was halted only when it reached the sea.

The rise of agriculture in the Midwest was an important influence on the use of forestland in the East. The dominant reason for land clearing in the East and the South had been to convert forestland to agricultural uses. As the frontier moved westward, the fertile lands of the Midwest became available for agriculture. Railroads improved access to eastern markets for the products of the high-fertility midwestern lands, creating stiff competition for eastern and southern agriculture. Cropland expansion slowed and then reversed in many previously forested regions. By the 1880s, net land abandonment was under way in the Northeast. However, in most of the Lake States cropland expansion did not peak until 1920 (Council on Environmental Quality, 1985), and the South was insulated from some of the early factors that resulted in abandonment because of its specialization in tobacco and cotton crops.

As wood consumption was rising dramatically during this period, so too was the real price—that is, the inflation-adjusted price—of the timber resource. The real price of lumber, the major product of the timber resource, doubled between 1850 and 1900 and increased another 50 percent by 1920 (Ulrich, 1988). Although massive volumes of timber were available in the forest, much of the timber was in the West away from the population centers. At the major markets, the growth in demand was outstripping the available supply, thereby forcing up the real prices of both delivered timber resources such as logs and major processed products such as lumber (Manthy, 1978).

Public Forests as Common Property

Exacerbating the problems arising because of the massive and continuing surge in timber demand were inappropriate institutions or unenforceable laws and regulations that encouraged economically excessive rates of deforestation and waste. For example, Nelson (1985) pointed out that

although much of the available timber was found on public lands, the public land laws had not been designed with timber production in mind. The Preemption, Homestead, and other key land laws were intended to promote agricultural settlement by small farmers. In most cases, they limited the sale or other disposal of land to 160 acres per individual. Originally, there were no special provisions for sale of timber.... The absence of any satisfactory way of obtaining public timber created incentives of the worst kind for those who actually harvested such timber. There was no reason for trespassers to be concerned about employing proper harvesting techniques or reforestation, since they would have no claim on future timber from the site. In essence, the public forests were a giant timber commons and the failure to establish effective property rights created the usual adverse incentives of the commons—to rush out to get ahead of others in exploiting the resource (Nelson, 1985, pp. 24–25).

Hence, in Nelson's view the problem was not, as sometimes charged, that capitalists were inherently shortsighted and were willing to dissipate their forests with no thought of the future. Rather, the institution of private property capitalism was never really operational for much of the nation's forest estate, and the laws governing the disposal of the lands were seriously flawed and often exacerbated the problem. Effectively, the forest belonged to no one; thus the timber was there for the taking. What ensued, in Nelson's view, was a variant of the classical "tragedy of the commons" (Hardin, 1968), intertwined with the widespread fraud and illegality that attended the disposal of the public lands. Although Congress tried to curb the abuses, it never addressed the basic failing of the land law that caused the abuses in the first place (Nelson, 1982; Gates, 1968).

Forest Management

The inattention to the longer-term management of American forests cannot be attributed solely to the lack of property rights. Although corruption and the lack of property rights contributed to the lack of care afforded the public forest, the absence of long-term forest management was also the rule on private lands. During the 1850–1920 period, there was little done that could be called active forest management. With but a few exceptions, the best situation provided only a loose stewardship; more often there was no stewardship at all. The primary reason that forest management and tree planting were rare, even on private

lands, was simply that these investments did not pay financially. Bernard Fernow, a German forester employed as the chief forester of the U.S. Department of Agriculture (USDA), reported in 1892 that forest owners failed to practice sustainable forestry because it did not pay; J. E. Defebaugh, a lumberman, expressed a similar view in 1893 (Robbins, 1985). Even the efforts of Gifford Pinchot, President Theodore Roosevelt's natural resources adviser, to apply European forestry practices to the North Carolina Biltmore estate of George Vanderbilt in the 1890s eventually proved unprofitable (Davis, 1983).

Efforts to manage the forests failed financially because timber in America was still plentiful and, as Nelson (1985, pp. 25–26) noted, "the huge supplies and very low price of timber provided little incentive to reforest. Like air or water, timber on the stump was close to a free good." The continent was covered by abundant forests, especially in the East, which was the location of the vast majority of the European settlements and economic activity for the first 200 years. The settlers viewed the century-old trees as impediments to agricultural development and as readily available for the cost of felling and transportation; thus, they did not expect the price of the trees to adequately cover the costs of planting and tending to maturity, a process that took 50 to 100 years. The European environment in which German and French forestry evolved was one in which timber was in relatively scarce supply. The lack of ready availability of frontier forests, and pressures on the small central European land base, created conditions of wood scarcity and high prices. This, in turn, provided incentives to care for and manage many European forests. By contrast, even in the early twentieth century wood was still plentiful in America and logging was essentially a foraging operation with little attention given to future timber supply. Absent were any incentives to promote more careful logging practices and reforestation. Furthermore, even when prudent practices seemed appropriate, there was little experience to draw on and American forest expertise was acquired only slowly (Clark, 1985). The result was that the settlers abandoned large areas of logged-over forestland and gave little thought to how humans might assist in promoting forest regeneration.

Perhaps the only management tool the settlers commonly used during this period was fire. They used fire not to promote forest growth but to prevent or limit regrowth, thereby facilitating the conversion of

A response to the perceived excesses of this period was the advent of a conservation movement, calling for major legislative action.

forest to cropland and pasture. Surely, agricultural land was more valuable than logged-over forest. In the Lake States, settlers viewed fire as a vehicle that contributed to the land clearing and facilitated ultimate conversion of the land to more useful and valuable agricultural lands. Perhaps for that reason, larger fires were common on cutover lands. For example, in 1871 the Peshtigo fire burned 1.3 million acres in Wisconsin and took 1,400 lives. Catastrophic fires occurred periodically in the Lake States, and to a lesser degree in the Northeast, into the first decades of the twentieth century. Large fires also occurred in the West. The Yacolt fire, which burned more than 1 million acres, led to the formation of private fire protection organizations in Washington and Oregon in the first decade of the twentieth century (Fedkiw, 1989). In many places rural people, like the Native Americans before them, used fire to prevent the excessive buildup of forest debris. In the South, settlers commonly used the annual burning of pine land as a management tool to promote grasses for pasture at the expense of woody vegetation; this practice contributed to the relative absence of catastrophic fires in this region (Pyne, 1982).

However, timber was gradually increasing in value. The real prices of wood in the United States had been rising since at least 1800 (see appendix 3, figure 3-A2). By the late 1800s, lumber real prices had increased more than fivefold over those that prevailed at the beginning of the century. This trend in the real price of lumber, a processed product, was mirrored in the prices of sawlogs (Manthy, 1978). Although still plentiful by European standards, the increased inaccessibility of the forests and increasing demands on the resource generated higher transportation costs and higher market prices. Nevertheless, before 1920 real prices had not yet risen sufficiently to justify financially even minimal forestry management in accessible locations under the existing conditions.

Rising Concerns: The Early Conservation and Preservation Movements and Legislation

In the context of the rapid expansion of logging and forest depletion, it is not surprising that Americans were raising concerns about the future of the American forest. From the perspective of the late nineteenth century, this alarm appeared to be well grounded. An extrapolation of late nineteenth-century trends in deforestation and in industrial and fuel-wood consumption suggested that these trends were not sustainable and soon would run up against limitations in resource availability. Certainly, the American forest could not continue to increase timber production in the first half of the twentieth century at the rate it had increased in the previous half-century—that is, by a factor of five in fifty years—without seriously compromising the sustainability of much of the remaining American forest.

The theme of a "timber famine" recurred periodically throughout the late nineteenth century and well into the twentieth in continuing discussions and debates about the role and capacity of the American forests. As early as 1849 the commissioner of patents, in his annual report, raised questions concerning "the waste of valuable timber in the United States" (Fedkiw, 1989). By the 1860s, a number of reports decried the destruction of the forests and its deleterious effects on a variety of timber, economic, and environmental values. In 1873, the American Association for the Advancement of Science organized a lobbying effort to convince Congress to establish forest reserves. The "Report of the Forests of North America," part of the 1880 census, projected that the remaining white pine forests of the Lake States would be exhausted in eleven to twelve years at the existing rates of harvest (Gates, 1968).

As forests declined in some regions, so too did the environmental services they provided. Reductions in forest habitat, together with intensive hunting, led to dramatic declines in some wildlife populations (see chapter 6). Also, watershed protection was sometimes compromised and erosion and flooding problems were exacerbated (see chapters 2 and 5). A response to the perceived excesses of this period was the advent of a conservation movement, calling for major legislative action. As early as 1877, Secretary of the Interior Carl Schurz had warned of timber shortages and predicted environmental disturbances:

> If we go on at the present rate, the supply of timber in the United States will, in less than twenty years, fall considerably short of our home necessities. How disastrously the destruction of the forests of a country affects the regularity of the water supply in its rivers necessary for navigation, increases the frequency of freshets and inundations, dries up springs, and transforms fertile agricultural districts into barren wastes, is a matter of universal experience the world over. It is the highest time that we should turn our earnest attention to this subject, which so seriously concerns our national prosperity. (Wilkerson and Anderson, 1987, pt. 5, at xvi)

The early interest in conservation of the forests was strongly influenced by individuals trained in the sciences. Gifford Pinchot, W. J. McGee, Frederick Newell, and John Wesley Powell were strongly influenced by the "progressive" view, which was based on two principles that dominated the progressive era: op-

position to the domination of economic affairs by narrow "special interests," and a fundamental belief in rationality and science (Culhane, 1981). Efficiency was a central theme of the progressive movement and led to the concept of "wise use" in natural resources. Another theme was the populist one of broadly distributing the benefits (Hays, 1959). Pinchot captured this concept in his principle: "Natural resources must be developed and preserved for the benefit of the many and not merely for the profit of the few."

The progressive conservationist movement was not the only voice protesting the degradation of the forest. Early preservationists such as Henry David Thoreau and John Muir espoused the preservation and protection of natural areas for their inherent, and even spiritual, qualities. Although the preservationist position would continue to be articulated in the mid-twentieth century and gain strength in the late twentieth century, the progressive conservationist movement, with its message of scientific management and wise use, was the dominant political force shaping forest legislation and institutions during the late 1800s and early 1900s.

Unrestricted logging (foreground) contrasted with U.S. Forest Service selective logging (background), 1908

One piece of legislation influenced by progressive conservationists was the Forest Reserve Act of 1891, which permitted the president to set aside portions of the public land as public reservations. By 1893, more than 17 million acres of forest were in the reserve and in 1896, 21 million more acres were added. The Organic Act of 1897 provided for use and management of the reserves. In 1905, the administration of the forest reserves, by that time totaling 85.9 million acres, was transferred from the Department of the Interior to the newly formed Forest Service, which came under the auspices of the USDA; Gifford Pinchot was named its first chief. During the administration of Theodore Roosevelt, who was a strong supporter of the conservationist movement, more land was added to the national forests, as they were renamed in 1907. By the end of Roosevelt's administration in 1908, nearly 194.5 million gross acres were within forest reserve boundaries (Robinson, 1975), although not all of that forestland was administered by the Forest Service. Through the Weeks Act of 1911, the Forest Service obtained the power to purchase forestland and cut-over land within the watersheds of navigable streams. The first purchases by the national forest system included 5 million acres in the White Mountains in New Hampshire, at a cost to the government of less than 5 dollars per acre. Between 1916 and 1920, nine national forests were established in the East. These eastern forests consisted mainly of unwanted land that was heavily logged over, often burned, and badly eroded, as well as abandoned farmland (Shands and Healy, 1974). In the South, much of this land was taken from marginal agriculture that had ceased to be productive.

The Post–1900 Decline in Wood Consumption

Ironically, at the same time that President Theodore Roosevelt, Gifford Pinchot, journalist Horace Greeley, and others were raising the specter of a coming timber famine, the total consumption of wood in the United States was beginning to decline—independently of any external intervention. The per capita decline in wood consumption for both industrial and fuel uses had begun as early as 1870 (Manthy, 1978). Although the population had continued to increase, after 1910 the rate of decline accelerated, and by 1920 per capita wood consumption for industrial and fuel purposes was not much more than one-half of its

> *Technologies in the form of longer-lasting products and wood substitutes had gradual but ultimately dramatic impacts on the demand for wood.*

1870 level. Only in another seventy years would total consumption challenge the peak achieved in 1907. The much-heralded timber famine did not arrive.

The reasons for this decline in wood consumption were many and complex. Throughout the nineteenth century, wood use had been changing significantly. The importance of fuelwood gradually declined as fossil fuels and other energy sources, beginning with coal and later supplemented by petroleum and natural gas, came into common usage. Timber and industrial wood consumption declined following the early 1900s as lumber lost its preeminence as a building material. Brick buildings increasingly replaced wooden structures, sometimes for legal reasons, as was the case after the great Chicago fire in the early 1870s. Newly introduced construction materials—cement, iron, steel, and reinforced concrete—replaced wood. In addition, the use of wood for road surfacing, which was common practice during much of the nineteenth century (Abbott, 1981), was all but abandoned in the twentieth century.

Many of these innovations were made possible by the development of technologies. Technologies in the form of longer-lasting products and wood substitutes had gradual but ultimately dramatic impacts on the demand for wood. For example, barbed wire was especially useful for controlling livestock. This product reduced the need for wood in the construction of fences, especially in the wood-scarce West during the 1880s and 1890s (Anderson and Hill, 1975). On the other hand, wood preservatives that dramatically extended the life of wood products, such as treated railroad ties, reduced the demand for wood replacements. From the 1870s to 1900, the railroads consumed nearly one-fourth of the nation's annual timber production. To extend the life of the crossties and other wood used in the construction of railroad facilities, chemical wood preservatives were used to prevent wood rot. Beginning modestly about 1900, the treatment of railroad ties with chemical preservatives increased to more than 50 percent of tie production by the early 1920s, and to nearly 100 percent by 1960. Furthermore, as techniques of wood preservation improved, previously unused wood species became suitable for ties. By the 1960s, railroad consumption of the total solidwood supply had fallen to 5 or 6 percent, or an absolute decline to about one-fifth of its level in 1900 (Olson, 1971).

The rise in the real price of timber that had continued almost uninterrupted since at least 1800 undoubtedly had contributed to the relative decline in the use of timber. Although most natural resource uses in the United States exhibited a constant or declining trend in real prices, industrial wood prices behaved quite differently (Manthy, 1978). For example, the real price of lumber increased an average 1.5 percent annually over the 120 years preceding 1920. Although this increase had begun from a low base, after decades of steady growth it began to influence wood usage. Rising real prices for wood, in the context of stable prices for most other materials, meant that the price of other materials was becoming increasingly competitive with wood, thus encouraging the development of wood-extending technologies and wood-substituting products.

Although the period following 1910 saw the beginning of the decline in lumber consumption both absolutely and in per capita terms, it also saw two developments that would lead to a continuing upward trend in the total consumption of industrial wood in the post–World War II period—the emergence of an industry that used woodfiber as feedstock for pulp for paper production, and the development of a fledgling wood panel industry (specifically, the slowly developing plywood industry).

Pressures on Forests in the Far West

The pressures on the forests of the Pacific Coast region were quite different from those experienced in the East. In 1920, the Forest Service estimated that 80 percent of the original forestland of the Pacific Coast states remained in forest. Virgin forest existed on 75 percent of the acreage—contrasting with the forest for the entire country, which was estimated in 1920 to cover only about 50 percent of the original forestland area (U.S. Department of Agriculture, 1928), with little of it remaining in virgin forest. Two factors that limited the extent of forest use and the conversion of forestlands to agriculture in the West were the area's isolation and limited access and the poor quality of the soils for agriculture (Cox, 1983).

Use of the region's timber resources began in the mid-1800s with the advent of the gold rush and the subsequent influx of population. By the 1880s, lumber manufacturing had become one of the region's leading industries. Although used locally, West Coast lumber generally was not competitive in Midwest markets before the 1890s because of high railroad costs. Inexpensive ocean shipping did allow Pacific Coast timber to find major international markets in the Pacific basin and elsewhere; however, even this commerce was limited before the advent of the Panama Canal in 1914.

Another feature that differentiated Pacific Coast forestry and therefore changed the land-use dynamics was the lack of acceptable soils that would allow cut-over land to be converted to productive agricultural uses. Few farms were cleared from forestland, and most land that was cleared, except in the few favorable sites such as low-elevation river valleys, proved to be marginal and soon was abandoned to the forest. The result was that the settlers there rarely converted

Although most natural resource uses in the United States exhibited a constant or declining trend in real prices, industrial wood prices behaved quite differently.

cutover forest to agriculture. Rather, they allowed it to remain idle and eventually regenerate naturally with a new crop of timber (Cox, 1983).

The End of an Era

In many respects, 1920 marked the nadir for the American forests. The area of timberlands was at its historic low of 464 million acres, considerably less than the 580 million acres estimated by Clawson, Held, and Stoddard (1960) for the early 1900s and somewhat below the current Forest Service estimate of 483.1 million acres (U.S. Department of Agriculture, 1988b). The total area of all forestland in 1920 was estimated by Clawson (1979) at slightly more than 600 million acres, considerably below the estimate of 728 million acres for current forestland. Even worse, the state of many of the forests in 1920 was poor in that their stocking levels were not managed constructively. The use of the nation's eastern forests for timber and the wholesale conversion of forestlands to agricultural uses that had begun around the mid-nineteenth century had ended. Conversion first swept the forestland of New England and then moved to the Lake State forests, which were intensively exploited by 1900. As the Lake State forests declined, timber interests moved to the South, with intensive logging beginning in the late nineteenth century and peaking during World War I. By 1920, the forests of the South, too, had been heavily depleted. Although it would be a mistake to characterize any of these regions as denuded of forests, the forests were certainly in far poorer condition than they had been sixty years earlier—or would be sixty years later. As the old forests were logged, what remained was often a degraded forest or a marginal agricultural field or pasture. With the forests of the Lake States and the South heavily depleted, the only remaining large stands of virgin timber were now found almost exclusively in the West.

By 1920, the concerns and pressures of the conservationist movement had succeeded in inducing Congress to undertake four steps designed to manage and preserve the forest resources: to set aside large and growing forestland as part of a national system of forest reserves; to legislate an organic act that would provide for the use and management of the forest reserves; to create a new and elite agency, the Forest Service, to administer and manage those lands; and

to provide for additions to those reserved lands under specific conditions. By that time, the federal government had established firm control over the some 150 million acres of public forestland—the national forests—that had ceased to be timber commons. Instead, the public forest was now under active public stewardship and protection. During this period, there was relatively little timber harvesting in the national forests. In addition, per capita timber consumption had been declining for almost two decades. There was growing concern, if not yet effective action, to control wildfire on both public and private lands. The remainder of the forest estate, still the majority of the nation's timberlands, was in private ownership of various types running the gamut from forest industry land to farm woodlots.

Rebirth of the Forest: 1921 Through World War II

During the 1920s, the United States experienced only modest economic growth together with weakening agricultural prices and a slight decrease in overall timber consumption. Clark (1985) characterized the agricultural situation in the South as follows:

> Immediately after 1920 there developed across the South a distinct lull, if not depression, in the region's economy. Farmers suffered serious reverses as results of falling cotton and tobacco prices, boll weevil damage, loss of markets, and a faltering credit system. Bankruptcy for the South in 1925 was a grim spectre, especially for little farmers and sharecroppers. Exhausted farm lands and cutover timber tracts could be acquired at buyers' bargaining prices. (Clark, 1985, pp. 50–51)

The situation of agriculture in the Lake States, as characterized by Hansen (1980), was similar: "During this period from about 1920 on through the Depression years of the 1930s, land abandonment in the poorer farming counties went on at a great rate. Millions of acres of farms were abandoned" (p. 79).

Also during that period, the condition of the forest could be characterized as poor by most criteria. Not only had the area in forestland reached its historic low in 1920, but much of the forest that remained in the East was low-quality, low-volume, degraded for-

Seedlings planted on barren slopes to control erosion

est, often used for grazing. Poor logging practices repeatedly fostered erosion and destroyed wildlife habitat. Forest watershed and flood control services in many cases deteriorated with the decline of the forest. Where wildfire had recurred excessively, soil degradation also occurred. The Forest Service described the condition of the forest as follows:

> By the early years of this century, the rapid harvest of timber, uncontrolled wildfires, and grazing by livestock had resulted in nearly complete clearing of the forest in many parts of the South. Observers in some areas could look for miles and see lands entirely stripped of trees. As in other regions, people generally assumed at the time that most cutover lands would be converted to crop and pasture use. The protection of forest cover was considered to be of little consequence. Most of the cutover lands were not developed for crops, however, but left untended and used by livestock, if used at all. There was little in the way of fire protection and replanting until the 1930s. Even then, the acres planted and protected were modest when compared to the total acreage. (U.S. Department of Agriculture, 1988b, p. 38)

Although the total U.S. land area in cropland use changed little between 1920 and 1950, the aggregate figures mask regional changes that were substantial (Frey and Hexem, 1985). The East showed a decline of 29 million acres in cropland between 1920 and 1940; the Northeast, Appalachia, and the Southeast continued that decline into the 1950s for a total decrease of cropland in the East of 31 million acres. In the South, the area of cultivated cropland remained high until the late 1930s. From that time, cropland in the South declined steadily to a low in the mid-1960s (Healy, 1985). For example, between 1937 and 1974 in Carroll County, Georgia, 90,000 acres were converted from agriculture to forest and only 8,000 acres were converted from forest to agriculture (Williams, 1988).

Until about 1930, ownership of land by the timber industry tended to be temporary, with cutover timberland sold for farming or other uses. Where markets for cutover lands were absent, these lands reverted to local governments in payment for back taxes (Council on Environmental Quality, 1985), and little interest was shown by either the industry or governments in timber growing. From 1925 to 1945, the southern forest industry planted an average of only 6,800 acres a year of its own land (Williston, 1980).

Wood Markets

After 1910, markets for wood products had ceased expanding, although market consumption remained high through World War I and into the 1920s. Real prices for wood had been stable after 1910 but then experienced a decline before 1920. After reaching new highs in the early 1920s, the real prices of industrial wood exhibited a decline that carried into the Great Depression and into the early 1940s. In the early 1900s, fledgling wood-using products such as plywood and woodpulp had begun to consume modest amounts of industrial wood. However, in a national context, these new products were negligible users of the total wood production in the 1920s and 1930s. The South initially was insulated from the decline in demand for industrial wood by the falloff in harvests from the Lake States. However, during the 1920s southern timber harvests also declined gradually and a slowdown in the economy of the South forced mills to close. Economic activity fell dramatically through the United States during the Great Depression. With this sharp decline in economic activity, including construction, came a more severe decline in industrial wood consumption. In 1932, U.S. wood consumption was only 60 percent of the wood consumption peak of the early twentieth century. The only major exception to the declining trend in wood consumption was the increase in the consumption of fuelwoods. This trend, unfortunately, reflected the lower living standards during the Great Depression. Only when World War II brought an end to the depression did economic activity increase and wood consumption begin to increase substantially. The real

The widespread abandonment of agricultural lands by farmers that occurred after 1930 . . . laid the foundations for the forest regrowth.

prices of wood resources reflected this upturn, although the rise was inhibited by price controls during the war.

The vast majority of the industrial wood consumed during this period was harvested from private forestlands. Despite the large national forests and the addition to substantial new areas of forest to the national forest system from 1920 to 1945, the harvests from the system remained limited until World War II, when those harvests were increased to meet the war effort. Even given the war effort, in 1945 total domestic production and consumption of both industrial wood and fuelwood was substantially lower than it had been in 1920.

Changing Land-Use Patterns

Although not apparent at the time, the period beginning about 1920 marked the onset of the rebirth of large portions of the nation's eastern forest. From 1850 into the early 1900s massive areas of forestland had been converted to agriculture, including large areas of private land, much of which had been transferred by a federal program to the private sector (see chapter 5). The conversion was reversed, unintentionally, as a result of benign neglect during the period 1920–1945 through a combination of a decline in wood consumption and the widespread abandonment of agricultural lands by farmers that occurred after 1930. In many parts of the East and South abandonment of lands allowed for the reintroduction of the forest, initially through natural regeneration and later through conscious tree planting and fire control. The decline in wood consumption laid the foundations for the forest.

The process occurred gradually, beginning as early as the 1870s in the Northeast, where agricultural lands that could no longer compete with the cheaper production of the fertile agriculture of the Midwest were abandoned. This process was accelerated by the depression, spreading to the South, Appalachia, and the Lake States in the 1930s, and continuing through the war years and into the postwar period (Hart, 1968).

With the decline of agricultural prices from a high during World War I, the opportunity to use cutover lands for economic agricultural production never returned to the South and the Lake States. As markets eroded and cotton was plagued by the boll weevil, even previously productive agricultural lands in the

South began to fall into disuse. As before in the Northeast, these southern lands could not be redirected readily into food and feed grain crops because of the competition of the superior midwestern prairies. Agriculture in the Lake States suffered a similar fate, especially on land recently converted from forest. These large areas of marginal agricultural lands throughout the East were abandoned. For a time the abandoned land was used as pasture; however, small-scale livestock operations became uneconomical. Abandoned areas that had once been converted from forest to agriculture reverted easily to a new cover of forest.

Although exacerbated by the Great Depression, the return of substantial cropland to forest was probably inevitable. The period of rapid forestland conversion was over and the consumption of timber had declined. Market forces in the context of technological developments in the wood industry put an end to the dramatic increase in the growth of wood consumption experienced in the late 1800s. The introduction of productivity enhancing technologies in the fertile agricultural land of the Midwest relieved the pressure to convert and maintain forestland in crops. Ignored by both farmers and loggers alike, converted and abandoned lands were left largely to the dictates of natural processes.

Forest Renewability

Despite the stresses inflicted by people, American forests showed an amazing resiliency. Having survived natural disasters in the past, they also demonstrated the capacity to recover from the impacts of logging and agriculture. Although not well recognized, the logging of old-growth forests created opportunities for new growth. Mature forests generate little net growth. Young forests, however, are typically vigorous, often exhibiting rapid growth in height and volume. Where the land was not converted to permanent nontimber uses, the intensive logging of the late 1800s and early 1900s had created a disproportionately young forest estate. Additionally, the decline of agriculture in the Northeast, South, and parts of the Lake States had left large areas of abandoned fields that were well suited for the natural regeneration of forests (Healy, 1985). Abandoned agricultural fields, if not used heavily for grazing or burned recurrently, typically remained unforested for only short

Although not well recognized, the logging of old-growth forests created opportunities for new growth.

periods before tree species quickly established themselves. Often, the pioneer species that reclaimed a site were different from the dominant species in the original forest. For example, the longleaf pine, which had inhabited vast areas of the southern coastal plain, was commonly replaced by a more effective pioneer species such as loblolly or shortleaf pine (Clark, 1985). In the Lake States, the pioneer species that often followed the logging of old-growth white pine forest was aspen. Elsewhere, other pioneer species led the regeneration. Much of New England was regenerated in pine forests that invaded abandoned agricultural fields and came to be known as "old field" pine.

Although in some cases repeated burning lowered the productivity of the land for forest growth, the pervasiveness and vigor of the regeneration exceeded the expectations of most observers. Clawson (1979) noted that almost all projections of future forest growth, even into the 1970s, badly underestimated the rate of forest growth that subsequently would be achieved. From an estimated 6 billion cubic feet in 1920, the net growth of U.S. forests increased to 13.9 billion cubic feet by 1952 and 22 billion cubic feet by 1986 (Haynes, 1988).

The early pessimism regarding growth potential is not surprising, given the dearth of scientific information about the ability of forests generally and pine in particular to regenerate naturally and to grow rapidly on favorable sites. Because most American foresters at the turn of the twentieth century had been trained in Europe, the European forestry tradition influenced early thinking in the United States about scientific forest management. Experience in Europe suggested much longer periods of regrowth than would be experienced in much of the United States, and particularly in the South.

By the 1920s, scientific interest in forest regeneration was developing in selected pockets in the South and elsewhere (Clark, 1985). In 1931, Henry Hardtner, one of the early pioneers who personally had been concerned with silviculture and forest renewal for more than thirty years, described the difficulties experienced by these early foresters to members at a Society of American Foresters meeting: "At first I had to pioneer every step in my investigation of the reproduction of longleaf pine. I thought it would take 60 to 100 years to grow a merchantable crop. No one could tell me what was possible. I had to work out the problem myself" (Clark, 1985, p. 55). In addition, at the time of land abandonment few people recognized the capacity of forestland to regenerate timber without any conscious intervention. However, American forestland, particularly in the South, responded quickly to the unusually favorable mix of climate, species, and soils that promoted both rapid natural regeneration and rapid growth. In fewer than ten years forest cover was firmly reestablished on many southern sites. Tall pines now stood on lands that only recently had exhausted their fertility for growing tobacco, cotton, and corn. This new forest became known as the South's "Second Forest."

The total volume of the nation's forest growing stock probably continued to decline for a period after 1920 as harvests continued to exceed the invigorated growth of the regenerated forests. Gradually, however, the area of regenerated forest expanded and the rate of forest growth increased. The decline in the nation's harvest after 1920 also contributed to redressing the imbalance between harvest and growth. Sometime around the early 1940s, forest growth nationally came into balance with harvests, and since that time growth has exceeded harvest.

Fire may have laid the foundation for a new forest, but wildfire discouraged tree planting.

Wildfires and Tree Planting

As with silviculture and forest renewal, the fire problem in the United States was quite different from that experienced in the cooler and wetter parts of Europe. Coert duBois (1914) wrote, "American foresters have found that they have a unique fire problem and that they can get little help in solving it from European foresters...." The ecology of fire, together with a philosophy and the techniques for controlling fire, had to be developed in the United States (Pyne, 1981).

Wildfire plays a number of important roles in the environment of the forest. Although wildfire can destroy timber, fire also prepares the forest floor for the next generation of forest. Particularly in the South, fire ensures the perpetuation of a pine forest. The thick bark insulates the trees from low fires that can destroy the competition of emerging hardwoods. Also, pioneer pine species are genetically programmed to respond to a fire environment, establishing young, vigorous forests literally out of the ashes of the fires.

Although wildfires were sometimes an act of nature and currently are often used as part of a vegetative control regime, they often were the result of careless acts. For example, logging techniques depended on steam skidders and logging locomotives, both of which were fire menaces (Clark, 1985). Furthermore, with burning being a common technique for managing pasture and controlling brush, the risk of the burn spreading to surrounding forest was great.

Fire may have laid the foundation for a new forest, but wildfire discouraged tree planting. In 1926, the total area of tree plantation was only 352,000 acres, most of that being in the North (Council on Environmental Quality, 1985). Statistics available from various issues of the Forest Service's *Forest Fire Statistics* reveal that the area of forest burned annually after 1924 exceeded 20 million acres into the early 1940s, and was sometimes as high as 50 million acres annually (see appendix 3, figure 3-A3). It was not until the latter part of the 1950s that there were substantial reductions. In addition, fires occurred predominantly on state and private forestland, not in national forests. These figures suggest that the majority of the fires occurred in eastern forest areas, probably on logged-over or young forests. With wildfire common and largely uncontrolled, the risks associated with tree planting were considerable because planted pine forests ran a substantial chance of being

small appropriations for tree growing. Together with the Knutson-Vandenberg Act of 1920, which provided monies for planting trees in national forests and abandoned cutover areas, these funds financed fledgling tree planting programs in the 1920s and 1930s. As early as the 1920s, large-scale state tree planting programs with federal cooperation were undertaken to promote reforestation, especially in the Northeast and in the Lake States. The Copeland Report, published in 1933, viewed tree planting as necessary to regenerate the American forest and suggested planting programs of 50 million acres (U.S. Department of Agriculture, Forest Service, 1979). Although these levels were never achieved during the 1930s, the amount of tree planting undertaken was substantial indeed. The Civilian Conservation Corps (CCC), created in 1933 in the depths of the depression, was active in conservation programs, particularly tree planting. In its first five years of existence, the CCC planted approximately 1 million acres of cutover lands (Clark, 1985).

The economics of tree planting in the interwar years were unattractive in the absence of substantial government involvement and subsidization. Fire control, too, would have to be a critical component in making tree planting economically viable. Without wildfire control, the risk of losing a young stand of trees was too great to justify the investment, even in the face of higher prices. In the presence of a high degree of fire risk, regenerated forests would have to come in naturally with no out-of-pocket costs to investors. If the risk of wildfire could be significantly reduced, however, tree planting might just pay. By the early 1940s, tree planting still averaged only 184,000 acres per year.

The Role of Government: Acquisitions for the Public Domain

The government was an important force contributing to the preservation and renewal of the forest, to some extent at the state and local levels, but primarily at the federal level. The conservationist fervor of the turn of the century was alive and well, and sentiment for public ownership and control of a large amount of forestland remained strong. By 1920, about 150 million acres of forest had been established as national forests. Additional eastern forests, often of degraded forestlands, were added during the 1920s,

destroyed before harvest. In this setting, most tree planting simply was not cost effective.

Although forest fires have played a role in American forests and large wildfires periodically have impacted the forest from the time of early settlement, Chief Forester William Greeley in the 1920s campaigned vigorously for fire-suppression programs, and the Clark-McNary Act of 1924 included funds for a cooperative federal/state fire-suppression system (Williams, 1988). The system was to involve both public and private lands. With the advent of active suppression programs in the 1930s and later, losses resulting from fires gradually began to decline and many of the young regenerated forests were protected to maturity.

In addition to making funds available for forest fire suppression, the Clark-McNary Act of 1924 provided

Reforestation, California, 1924

and the depression stimulated the establishment of twenty-six national forests in the East from Missouri to Vermont and Wisconsin to Florida (Shands and Healy, 1974). Between 1934 and 1946, the federal government acquired nearly 11.3 million acres in forty-five states and redeveloped 9.5 million acres in forest, range, and related multiple uses such as wildlife habitat, watershed protection, and recreation. The government converted another 1.8 million acres to parks and wildlife refuges (Fedkiw, 1989). During the 1930s, states such as Michigan, Minnesota, Wisconsin, New York, and Pennsylvania took over large areas of tax-delinquent land, many of them cutover forestland, which were subsequently incorporated into state and local forests. Between 1920 and 1950, the Forest Service added 22 million acres to the net area of national forests (Clark, 1985); most of these additions were made during the depression.

In addition to its emphasis on tree planting, the Copeland Report of 1933 reflected some of the depression-era confidence in the efficacy of planning and in an increased governmental role through its recommendations for a massive extension of public acquisition of forestland and broad public regulation of forest activities (Clawson, 1983). The report recommended federal or state purchase of 244 million acres of private forestland with extensive public regulation. In his letter of transmittal with the report, Secretary of Agriculture Henry Wallace stated the controversial proposition that "practically all of the major problems of American forestry center in or have grown out of private ownership" (Wilkerson and Anderson, 1987, p. 27). Congress, however, did not appropriate adequate funds to fully implement the recommendations of the report. Although controversy continued to surround many of the recommendations for increased government ownership and regulation of forestland, the sentiment for such reforms waned and largely were abandoned by the Forest Service after World War II.

Successful Regeneration

The period following 1920 until the end of World War II was a time of confluence of a number of forces that helped curtail the decline of America's forest estate and contributed to its significant renewal. Initially the renewal was almost imperceptible, but gradually it grew and became more apparent. After declining for years—in fact, for several centuries—the forest began to experience widespread recovery. The recovery reflected changes in the use of timber and fuelwood as well as changing agricultural conditions that modified society's requirements for agricultural land, particularly land of low productivity that originally had been in forest. The inherent regenerative capacity of the forest made the recovery possible, even in the absence of deliberate regeneration efforts. In addition, the government took a proactive role not only in setting aside areas of forest but in beginning to undertake policies and activities to protect and promote forest growth and to deal with wildfire. Industrial forestland acquisition also began during this period. The recovery of the forest provided the basis for recovery of many of the environmental services provided by the forest. Watershed protection, erosion and flood control, and wildlife habitat all experienced renewal as a result of the rebirth of the forest. More detailed discussions of the provisions of these services appear in the chapters on water (chapter 2), crops (chapter 5), and wildlife (chapter 6).

Improved Management: Post–World War II to the Present

The burst of economic activity associated with World War II brought wood production out of the low levels of the depression. In the early postwar period, the United States continued to experience significant growth both in its population and its economy. Consumption of nonmilitary goods and services increased dramatically in the early postwar period, reflecting the release of the pent-up demand associated with the frustrations of the depression and the rationing of the war. Forest products were no exception. The U.S. housing stock and other structures had been largely ignored during the depression and the war, but in the prosperous postwar environment consumers demanded new housing and a variety of other new structures. The baby boom of the late 1940s and 1950s contributed to the longevity of the housing boom. Industrial wood production, which had surged during the war, remained at high levels in the early postwar period. Lumber production in 1948 was just slightly above its wartime high, but nearly three times the production levels during 1932—the lowest point of the depression—and more than 50 percent above that of 1938 (U.S. Department of Commerce, Bureau of the Census, 1975).

With the high demand levels of the postwar period, the role of the national forests as a source of industrial wood began to increase dramatically. For the first time, timber harvesting became a major activity of the Forest Service. Between 1950 and 1959, the timber harvest on national forest land increased from 3.5 billion to 8.3 billion board feet annually. Clawson (1984) characterized this period as one of "intensive timber management" of the national forests. In the 1960s, private sector forestry also began to experience a fundamental change. Not only was the timber industry interested in logging, but the private sector discovered that investments in forestry could pay substantial dividends; thus the private sector began to expand dramatically in its role as a timber grower. However, the early postwar consensus that the public forests would increase their harvests and the intensity of timber management would increase was soon replaced by a "consultation and confrontation" period (Clawson, 1984).

Although only rather modest changes in the area of forest and timberland have occurred during the postwar period from the mid- to the late 1960s the area of forest and timberland increased slightly, even as the area of cropland declined (Darr, 1988). However, the inventory volume on timberland increased substantially. The favorable agricultural prices of the 1970s were associated with some declines in forestland as people devoted land to crops (Bones, 1988). But during the 1980s, the area of land in crops declined and the area of forestland stabilized. The major area where forest conversion continued was the rich river bottomland where people continued to convert the hardwood forest into cropland, in part as a consequence of flood control and drainage programs (Stavins and Jaffe, 1990).

Timber, however, was not the only output the public was demanding of the forest. Although consumers exercised their influence in the market by purchasing wood and wood products, they increasingly began to recognize and value the nontimber uses of public land. The prosperity of the postwar period, with the mobility afforded the population through widespread use of the automobile, led to a burgeoning demand for outdoor recreation. From 1950 to 1960, for example, recreational visits to the national forests increased from 26 million to 81.5 million visitor days (a visitor day is one visit by one visitor for one day). Recreation visitor days in the national forests peaked in 1980 (at 233 million) and actually declined slightly through the 1980s.

Coincidentally with the emergence of new interest in a variety of the forest outputs, earlier concerns about environmental interests reemerged. The preservationist legacy of John Muir has once again chal-

After declining for years—in fact, for several centuries—the forest began to experience widespread recovery.

lenged the utilitarian philosophy of Gifford Pinchot and the conservationists. People now value forests not only for their timber, watershed, and recreational services, but also for their provision of other environmental services. Considerations and concerns that first had been expressed under the rubric of species preservation were by the late 1980s being expanded and refined to include concerns about the maintenance of ecosystems and biodiversity. During the postwar years, various interest groups increasingly have been engaged in conflicts over the management of the nation's forests, especially its public forests. Moreover, environmentalists increasingly have viewed timber outputs of the forest as competitive with other forest outputs, especially a set of outputs tied to ecological considerations. The arena in which these conflicts have been fought has not been the traditional marketplace, but politics.

By the 1990s, concerns about the American forest had shifted dramatically from a largely utilitarian concern about the protection of its watersheds and the adequacy of its timber resources in the context of an expected impending timber famine to a preservationist concern for the protection of old growth and the maintenance of biodiversity within the context of the forest ecosystem. The old-growth controversy, for example, hinges on a judgment about the relative social value of the old-growth forests of the Pacific Northwest as habitat for maintaining ecological biodiversity. Furthermore, because substantial areas of old-growth forest still exist, it requires a judgment of how much preservation is required. Biodiversity is a much more esoteric concept than, say, flood control, and ascertaining its value is much more judgmental and elusive.

Wood Products and Markets

Although the production of industrial wood expanded throughout much of the early postwar period, total wood consumption including fuelwood increased slowly. It was not until the mid-1960s that total industrial wood production exceeded the levels of the early 1900s. Although the value of manufacturing shipments of wood products increased by a factor of nearly three in constant 1982 prices from 1950 to 1986 (Haynes, 1988), much of this value was attributed less to the timber resource than to the value added in processing.

The most unstable component of wood production in the postwar period was fuelwood. Fuelwood production in 1948 was about one-half that of 1932, and by 1975 production had dropped to less than one-fifth of its 1948 level, an almost negligible level. In the mid-1970s, fuelwood had almost ceased being a significant wood use, reflecting the continuing substitution of fossil fuels for wood fuels. Total wood use—industrial wood and fuelwood together—did not exceed the 1907 peak until 1978. Primarily because of the energy crisis of the late 1970s, a number of fuelwood-promoting actions were set in motion, such as auxiliary wood-burning electrical power generation and greater use of wood energy at pulp and paper mills. It had taken seventy years for total U.S. wood removals to again reach the record levels of the first decade of the twentieth century.

By the mid-1980s, fuelwood consumption approached the levels experienced in the early 1930s, largely as a result of the more complete use of wood waste and residue that grew out of the energy crisis of the 1970s rather than the large-scale reintroduction of wood for home heating. Although fuelwood production was declining, the amount of domestic wood production that was directed into woodpulp to produce paper and paperboard grew dramatically, more than doubling between 1938 and 1948, doubling again by 1965, and increasing again by 50 percent by the mid-1980s.

In addition, during the postwar period certain U.S. wood requirements, especially lumber, have been met by increased lumber imports from Canada. By the early 1980s, Canadian lumber constituted more than 30 percent of U.S. consumption. At the same time, however, the United States has become more active in international markets, particularly the Japanese and other East Asian markets. U.S. log exports increased from negligible levels in the late 1940s to substantial volumes, especially after 1970. Through much of the postwar period, the United States has been a modest net importer of forest products, with imports from Canada exceeding U.S. exports to other countries (Sedjo and Radcliffe, 1981).

Technology and Forest Products

Perhaps the major explanation for the modest growth in U.S. industrial wood production in the postwar period is the continuing introduction of technology

that has increased the efficiency of timber use. Across the industry, mills have become more efficient in their use of raw timber through innovations that reduce processing waste. For example, small log use reduces waste, thin sawblades reduce losses to sawdust, and computers use lasers to direct sawing operations to maximize the value of output for each individual log. In addition, "wood-saving" products have allowed for the production of an acceptable product that uses less wood input. One example is the use of wood trusses in building construction; trusses provide the required strength but use substantially less wood than earlier methods. Likewise, low-quality wood has been used to produce substitutes for higher-quality wood products. For example, waferboard and oriented strand board are produced from the previously largely underused aspen forests of the Lake States. These products are competitive with lumber and plywood, both of which use more expensive wood sources

(Haygreen and coauthors, 1986). In the pulp and paper industry, a number of important wood-saving innovations have been introduced. For example, the chemithermalmechanical pulp process reduces the wood requirements for certain types of woodpulp by almost one-half.

The composition of wood products during this period has also changed substantially as newly developed wood products encroach on the markets of traditional wood products. U.S. lumber consumption, for example, increased only modestly—by about 30 percent—between 1950 and 1986 (Ulrich, 1988), largely because of the growing role of plywood and other composite wood products in construction. During the postwar period, plywood production has increased by a factor of almost five (U.S. Department of Commerce, Bureau of the Census, 1975).

Not only has the composition of products changed, but so too has the composition of wood types and

*In general, the
effect of
technology on
forest products has
tended to move
toward both
reducing the
required wood
inputs and
increasing the use
of a greater range
of wood types,
wood residues,
and wood fibers.*

species as technological innovations have allowed wood types previously viewed as inferior to be substituted, in many uses, for higher-quality woods. For example, hardwoods, which have short wood fibers and previously had not been usable in many types of pulp and paper production, constituted about 38 percent of the feedstock for woodpulp by 1986—up dramatically from 14 percent in 1950—because of technological advances in pulp and papermaking (Ulrich, 1988). The result has been that, although the hardwood timber used for lumber showed no trend in the 1950–1986 period, hardwood pulpwood use increased by a factor of more than eight. By the mid-1970s, hardwood used as pulpwood exceeded that used in lumber production.

In general, the effect of technology on forest products has tended to move toward both reducing the required wood inputs and increasing the use of a greater range of wood types, wood residues, and wood fibers (Sedjo and Lyon, 1990). These two factors imply that the wood from a given forest is capable of producing a greater amount of forest products.

Wood Prices

The real price of most important wood resources has shown a great deal of volatility in the postwar period, especially during the 1970s. However, since 1950 the inflation-adjusted price of the most important wood resources has exhibited at most only a modest increase. The real price of lumber, for example, which had risen for about 150 years—averaging about 3 percent annually from 1805 to the early 1950s—increased less than 10 percent overall between 1950 and 1986. Similarly, southern pine sawlogs have exhibited little real price rise since 1950. Real prices for pulpwood have never exhibited the long-term upward trend experienced by some wood resources (Manthy, 1978; Sedjo and Lyon, 1990), although they have experienced cyclical variability. However, the price of Douglas fir logs has continued to exhibit substantial increases (Ulrich, 1988).

The price behavior of lumber and sawtimber before 1950 suggests that demand was continually outrunning supply, even during periods when total demand exhibited little growth. This behavior is consistent with conventional wisdom that views natural resources as becoming increasingly scarce as demand outstrips supply. However, for most natural resources, the long-term stability of real prices is the norm. As noted by Potter and Christy (1962), the long-term rise in lumber prices before the 1950s was the exception for natural resources and not the rule. The relative long-run stability of lumber price behavior for the 1950–1990 period suggests the possibility of a fundamental change in the long-term balance in the supply and demand for industrial wood in the United States (Manthy, 1978).

Sustainability, Management, and Forest Renewal

In regard to the forest resource, the post–World War II period can be characterized as one of management and forest renewability. Over this time, foresters have become attentive to the need for sustainability of the forest resource and have begun to seriously practice forest management.

Traditionally in the United States, wood resources have been obtained through a foraging-type process in which logging simply has been done on forests that are suitable in terms of location, access, wood quality, species, age, and so forth. The sites of natural forests are chosen by nature. Forests that have been accessible and well situated with respect to markets, or that have promised lucrative other land uses, have generally been harvested. Forests that have been inaccessible by virtue of location or terrain, or have otherwise been less readily exploitable, have been passed by. At low prices, logging may be a viable economic activity while tree planting is not. As the natural forests across the country have been harvested, more of the nation's forest resources have consisted of regenerated second-growth forest. In most cases, the current mature second-growth forest is simply the outgrowth of natural regeneration from cutover forestlands or abandoned agricultural lands. In the absence of conscious efforts to effect regeneration, the harvested forest is replaced by a new second-growth forest, the species composition of which is determined by the local conditions and the forest's ecology.

It is obvious, however, that the harvest cannot exceed growth indefinitely because eventually the forest inventory would run out. It is less obvious—but equally true—that forest growth cannot exceed harvest removals indefinitely. The volume of mature forest is limited by the biological potential of the site as determined by temperature, moisture, and soil conditions. Ultimately, growth cannot exceed the natural mortality of the forest, and the net growth of the stand will equal zero. A harvest can be viewed as allowing for the capture of useful timber before it is ultimately lost to mortality.

The forester's ideal has come to be viewed as a sustained-yield (or steady-state) forest in which harvest equals net growth. To provide equal annual harvests, the forest requires an even age distribution of the trees. In a forest where all sites are of equal productivity, each age class would be represented by an equal area. Each year the oldest age class would be harvested and the cutover area reforested, resulting in a sustainable output. Theoretically, a forest could approach that ideal by undergoing periods of forest stock buildup and periods of stock drawdown that would allow the age distribution of trees to adjust to the configuration required for sustained-yield harvests. Adjustment would also have to be made to reflect the productivities of different sites. In addition, the sustained yield or annual harvest of U.S. forests could be increased through improved forest management that would increase the rate of growth.

In one economic view of the forest, the forest has been seen as a timber-producing renewable resource, from which timber should be harvested as an intertemporal stream that maximizes the discounted present value of returns to the forestland. Given this objective, a sustained yield harvest is not necessarily the desired outcome. However, for many forests the result would be a long-term sustainable harvest at a somewhat younger harvesting age than the forester's ideal (Lyon and Sedjo, 1983).

A broader view of the economics of the forest has emerged that also includes considerations of other uses and outputs in addition to timber. In this view, water, wildlife, erosion control, recreational uses, and preservation of the ecological system all provide social values. Some of these values are transacted in markets, but others are referred to as nonmarket values. A forest can be managed to achieve a maximum discounted present social value that reflects both nonmarket and market values. In this view, the economist's objective is to maximize the net present value of the mix of all forest uses, both timber and nontimber (Bowes and Krutilla, 1985).

In many cases, these resource uses are not in conflict—for example, young plantation forests and mature old-growth forests both provide similar watershed protection and erosion control. However, at times conflicts do exist. Mature forests provide better habitat for some wildlife species and young forests provide better habitat for others. The societal question relates to providing a mix of forest outputs that optimizes the total value to society of all the forest uses.

Harvest cannot exceed growth indefinitely because eventually the forest inventory would run out. It is less obvious—but equally true—that forest growth cannot exceed harvest removals indefinitely.

*Copper Creek area in Montana, clearcut in 1960 and planted with spruce,
lodgepole pine, and Douglas fir in 1972 (foreground)*

Although industrial forests are typically established to produce industrial wood, environmental services associated with forests typically are generated in the process. Furthermore, government regulations are usually in place to ensure environmentally safe management practices. There is growing evidence that private owners—even large industrial operators—often explicitly manage for some nonwood uses such as wildlife (Lassiter, 1980).

Plantation Forestry

It was not until the postwar period that forest management involving tree planting became common practice. Management has been applied increasingly to the forest to promote growth of species and trees with desirable characteristics. In the late 1950s and early 1960s, tree planting in the United States increased dramatically. The level of tree planting by all owners has risen from approximately 500,000 acres in 1950 to about 3 million acres per year in 1987. In

the mid-1980s, approximately 2 million acres per year were planted in the South, 400,000 acres in the Pacific Northwest, and roughly 150,000 acres per year in the North, with the remainder in the Rocky Mountains and elsewhere (Haynes, 1988). The increase has been relatively steady and continuous with the exception of the huge upsurge in tree plantings as a result of the Soil Bank program of the late 1950s, which heavily subsidized tree planting.

Artificial regeneration—planting and direct seeding—requires an initial investment, but generally allows for prompt regeneration and control of the species (Haynes, 1988). In the most intensive form of forest management, the forest is managed in a manner akin to agricultural cropping, from the initial site preparation through planting, tending, and on to harvest. An important feature under the control of the investor is the location of the plantation. As with agriculture, soil, water, and climate conditions must be favorable to justify investment in planting the forest crop. Rugged terrain raises costs of planting, tending, and harvesting. Only desired species are planted. If seedlings are to be planted, it may be economic to introduce only superior genetic stock, which will allow for some control over growth rates, stem form, wood fiber characteristics, and so forth (Sedjo, 1983). Planting also offers the ability to control species composition and introduce seedlings of superior genetic quality, as well as to direct intensive management on a highly productive, well-situated site.

Plantation forestry can generate acceptable financial returns under some conditions. However, as with most investments, it is the specifics of the situation that determine whether the project will pay acceptable returns. In the United States, the prime region for plantation forestry on private land is the South, where in recent years more than 80 percent of the tree planting has occurred. Not only are biological conditions for forest growth favorable in the South, but the harvest rotation there is shorter than in most other regions of the United States, thereby generating generally better financial returns. In addition, the terrain is relatively flat, allowing for low-cost planting, tending, and harvesting, and the South has a well-developed infrastructure that contributes to lower-cost operations. Contributing to the favorable situation of plantation forestry in the South is the relatively low price of land there. In addition, the desired species are indigenous southern pines, primarily loblolly and slash pine, which are rapidly growing pioneer species that do well on both logged-over forest and on sites formerly in agriculture. Moreover, southern land, although usable for cropping, is generally of lower productivity than farmland in many other areas of the United States, and thus forestry is not forced to pay prohibitive prices to bid land away from what is often only marginal agricultural uses. Finally, the South has good access to markets, both domestic and foreign.

Plantation forestry is also practiced elsewhere in the United States, with the Pacific Northwest next to the South in importance and potential. Although conditions in the Pacific Northwest differ from those of the South—especially with respect to terrain and species type—rotation age, favorable growing conditions, accessible markets, and intensive wood use suggest acceptable rates of returns for private investors. In addition, state laws in this region generally require that forestland be regenerated.

Foresters have expressed concern about the future availability of the more valuable pine rather than the lower-valued hardwood (Boyce and Knight, 1979).

With the steady rise in artificial plantings, foresters have been influencing the forest's species composition. For example, in the South, the quintessential tree-planting region in the country, the preponderance of artificial planting has been in pine. By 1985, tree plantations covered 20.9 million acres, or 24 percent of the total area of pine and pine-hardwood types (U.S. Department of Agriculture, 1988b). Furthermore, the genetic quality of the pine seedlings has been vastly improved. Early planting came from randomly selected, often genetically inferior seed. However, genetic programs begun in the mid-1950s gradually supplied more and more seed from genetically improved seed orchards. Today the vast majority of pine plantings are of genetically superior seedlings, which should help increase pine availability.

The Private Sector's Role in Forest Renewal

The postwar period has seen the confluence of a number of factors that have dramatically improved the economics of tree planting and forest management. The increases in the real prices of timber, which occurred largely before 1950, improved the potential financial returns to tree planting and forest management. The efforts to control wildfire, which began in the 1920s, were by the 1950s resulting in a significant reduction in the areas affected by fire. In the late 1950s, fire was affecting only about one-tenth of the area affected twenty years earlier. In addition, some additional acreage was withdrawn from agriculture during the 1950s (see chapter 5). That land became available for forestry, often at low prices. Moreover, the postwar financial environment had been made more attractive for forestry by the 1943 revised Internal Revenue Code that allowed capital gains treatment to be extended to income from timber harvests (U.S. Department of Agriculture, 1988b). By the end of the 1950s the Soil Bank program, which created incentives to withdraw land from agriculture and put it into uses such as forestry, had been created. Finally, the development of genetically improved seedlings and other technological advances has offered plantation forestry the potential to obtain large increases in productivity from intensive management.

There is no question that the economics of private sector tree planting has progressively improved during the postwar period. In the early 1950s, total private sector plantings—those of the forest industry and the nonindustrial private forests—were about 400,000 acres annually. It was only after the mid-1950s, when wildfire risks had been substantially reduced, that private planting of timber began to occur on a large scale. By 1960, total private plantings had risen to about 2 million acres annually. However, this level reflected the subsidies of the Soil Bank program, and declined with its termination. After falling to more modest levels in the mid-1960s, private sector planting has continued to expand, reflecting improved fire control, low-cost availability of highly productive forest lands, and genetically improved seedlings. By the mid-1980s, the forest industry and the nonindustrial private forests were averaging close to 2.5 million acres of planting annually.

Although the forest industry often has led in establishing plantation forests and in developing technologies that are likely to increase productivity—for example, genetically improved seedlings—plantings by the nonindustrial private forests have been substantial. Yet some observers have expressed concern about the willingness of the nonindustrial private forests, which control 58 percent of U.S. forestland, to invest in tree planting (Sedjo and Ostermeier, 1978; Brooks, 1985; U.S. Department of Agriculture, 1988b). Nevertheless, in 1987 for the first time since the Soil Bank years, artificial regeneration on nonindustrial private land equaled or exceeded regeneration on forest industry lands (Haynes, 1988)—both regenerated about 1.4 million acres. This surge in nonindustrial plantings certainly resulted in part from the newly instituted Conservation Reserve Program (CRP), which provides incentives for forestry and other nonagricultural uses of erodable lands. In 1987, nonindustrial forest owners achieved a level of planting that was nearly three times the level of the mid-1970s.

The continued high level of planting has been somewhat surprising, as the Federal Tax Reform Act of 1986 eliminated a special capital gains treatment. However, the change did not affect a number of tax provisions that forest growers desired, such as the amortization and tax credit for reforestation and the expensing of annual management costs (U.S. Department of Agriculture, 1988b). Also, studies suggest that recent investments in forest plantations in the South and in the Pacific Northwest have generated favorable economic returns (Sedjo, 1983). Public programs have contributed directly to the regeneration of the forests, and have provided an environment that is conducive to private investments in reforestation and forest management. Other events, too, may have contributed to the increasing interest by the private sector in forestry investments. For example, the Forest Industries Council (1980) undertook a widely publicized study that reported that significant financial returns were readily available on a variety of forestry investments, particularly in the South and Pacific Northwest. Such a study might have helped to alert the private sector to the opportunities available.

Today, the forest industry, which has often been criticized for having little interest in maintaining forestlands after harvesting old growth, is actively involved in what can best be described as tree farming on a large scale. Although at one time it could accurately be stated that "forestry does not pay," today profit-seeking firms are planting, growing, and harvesting forests on an unprecedented scale. In many respects, forestry in the United States is experiencing a transition similar to that made 2,000 years earlier by agriculture, from a foraging activity that relied on the resources provided by nature to a cropping activity that requires planting, tending, and harvesting. The rising real price of timber, together with technical changes that allow for increased uses of fast-grown wood, has made plantation forestry economically attractive. As investments are now being made in planting, it makes economic sense for investors and managers to try to control an array of variables formerly left to nature. The United States experience parallels the experience in much of northern and western Europe, where planting and intensive management have come to be commonly practiced over the past 100 years as wood has become increasingly scarce.

Today profit-seeking firms are planting, growing, and harvesting forests on an unprecedented scale.

The Federal Role in Forest Renewal

In the postwar period, the public sector, led by the Forest Service, has continued its active role in promoting the renewal of the American forest. Perhaps the most important single activity has been the control of wildfires. It was not until the early 1950s that fires were reduced to below 10 million acres annually. According to *Forest Fires Statistics*, by the late 1950s the area disturbed by forest fires was further reduced to an average of about 5 million acres per year (see appendix 3, figure 3-A3). By the 1970s, the area disturbed by wildfire had fallen to an average of less than 3 million acres annually, less than one-tenth of the average acreage affected during the 1930s. Also, the average size of the area affected by each fire had declined dramatically, indicating an improved capacity to detect fires and limit their spread. In 1988, a year characterized as having a serious forest fire problem (such as the Yellowstone fire), the total area burned was about 6 million acres. Although this is significantly above the average of the 1980s, it is far below the levels that prevailed before the late 1950s (appendix 3, figure 3-A2).

In addition to fire control programs, the public sector has undertaken a variety of public programs to promote reforestation and better forest management. From 1950 into the mid-1980s, the public sector increased its tree planting from 100,000 to more than 400,000 acres annually. The Soil Bank program of the late 1950s helped to establish several million acres of planted forest on land previously in agriculture. Other public programs designed to promote tree planting and forest management, particularly among the nonindustrial private forest ownerships, have included state forest practices acts, currently in effect in eighteen states; forestry assistance programs designed to share costs and provide technical assistance (beginning with the Clark-McNary Act of 1924 and including the Federal Forestry Incentives Program of 1973 and a growing number of subsequent state forestry incentives programs); and various tax benefits—federal, state, and local—that have provided incentives for investments in timberland and tree growing. Also, the Conservation Reserve Program, which began in 1986, has provided incentives for landowners to convert highly erodible agricultural land into forest. Through 1989, more than 2 million acres of CRP land had been contracted for conversion to tree plantation, most of it in the South.

In recent years the Forest Service and other public forest management agencies have been subject to considerable criticism for their management of the public forests.

The effect of public programs on the American forest has often been difficult to assess. In recent years the Forest Service and other public forest management agencies have been subject to considerable criticism for their management of the public forests. Environmentalists have criticized the Forest Service for focusing on timber outputs and values at the expense of nontimber outputs and values (O'Toole, 1988; The Wilderness Society, 1989). Economists have charged that Forest Service operations are sometimes inefficient, with forest management expenditures often not being related to returns (Deacon and Johnson, 1985). Nevertheless, Teeguarden (1985), assessing the theoretical effects of a number of government programs and policies related to the direct management of public timberlands and those designed to encourage investments in forestry, found evidence of the benefits of fire suppression programs and other programs in reducing timber damage, in providing physical and financial environments conducive to forest growth and tree planting, and in providing more direct incentives to forest management through technical assistance and cost sharing. He also found that incentives were provided through measures such as tax advantages. On the other hand, in what has been perhaps the only attempt to systematically evaluate the effects of government policy on a major economic sector of the economy, Boyd and Hyde (1989), in evaluating the impacts of public regulation on the forestry sector, found little direct evidence that government programs generally improve the overall performance of the forestry sector, although some individual programs did show evidence of important social benefits.

Conflicting Demands and Legislation

Americans during the postwar period have placed an increasing array of demands for outputs on the forests—particularly the national forests—reflecting the diverse preferences of the American society. Inevitably, the competing demands have led to conflict over the uses and the management of the public land and, to a lesser extent, private forestland. However, the nature of these conflicts was not wholly evident in the early postwar period. During that time, the energies of the populace were largely engaged in the postwar economic boom that entailed, at least in part, the renovation and reconstruction of the United States after almost two decades of neglect as a result of the depression and the war. Clawson, Held, and Stoddard (1960) characterized the early postwar period as one of "intensive management" of the public forest, and one when harvests from public forests increased significantly. The conflicts, however, have become more sharply focused as the postwar period has continued into the present. To a large extent, they reflect a modern version of the disputes between conservationists and preservationists a century earlier. Although Pinchot and the conservationists' utilitarian view, with its focus on the wise use of the timber resource, had become the dominant view, the preservationist philosophy of John Muir and his contemporaries has reemerged in the postwar period.

As the conflicts among the various demands on the public forest have become more obvious and more contentious, Congress has enacted legislation to alleviate the problems. The Multiple-Use, Sustained-Yield Act of 1960 codified a multiple-use mandate for the Forest Service in its management of the national forests, giving the various nontimber uses statutory comparability with timber and water. The Wilderness Act of 1964, which promoted wilderness planning, was followed by the National Environmental Policy Act of 1969, which mandated the protection of the environment and either encouraged or required the Forest Service to apply environmental criteria to many of its activities. The Resources Planning Act of 1974 required the Forest Service to prepare an assessment of the nation's public and private resources every ten years, and proposed a program for setting long-term

resource goals every five years. The National Forest Management Act of 1976 (NFMA), an amendment to the Resources Planning Act of 1974, established comprehensive planning for the national forests within the confines of well-defined standards and a greater role for public participation. The NFMA also stated that forest plans should "provide for diversity of plant and animal communities" (Wilcove, 1988), thereby reinforcing the Endangered Species Preservation Act of 1966 that had focused on habitat protection, and that was followed by additional endangered species legislation in 1973 and 1978 (see chapter 6).

The general thrust of the legislation has been to encourage and require that public land be managed for a variety of values in addition to timber; that greater areas of public land, particularly forests, be set aside for recreation, wilderness, and habitat; that the management and use of the public forest be subject to more comprehensive intensive planning (Leisz, 1983) to ensure the efficient provision of a variety of outputs (Haigh and Krutilla, 1980); and that the public be more involved in the planning process. Much of the contention surrounding these issues has related to the values of the nonmarketed forest outputs and questions of tradeoffs between the various outputs, including wildlife, wilderness, recreation, and endangered species, as well as the priorities each of the various uses should receive in public forest manage-

The area of forest in New England in 1980 had returned to levels that were substantially higher than those of the mid-1800s. The same story has been repeated in other places in the East, the South, and the Lake States.

ment (on evaluation procedures, see Peterson and Randall, 1984).

Although it is difficult to identify any particular legislation as the cause, timber harvests from public land leveled off after having increased rapidly into the mid-1960s. Timber sales from the national forest system remained in the 11 billion to 12 billion board-feet range in the 1980s. In addition, by the end of the 1980s, 32.5 million acres in thirty-six states became part of the permanent National Wilderness Preservation system. Much of the land in this system has been designated as wilderness in recent years, with 7.4 million acres of national forest land receiving wilderness designation and protection between 1981 and 1988 (U.S. Department of Agriculture, 1989).

The Current Condition of the American Forest

In 1987 forests occupied about 728 million acres, or roughly 32 percent of the land area of the United States. The area in forest remained essentially stable through the 1980s. Of this, some 483.1 million acres were in timberland or what was until recently referred to as commercial forest (U.S. Department of Agriculture, 1988a). Timberlands are the forests from which almost all of the industrial wood and most of the fuelwood are drawn. Although the area classified as timberland declined by 8 million acres from an earlier inventory in 1977, the decline is accounted for by the withdrawal of forests from timberland into reserve status (for instance, for wilderness). In Alaska, for example, 4 million acres were withdrawn, and a substantial area was withdrawn in the Pacific Northwest (U.S. Department of Agriculture, 1988a). Total areas dedicated to wilderness increased from 25.1 million acres at the end of 1980 to 32.5 million acres in 1988 (U.S. Department of Agriculture, 1989), although not all of the area dedicated as wilderness was formerly classified as timberland. In addition, much of the remaining decline in the area classified as timberland is explained by reclassification.

U.S. timberland was about 72 percent privately owned and 28 percent publicly owned in 1987. The forest industry owned approximately 14 percent of

the total; other private interests, 57 percent; the national forests, 18 percent; and other public interests, about 11 percent. In 1986, timber harvests (removal of growing stock) totaled 17.0 billion cubic feet, compared with 14.2 billion cubic feet in 1976, and 10.8 billion cubic feet in 1952. For recent periods, growth has exceeded removals. This favorable relationship exists for both softwood and hardwood. Fuelwood, the use of which has declined for decades, showed a sharp increase in usage following the energy crisis of the mid-1970s and through 1986, the latest year for which data are available.

Although providing society with an increasing volume of industrial wood, and despite the withdrawals and reclassifications that have reduced the area defined as timberland, the total volume of growing stock inventory on American timberland continued to rise uninterrupted through the five inventories taken from 1952 to that reported in 1988. Some restructuring of the forest occurred during this period, however. The percentage of hardwood forest inventories grew more rapidly than that of softwood inventories, in part because of withdrawals and reclassifications; however, these inventories reflect the greater relative demand on the softwood resource compared with the demand for the hardwood resource. In addition, timber inventories grew much more rapidly in the relatively young forests of the South, the Northeast, and the north central region than in the old-growth forests of the West.

In certain regions the long-term changes have been dramatic. For example, the area of forest in New England in 1980 had returned to levels that were substantially higher than those of the mid-1800s (see table 3-1) (Barrett, 1980). The same story has been repeated in other places in the East, the South, and the Lake States. Furthermore, changing technology has allowed for greater use of a wide range of types of wood for industrial purposes.

Table 3-1. New England's Growing Forest (percentage of area forested)

State	Mid-1800s	1980
Maine	74	90
New Hampshire	50	86
Vermont	35	76
Connecticut, Massachusetts, and Rhode Island	35	59

Source: Adapted from Barrett (1980), pp. 25, 37.

An important measure of the nation's forest resource is its volume of forest, sometimes called growing stock. As noted earlier, probably during the late 1930s or 1940s the net growth of the nation's timberland exceeded the level of timber removals, resulting in an increase in the growing stock or volume of the nation's forest. Beginning in 1952, systematic nationwide estimates were made periodically of the nation's forest inventory, forest growth, forest mortality, and so forth. The net growth and forest growing stock increased with each of the four subsequent inventories. Although harvests were high during this period, reflecting the general level of prosperity and economic activity, net growth of the forest persistently exceeded harvest. Thus the total volume of timber in the nation's forest estate has increased throughout the postwar period, so that by 1987 the

total inventory of growing stock on the nation's timberland was 27 percent larger than it had been in 1952.

The higher timber inventory volumes reflected both an increase in the average volumes per unit of timberland and the initial increase in the area of timberland. Throughout the early postwar period and into the 1960s, the land area in timberland increased as cropland from regions in the East continued to be abandoned and revert to forests. After the mid-1960s, the area in timberland began to decline modestly, in part as a result of the once-again expanding demands for agricultural land that occurred in the 1970s, but also because public authorities have taken some existing public timberland together with land purchased from private owners and have designated these lands as parks, preserves, and wilderness areas to protect them from commercial exploitation. However, this modest decline in land area has been more than offset by continued and increasing forest growth on timberland. Thus, despite numerous studies warning of impending limits and downturns in the growing stock volume (Clawson, 1979), the nation has experienced a continuing buildup of its timber volumes throughout the entire postwar period.

As the stocks of the nation's forest resources have increased, the pressures of real rising prices have abated. After 1950 came a substantial reduction of the long-term growth in the real prices of the timber resource as supply and demand apparently moved into a more balanced relationship (Sedjo and Lyon, 1990). In addition, in the postwar climate many of the earlier pressures to nationalize private forestland have abated. In fact, the early 1980s even saw a movement toward privatization of federal land, a movement that appears largely to have dissipated. Currently, although the ownership of private forestland appears secure, management of private forestland increasingly has come under public regulation. Often, extensive state regulations have been the instrument by which the public regulates such land (Vaux, 1983), and the courts frequently have intervened in the management of private timberland to impose social goals (Johnson, 1983). Recently, much of the conflict over how forestland in general and public forestlands specifically ought to be managed has focused on threatened and endangered species and on the conflicts regarding the preservation of certain valued or unique ecosystems.

Currently, American forests are a mix of old-growth stands, naturally regenerated forest, and planted forest. In the West, large areas of old growth remain in the Pacific Northwest, parts of California, and much of the Rockies. East of the Mississippi River, much of the forest is second-growth, naturally regenerated stands. In some cases the land never was converted to agricultural use but selective logging was common. The species found in these stands are usually similar to those that would have existed there at settlement. Forest plantations, although increasingly common, still account for only between 30 million and 40 million acres of the U.S. forestland (Postel and Heise, 1988), or less than 10 percent of the total timberland area in the nation. Even in most forest plantations in the United States the species composition mimics the forest that would have naturally regenerated there. For example, planted loblolly pine in the South typically substitutes for the naturally regenerated pine forest that nature would have provided. In the Pacific Northwest, young planted Douglas fir forests replace older, often homogeneous stands that nature had established, albeit the planted stands typically skip an intervening stage when red alder would have dominated.

The United States is the world's leading producer of industrial wood, far outdistancing the Soviet Union and Canada in production. Forests in the United States are now providing the largest harvests in history. Despite these high levels of harvest and consumption, the forest stock and forest inventories are continuing to expand. Although a significant portion of U.S. lumber consumption is provided by Canada, the United States has nevertheless become the dominant external supplier of conifer logs to much of East Asia.

Well-managed, planted forests typically grow timber more rapidly than a naturally generated forest. This factor has provided a major justification for investments in plantation forests. Furthermore, the outputs of American forests are being used more efficiently. Technology is allowing a given resource to provide more service through wood-saving and wood-extending innovation. These considerations have encouraged growing optimism among many analysts about the long-term availability of timber from U.S. forests; concerns are rarely expressed today about a timber famine. Concerns today do involve the penetration of foreign markets by competitors, the need to fend off foreign competition in domestic markets, and near-term regional imbalances between supply and demand.

The mix of old, secondary, and recently established young stands also provides an array of amenity and

Forests in the United States are now providing the largest harvests in history. Despite these high levels of harvest and consumption, the forest stock and forest inventories are continuing to expand.

environmental services, including watershed protection, erosion control, wildlife habitat, and other values. These are some of the same environmental services that the forests provided at the time of early settlement. In the last half-century, however, the provision of these services has improved markedly. Many of the renewed forests are now managed for wildlife, recreation, and other values, as well as for timber. Management for these amenities and services is mandated for public forestland by the Multiple-Use, Sustained-Yield Act of 1960, and often is practiced on private forestland as well. It has been well established that many nonindustrial private forest owners place higher emphasis on nontimber values, such as wildlife and recreation, than on timber values (Sedjo and Ostermeier, 1978). In recent years, many large private timber companies have also managed their forests for outputs—particularly wildlife—other than timber (Lassiter, 1980). The revitalization of the eastern forest habitat, in concert with actions of forest owners both public and private, has contributed to the renewability of many wildlife populations (see chapter 6).

Perhaps the most difficult question concerning the management of U.S. forests today relates to emerging concerns about the maintenance of ecological values, such as biodiversity. This issue is embodied in the spotted owl and the old-growth controversy. Forests in temperate climates generally differ from tropical forests in that the former tend to have lower levels of biological diversity and this diversity tends to be less endemic. These characteristics suggest that a smaller area of temperate forest may be required to preserve the essence of the temperate forest and its unique biodiversity than would be the case with a tropical forest. Nevertheless, the issue is not "to save or not to save" an individual species or indeed an ecosystem; rather, the issue is the more subtle one of "how much should be saved," and hence "how much should not be saved." Although science can provide some measure of the parameters involved in preserving a species, many of the issues relate to values and are not scientific questions.

In the United States, the forest estate consists of a wide array of forest types and ages. In this regard it is not too different from the mosaic of forest types present during the time of early settlement. The creation of many national parks and wilderness areas, now totaling more than 90 million acres, has resulted in an increase in the portion of older, relatively undisturbed forest protected in perpetuity. These preserves have been created, in part, to address the concern for maintaining natural habitat and biodiversity. The current outstanding issues are whether the size and range of wilderness and other protected areas are adequate to preserve ecological values, and the extent to which forests might be managed for both ecological values and other outputs, including timber (Franklin, 1989).

Interpreting the Historical Experience of the Forests

The current favorable condition of U.S. forests is remarkable in light of the historical experience of those forests. In colonial times and in the early period of the republic, the surfeit of forests was such that human-induced changes had little effect on the total forest and environmental system. Gradually, the impacts on the resource and the environment became significant, especially after 1850. The rising real price of wood, together with technical change, moved toward lengthening the life of wood products and the development of nonwood substitutes for a wide array of uses. The advent of the age of fossil fuels would

substantially reduce the pressure on the U.S. forest resource as a source of wood energy. Furthermore, increases in agricultural productivity would reduce the pressure to add new land to the agricultural base and thereby reduce the rate of conversion of forestland to agricultural land. The availability of agricultural land in the Midwest, much of which was never forested, made continued agricultural production uneconomic on marginal land in the East and the South, thus allowing the reversion of large areas of land to forest use.

Between 1920 and the mid-1980s, the U.S. population more than doubled. In addition, the gross national product increased by a factor of six, while per capita output increased by a factor of three. The conventional wisdom would suggest that increasing population and production would increase the pressures on the natural resource base, including the forests. True, total roundwood consumption in 1987 was 50 percent above its 1920 level. However, by the mid-1980s per capita consumption had fallen to about three-fourths of its 1920 level. Clearly, even as the population was growing and becoming wealthier, per capita wood consumption was continuing its decline, no doubt as a result of wood-saving innovations induced partly by higher market prices. Perhaps more important, despite the postwar increase in total wood consumption, U.S. forests continued to grow at a pace that substantially exceeded harvests.

In the context of an improving forest resource, how should the historical experience of the U.S. forest be interpreted? The period from the mid-1800s to 1920 in the United States was one of wanton and unjustified destruction of forest resources, according to some critics. Without defending the excesses of the time, that period also could be viewed as one when hitherto relatively unproductive forest assets were converted to more productive capital assets in the form of harvested timber and, in some cases, agricultural uses that produced higher returns. The previously unproductive forest assets generated commodity outputs in the form of construction materials, fences, pit-props for mines, railroad ties, and fuel for home and industry, among others. From the newly converted agricultural land came an increasing flow of agricultural products. Undoubtedly, the use of forest timber for buildings and transportation networks and the conversion from forestland to agricultural land contributed significantly to much of the nation's early development.

The conversion of forests to capital assets and land to agricultural and other beneficial uses, however, was not without cost. The costs were borne in the form of many denuded hillsides, widespread soil erosion and loss of soil fertility, silted rivers, exacerbated downstream flooding, and destruction of wildlife habitat. Were these costs worth the gains to a newly formed nation trying to establish a viable society out of what was then referred to as the wilderness? It may never be possible to find a definitive answer to that question. Libecap and Johnson (1975) have argued that the rate of timber harvesting in the Lake States forest during the latter part of the nineteenth century was not excessive from an economic perspective. They argue that given the wide availability of the timber resource elsewhere in the United States and the value of that resource to the development of the American economy, the highest social use of the forest was to convert it into socially and economically valuable and useful products, and that exploitation of the forest resource could be viewed as a rational way for the colonial and early U.S. societies to cope and survive in the hostile environment in which they found themselves.

Whether the rapid forest conversion was justified, the United States today is fortunate that the forests are a renewable resource that is responsive both to natural forces and to human forest management. In light of the decades of use and reported abuse to which the U.S. forest has been subjected, to what can one attribute the healthy forest estate? The answer appears to lie in a confluence of benevolent factors, including the substantial reduction in pressures on the forest from both logging and land-use conversion activities that began after 1920; the resiliency of the forest resource itself, which allows it to regenerate naturally in many places; reduced relative pressures on the forest resource in the postwar period as a result of technological innovation that made wood use more efficient; and the widespread substitution of fossil fuels for wood energy. Furthermore, the government's active role in protecting and maintaining the forests—ranging from controlling wildfire to direct forest protection and technical assistance—as well as tax and incentive programs to promote tree planting have undoubtedly played a critical role. The single most effective public policy in the renewal of the U.S. forest probably has been the control of wildfire. This action not only allowed the existing forest to grow toward maturity, but also reduced the risks to the private sector of investments in planting and management. In the postwar environment of higher real prices for delivered wood and lower risks to young forest stands, the private sector has taken the lead in generating the improvement of the nation's forests by way of management and widespread tree planting.

The American people have had the opportunity to reap the bountiful benefits associated with using their forests, sometimes exploitively, and still find themselves with one of the most productive forest estates in the world. This fortuitous situation appears to be less the result of collective foresight than it is the result of the amazing resilience with which nature has endowed the nation's renewable forests.

The Future of the U.S. Forest Estate

By most criteria, U.S. forests are in excellent condition. Although the forests will never return to their precolonial condition, there can be little doubt that the forests at the end of the 1980s were in much better condition than they were in 1920. Both the area of forestland and the total volume of forest inventories are larger now than they were in 1920.

Were these costs worth the gains to a newly formed nation trying to establish a viable society out of what was then referred to as the wilderness? It may never be possible to find a definitive answer.

Other measures of the forest condition, such as wildlife populations, generally present an improving picture.

The trend over the postwar period has been favorable. The forests have had time to recover from their low point in the 1920s, with net growth increasing and growth continually exceeding harvests. Although growth certainly cannot exceed harvests indefinitely, U.S. forests have shown the potential to deliver large volumes of wood on a sustainable level into the indefinite future (Sedjo and Lyon, 1990).

The Forest Service is responsible for large areas and volumes of the U.S. forest estate. Although observers may disagree about how best to manage these forests, most would agree that a significant deterioration of the national forest system is unlikely. In addition, it is clear that timber owners, both industrial and nonindustrial, have now actively embarked on a path of creating and managing existing and new forests. Private tree planting is at levels that would have been viewed as fanciful only two decades ago. Private investors increasingly believe that tree growing is an investment that can generate attractive financial returns under contemporary conditions. Furthermore, society continues to reforest logged areas and to move toward a genetically superior, more rapidly growing forest stock. It is difficult to envision physical conditions that would radically alter current trends, and therefore it is difficult to envision serious timber supply problems, or a significant deterioration in the condition of U.S. forest that would result in inadequate timber supplies or in inadequate provision of nontimber outputs.

If there is to be a future problem with the availability of domestic timber or other, nontimber outputs, it will almost surely be the outcome of political, rather than biological, forces. Society does have to address difficult issues, such as the appropriate mix of productive forests, wilderness areas, biodiversity, and amenity outputs. Environmental concerns have led to increased areas of forest being withdrawn from the timber base, largely from the federal forest estate. In addition, public policies can affect the willingness of private timberland owners to plant and harvest timber. Other concerns, such as endangered species requirements, could result in additional and possibly quite large withdrawals from the timber base. On a large scale, such actions could significantly reduce the domestic timber base and hence the supply potential. However, the aggregate effect of such actions on U.S. domestic consumption of forest products is problematic. The worldwide industrial wood market has become truly integrated. A reduction in domestic production is likely to be offset by both decreased exports and increased imports. Additional supplies could be forthcoming initially from Canada, and from a variety of other sources. Although some analysts (Darr, 1988) have suggested that the ability to increase Canadian harvests is limited, others (Williams, 1986) have suggested that the potential supply from Canada is indeed massive and would require only strong economic incentives to be released.

Another concern relates to the future effects of a possible global warming on the U.S. forest estate. Although the long-term effects of warming on the nation's forests are unclear, some analyses indicate that they are likely to reduce modestly the area and volume of forest both worldwide and in the United States (Sedjo and Solomon, 1989). Another unknown is the nature of the transition of the forest from its present configuration to one consistent with the climate conditions associated with a warming. Such a transition could provide abundant timber supplies in the short run in the form of salvage logging. In the longer term, however, timber supplies could be affected adversely if productivity were affected negatively.

In the absence of a global catastrophe, the physical potential of the United States to produce the vast majority of society's wood needs appears certain. The economic potential also exists. Timber can be harvested from existing forests and delivered to mills at economically acceptable costs. If timber supply problems arise in the United States, they would almost surely result from decisions to withdraw massive amounts of public timberland from the timber base, or from federal or state policies that discourage the private sector from continuing to make large investments in timber growing.

Notes

This draft has benefited from the suggestions and comments of Perry Hagenstein, John Fedkiw, Robert Nelson, John McMahon, R. N. Pierson, Lester Holley, Pierre Crosson, Ken Frederick, Marion Clawson, Robert Wolf, John Zivnuska, and a number of anonymous reviewers at the U.S. Department of Agriculture. In addition to his detailed comments, Fedkiw's own work was a valuable source of some of the historical information used in this chapter.

Appendix 3

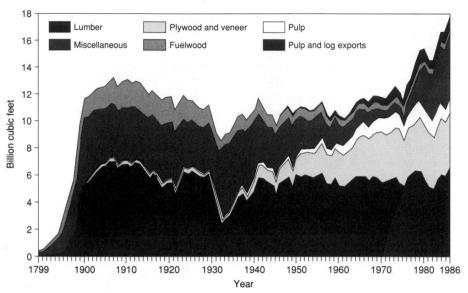

3-A1. Domestic production of timber in roundwood equivalent, 1799 to 1986
Sources: U.S. Department of Commerce, Bureau of the Census (1975); Steer (1948).

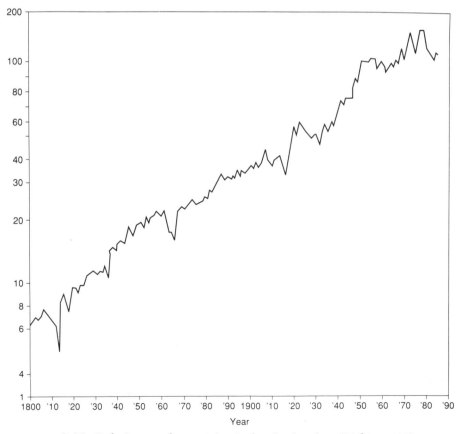

3-A2. Relative producer price index for lumber (1967 = 100)
Source: Ulrich (1988).
Note: Relative index derived by dividing the actual price index by the all commodities price index.

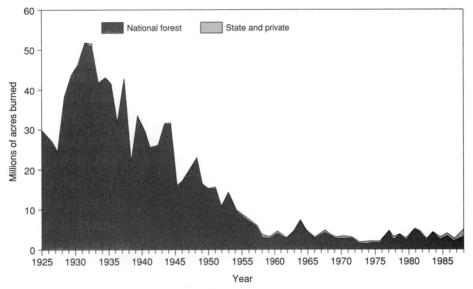

3-A3. Forest fires in the United States, 1924–1987

Sources: U.S. Department of Agriculture, Forest Service (1926–1967; 1968–1989).

References

Abbott, Carl. 1981. "Plank Roads and Wood-Block Pavements." *Journal of Forest History* 25, no. 4 (October): 216–218.

Anderson, Terry L., and P. J. Hill. 1975. "The Evolution of Property Rights." *Journal of Law and Economics* 18 (April):163–179.

Barrett, John W. 1980. "The Northeast Region." In *Regional Silviculture of the United States*, edited by John W. Barrett, 25–66. New York: John Wiley and Sons.

Bones, James T. 1988. "An Analysis of the Land Base Situation in the United States: 1989–2040. A Technical Document Supporting the 1989 USDA Forest Service RPA Assessment." U.S. Department of Agriculture. Typescript.

Bowes, Michael D., and John V. Krutilla. 1985. "Multiple-Use Management of Public Forest Lands." In *Handbook of Natural Resource and Energy Economics*, vol. 2, edited by Allen V. Kneese and James L. Sweeney, 531–569. Amsterdam, The Netherlands: Elsevier Science Publishers.

Boyce, Steve G., and H. A. Knight. 1979. "Prospective Ingrowth of Southern Hardwoods Beyond 1980." Research Paper SE-203, U.S. Department of Agriculture, Forest Service, Southeast Forest Experiment Station, Asheville, N.C.

Boyd, Roy G., and William F. Hyde. 1989. *Forest Sector Intervention*. Ames, Iowa: Iowa State University Press.

Brooks, David J. 1985. "Public Policy and Long-Term Timber Supply in the South." *Forest Science* 31(2):342–357.

Brown, Nelson C. 1919. *Forest Products—Their Manufacture and Use*. New York: John Wiley and Sons.

Clark, Thomas D. 1985. *The Greening of the South*. Lexington, Ky.: University Press of Kentucky.

Clawson, Marion. 1979. "Forests in the Long Sweep of American History." *Science* 204, no. 15 (July):1168–1174.

—————. 1981. "Competitive Land Use in American Forestry and Agriculture." *Journal of Forest History* 25, no. 4 (October):222–227.

—————. 1983. *New Deal Planning*. Washington, D.C.: The Johns Hopkins University Press for Resources for the Future.

—————. 1984. "Major Alternatives for Future Management of Federal Lands." In *Rethinking the Federal Lands*, edited by Sterling Brubaker, 195–234. Washington, D.C.: Resources for the Future.

Clawson, Marion, R. B. Held, and C. H. Stoddard. 1960. *Land for the Future*. Baltimore, Md.: The Johns Hopkins University Press for Resources for the Future.

Council on Environmental Quality. 1985. *Environmental Quality: 16th Annual Report of the Council on Environmental Quality*. Washington, D.C.: Council on Environmental Quality.

Cox, Thomas R. 1983. "Trade, Development, and Environmental Change: The Utilization of North America's Pacific Coast Forest to 1914 and Its Consequences." In *Global Deforestation and the Nineteenth-Century World Economy*, edited by Richard P. Tucker and J. F. Richards, 14–29. Durham, N.C.: Duke University Press.

Culhane, Paul J. 1981. *Public Lands Politics*. Baltimore, Md.: The Johns Hopkins University Press for Resources for the Future.

Darr, David R. 1988. "The 1989 RPA Assessment of the Forest and Range Land Situation in the United States." U.S. Department of Agriculture, Forest Service. Typescript.

Davis, Richard, ed. 1983. *Encyclopedia of American Forest and Conservation History*. New York: Macmillan.

Deacon, Robert T., and M. Bruce Johnson. 1985. *Forestlands: Public and Private*. Cambridge, Mass.: Ballinger Publishing Co.

duBois, Coert. 1914. "Systematic Fire Protection in the California Forests." Washington, D.C.: U.S. Forest Service.

Fedkiw, John. 1989. *The Evolving Use and Management of the Nation's Forests, Grasslands, Croplands, and Related Resources. A Technical Document Supporting the 1989 USDA Forest Service RPA Assessment*. Fort Collins, Colo.: U.S. Department of Agriculture, Forest Service, Rocky Mountain Forest and Range Experiment Station.

Forest Industries Council. 1980. "Forest Productivity Report." Washington, D.C.: National Forest Products Association.

Franklin, Jerry. 1989. "Toward a New Forestry." *American Forests* 95 (November/December):1–8.

Frey, H. Thomas, and Roger W. Hexem. 1985. "Major Uses of Land in the United States: 1982." AER 535, U.S. Department of Agriculture, Economic Research Service. Washington, D.C.

Gates, Paul W. 1968. *History of Public Land Law Development*. Washington, D.C.: GPO.

Hagenstein, Perry R. 1988. "Forests in the Long Haul." Paper presented to the American Forestry Association conference on Natural Resources for the 21st Century, Washington, D.C., November 14–17.

Haigh, John A., and John V. Krutilla. 1980. "Clarifying Policy Directives: The Case of National Forest Management." *Policy Analysis* 6, no. 4:409–439.

Hansen, Henry L. 1980. "The Lake States Region." In *Regional Silviculture of the United States*, edited by John W. Barrett, 67–106. New York: John Wiley and Sons.

Hardin, Garrett. 1968. "The Tragedy of the Commons." *Science* 162:1243–1248.

Hart, J. Fraser. 1968. "Loss and Abandonment of Cleared

Farm Land in the Eastern United States." In *Annuals*, 58. Washington, D.C.: Association of American Geographers.

Hawke, David F. 1988. *Everyday Life in Early America.* New York: Harper & Row.

Haygreen, John, Hans Gregersen, Irv Holland, and Robert Stone. 1986. "The Economic Impact of Timber Utilization Research." *Forest Products Journal* 36, no. 1:1–18.

Haynes, Richard W. 1988. "An Analysis of the Timber Situation in the United States: 1989–2040." Part I and part II: "The Future Resource Situation." U.S. Department of Agriculture, Forest Service. Typescript.

Hays, Samuel P. 1959. *Conservation and the Gospel of Efficiency: The Progressive Conservation Movement, 1890–1920.* Cambridge, Mass.: Harvard University Press.

Healy, Robert G. 1985. *Competition for Land in the American South.* Washington, D.C.: The Conservation Foundation.

Johnson, M. Bruce. 1983. "Regulations of Private Forest Lands: The Taking Issue." In *Governmental Interventions, Social Needs, and the Management of U.S. Forests*, edited by Roger A. Sedjo, 276–295. Washington, D.C.: Resources for the Future.

Lane, Leighton, E. 1959. "Origin and Development of the Small Woodlot in the Northeast." Master's thesis, State University College of Forestry at Syracuse University.

Lassiter, Roy L., Jr. 1980. *Access to and Management of the Wildlife Resources on Large Private Timberland Holdings in the Southeastern United States.* College of Business Administration Monograph Series, no. 1. Cookeville, Tenn.: Tennessee Technological University.

Leisz, Douglas R. 1983. "Impact of the RPA/NFMA Planning Process on the Management and Planning in the Forest Service." In *Governmental Interventions, Social Needs, and the Management of U.S. Forests*, edited by Roger A. Sedjo, 245–258. Washington, D.C.: Resources for the Future.

Libecap, Gary A., and Ronald N. Johnson. 1975. "Property Rights, Nineteenth Century Federal Timber Policy and the Conservation Movement." *Journal of Economic History* 39, no. 1:129–142.

Lyon, Kenneth S., and Roger A. Sedjo. 1983. "Application of Optimal Control Theory to Estimate Long-Term Supply of Timber." *Forest Science* 29, no. 4:798–812.

Manthy, Robert S. 1978. *Natural Resource Commodities—A Century of Statistics.* Baltimore, Md.: The Johns Hopkins University Press for Resources for the Future.

Nelson, Robert H. 1982. "The Public Lands." In *Current Issues in Natural Resource Policy*, edited by Paul R. Portney, 14–72. Washington, D.C.: Resources for the Future.

———. 1985. "Mythology Instead of Analysis: The Story of Public Forest Management." In *Forestlands: Public and Private*, edited by Robert T. Deacon and M. Bruce Johnson, 23–76. Cambridge, Mass.: Ballinger Publishing Co.

Olson, Sherry H. 1971. *The Depletion Myth.* Cambridge, Mass.: Harvard University Press.

O'Toole, Randal. 1988. *Reforming the Forest Service.* Washington, D.C.: Island Press.

Peterson, George L., and Alan Randall. 1984. *Valuation of Wildland Resource Benefits.* Boulder, Colo.: Westview Press.

Postel, Sandra, and Lori Heise. 1988. "Reforesting the Earth." Worldwatch Paper no. 83. Washington, D.C.: World Watch Institute.

Potter, Neal, and Francis Christy. 1962. *Trends in Natural Resource Commodities.* Baltimore, Md.: The Johns Hopkins University Press for Resources for the Future.

Pyne, Stephen J. 1981. "Fire Policy and Fire Research in the U.S. Forest Service." *Journal of Forest History* 25, no. 2 (April):64–77.

———. 1982. *Fire in America—A Cultural History of Wildland and Rural Fire.* Princeton, N.J.: Princeton University Press.

Robbins, William G. 1985. *American Forestry—A History of National, State, and Private Cooperation.* Lincoln, Neb.: University of Nebraska Press.

Robinson, Glen O. 1975. *The Forest Service.* Baltimore, Md.: The Johns Hopkins University Press for Resources for the Future.

Sedjo, Roger A. 1983. *The Comparative Economics of Plantation Forestry.* Washington, D.C.: Resources for the Future.

Sedjo, Roger A., and Kenneth S. Lyon. 1990. *The Long-Term Adequacy of Global Timber Supply.* Washington, D.C.: Resources for the Future.

Sedjo, Roger A., and David M. Ostermeier. 1978. *Policy Alternatives for Nonindustrial Private Forests.* Grosvenor, Md.: Society of American Foresters.

Sedjo, Roger A., and Samuel J. Radcliffe. 1981. *Postwar Trends in U.S. Forest Products Trade: A Global, National, and Regional View.* Washington, D.C.: Resources for the Future.

Sedjo, Roger A., and Allen Solomon. 1989. "Climate and Forests." Chapter 8 in *Greenhouse Warming: Abatement and Adaptation*, edited by Norman J. Rosenberg, William E. Easterling III, Pierre R. Crosson, and Joel Darmstadter. Washington, D.C.: Resources for the Future.

Shands, William E., and Robert G. Healy. 1974. *The Lands Nobody Wanted.* Washington, D.C.: The Conservation Foundation.

Stavins, Robert N., and Adam B. Jaffe. 1990. "Unintended Impacts of Public Investments on Private Decisions: The Depletion of Forested Wetlands." *American Economic Review* 80, no. 3 (June):337–352.

Steer, H. B. 1948. "Lumber Production in the United States, 1799–1946." U.S. Department of Agriculture, Miscellaneous Publication no. 669. Washington, D.C., October.

Teeguarden, Dennis E. 1985. "Effects of Public Policy on

Forestry Investments." In *Investments in Forestry*, edited by Roger A. Sedjo, 215–240. Boulder, Colo.: Westview Press.

Ulrich, Alice H. 1988. "U.S. Timber Production, Trade, Consumption, and Price Statistics, 1950–1986." U.S. Department of Agriculture, Forest Service, Miscellaneous Publication no. 1460. Washington, D.C., June.

U.S. Department of Agriculture, Forest Service. 1926–1967. *Forest Fire Statistics*, various annual issues.

————. 1928. "Timber Depletion, Lumber Prices, Lumber Exports, and Concentration of Timber Ownership." Report on Senate Resolution 311. 3d ed. Washington, D.C.: GPO.

————. 1968–1989. *Wildfire Statistics*, annual issues.

————. 1979. *A National Plan for American Forestry*. The Copeland Report. S. Doc. 12, 73 Cong., 1 sess. Reprint.

————. 1988a. "An Analysis of the Timber Situation in the United States, 1989–2040." Part 1: "The Current Resource Situation and Use." Draft.

————. 1988b. *The South's Fourth Forest: Alternatives for the Future*. Forest Resource Report no. 24. Washington, D.C., June.

U.S. Department of Agriculture, Office of the Assistant Secretary. 1989. "Performance Report: Natural Resource and Environmental Policy and Program Area 1981–1988." Assistant Secretary for Natural Resources and Environment. Memorandum, January.

U.S. Department of Commerce, Bureau of the Census. 1975. *Historical Statistics of the United States, Colonial Times to 1970*. Washington, D.C.

Vaux, Henry J. 1983. "State Interventions on Private Forests in California." In *Governmental Interventions, Social Needs, and the Management of U.S. Forests*, edited by Roger A. Sedjo, 124–169. Washington, D.C.: Resources for the Future.

Walker, Laurence C. 1980. "The Southern Pine Region." In *Regional Silviculture of the United States*, edited by John W. Barrett, 231–276. 2d ed. New York: John Wiley and Sons.

Wilcove, David S. 1988. *Protecting Biodiversity*. Vol. 2 of *National Forests: Policies for the Future*. Washington, D.C.: The Wilderness Society.

The Wilderness Society. 1989. *National Forests: Policies for the Future*. Vols. 1–5. Washington, D.C.: The Wilderness Society.

Wilkerson, Charles F., and H. Michael Anderson. 1987. "Annual Report of [the] Secretary of [the] Interior," 45 Cong., 2 sess., 1877. H. doc. no. 1. Reported in *Land and Resource Planning in the National Forests*. Washington, D.C.: Island Press.

Williams, Douglas. 1986. "The Economic Stock of Timber in the Coastal Region of British Columbia." Report no. 86–11, vols. 1 and 2, *Forest Economics and Policy Analysis Project*. Vancouver, B.C.: University of British Columbia.

Williams, Michael. 1983. "Ohio: Microcosm of Agricultural Clearing in the Midwest." In *Global Deforestation and the Nineteenth-Century World Economy*, edited by Richard P. Tucker and J. F. Richards, 3–13. Durham, N.C.: Duke University Press.

————. 1987. "Industrial Impacts of the Forests of the United States 1860–1920." *Journal of Forest History* 31, no. 3: 108–121.

————. 1988. "The Death and Rebirth of the American Forest: Clearing and Reversion in the United States, 1900–1980." In *World Deforestation in the Twentieth Century*, edited by John F. Richards and Richard P. Tucker, 212–229. Durham, N.C.: Duke University Press.

Williston, Hamlin L. 1980. "A Statistical History of Tree Planting in the South, 1925–79." Miscellaneous Report no. SA-MR8. U.S. Department of Agriculture, Forest Service. Atlanta, Ga.

4

Rangeland Resources: Changing Uses and Productivity

B. Delworth Gardner

Rangeland in the United States, particularly in the West, has been and increasingly continues to be a resource of tremendous value to the nation. Rangeland may consist of natural grassland, savannas, deserts, shrubland, tundra, alpine plant communities, coastal marshes, wet meadows, and introduced plant communities managed like rangeland (U.S. Department of Agriculture, 1988b). Rangeland—much of it privately owned—produces native vegetation such as grasses, grasslike plants, forbs, and shrubs. This land is suitable for grazing or browsing by domestic livestock and wild animals.

U.S. forests and rangeland provide forage and browse for more than 70 million cattle, 8 million sheep, 55,000 wild horses and burros, 20 million deer, 400,000 elk, and 600,000 antelope (Darr, n.d.). The quantity of livestock grazing is reckoned in animal-unit-months. An animal-unit-month (AUM) of grazing is approximately the quantity of forage needed to maintain a mature cow for one month. AUMs produced on private rangeland represent nearly 86 percent of the total forage consumed by livestock nationwide. Private irrigated pastures supply 2 percent and crop residues 5 percent of the total. Often private rangeland is used by ranchers in a complementary way with public rangeland managed by federal and state governments. AUMs of grazing produced on public land constitute about 7 percent of the total (Joyce, 1989). Many private ranches would not be viable economic units if they did not have access to public grazing. Hence the aggregate value of public and private rangeland used for grazing is probably higher than the sum of the separate parts.

Currently, an estimated 1.6 billion acres, or about 66 percent of the nation's total area, are classified as forest or rangeland or are covered by water. Less than 50 percent of this area, however, actually is rangeland (Joyce, 1989). Most of the rangeland is located in the seventeen western states. Rangeland in four states accounts for nearly 50 percent of the total range area: Alaska, 173 million acres; Texas, 96 million acres; Nevada, 60 million acres; and New Mexico, 51 million acres (Schlatterer and coauthors, n.d.).

Slightly more than 40 percent of the nation's rangeland currently is in federal ownership—most of it in the Rocky Mountain and Great Plains states and in Alaska (Joyce, 1989). Consequently, rangeland has come to have a regional and even a cultural connection. Americans generally associate rangeland with the wild land and open spaces of the West, at least partly because of the romance in the American psyche

Considering the variety of rangeland uses, the institutional arrangements used to govern the production and disposition of range resources tend to be complex and often conflict.

associated with ranching, the American cowboy, and "home on the range." Few Americans would consider livestock pastures in the East and South to be rangeland, although technically they fit the definition and are so considered by range professionals.

Rangeland has unique characteristics that make it complex to classify and describe. Historically, even though its primary purpose has been for the grazing of domestic livestock, rangeland—particularly but not exclusively that in the public domain—also has been used for watersheds, habitat for wild animals, and recreation. Thus most Americans have a direct interest in how this land is used and governed. In addition, rangeland varies in the types and quantities of vegetation produced, depending on physical terrain, soils, moisture, altitude, and latitude. Generalizations about rangeland characteristics, or belief that certain policy prescriptions would apply to all rangeland equally well, are therefore inappropriate. Moreover, many products that have commercial value derived from rangeland are produced indirectly. For example, unlike forestland timber that is harvested and marketed directly, the vegetation from rangeland is ingested by livestock and wild animals, which, in turn, ultimately become the object of value to users. Considering the variety of rangeland uses, the institutional arrangements used to govern the production and disposition of range resources tend to be complex and often conflict.

The acreage in rangeland has fluctuated in the past and undoubtedly will in the future because land has so many uses. Land used for domestic livestock and wildlife—the principal uses of rangeland—has a relatively low economic value compared with land used for other purposes such as urban development, highways, airports, railways, and agricultural crops. As a consequence, land classified as range generally is considered "residual," or land that is left over after other demands have been satisfied. To the extent that demand for other land uses changes over time, the land remaining in rangeland probably will change over time also. The concept of "residual" land largely explains the existing extensive acreage in public rangeland. The Homestead acts of 1862, 1873, and 1877 removed from public ownership much of the land suitable for growing crops. The government also gave huge grants of public land to railroad companies to expedite the building of the transcontinental railways, as well as to the states to support education. Much of this private and state land continues to be classified as rangeland, however, because of a lack of more valuable uses.

A more difficult and controversial classification concerns that of range quality or productivity. How does one judge whether the productivity of the range resource is improving or declining? The range ecologist studies the range vegetation, soil, and supporting water resources to make such a judgment. However, rangeland users do not separate range productivity from their own economic interests. It is likely that much of the confusion and many of the resulting disputes about trends in range productivity can be traced to ambiguities in criteria for judging range productivity.

This chapter examines classification of rangeland in terms of its quantity (acreage) and quality (health or condition). The chapter focuses principally on changes in the quantity and quality of rangeland resources through time, and explains and evaluates these changes in light of physiological, cultural, political, and socioeconomic factors that have affected trends in both quantity and quality. Three periods are addressed: the Cenozoic era up to 1890, the year when the federal government first imposed regulation of livestock grazing on the forest reserves; 1890 to 1934, the year when the government regulated livestock grazing on the remaining federal land called the public domain; and 1934 to 1990. The selection of periods is somewhat arbitrary; however, the changes in the range resource and the factors influencing those changes are more conveniently described in these periods than they would be in others. To provide a context for this historical discussion, the chapter first traces the evolution of criteria for determining range condition.

Criteria for Measuring Range Condition

Professionals working in the field of range management use the term "range condition" as a measure of the productivity or health of the rangeland ecosystem (Society for Range Management, 1989). The original concept of range condition usually referred to range productivity in terms of the principal use—livestock grazing—and was based on a comparison of actual forage production with some ideal or potential forage production. That concept has evolved to a view of range condition based on ecological status—that is, a concept that relates the actual production of vegetation to the quantity and quality of plants most suitable for the desired use of the range.

By the late 1940s and early 1950s, the primary federal range management agencies—the U.S. Department of Agriculture (USDA), Forest Service (FS), Bureau of Land Management (BLM), and Soil Conservation Service (SCS)—had adopted some type of range condition classification system (Secrist, 1988). One description of the standard process for determining range condition was as follows:

> The range is first assigned to a specific range site. Condition is judged by determining the percent similarity of species composition of the present vegetation to that of the climax for the site. Condition guides are developed by study of relic areas, exclosures or other areas representing undisturbed vegetation. Four condition classes based on percent of climax are used: excellent, 76–100%; good, 51–75%; fair, 26–50%; and poor, 0–25%. Change in range condition through time is referred to as "trend." (Smith, 1984, p. 817)

Early conceptions of range condition and trend as described by Smith, however, were inadequate. With shifts in rangeland use after World War II, the question of productivity became more complex. Other concepts have emerged because the "optimal" quantity and quality of vegetation produced depended on desired rangeland use.

Emerging Range Condition Criteria

Statutes such as the Multiple-Use, Sustained-Yield Act of 1960 and the Federal Land Policy and Management Act of 1976 mandated that federal agencies look beyond livestock grazing in accounting for their stewardship of public land. Such legislation encouraged these agencies to recognize the variety of rangeland uses: wildlife habitat, outdoor recreation, hunting and fishing, scenery, fresh air and open spaces, territory for roaming wild horses, soil stability, water quality, economic diversity, protection of endangered species, ecological diversity, community stability, and a rural life-style (Comanor, 1988). Thus arose a need to measure range management goals and accomplishments in terms that more accurately portrayed, to both administrators and the public, the entire scope of range vegetation management (U.S. Department of Agriculture, 1988b).

Recognizing the inadequacy of existing criteria, the Society for Range Management in 1978 established the Range Inventory Standardization Committee (RISC), an ad hoc subcommittee of the Research Affairs Committee, to examine these issues. In 1983, RISC recommended that terminology be standardized, that assessors of range ecosystems classify those ecosystems uniformly, and that the focus shift from "range condition" to "ecological status." In addition, RISC recommended that the basic unit for inventory, analysis, monitoring, and interpretation be the "ecological unit." Units would be classified as a certain "ecological type," which would provide a common land-based system for describing, comparing, grouping, predicting responses, and reporting for a particular unit of land for all resources involved (U.S. Department of Agriculture, 1988a). To make range condition more ecological and to free it from livestock "bias," RISC recommended that the four indicators in the SCS conventional system (that is, excellent, good, fair, and poor) be replaced by four new indicators: potential natural community or climax, late seral, midseral, and early seral, respectively (Pendleton, 1984, p. 855). "Seral" is an ecological term used to classify rangelands; and the modifiers "early," "mid," and "late" describe the composition of the forage toward its highest or climax level (Pearson and Thomas, 1984, p. 759).

Changing the classification system, however, did not eliminate the problem of determining the "ideal" vegetative cover for various purposes. Thus the classification system was modified to identify an ideal vegetative cover (Smith, 1984, p. 823); it was called a "desired plant community." The following procedure was recommended for selecting the desired plant community for a given site:

> Identify from the land-use plan the multiple-use values that are affected or dependent upon vegetation. Then, identify the vegetation characteristics or attributes that provide for the desired uses and values. Next, analyze the seral plant communities occurring on a site and assess their capability for providing the desired attributes. Finally, select a community or communities that best represents the desired attributes. This community becomes the [desired plant community] and the vegetation management objective. (Secrist, 1988, p. 5)

In 1988, a Forest Service Vegetation Analysis Task Group strongly recommended that the Forest Service adopt this ecological status and seral stages process to evaluate its rangeland and forest ecosystems (U.S. Department of Agriculture, 1988c). The Bureau of Land Management would follow in the same year (Secrist, 1988).

Before 1979, the Bureau of Land Management did not classify rangeland according to its potential. Therefore it is probable that pre–1979 BLM range condition data are primarily forage value ratings. Some rangeland classified as being in poor condition, rather than in a truly deteriorated state, may simply have had a low productive potential. After 1979, however, the BLM followed the SCS procedures for classifying and mapping range sites and range condition—that is, the current productivity of a range relative to what the range is naturally capable of producing. The Bureau of Land Management described range condition on its land as a comparison with a potential natural community: excellent, 75–100 percent similarity with the potential natural community; good, 50–75 percent; fair, 25–50 percent; and poor, 0–25 percent (Joyce, 1989).

The Soil Conservation Service, on the other hand, elected not to adopt the new seral stages system, apparently because it is regulated by different statutes than the public land range management agencies and appears to be less constrained by multiple-use management requirements. It also has primary responsibility for estimating range condition on private land where livestock output still dominates use decisions. A pioneer in developing range condition criteria since the early 1950s, when it introduced a "deviation from climax" basis for determining range condition that now is used by all the land management agencies (Society for Range Management, 1989), SCS continues to use the old terminology of "range condition" and "trend" (Joyce, 1989).

However, one of the consequences of changing range condition concepts and the use of different criteria by the various agencies is that even range professionals sometimes have difficulty determining what is meant by range condition statements in certain surveys. Box (1990) points out that

> Congress has directed the Forest Service and the Soil Conservation Service to report the condition of public and private rangeland, respectively, at least once each decade. These laws have led to range condition reports at least every five years. Unfortunately, the agencies release the reports at different times, using different techniques and differing formats. This has contributed to

each private interest group using the agency's data to make whatever point is favorable to them. Confusion continues, or perhaps has increased, because of the variable reporting systems. (pp. 109–111)

In addition, an important implication is that the change in the classification system itself implies an improvement in *observed* range condition. Rangeland is evaluated by a criterion that brings into juxtaposition vegetative cover and intended use. For example, if the intended range use were cover for wild animals and birds and the vegetation were woody plants, the rangeland currently would have a high resource-value rating, whereas it probably would have been rated "poor" under the old classification system because the condition was associated only with livestock grazing. Apparently, universal adoption of the new concepts would expedite a common understanding and interpretation of range productivity data that are so badly needed. Complete uniformity seems desirable because the ecological status framework permits range performance to be more realistically and objectively determined in the current multiple-use planning environment.

The Optimal Condition Problem

Measurement and criteria problems aside, one question remains: What is an "optimal" range con-

dition? The optimum obviously should be influenced by *intended* range use, the costs and benefits of use, and the vegetation produced. For example, different ungulates, such as cattle, sheep, goats, deer, and elk, prefer different plant species. How suitable the range is for grazing depends on both the quantity and quality of plant growth and the preferences of the grazing animals using the range.

The conventional methods of determining range condition compare the existing vegetation on the range with what is ideally or potentially produced. But is the ecological climax condition necessarily the optimal condition? Consider the rancher who is attempting to maximize the animal output produced on the range. The rancher might well see the optimum as falling short of ecological climax. Maximizing increases in animal output might require heavy grazing of the most palatable forage species, leaving less for regeneration than might be needed to maintain climax range condition. On the other hand, public range managers, charged by legislation with stewardship of the biological and soil resources on the range as well as active consideration of multiple uses, might be expected to see an optimum defined in terms of climax or near-climax, and could well judge the rancher's optimum as overstocking.

Perhaps this conflict over optimal range condition can help to explain two observed and puzzling phenomena. The first is that rancher permittees whose livestock graze federal allotments have almost always resisted grazing cuts, often strenuously, whenever public land agencies have proposed those cuts (Rowley, 1985). If, as the public range managers frequently argue, the cuts were necessary to protect long-range productivity, why did the permittees not agree readily to the cuts? After all, their livelihood and wealth depend critically on the productivity of the public grazing over the long run. Perhaps one explanation is that grazing tenure might be so insecure that once cuts were begun the permittees would fear losing all their public grazing. This explanation is unconvincing, however, because permits normally are issued for ten years. Why, then, should the permittees have resisted the cuts unless there were fundamental differences of opinion about which range condition and stocking rates were optimal?

The second puzzling phenomenon focuses on what studies have concluded about actual range condition on private ranges. For example, a 1989 report on range condition indicates that more than 60 percent of private ranges are in fair or poor condition (Society for Range Management, 1989; see also table 4-12). Workman (1986) has argued that ranchers may intentionally abuse their own ranges in the short run because of temporary exigencies, such as drought or unfavorable prices, but cannot afford to do so in the long run if it means depletion of the range resource. Ranchers have property rights to stock at whatever level they wish on their own land. Why should they overstock and deplete their ranges when the inevitable result would be a reduction in livestock product and a diminution in their wealth in the long run?

Some might argue that existing range condition simply reflects a rancher's limited knowledge—that the rancher is cognizant only of the short-term economic profits connected with livestock output and not the health of the range resource. This view is hardly convincing, given the stakes for the rancher. Plenty of means exist for acquiring knowledge and management skills that would enhance wealth if the rancher managed the range optimally. A rancher could always invest in range improvement, if it were economic.

Another view suggests that ranchers are forced to overgraze because of hard economic times or because of their inability to secure capital to improve the range or to acquire other feed. These situations could arise on rare occasions because of capital shortages; however, this view lacks credibility as an explanation for overstocking on a permanent basis. Investment capital usually is available to ranchers from private lenders and through government programs, often at subsidized interest rates.

The more convincing explanation for the observed fair and poor range condition on private ranges is that the range condition criteria themselves do not adequately reflect the optimal level of range productivity. Therefore, measuring range condition continues to be problematic. Nevertheless, awareness of the evolution of range condition criteria provides a basis for understanding historical changes in the quality of rangeland resources.

Overgrazing and Poor Climate: The Cenozoic Era Up to 1890

Rangeland of the western United States has changed from subtropical to arid over a very long time. At the end of the Cretaceous period some 60 million to 70 million years ago, the United States was dominated by the broadleafed pan-tropical forest geoflora (Dix, 1964). During that period, the Rocky Mountains, the Mexican Plateau, and the Sierra Madres uplifted. This development produced a blockage of warm, moist air in the western United States, thus creating warmer and drier climates (Axelrod, 1979). Then, during the Cenozoic era (70 million years ago to the present), the same region was subjected to at least four major glacial stages, at the close of the Pliocene epoch (about 2 million years ago) and during the Pleistocene epoch that followed (Kendeigh, 1974). By the close of the most recent glacial stage—the Wisconsin, which ended some 5,000 to 8,000 years ago—the vegetation was dominated by grass, but also included scattered woody plants across the general region of the Great Basin (Dix, 1964). Thus the arid vegetation found in modern times in the western United States is of recent origin (Axelrod, 1958; Dix, 1964).

Rangeland Acreage and Uses Increase

The ancestors of the modern horse, rhinoceros, camel, and other mammals were active grazers of the prehistoric rangeland in the United States (Dunbar, 1960). Although wild game numbers have not been accurately estimated for the Cenozoic era up to 1890, much anecdotal evidence suggests that large numbers of bison, elk, mule deer, white-tailed deer, and antelope also inhabited the rangeland and forestland of the country. Native Americans had harvested these animals for centuries; the animals were essential to the Native American livelihood, as food and as a source of clothing and lodging materials. Eventually, European settlers arrived. In 1539, the Spanish conquistador Coronado brought cattle, sheep, horses, and mules to the western rangeland of the United States (Sampson, 1952). Colonial settlers also introduced cattle and sheep in the East and South; the livestock grazed on the frontier woodland as well as on developed pastures.

By approximately 1780, the United States consisted of the land area east of the Mississippi River, except for Florida (Fedkiw, 1989). Most of the cropped land, however, was in the original thirteen colonies, and the remainder was largely wild land in the public domain. By 1853 the present geographic dimensions of the contiguous forty-eight states, consisting of about 1.9 billion acres, had been reached. The U.S. government acquired land primarily through various state cessions of land, the Louisiana Purchase, a treaty with Spain, the annexation of Texas, the Oregon Compromise, the Mexican Cession, and the Gadsden Purchase of land in the Southwest. The government later acquired Alaska from Russia in 1867 and annexed Hawaii in 1898 (Fedkiw, 1989).

Between 1880 and 1890, acreage in major classifications of land use shifted. Land devoted to cropland increased by 60 million acres and that devoted to range decreased by 43 million acres, following a trend that would last until the 1930s, when cropland would reach its peak (see appendix 4, table 4-A1). The residual land concept explains the increase in cropland and the reduction in rangeland during this period. A strong ethos existed in the country to get farmers on the land to establish homes and communities, and land disposal policy was directed to that purpose. However, perhaps the most important policy instrument for land disposal was the Northwest Ordinance of 1785, which set the basic directions for settlement and development of the public domain. Land was auctioned off and sold for cash at a minimum of $1 per acre. The Homestead Act of 1862 gave eligible settlers free title to 160 acres of public land after five years of residence on the land and homestead improvements, or after six months of residence with suitable improvements and payment of $1.25 per acre (Fedkiw, 1989). By the end of 1862, of the

1.31 billion acres in the public domain, the government had sold or granted 320 million acres to individuals and states. The transfer of public land to individuals increased in the 1880s, averaging more than 7 million acres per year until 1920. Transfers of public land to private ownership from 1880 to 1920, including sales and homestead entries, totaled nearly 325 million acres, which was one-third of the public domain that remained in 1862. The land transfers generally occurred in the arid and semiarid regions between the 100th meridian and the Sierra and Cascade mountains of the Pacific Coast (Fedkiw, 1989).

Development of rangeland continued as cattle raising became largely a frontier industry. Drovers trailed herds from the Ohio country to the East from 1818 to 1845. By 1865, the cattle industry had moved to Illinois, Iowa, and Missouri, and then to the West Coast (Rassmussen, 1974). Cattle numbers in the nation as a whole increased from 21 million head in 1970 to 45 million head in 1890. From 1870 to 1884, sheep numbers increased from 36 million head to 50 million head (U.S. Department of Commerce, 1975). These large increases suggest that landowners were using pasture and rangeland for more intensive grazing during this period. However, without some knowledge of the precipitation that fell at that time, which would be closely correlated to the production of forage, it cannot be concluded definitively that these increasing numbers imply overgrazing. No direct estimates of carrying capacity at the time are available.

After European settlement, the great bison herds that had roamed the Plains and Rocky Mountain states faced near extinction, thus freeing the forage for use by domestic livestock. As livestock replaced wild

---

By the end of 1862, of the 1.31 billion acres in the public domain, the government had sold or granted 320 million acres to individuals and states.

*Development of
rangeland
continued as cattle
raising became
largely a frontier
industry.*

grazers on rangeland, the ecosystem changed as a result of a number of factors. Cattle could be raised much farther from the markets with the advent of refrigeration and rail shipment. New technology that produced irrigation in the semiarid West, the windmill, and improved forage species allowed both a more varied and improved feed mix and improved livestock distribution (Joyce, 1989).

By the 1870s and 1880s, drovers were bringing large herds of cattle and sheep out of Texas to graze other areas of the West. Most of these ranges also were grazed by the "permanent" ranchers who had earlier settled in the region but did not have title to most of the grazing lands. This situation resulted in conflicts that have become part of the folklore of the region, and later became a significant factor in the development of range policy. Cattle herding continued to expand. By the late 1880s, 7.6 million head of cattle alone existed in the eleven western states (U.S. Congress, 1936). In the 1870s and 1880s, cattle herding also increased in the Northern Plains. However, livestock growers in Montana and Wyoming, fearing the growing influx of southwestern cattle onto the public ranges of the northern Great Plains, persuaded the National Cattlemen's Convention in 1884 to pass a resolution asking Congress to consider leasing public land to local stockraisers (Muhn, 1987). This is one of the first known efforts of the kind; the government did eventually give preference to local ranchers when issuing grazing permits on public land, as discussed below in the section on Rangeland Protection, 1890–1934.

Factors in Deteriorating Range Condition

Several factors led to deteriorating range condition in the period just before 1890. The active coloniza-

tion that was encouraged by the federal government through land sales, the Homestead acts, and grants of land to the railroads and the states brought an influx of population to the rangeland region. Most rangeland was not privately owned, however, and thus the "law of capture" prevailed; that is, the forage was harvested by those who could position themselves to capture it. This lack of property rights led predictably to a "tragedy of the commons," a term made famous by Hardin (1968). No incentives existed for an individual rancher to conserve the available forage for later use because each grazier knew that if he or she did not take the forage, another grazier would. Under these conditions, it is hardly surprising that ranchers soon regarded the ranges as overstocked and began to look toward regulation (Donart, 1984).

The first warning of trouble ahead for livestock graziers came during the late nineteenth century when the dry summers were coupled with severe winters (U.S. Congress, 1936). Dry summers would reduce forage production and diminish the ability of livestock to endure harsh winters. During the winters of 1886 and 1887, cattle ranchers on the Northern Plains apparently lost from 30 to 80 percent of their cattle (Schlebecker, 1963).

Many factors combine to determine vegetation on rangeland: climate, elevation, soils, fire, adaptability of plants, and animal-grazing relationships. Because all interact simultaneously. Without precise experiments that allow changes in one variable at a time it is difficult to determine what variables result in changes in range condition. Ecologists have attempted to estimate long-term changes in vegetation on western rangeland. Although comprehensive surveys of range condition in the entire region were not conducted until the 1930s, scholars have tried to infer what range conditions were like before 1890.

Some scholars believe that the condition of rangeland in the Southwest deteriorated from the time of European settlement onward. At the very time that livestock grazing was increasing during the last half of the nineteenth century, precipitation was declining (Hastings and Turner, 1965), a warming trend was occurring (Dix, 1964), and the pattern of precipitation was yielding fewer but heavier storms (Leopold, 1951). Any of these factors could have contributed to an increase in brush and woody plants and a corresponding decrease in perennial grass density, a result usually associated with deteriorating range condition. York and Dick-Peddie (1969), in an examination of land survey records of 31 townships in southern New Mexico, concluded that before overgrazing occurred in the latter part of the nineteenth century, that area predominantly grew grass rather than the desert shrubs and woody plants characteristic of the region today. Likewise, Buffington and Herbel (1965), who reviewed survey records dating back to 1858 to assess vegetative change from 1858 to 1953 on the Jornada Range Experiment Station in New Mexico, found evidence that good grass covered 90 percent of the area in the 1850s. This area has since been invaded continuously by woody plants, however. On the other hand, Hastings and Turner (1965), in reviewing comparative photographs of plots of land in southern Arizona to assess vegetative change over approximately one century, found increases in woody plants in some areas but decreases in others.

One explanation for at least some of the invasion of woody plants in the Southwest has been advanced by Bahre (1985). He surveyed early newspaper articles from communities in southeastern Arizona to determine the frequency and intensity of wildfires. Bahre argued that frequent and hot wildfires in the period before overgrazing in the 1870s and 1880s permitted grasses to survive and even flourish while seriously reducing the competition of woody plants. Two factors introduced by humans disturbed the biologic equilibrium of the dominant grass cover: overgrazing, which removed grasses, the primary source of fuel for fire-spreading; and the active suppression of fires by the European settlers, which increased the competitive ability of the invading woody plants.

Evidence that controlling grazing has significantly influenced the changes in rangeland vegetation has been presented by Bahre and Bradbury (1978). They analyzed photographs taken periodically at markers that divide the United States from Mexico, and observed striking changes in vegetation. For instance, photographs from 1892 depict a landscape devastated by severe drought and overgrazing on both sides of the border. Plant cover was dramatically improved in later periods, however, by grazing management on the American side of the border, whereas on the Mexican side, where uncontrolled grazing has continued to exist, few changes in range condition have been observed.

Johnson (1987), however, found that changes in range condition resulted from factors other than overgrazing or mismanagement, but he studied a different region. To appraise the effects of 115 years of rangeland use and management in Wyoming, Johnson determined the location of fifty-six sites photographed by William Henry Jackson in 1870 during a U.S. Geological and Geographical Survey expedition through southern Wyoming; he then had new photographs of the same sites taken during the period from 1974 to 1984. By comparing his photographs with Jackson's, he was able to assess changes in ecological condition since 1870. Johnson concluded that,

overall, range condition has changed relatively little and that plant communities have been fairly stable over the period. Seventy percent of the photo sites revealed little or no detectable change in either soil resources or plant communities. The sites exhibiting significant or fundamental change had been modified by people through construction, cultivation, changes in streamflow, and fire, but the changes were not the result of overgrazing or mismanagement. Johnson's study has been criticized on the grounds that the sites photographed in 1870 had already been grazed for decades by livestock accompanying emigrant wagon trains, and thus might have been in a depleted condition when Jackson photographed them.

This view of the relative stability of vegetative cover, at least in the sagebrush regions of the intermountain area (Great Basin and northern Rocky Mountains) has been corroborated by Vale (1975). He found descriptions of the existing vegetation in twenty-nine journals written by people who passed through the area before heavy emigration began along the Oregon Trail in 1843 and along the Humboldt River in Nevada in 1849. Vale concluded that the pristine vegetation was dominated by shrubs, whereas stands of grass were confined largely to wet valley bottoms, moist canyons, and mountain slopes, much as they are today.

In summary, by 1890 a combination of overgrazing, climate, and other factors contributed to a deteriorating range condition in the Southwest, as evidenced in the shift from grass to woody shrubs. However, evidence of range depletion on a large scale was not nearly so compelling in the Plains and northern Rocky Mountain states. But even in these areas there was a substantial risk that depletion would eventually occur in the absence of public regulation as long as the government continued to own and manage the public lands.

Rangeland Protection Policies: 1890–1934

Between 1890 and 1930, the area in rangeland fell by about 184 million acres and that in cropland and forestland increased by 165 million acres and 3 million acres, respectively (see appendix 4, table 4-A1).

Preservationists, such as John Muir, were adamantly opposed to livestock grazing—especially sheep grazing—on western public land.

Other land uses rose by 16 million acres. Thus the dominant factor in changing land use during this period was conversion of rangeland to cropland. Despite this significant reduction in rangeland acreage, however, it was the productivity of rangeland and measures to protect and enhance it that appeared to dominate the concerns and policy of the period.

Initiation of Grazing Policy and Regulation

As long as access to public land was open, people used the land if they could protect their position. When conflicts arose between individuals, sometimes appeals for mediation could be made to the grazing-user associations that constituted a higher authority. Otherwise, conflict was often accompanied by violence as competing interests fought for supremacy.

Policy to control grazing on public forestland was initiated early in the period following 1890. Preservationists, such as John Muir, were adamantly opposed to livestock grazing—especially sheep grazing—on western public land because, they alleged, devastation to vegetation and soil resources would occur (Rowley, 1985). They demanded government action to eliminate or reduce grazing. The livestock-raising community just as firmly opposed regulation. These divergent views eventually culminated in the following order by the secretary of the interior on June 30, 1897:

The pasturing of livestock on public lands in forest reserves will not be interfered with, so long as it appears that injury is not being done to the forest growth, and the rights of others are not thereby jeopardized. The pasturing of sheep is, however, prohibited in all forest reserves except those in the states of Oregon and Washington, for the reason that sheep grazing has been found injurious to the forest cover, and therefore of serious consequence in regions where the rainfall is limited. (U.S. Congress, 1897, p. 10)

Subsequently, the Department of the Interior requested that the U.S. Department of Agriculture appoint a USDA botanist to undertake a study and make recommendations on the basis of scientific evidence. The resulting Colville report deplored the uncertainty that surrounded forest reserve policies. Botanist Colville recommended that grazing be regulated, but not abolished, on the public land (Rowley, 1985). The government eventually implemented this recommendation on most public rangeland.

Additional evidence of a need for regulation of grazing was revealed in a report from the Public Land Commission that alleged overgrazing of ranges by livestock and the accompanying ruin of millions of acres of valuable rangeland (Fedkiw, 1989). In response to the allegation, the government allowed grazing on the forest reserves under a system of per-

mits. The Forest Management Act of 1897 authorized the management of the forest reserves to improve and protect the forest, ensure that favorable conditions of water flow were present, and furnish a continuous supply of timber. In 1900, the General Land Office published rules and regulations for issuing permits. The AUMs authorized by the permits were based on the number of animals the forestland could support consistent with the welfare of the forest and the livestock (Fedkiw, 1989). Thus the government issued grazing privileges to permittees who met certain eligibility requirements. The permits limited the number of AUMs of grazing, fixed the seasons of grazing use, and established the type of livestock that could be grazed (Gardner, 1962b).

In 1905, congressional legislation transferred management of the forest reserves from the General Land Office in the Department of the Interior to the USDA Bureau of Forestry, which later became the Forest Service (Rowley, 1985). The bureau introduced grazing fees. In addition, the secretary of agriculture, James Wilson, prepared a landmark letter of transmittal outlining the administrative duties of the Bureau of Forestry. The letter stated that "all land is to be devoted to its most productive use for the permanent good

of the whole people and not for the temporary benefit of individuals or companies" and that "where conflicting interests must be reconciled, the question will always be decided from the standpoint of the greatest good of the greatest number in the long run" (Rowley, 1985, p. 54).[1] The philosophy set forth in this letter has been highly influential in governing range policy over the decades since.

These maxims have been a rallying point for preservation, conservation, and environmental organizations that have opposed grazing on public land. Given a technical interpretation, however, the last maxim is a logical contradiction: it may be possible to maximize the gains to a few people or to maximize the number of parties (individuals) who gain, but to maximize both simultaneously is impossible. If conservationists postpone consumption of resources in the present to have more for future consumption, then it is likewise impossible to maximize the present consumption of forage (by whomever) and at the same time to conserve it. However, the popular interpretation of the maxim has been that broad social goals rather than narrow private interests should dominate decisions about resource use. In this view the clear implication for using the public land is that broad social interests such as wildlife protection and wilderness preservation would receive priority over narrow commodity interests such as timber production and livestock grazing.

Most ranchers who had used the public ranges under open access conditions in the nineteenth century actively opposed government regulation. At that time,

> most of the public rangeland that was surveyed and open to entry was made available for appropriation only under the settlement laws and not the auction and cash sale system that enabled individuals to acquire unlimited acreage. This policy limited the amount of public land to which ranchers could obtain title. Unable to acquire the acreage they needed legally, western graziers adopted illegal means to take and hold the public land they used. (Muhn, 1987, p. 9)

In addition to the property rights issue, grazing fees were a source of continuing conflict between user groups and agency administrators. The government argued that efficient management would require the imposition of fees to defray the cost of bringing order and protection to grazing lands. At first, the government suggested that fees should at least cover the cost of public administration; however, those fees would have little relationship to the value of the forage. The stockmen, however, argued that only Congress could levy taxes, that fees were indeed taxes and thus were illegal (Rowley, 1985). The political compromise reached was that fees would be charged but were to be set below the value of the forage. This decision made necessary nonprice eligibility requirements that resulted in misallocated public range permits (Gardner, 1962b).

With the implementation of the permit system, ranchers who had used the public ranges were concerned that loss of "their" forage to "permitted" graziers and other classes of users would cripple their year-round ranching operations. Thus, to make regulated grazing more palatable politically, the government imposed eligibility requirements that favored "bona fide" local ranchers who previously had grazed these ranges. These requirements, according to some scholars (Dana and Fairfax, 1980), stabilized the livestock industry by protecting it from fluctuating influences that were not under the control of local people. The requirements did effectively eliminate from consideration for permits the itinerant ranchers who did not own local ranch property but moved their stock among various geographic areas, often on a seasonal basis, where forage was available. However, whether the requirements "stabilized" the industry by reducing fluctuations in employment or prices is arguable. The requirements certainly favored one group of ranchers over another group by using non-efficiency criteria. Therefore, the eligibility requirements were inefficient economically because they prevented the allocation of federal forage to those ranchers who would value it most (Gardner, 1962b).

Most ranchers who had used the public ranges under open access conditions in the nineteenth century actively opposed government regulation.

Moreover, controversy arose over whether to allocate the allowable public forage to large or small permittees. Carrying capacity of the public ranges could not accommodate all interested graziers, especially because fees were set below the value of the forage, thus creating excess demand. Congress, sensitive to the allegation that grazing laws and regulations were transferring wealth to large and wealthy permittees, favored small permittees by placing upper limits on allowable AUMs. The large permittees naturally believed that the small ones were not really serious ranchers and thus were using the forage inefficiently. The issue of requiring large permittees to give up public forage so that it could be reallocated to other qualified (and generally smaller) ranchers was known as the "distribution" problem (Rowley, 1985), and it continues to fester even today.

Although many ranchers continued to oppose government regulation of rangeland, the experience of some ranchers in Montana eventually led to acceptance of federal regulation of grazing on the remaining public domain administered by the BLM under the Taylor Grazing Act of 1934 (Muhn, 1987). In Montana, a small group of ranchers could see federal control of the nonforested public domain coming and wanted to establish a foothold for themselves (Dana and Fairfax, 1980; Muhn, 1987). They convinced Congress to pass legislation that would lease to them the public land adjacent to their private holdings as an experiment to determine whether regulation of grazing on the public domain would benefit the western livestock industry. Congress passed the Mizpah-Pumpkin Creek Grazing District bill, and President Calvin Coolidge signed it into law on March 29, 1928. The association of ranchers issued grazing permits to members, collected fees, reduced stocking rates, and made range improvements. Range condition improved dramatically. Although the Montana experience was apparently successful, it is necessary to point out that an association of ranchers managing public land in its self-interest may produce results different from those of a regulating federal bureaucracy that has many competing interests, including its own, to worry about.

The issue of land ownership surfaced again (and would continue to come up again and again until it was largely settled in the 1970s) after Herbert Hoover was elected president in 1928. Hoover held the view that decentralized government was more efficient than government from the top in Washington, D.C. Ac-

It became clear from the beginning of federal regulation that if government control of the public ranges was to be irrevocable, the permitted grazing must be considered a "privilege" and not a "property right."

cordingly, the Hoover Commission on the Public Lands recommended the transfer of federal land to the states in which the land was located (Rowley, 1985). Forest Service personnel strongly resisted this recommendation, arguing that such a move would imply that the federal government was not managing the public land effectively. The proposal, however, never reached fruition because the states refused to accept the offer; state officials believed that the costs of administering this land would be prohibitive in the then-depression era. Beyond that, the federal government refused to confer the mineral rights along with the surface rights, and the states saw correctly that mineral rights were potentially more valuable.

In light of the property rights controversy, it became clear from the beginning of federal regulation that if government control of the public ranges was to be irrevocable, the permitted grazing must be considered a "privilege" and not a "property right." As early as 1911, the U.S. Supreme Court held that "any previous implied license to graze stock on public lands did not confer any vested rights on the users, nor did it deprive the United States of the power of recalling such licenses" (Dana and Fairfax, 1980, p. 89). Over the decades the government generally has held that it could revoke privileges without any compensation to permittees. Quite naturally, the permittee users

have seen this policy as an impediment to good stewardship and private investment on their grazing allotments. The government did try to minimize this problem by granting permits for ten-year periods, which provided some security of tenure to the permittees, although the AUMs authorized in the permit could be cut at the government's discretion.

Another mechanism the government designed to weaken political opposition to federal control of public rangeland was to give stockmen a voice in making and enforcing the rules and regulations for the management of local ranges. The government accomplished this effort through the establishment of forest advisory boards (Rowley, 1985). The federal government used exactly this same vehicle later in the Taylor Grazing Act of 1934, which created the Grazing Service that later became part of the BLM (Dana and Fairfax, 1980). In recent years, the government has broadened advisory boards to include other interest groups, including the "public" interest.

The concern for grazing on rangeland during this period also expanded to include consideration of the status and health of the nation's watersheds, particularly those in the West where established communities were growing at a rapid rate. Severe summer thunderstorms on denuded watersheds produced flash floods that destroyed property and were life-threatening in many instances. The premature siltation of reservoirs also became a problem. Such a severe storm occurred in 1923 in Davis County, Utah, where floods did much damage (U.S. Army Corps of Engineers, 1984). Public sentiment for the elimination of livestock grazing on some of these critical watersheds became intense, and the government responded to the public concern. These ranges have not been grazed since, even though forage production levels have increased sharply.

Range Condition: Perceived Improving Forest Ranges, Worsening Public Ranges

At the turn of the twentieth century, range condition was viewed as so poor in the West, especially on the forestland, that federal regulation and control were absolutely necessary. Still, because scientists did not undertake studies until later, firm evidence for poor range condition at that time is fragmentary, and some anecdotal evidence may even be interpreted as contradicting this conclusion. For example, around 1900, shortly after his installation as director of grazing in the Forest Service, Gifford Pinchot concluded that "range conditions were satisfactory and that stockmen enjoyed a prosperity which gave them confidence in the future" (Rowley, 1985, p. 74).

Moreover, in 1915, more than a decade after it had assumed control of the forests, the Forest Service estimated that there was more than a 50 percent increase in the number of animals actually using forest ranges.

> About 38,000 more cattle and horses and 347,000 more sheep and goats were under permit. All this meant, according to forest officials, that carrying capacity of the range was increasing under better management, especially in the areas of distributing and handling stock. (Rowley, 1985, p. 93)

These data hardly support the view that government regulators were desperate to reduce stocking levels because of overgrazing. However, perhaps they saw themselves as supporting the war effort on a temporary basis, and thus one should not interpret their actions as failing to observe overgrazing. Yet the official line was that, under regulation, the productivity of the forest ranges was improving while that of the public range outside the forests was deteriorating (Rowley, 1985). To be fair to the agency, the Forest Service would later use these World War I statistics for meat and wool production to argue against similar "overuse" of the ranges during the next wartime emergency, in World War II (Rowley, 1985).

The position that ranges were in a seriously depleted condition by 1934, however, was strongly reinforced by the publication of the first purportedly systematic study of range condition: *A Report on the Western Range* (U.S. Congress, 1936). Moreover, the study revealed that ranges administered by the Forest Service were then in significantly better condition than any others, private or public, and that forest ranges had improved from 1905 to 1934, whereas private and other public ranges had deteriorated significantly.

Others claimed that ranges were not as depleted as some often alleged, especially in certain areas of the West. Branson (1985) confirmed this view in his discussion of a study based on compared photographs, similar to the one conducted earlier by Kendall Johnson. Branson did not reveal exactly where his study photos were taken—only that they were from the northern Great Plains region. Sites photographed by Homer L. Shantz during the years 1908–1927 were again photographed in 1958, 1959, and 1960 (Phillips, 1963). Vegetation in many of the photos had changed little, but of sites that were in native vegetation in the photographs compared, more ranges improved than declined (Branson, 1985).

Developments in Measuring Range Condition

In 1910 the Forest Service established the Office of Grazing Studies to coordinate and promote range research and to collect technical range management information. An appointed director launched a grazing "reconnaissance" of specific forest ranges, probably the first systematic effort to appraise range condition. Later this task would be called the "range survey" or "range-resource inventory." The ultimate goal of the survey was to find a simple, reliable method for rating empirically the condition of the range and also for determining whether the range was improving or deteriorating. By 1915, the Office of Grazing Studies had become the leading government agency in the field for range research (Rowley, 1985).

In addition to this effort, Arthur W. Sampson, a prominent pioneer in range science, helped to organize the first experiment station devoted mainly to range research on the Manti Forest near Ephraim, Utah. In articles published in 1917 and 1919, Sampson argued that the effectiveness of range management could be measured in terms of plant succession—the progressive development of a simple, sparse vegetation into more complex, abundant forms (Rowley, 1985). Sampson believed that progressive development could "be greatly expedited by cropping the herbage in such a manner as to interfere as little as possible with the life history and growth requirements peculiar to the different successional plant states" (Rowley, 1985, p. 103). A working knowledge of plant succession could assist in judging what was overgrazing or undergrazing. Sampson's views have become pillars of modern range science.

Shifts in Land Use Demand: 1934–1990

Changes in Rangeland Acreage and Uses

Acreage in rangeland increased from 708 million acres in 1930 to its peak of 723 million acres in 1940 (see appendix 4, table 4-A1). A steady decline occurred thereafter through the 1950s, 1960s, and 1970s, and reached a low of 659 million acres by 1982. In contrast, during this period the cropland base was roughly constant at approximately 400 million acres. Thus it was the "other" uses of land that increased steadily at the expense of rangeland during this period (from 176 million acres in 1930 to 266 million in 1982). The period after World War II, particularly, saw rapid expansion of urban areas, roadways, and land set-asides for watersheds, recreation, and conservation, all of which would be included in the "other" category. The acreage trends reflected the shifts in demand for the various uses of land. However, rangeland continued to be used predominantly for grazing domestic livestock and wild animals—its predominant use today as well.

DOMESTIC LIVESTOCK

The historical peak in cattle numbers in the United States was 132 million head in 1975 (Joyce, 1989). There was a decline to 105 million head by 1986. The decline was much greater in the eastern region than in the western region where most of the rangeland exists, however. In contrast, sheep numbers peaked in the depression year of 1935 at about 56 million head and dropped steadily to approximately 10 million head in 1982. Horses on farms declined from a peak of nearly 20 million head in the 1920s, when the tractor was first introduced, to about 2 million by 1982. Mechanical power was substituted for animal power on American farms. The number of goats has always been relatively small compared with the number of other grazing animals, and goats are significant grazers only in Texas (Joyce, 1989).

Among classes of domestic livestock, range forage use currently is dominated by cattle and sheep, although dairy cattle, goats, and horses also use small amounts of grazed forages. Forage sources for grazing animals can be classified as nonirrigated private ranges, irrigated private pastures, public grazing lands, and residues from cropland. The main source of grazed forages for beef cattle in the entire country is from deeded nonirrigated rangeland (Joyce, 1989). For the country in 1985, 89 percent of the cattle AUMs came from private ranges and irrigated pastures, 6 percent from public ranges, and 5 percent from residues from cropland. For sheep, 63 percent came from private ranges and pastures, 11 percent from public ranges, and 26 percent from crop residues (Joyce, 1989). Joyce also reports that harvested and grazed forages supply 61 percent of the nutrients consumed by dairy cows, but less than 1 percent of dairy feed costs are for pasture. Harvested forage, such as hay and concentrates, provides most of the diet of dairy cattle. Moreover, grazed forages supply approximately 61 percent of annual beef cattle feed requirements (excluding cattle in commercial feedlots) and 90 percent of the annual requirements for sheep. The reason for this difference between cattle and sheep is that most areas of the United States with large beef cattle inventories do not have year-round forage available; thus, beef ranchers must obtain supplemental feeds. Little supplemental feed is needed in the production of sheep in the seventeen western states, however, except in the northern Great Plains (Joyce, 1989).

In 1986, public land statistics from the Department of the Interior indicated that the Bureau of Land Management had about 163 million acres under grazing permits or leases in sixteen western states. About 20,000 operators grazed nearly 4 million head of livestock under these permits and leases, or approximately 10.5 million AUMs. The Forest Service had about 102 million acres under 10,387 allotments in thirty-six states, but most of these were located in the seventeen western states. The Forest Service administered 13,805 permits, and actual forage use was 8.6 million AUMs (Joyce, 1989).

How important, then, is the public land for supplying forage for domestic livestock? The Department of Agriculture has estimated that federal land produces only approximately 7 percent of the total AUMs of grazed forage nationwide (Joyce, 1989). In 1960 in eleven western states, however, public land supplied nearly 17 percent of all livestock forage (Gardner and Roberts, 1963). Although the regions do not correspond exactly to those in the Gardner-Roberts study, 1985 data from the Pacific Northwest, California, the Southwest, and Rocky Mountain states show that 13.25 percent of the total AUMs of forage for beef cattle and sheep came from grazing on the public lands (Joyce, 1989). If anything, these figures understate the importance of federal land to the local ranching economies, because public land often is used in a complementary grazing rotation with private grazing and haying land. If public grazing were unavailable and had to be replaced with more costly private grazing or supplementary feeds, the economic feasibility of many existing ranching operations would be questionable (Gardner and Roberts, 1963).

Despite the importance of federal land to local ranching, domestic livestock grazing on national forest system land has declined slightly since 1953, primarily because of a decline in the number of grazing sheep and goats. Cattle allotments have declined in some regions as well (Joyce, 1989). Moreover, the percentage of domestic livestock grazing on BLM public domain land has declined more than on the forestland, for two reasons: the government reduced the quantity of allowable grazing on some allotments, and the government transferred some BLM-administered land to other agencies. In the

northern Rockies alone, Bureau of Land Management AUMs declined from nearly 9 million in 1969 to fewer than 8 million in 1986. Sheep use declined by approximately 50 percent.

Nevertheless, Joyce (1989) projects that forage outputs on national forest system land will increase slightly from 9.8 million to 10.3 million AUMs between 1989 and 2040. This projected increase in AUMs on national forest land is less than that projected for private land, however; the difference in these projections reflects pressures on the national forest system to increase other uses of the public land, such as for recreation, improved riparian habitat, and wildlife production.

WILDLIFE

Western rangeland is used by significant and generally increasing numbers of domestic livestock and wild game animals; thus this rangeland is extremely important to the economies of the region. Wildlife such as migratory game birds, including waterfowl—ducks, geese, and swans—and webless migratory species such as woodcock and mourning doves, use rangeland. However, the country's duck population has declined from 44 million birds in the early 1970s to about 30 million birds in the mid-1980s because of a deterioration in the quantity and quality of wetland areas (Darr, n.d.). Moreover, undoubtedly the decline has been affected by the profitability of converting wetland into cropland because of high and often subsidized agricultural commodity prices.

Assessing the land area grazed by wild herbivores is a difficult task at best. Federal and state agencies estimate numbers of wild herbivores only periodically. Although population estimates for Forest Service land are available, the figures may be misleading because the animals also use surrounding private and other public land (Joyce, 1989). Wild animals move across the landscape and across ownerships and plant communities. The extent of wildlife grazing on nonfederal rangeland has never been accurately estimated.

Given the estimates that are available, it is difficult to infer the level of range conditions from animal numbers alone. Wild animal populations appear to be somewhat stable, and probably do not themselves indicate either undergrazing or overgrazing. Therefore the controversy about range condition cannot be settled by appealing to data on wild animals. The same conclusion also appears to be valid with respect to domestic livestock numbers. Increasing numbers do not imply overgrazing if the productivity of the range is increasing. If overgrazing is occurring, then one must seek the proof in the quantity and quality of forage produced, not in the numbers of animals using the forage.

Studies of Range Condition

Compared with the two previously discussed periods, the period since 1934 has seen large increases in data relating to range condition. Regional range condition studies (some of them covering private rangeland) that rely on data measurements through time, as well as a number of studies conducted by government agencies, have produced disparate assessments of range conditions and range trends. A sample of those studies is reviewed here, as are opinions on range condition obtained from range professionals. A study of the trend and condition of riparian rangeland is also examined.

REGIONAL STUDIES

The Southwest. Several studies conducted in the Southwest reveal a declining range condition. From 1932 to 1949 at the Santa Rita Experiment Station in southern Arizona, Glendening (1952, p. 327) found that "mesquite, a woody plant, more than doubled in number and crown area while perennial grass density decreased more than 95 percent under all grazing treatments." He believed that unless the various brush species were controlled, the observed trend toward mesquite and cacti would result in large areas of semidesert grassland being converted to a desert shrub type of much lower grazing value. Glendening's findings reinforced the trends reported previously from other studies covering earlier periods in the region. Likewise, Humphrey and Mehrhoff (1958) showed that from 1904 to 1954 in Arizona woody plants had increased markedly in both area and abundance. In yet another study, Johnston (1963, p. 464) stated, "In many areas the woody vegetation is now thicker and more nearly exclusive of grasses and forbs than formerly."

The exceptionally dry years of 1950–1957 could have exaggerated the trend toward deterioration, which might not have existed with more favorable weather.

Several of these studies of the Southwest were terminated during a period of drought, and the region may have since recovered because of more favorable weather (Goldberg and Turner, 1986). On the other hand, because most studies took actual measurements at several points over a long period and each measurement showed an overall trend of deterioration, the drought explanation does not seem to account for the overall trend. Nevertheless, although these studies attribute the decline to different causes, they seem to agree that on the whole the condition of the rangeland in the areas studied clearly is deteriorating.

In contrast, other studies appear to show that the range in the Southwest is either in a stable, static condition or even may be improving slowly. In a study conducted from 1906 to 1978, Goldberg and Turner (1986, p. 711) found "no consistent, directional changes in the composition of vegetation . . . despite large fluctuations in absolute cover and density of the component species." Smith and Schmutz (1975) studied two areas, one grazed and one protected, from 1941 to 1969. Their results indicated that the grazed range was "low" in range condition but was slowly improving. They also pointed out that the grazed range would probably not improve much more unless the managers of the range could control the mesquite by mechanical means or by the application of chemicals, or unless grazing was reduced. The condition of the protected range was intermediate and improving, yet also was threatened by the invading mesquite.

However, it is difficult to generalize the causes of changing range condition, as is evident from a study from Arizona (Martin and Turner, 1977). It was found that some species formerly thought to be indicators of overgrazing were even more responsive to short-term changes in climate. For example, burroweed invaded an area studied twice during the years 1922 to 1977. In 1922, there was almost no burroweed, but in 1935 it had become the dominant plant. In 1947, there was much cholla grass but little burroweed, and in 1969, after two wet winters, a new strand of burroweed existed. In 1975, following several dry winters, much of the burroweed died; yet, in response to above-average summer rains, more perennial grass was present. As Branson (1985, p. 38) has observed, "because the kind of vegetation on a semidesert site changes greatly from time to time due to natural causes, there is no combination of plant species that can be said to be nature's choice for all time." This statement appears to take issue with the

To left of fence, sample plot of rangeland protected from grazing

"climax" notion, and implies that any definitive determination of "potential vegetation" for a site may be impossible.

The Great Plains. Studies of range condition on both public and private grazing land have been made in the Great Plains since 1934, but, like studies of southwestern range condition, they do not tell a consistent story.

Changes in the native vegetation on grazed private ranges in western North Dakota were evaluated by Whitman, Hanson, and Peterson (1943) from 1932 to 1942. During the first half of the period, ranges deteriorated, mostly as a result of a prolonged drought that lasted seven years (Branson, 1985), but partly because of heavy grazing. Range condition declined sharply from 1933 to 1936, after which the vegetation showed continued improvement as a result of the cessation of drought and the removal of large numbers of livestock from the range by their owners because of unprofitable grazing conditions. Drought injury was not so severe in western North Dakota as it was in Montana and in the central and southern Great Plains (Whitman, Hanson, and Peterson, 1943).

Despite the increasing attention given to management to improve ranges as well as a general awakening to the nature and value of grassland, the condition of ranges in the northern Great Plains was not good:

Drought, overstocking, uneven distribution, and unwise breaking of native sod are important causes of material deterioration on an estimated 25 million to 40 million acres of range land. Evidence of this subnormal condition is widespread in the form of accelerated soil movement; reduced height growth, or density; change in composition from valuable to less desirable species; and excessive erosion and run-off. (Hurtt, 1950, p. 24)

Weaver and Albertson (1956, p. 255) observed similar conditions:

Such [excellent] ranges, which closely approach the climax condition, can still be found, as well as many good ranges. The great majority have deteriorated into the fair and poor condition classes. ... Thus, the vast area of grassland which formerly covered both High Plains and Piedmont of Colorado has been greatly changed by destructive grazing and by plowing. The two-layered prairie with its host of nongrasslike herbs has either been plowed or nearly all reduced to a short-grass sod in which blue grama alone often furnishes the bulk of present-day forage and in which the palatable forbs have been largely replaced by weeds. Improving depleted ranges and maintaining those still in good condition are extremely important economic problems.

However, Branson and Miller (1981), who sampled fifteen plant communities on public land in the Willow Creek basin near Glasgow, Montana, in 1960 and again in 1977, found that ground cover and forage production improved in most of the communities. They attributed this improvement to factors such as higher precipitation that occurred between the first and second sampling, and, less certainly, to improved management practices such as land treatments and the application of rest-rotation grazing systems. The results of the Branson and Miller study challenged the generally held view that western rangeland had deteriorated significantly.

More recent studies also suggest better range condition in the Great Plains. At a Society for Range Management symposium in 1978, Alex Johnston (1978) reported that in 1970 nearly 75 percent of U.S. rangeland was in fair or poor condition. The plains and prairie grassland ecosystems and ranges in the northern Great Plains were in good condition. In addition, the northern mountain valleys were in better condition than the ranges of the Southwest or of California. Likewise, in an article Ross and Taylor (1988) indicated that more than 50 percent of Montana's rangeland is in good to excellent condition. This finding is consistent with Daughterty's (1989, p. 12) report that the "Northern Plains had the highest proportion of range rated as 'excellent or good' in the 1982 SCS inventory of nonfederal rangelands."

Although drought has often seemed to be the principal culprit in rangeland deterioration, it is unlikely that all the deterioration in range condition can be attributed to unfavorable climate. Experiments in west-central South Dakota at the Cottonwood Range Field Station demonstrated clearly the serious effect that overuse has on subsequent foliage production and consequently on livestock (Johnson and coauthers, 1951). Continued heavy grazing reduced range condition from 70 percent in 1942 to 50 percent in 1949. Under moderate grazing, range condition remained about the same, whereas under light grazing it im-

proved from 73 percent in 1942 to 82 percent in 1949.

Some reasonably clear conclusions seem to emerge from these Great Plains studies as a composite. The studies covering the period of the 1930s, 1940s, and 1950s indicate poorer range condition than those of recent years. A wetter climate, and possibly other factors leading to improved productivity, produced a higher level of range condition.

FEDERAL STUDIES

Federal agencies have measured range condition within the United States since 1934. However, like the regional range condition studies, no federal study is really definitive in assessing range condition or in projecting trends for an entire region. The reason is that the studies used different range condition criteria and measurement standards and covered different geographic areas. Several federal range condition studies are reviewed here chronologically.

The 1936 western range study. The first national assessment of rangeland undertaken in the United States was a compilation of thirty-five reports by range experts working in the Forest Service (U.S. Congress, 1936). The findings were quite alarming and highly critical of existing grazing administration outside of the U.S. Department of Agriculture. Generally, findings revealed that across all classes of ownership the condition of the nation's rangeland was materially to severely depleted in 1936 (table 4-1). The national forests were in significantly better condition than the rest of the public land; public domain land was in the worst shape. Even private rangeland was seriously depleted, with more than 50 percent of the acreage materially or severely depleted.

Academic scholars have called the 1936 study more of a political document than a biological survey.

Table 4-1. Percentage of Rangeland Acreage in Depletion Classes, by Ownership, 1935

	Depletion class			
Ownership	Moderate	Material	Severe	Extreme
Federal				
National forest	46.5	40.0	12.0	1.5
Indian land	6.6	35.8	54.0	3.6
Public domain	1.5	14.3	47.9	36.3
Other federal	2.0	21.2	50.1	26.7
All federal	16.1	26.4	38.1	19.4
State and county[a]	7.1	47.4	37.0	8.7
Private	11.7	36.9	36.4	15.0
All ownerships	13.0	33.7	37.1	16.2

Source: U.S. Congress (1936).

[a]Row may not total 100 percent because of rounding.

The 1936 report also indicated changes or trends in range forage depletion from 1905 to 1935 (table 4-2). These trend data revealed that only on the national forests was the condition generally improving, whereas on the remainder of the public land and on private land the condition was deteriorating sharply. If these results were in fact true they constituted justification for the governmental regulation of grazing on the public domain embodied in the Taylor Grazing Act of 1934, passed two years before.

In light of the 1936 study findings, the Forest Service recommended several remedial measures: a more equitable distribution of grazing privileges among ranchers; a sharp reduction in the numbers of livestock on the range because ranges were allegedly overstocked by 43 percent; consolidation of range administration—both in the national forests and in the unreserved portions of the public domain; avoidance of any move by users to establish prescriptive or property rights to the range; and revision of the grazing act to prevent a conflict between federal and state authorities (Rowley, 1985).

Academic scholars have called the 1936 study more of a political document than a biological survey (Box, 1990), but explanations for the tone and findings of the study vary. The recommendations could represent a heightened proprietorial attitude on the part of the Forest Service and a desire to assume federal control of grazing on the unregulated public domain (Rowley, 1985). Another interpretation was that Harold Ickes, Franklin Roosevelt's ambitious secretary of the interior, wanted grazing control consolidated in the Department of the Interior, and that the range

condition report was a defensive measure on the part of the Forest Service and the USDA to at least maintain their control of grazing on the national forests (Rowley, 1985). At least part of the rationale was that at the time the Forest Service was unpopular with the ranching community for cutting the quantity of grazing and for attempting to raise grazing fees, ostensibly making it somewhat vulnerable to a transfer of its grazing management to the Department of the Interior.

After publication, the livestock graziers and some government officials strongly denounced the report as being full of inaccuracies and for being excessively complimentary to the Forest Service and antagonistic toward the Department of the Interior. Evidence was said to have been manipulated to show a greater contrast between national forest ranges and the unreserved and unregulated public domain than was actually the case (Dutton, 1975).

Table 4-2. Trends in Range Forage Depletion, 1905–1935

	Percentage of acreage by trend class		
Land control	Improved	Declined	Unchanged
National forests	77	5	18
Indian land	10	75	15
Public domain	2	93	5
Other federal	7	81	12
State and county	7	88	5
Private	10	85	5
Total grazing land	16	76	8

Source: U.S. Congress (1936).

Table 4-3. Percentage of Rangeland Acreage Depletion by Condition Class, 1961, 1966, and 1972

	Condition class		
Year	Excellent and good	Fair	Poor
1961	16.6	53.1	30.3
1966	18.9	51.6	29.5
1972	17.6	50.0	32.4

Sources: For 1961 and 1966, Pacific Consultants (1970); for 1972, U.S. Department of Agriculture (1972).

Note: On differences between the Pacific Consultants (1970) and U.S. Department of Agriculture (1972) studies, see the text pp. 146–147.

What were the substantive findings of this controversial study? It reported range condition in terms of stages of depletion from some "ideal" condition. The reference point was vague: some ideal "potential" productivity of the range. Range condition expressed in terms of deviation from an ecological ideal or climax did not become widespread until after Dyksterhuis (1948) published his influential paper, "Condition and Management of Rangeland Based on Quantitative Ecology" (Box, 1990).

The 1961 and 1966 Pacific Consultants study. After the western range study, no national range condition assessments were made during the next twenty-five years. This is surprising given the serious depletion of rangeland alleged in the 1936 report. In the early 1960s, however, Congress considered changing the laws regulating the public land and established the Public Land Law Review Commission. The commission contracted with the firm Pacific Consultants to evaluate the condition of the nation's rangeland and report back to the commission.

Pacific Consultants did not make on-the-ground surveys, but compiled data from "various sources" for the years 1961 and 1966. The study reported range condition in four classes: excellent, good, fair, and poor, but it is unclear what criteria the researchers

used to establish range condition classes. Moreover, the data are aggregated across land ownership classes (table 4-3). From the study findings, it appears that a slight improvement occurred between 1961 and 1966 since the percentage in the excellent and good categories rose by 2.3 percentage points and the fair and poor categories showed a small decline. Sampling error alone might have resulted in these small differences, however, to say nothing of measurement error, which, given the procedures used, must have been large.

The 1972 Forest Service study. Findings from a 1972 Forest Service study (U.S. Department of Agriculture, 1972) of range condition on federal rangeland, which relied primarily on off-the-shelf data from old surveys (Box, 1990), generally agreed with the Pacific Consultants study (table 4-3). Because it is unclear from the published reports whether the Forest Service used different data than those used by Pacific Consultants, no persuasive evidence exists that range condition changed significantly over the 1966–1972 period.

The 1975 Bureau of Land Management study. The Bureau of Land Management made a major effort to assess range condition on public domain land in the 1970s (U.S. Department of the Interior, 1975). According to its report, many of the statistical data were estimated, but were based on the most recent information available in BLM field offices. Findings from the study indicated that Bureau of Land Management personnel had classified 83 percent of the BLM range as being in fair, poor, or bad condition (table 4-4). This finding is nearly identical to findings in the 1936 western range report (a report that was critically received because of its alleged bias), which indicated 84.2 percent of the public domain land was "severely" or "extremely" depleted. Given the changing criteria and classification systems between 1936 and 1975, however, it would be a mistake to give great importance to the nearly identical numbers. Perhaps a safe conclusion would be that both studies indicated that

Table 4-4. Range Condition Depletion by Condition Class, 1975

	Condition class				
Measure	Excellent	Good	Fair	Poor	Bad
Percentage of acreage	2	15	50	28	5
Acres (in millions)	3.2	24.4	81.5	45.6	8.2

Source: U.S. Department of the Interior (1975).

Table 4-5. Erosion on Bureau of Land Management Land by Condition Class, 1975

Measure	Condition class				
	Stable	Slight	Moderate	Critical	Severe
Percentage of acreage	9	46	35	9	1
Acres (in millions)	12.8	67	50.6	13	1.3

Source: U.S. Department of the Interior (1975).

much of the BLM range in both periods was in a seriously depleted condition.

Specifically, the BLM report indicated that erosion was slight or soil was stable on approximately 55 percent of BLM ranges (table 4-5). Erosion was critical or severe on 10 percent, however. The study also reported trends in range condition (table 4-6). The trend was static on 65 percent of BLM acreage, with 19 percent improving and 16 percent declining.

The 1977 Soil Conservation Service study. Unlike the previously mentioned federal studies, the SCS study assessed range condition on *nonfederal* rangeland in 1977 (U.S. Department of Agriculture, 1984). This study is significant because few studies were conducted on range condition on private rangeland. The SCS randomly sampled 17 percent of all the nation's counties according to sampling procedures from the 1967 SCS Conservation Needs Inventory. The primary purpose of the study was to ascertain existing land use and the constraints on converting range, pasture, and forestland to cropland use. The SCS also requested that state range conservationists provide information on range site and condition levels (table 4-7). Definitions for each range condition class expressed the degree to which the composition of the existing plant community resembled that of the climax plant community. About 40 percent of private

ranges were in excellent or good condition. This was a higher level of condition than that revealed in comparable studies of public land. Unfortunately, the SCS study was unclear on whether the trend was up or down from 1934 to 1977. The 1936 study indicated that 48.6 percent of the private ranges were moderately or materially depleted (the top two range condition classes), but comparability of these depletion classes with the condition classes used in the 1977 report is so dubious that no reliable comparisons can be made. However, Pendleton (1984) believes that most range scientists agree that considerable improvement had been made in private range condition over the 1967–1977 period.

Another important finding in the 1977 SCS study was that 89 percent of all *nonfederal* rangeland was being adequately protected and therefore not deteriorating in condition through time. However, this finding is curious, given that only 40 percent of the acreage was in either excellent or good range condition. Apparently excellent and/or good condition was not deemed by the analysts to be a prerequisite for rangeland being "adequately" protected.

The 1982 Soil Conservation Service study. This study (U.S. Department of Agriculture, 1984) inventoried more than 400 million acres of nonfederal rangeland; data were for the forty-eight conterminous states and Hawaii, but excluded Alaska (Daugherty, 1989). The

Table 4-6. Trends in Range Condition on Bureau of Land Management Land, 1975

	Trend		
	Improving	Static	Declining
Percentage of acreage	19	65	16
Acres (in millions)	31	106	25.7

Source: U.S. Department of the Interior (1975).

Table 4-7. Percentage of Nonfederal Range Acreage by Condition Class, 1977

Condition class			
Excellent	Good	Fair	Poor
12	28	42	18

Source: Pendleton (1978).

Table 4-8. Percentage of Nonfederal Range Acreage by Condition Class, 1982

Condition class				
Excellent	Good	Fair	Poor	Other[a]
4.1	29.6	44.9	16.4	5.0

Source: U.S. Department of Agriculture, Soil Conservation Service, and Iowa State University Statistical Laboratory (1984).

[a]Range is classified as "other" if it has been seeded to an introduced species. Therefore, "other" range is not applicable to natural range conditions and was not rated as excellent to poor.

inventory undertook a qualitative assessment of range condition according to condition classifications that defined the degree to which the amounts, proportions, and types of plant species resembled the climax vegetation for the area studied (table 4-8).

Findings revealed that only 34 percent of nonfederal range was rated as excellent or good in 1982, compared with 40 percent in 1977. However, because the SCS added the "other" category, there is no convincing proof that deterioration of range condition had occurred. Presumably the SCS might have classified rangeland having introduced species of vegetation as excellent or good instead of as "other." The northern Great Plains had the highest proportion of range rated as excellent or good, with more than 64 percent included in the two classes.

The 1984–1987 Bureau of Land Management study. This BLM study showed an increase for land in the "unclassified or unsuitable" class and only minor changes in the other categories (table 4-9). "Unclassified" meant that the BLM did not have the time or resources to classify all of its land in a given year. The question is, what class would "unclassified" land have fallen into had it been classified? Assuming that the

increase in the observed "unclassified or unsuitable" category represents an increase in the quantity of land that the bureau simply did not measure, it might be reasonable to assume also that the land would be representative of all BLM land. Thus the "unclassified" land could be distributed on a proportionate basis throughout the other categories if comparability between years were desired.

However, land appeared to be "unsuitable" as a result of "physical and ecological limitations or because certain lands presently grazed will be designated for other priority uses" (U.S. Department of the Interior, 1975). If land was unsuitable because it was or would be used for purposes other than grazing or was inaccessible to grazing, then it may well have represented all BLM land and should be distributed proportionately over the other condition categories. However, if land that was "physically" or "ecologically" limited was rated "unsuitable" because it was too poor to graze economically, then the bureau probably would have classified it as being in poor condition. Perhaps the best assumption (certainly a conservative one for avoiding upward bias in range condition through time) is that these "unclassified" and "unsuitable" lands should be grouped with land in the poor and bad condition categories, which was done in the study comparisons that follow.

Comparison of public domain land studies, 1934–1987. A comparison of the studies conducted from 1934 to 1987 reveals that the percentage of BLM land classified as excellent and good was higher in the 1980s than in earlier periods (table 4-10). For land classified as poor, bad, unclassified or unsuitable, the percentages were sharply down from the 1936 figures. Even discounting the reliability of the 1936 data, BLM-administered rangeland still showed improvements in condition from the 1960s to the 1980s.

Table 4-9. Percentage of Bureau of Land Management Range Acreage by Condition Class, 1984–1987

Year	Condition class				
	Excellent	Good	Fair	Poor	Unclassified or unsuitable
1984	5	31	42	18	4
1985	4	31	42	17	6
1986	4	30	41	18	7
1987	3	30	39	19	9

Source: U.S. Department of the Interior (n.d.a.).

However, the quality and lack of comparability of the various studies are unsettling. The Bureau of Land Management did not randomly select small areas to be studied through time. Instead, it collected data needed to meet the requirements of the environmental impact analyses required by the National Environmental Policy Act of 1969 on certain allotments. This is not to say that these data are of no value or were not estimated as carefully as circumstances and resources permitted. But they were not measured in accordance with the best scientific practices known to the range management profession, simply because of time and financial constraints. Box (1990) shares these misgivings. He considered it alarming that the condition of more than one-fourth of the nation's rangeland, public and private, is simply unknown. These conclusions are strongly supported by a recent study by the U.S. General Accounting Office (GAO) (U.S. General Accounting Office, 1988b) for Congress.

The General Accounting Office studies. In one study reported in 1988, the General Accounting Office (U.S. General Accounting Office, 1988b) surveyed nearly 800 range managers from the Forest Service and the Bureau of Land Management to obtain data on range condition. Although both agencies are required by law to maintain a current inventory on range condition and trend, the GAO discovered that much of the data in both agencies' inventories were more than five years old and probably did not represent current conditions. Agency officials openly took the position that data on public range condition and trends may be unreliable because the agencies lack the staff resources needed to adequately monitor the condition of the vast amount of public range they manage. (Federally owned rangeland is divided into 31,000 livestock grazing allotments covering 268 million acres. The average allotment is more than 8,500 acres in size—about 13 square miles.)

What the GAO found most disturbing was that neither the BLM nor the Forest Service was concentrating its management attention or range improvement resources on those grazing allotments that their range managers believed were threatened with further deterioration. The most recent reports of the Forest Service and the BLM showed that more than 50 percent of the public rangeland remained in either poor or fair condition, a finding roughly similar to the findings of earlier studies. Moreover, the GAO survey of the professional opinions of range managers showed that they believed that 19 percent of BLM and Forest Service grazing allotments may be threatened with further damage because authorized livestock grazing levels were higher than the land could support. The survey also revealed that the condition of about 8

Table 4-10. Percentage of BLM Range Acreage in Three Condition Classes, Various Years, 1936–1987

	Condition class		
Year	Excellent or good	Fair	Poor, bad, unclassified, or unsuitable
1936[a]	1.5	14.3	84.2
1961[b]	16.6	53.1	30.3
1966[b]	18.9	51.6	29.5
1972[b]	17.6	50.0	32.4
1975	17.0	50.0	33.0
1984[c]	36.0	42.0	22.0
1985[c]	35.0	42.0	23.0
1986[c]	34.0	41.0	25.0
1987[c]	33.0	39.0	28.0

Sources: U.S. Congress (1936), Pacific Consultants (1970), U.S. Department of Agriculture (1972, 1984), U.S. Department of the Interior (n.d.a, 1975).

[a]Box (1990) reported that range condition classes were not reported as found in this table but were inferred based on the reported depletion.

[b]Box (1990) indicated that the database for these estimates includex all federal ranges; other estimates, except for the 1936 study, only include BLM land.

[c]These estimates do not include a classification "bad." These inventories include a new classification, "unclassified or unsuitable."

percent of the grazing units was actually declining, a figure that seems inconsistent with responses by field managers that about 18 percent of the BLM allotments and 21 percent of Forest Service allotments are overstocked. One might assume that overstocked ranges would be in deteriorating condition. This does not necessarily follow, however, because overstocking may simply prevent deteriorated range from recovering rather than causing additional decline.

The range managers explained to the GAO that they did not schedule adjustments to the authorized livestock grazing levels in 75 percent of these cases for a number of reasons. One reason was insufficient data. Because most grazing reductions are challenged by range users, often in adversarial hearings, public range managers are wary about making cuts unless they have sufficient data to make a persuasive case. Other reasons included permittee resistance, outside political climate, agency political climate, pending range improvements, and nonuse of allowable AUMs by permittees (U.S. Government Accounting Office, 1988b).

Another finding the GAO analysts found disturbing was that many of the range improvements that were funded by the BLM and the Forest Service were made on grazing allotments with low usage and stable-to-improving range trends. At the same time, projects proposed for overused and declining allotments remained unfunded. The criteria for selecting which range improvements to fund included factors such as

A survey of agency personnel, primarily in the BLM, revealed that those personnel do not believe their work will be supported by agency management if it is opposed by ranchers who use the public rangeland.

benefit-cost analysis, but neither agency emphasized funding for projects on declining and overstocked allotments. The GAO recommended that both the BLM and the Forest Service focus attention on those allotments that are overstocked or are declining when conducting the assessments needed to establish appropriate grazing levels, to plan funding for range improvement projects, and to develop allotment management plans. This recommendation is yet another example of the "worst first" investment strategy that is of questionable validity. Indeed, it is quite probable that the most unproductive allotments are those that will respond least to investment in range improvement, because areas of low condition are often the most fragile and the least responsive to treatment. Even critical land, such as riparian land, should be evaluated in terms of its responsiveness to improvement practices. This is precisely what the BLM currently is attempting to do under a classification system in which the bureau prioritizes allotments according to their improvement potential (U.S. Department of the Interior, 1982a, 1982b).

In another study (U.S. General Accounting Office, 1988a), the GAO examined the trend and condition of riparian rangeland. Many public resource managers believe that conflict over the management of the riparian zones of rangeland is a potentially explosive issue (Prouty, 1987). More than 90,000 miles of streams and rivers, providing 3 million acres of riparian habitat, are administered by the Forest Service and the BLM alone. Although riparian areas represent only 1 percent of the more than 250 million acres of federally owned rangeland, they are of critical importance because

they provide food, water, shade, and cover for fish and wildlife and forage for both wild and domestic grazing animals. They remove sediment from the water flowing through them, act as sponges to hold water in streambanks to provide a higher water table and a more stable stream flow, and help dissipate the energy of flood waters. The riparian areas also provide many recreational opportunities. (U.S. General Accounting Office, 1988a, p. 2)

Riparian land is especially vulnerable to despoliation because grazing livestock tend to congregate in the riparian areas, overgraze the vegetation, and trample the streambanks (U.S. General Accounting Office, 1988a). Such potentially destructive use can affect other beneficial uses provided by both riparian and nonriparian areas.

Table 4-11. Summary of Range Conditions and Trends for Public and Private Land, 1989

Range condition	Agency lands covered (percentage)		
	Forest Service[a]	Bureau of Land Management[b]	Soil Conservation Service[c]
Excellent or potential natural community	3	4	4
Good or late seral	36	30	30
Fair or midseral	44	41	45
Poor or early seral	16	18	16
Other		7	5
Trend			
Upward	43	15	16
Downward	13	14	14
Static	43	64	70
Undetermined		6	

Source: Society for Range Management (1989).

Note: Columns may not total 100 percent because of rounding.

[a]Figures are for public forestland administered by the Forest Service.

[b]Figures are for public land administered by the Bureau of Land Management.

[c]Figures are for private land surveyed by the Soil Conservation Service.

The GAO study reported in 1988 revealed that over the past twenty years the BLM and the Forest Service had restored a number of degraded riparian areas on the public rangeland in the West, primarily by improving livestock management, which implies that there are no technical barriers to improving riparian areas and that better management will go a long way toward improving all riparian areas on federal rangeland. Despite these successes, however, the GAO observers estimate that much more needs to be done. They are not confident that the pace of improvement will be rapid in light of a survey of agency personnel, primarily in the BLM, which revealed that those personnel do not believe their work will be supported by agency management if it is opposed by ranchers who use the public rangeland. The key to rancher cooperation and support appears to be the management of livestock through the use of fencing and herding until the vegetation can be restored. The GAO found that although an increasing number of ranchers accept the benefits of healthy riparian areas, many continue to oppose restoration initiatives.

What was conspicuously missing in the GAO study, however, was any indication that land restoration or improvement of riparian zones is economically feasible. An implicit assumption seemed to be that some land should be improved regardless of the costs and benefits. Riparian areas may be scarce and valuable, but capital needed for restoration is also scarce and has valuable alternatives. All investment resources proposed for riparian improvement, like those for all grazing lands, should pass a rigorous benefit-cost analysis before being allocated and spent.

The Society for Range Management study. The best and most recent data on ecological status, condition, and trend of U.S. rangeland, according to a special committee of the Society for Range Management, are presented in a report prepared by that committee (Society for Range Management, 1989). The report, which used data obtained from the Forest Service, the BLM, and the SCS, does not evaluate or interpret current conditions, but serves as a baseline on which to base future range condition surveys and perhaps to point out where agency procedures could be better integrated (table 4-11).

The study admits some weaknesses. For example, large acreages of rangeland are not represented in the report, some data are as much as twenty years old and do not necessarily reflect current conditions, and the data reflect only ecological status or range condition in relation to climax or potential natural plant community for a given site, along with the trend toward or away from that composition of vegetation. Thus the information does not describe the ability of rangeland to support specific uses, produce goods and services, or describe its impact on other resource values. This last limitation is significant given the discussion of optimum range condition that stresses the importance of relating condition and trend to actual and intended use. Moreover, the results reported are strikingly similar to those found in earlier studies. The report did not develop new data, nor did it use new evaluation procedures. The similarity may imply that the reliability of those earlier studies is better than is often alleged.

CONTEMPORARY RANGELAND PROFESSIONALS' OPINIONS ON CONDITION AND TREND

As the data from formal range condition studies are inconclusive and therefore are widely debated and questioned, perhaps the opinions of range professionals on range condition and trend might have merit. No effort has been made to take a scientific sample, but neither have opinions been chosen for their particular points of view.

Marion Clawson, a former director of the Bureau of Land Management, has been an astute observer of western rangeland for more than half a century. Although he believes that scientific proof is scant, Clawson contends that on the whole western rangeland is in better condition today than at any time during the twentieth century (Clawson, personal communication to the author, May 1989). Box (1990) essentially agrees with Clawson. Box believes that the worst despoliation of the range occurred shortly after the Europeans settled the West. He argues that with the establishment of grazing regulations in 1905, the national forest rangeland improved and continues to improve to the present. Box is careful, however, to qualify such statements with the caveat that more range improvement is desirable. Most ranges are still producing far less than their potential (even when potential is reckoned in terms of highest valued use rather than ecological climax) and will require treatment to reach their potential.

Box also argues that the public domain land administered by the BLM did not improve as rapidly as the forest rangeland because the public domain land is more arid, and because grazing control was not instituted until the 1930s. He and others find that the condition of these arid ranges is variable, and that as a whole they are producing less than half their biological potential (Box, Dwyer, and Wagner, n.d.).

The higher the fee revenues, the more can be dispersed to counties and states, a visible and politically popular practice.

Like Clawson and Box, Renner (1954) observed marked improvement in range conditions throughout almost all of the seventeen western states during the period he studied, which was from 1928, when vast areas of private range were eroded, overgrazed, and depleted, to 1953. Moreover, Cholis (1952) has suggested that recent range condition in the Northwest is superior to that existing at the turn of the century. For example, he indicates that grazing areas in Washington state have improved because

> (1) the ranges have been brought under control through extension of private ownership and fencing, (2) the homeless horse has become a rare sight on Washington ranges, and (3) the conviction on the part of stockmen that the responsibility for the proper use of land under their control rests in their hands, and that better management pays off. (Cholis, 1952, p. 134)

Likewise, Branson (1985), in one of the most comprehensive surveys of vegetation changes on western rangeland, has indicated that the ranges that had undergone drastic deterioration late in the nineteenth century and into the twentieth century had improved recently, especially in the West. He attributes some improvement in range condition during the moist years that followed 1960 to better range management practices (such as grazing in the proper season and with proper intensity), better livestock distribution, control of undesirable species, and land-surface modification to retain soil moisture for forage production. However, Branson finds that some of the changes have been undesirable but appear to be irreversible. For example, creosote bush has replaced grass, and topsoil has been lost to erosion in many areas of the arid Southwest. He also concludes that pristine conditions in the Great Basin cannot be restored, even if domestic animals are removed. Instead, a balance between grasses and shrubs is the best that can be done to stabilize the plant communities (Branson, 1985).

Not all observers agree that range condition is improving. The Comptroller General of the United States (1977), in a report to Congress, has observed that the nation's public rangeland is deteriorating and not improving primarily because of poorly managed livestock grazing. And the environmental community has strongly condemned overgrazing, although it has never produced convincing proof that overgrazing is creating deteriorating range conditions.

Bias in Assessing Range Condition and Trend

Some critics of the 1936 western range report have alleged that it was politically motivated and thus the results are somewhat suspect. The same could well be true of many of the other reports. This credibility problem would likely be most severe if the studies were made by the same agency that manages and administers the rangeland studied.

The direction of the bias may not always be obvious, however. On the one hand, agency employees may desire to show that their stewardship of the resources has been exemplary, thus producing the possibility of an upward bias in range condition estimates—which is the allegation levied at the 1936 report. On the other hand, in the competition for budget for range administration, management, and improvement, incentives could exist for understating range condition in order to make a stronger case for larger budgets. Moreover, agency analysts may encounter pressure to respond to the signals coming from higher echelons of government. An administration that gives environmental issues high priority may expect employees to be more sympathetic to environmental interests and thus to overstate range depletion in order to strengthen the case for the lowering of stocking rates; if the administration apparently favors commodity interests, the direction of bias would be reversed.

The practices of sharing user fees with local and state governments and also using a portion of the fees for range improvements, both required by law, may likewise bias assessments of range condition. The higher the fee revenues, the more can be dispersed to counties and states, a visible and politically popular practice. Thus, because grazing fees are determined by the number of permitted animals, local government officials might wish to permit higher numbers of grazing animals, which would in turn anticipate higher levels of range condition.

Like the agencies, user groups are not free of bias. Because the physiological relationships between livestock and wildlife grazing are complex, one frequent critical issue is the type of vegetative cover on the rangeland. In most cases, livestock and wildlife compete for forage only over a limited range. Cattle and wild horses, for example, are primarily grass foragers; deer and elk prefer shrubs and browse (Wagner, 1978). Thus livestock producers would opt for more grass production, whereas those people more interested in game animals might desire less grass and more shrub production. The result is a continual tug-of-war between competing interests, with the range condition issue becoming part of the battleground. Each side has incentives to show overgrazing by the other so that government agencies could be pressured to shift the available forage in the direction of the favored use.

These different perspectives are evident from Bureau of Land Management data collected in the 1975 BLM report (U.S. Department of the Interior, 1975). The bureau had asked concerned parties throughout the western United States to respond to questions

Livestock producers would opt for more grass production, whereas those people more interested in game animals might desire less grass and more shrub production.

such as: "What is your assessment of range condition on BLM lands in your state for wild horses and burros, watershed, wildlife, aesthetics, etc.?" Respondents from the livestock industry rated range condition and trend significantly higher than did respondents from environmental groups (table 4-12). Officials from state and county governments were also more positive than were federal officials, who were the most negative of all. It might have been interesting to survey the opinions of professional range scientists, including those in the universities. A conjecture would be that they would point out how little people know about range condition, and thus how critical the need is for public funds to support the research to find a more definitive answer.

To give range management a more scientific basis and focus, the Society for Range Management was established in 1948; it was initially called the American Society of Range Management (Rowley, 1985). Generally, the membership was made up of forestry and range professionals in government, university faculties, and people working in the private sector (Culhane, 1981). The membership has gradually expanded to include range professionals from many nations. The society disseminates the results of range research through the *Journal of Range Management* and *Rangelands*, and in the conferences and symposia it sponsors.

Developments in Range Policy

The federal agencies managing public land and livestock permittees became involved in bitter disputes in the period after World War II. The Forest Service was convinced that it needed to make grazing cuts to restore the range to satisfactory condition. Permittees reacted negatively, arguing that Forest Service data were unconvincing in showing that overgrazing was occurring. They believed that the agency was unjustifiably caving in to pressures for reduced livestock grazing brought by environmentalists and conservationists. Members of Congress from the western states actively challenged the actions of the agencies on behalf of these rancher constituencies (Rowley, 1985; Dana and Fairfax, 1980). For the most part the agencies stood firm against any proposals to weaken their authority over the administration of grazing land, but they did occasionally bow to political expedience. For example, to reduce grazing, federal agencies began to cut the quantity of permitted AUMs when the permit was transferred from one eligible permittee to another, rather than to cut all permits proportionately (Rowley, 1985). This policy impeded transfers to more efficient permittees because the transferee would get fewer AUMs than were originally allotted to the person who transferred, thus increasing the costs of transfer.

Table 4-12. Percentage of Respondents Giving Positive and Negative Assessments of Public Land Range Condition, by Interest Group, 1975

Interest group	Percentage of respondents making assessments[a]							
	1	2	3	4	5	6	7	8
Livestock ($n = 54$)	35	20	26	2	7	0	6	4
Environmental ($n = 55$)	9	62	7	4	0	0	16	2
Federal government ($n = 8$)	0	63	0	13	0	0	25	0
State government ($n = 16$)	31	25	19	0	6	6	13	0
County government ($n = 11$)	64	27	9	0	0	0	0	0
District advisory ($n = 26$)	54	0	23	0	8	0	0	15
State advisory ($n = 2$)	50	50	0	0	0	0	0	0
Others ($n = 26$)	12	65	12	0	4	8	0	0
All groups ($n = 198$)	27	38	16	2	4	2	7	4
Livestock and advisory boards ($n = 82$)	41	15	24	1	7	0	4	7

Source: U.S. Department of the Interior (1975).

Note: Rows may not total 100 percent because of rounding.

[a] 1, positive statement concerning range condition; 2, negative statement concerning range condition; 3, range condition has improved; 4, range condition has deteriorated; 5, positive statement, and condition has improved; 6, negative statement, and condition has improved; 7, range condition varies; 8, range condition is temporarily low as a result of drought. No Bureau of Land Management employees were included in the sample.

The acquisition of 4 million acres of national grassland by the Forest Service in 1954 had a salutary effect on federal rangeland policy. This grassland, formerly administered by the Soil Conservation Service, had originally been acquired under the New Deal Agricultural Adjustment Administration program to purchase submarginal farmland during the Great Depression. Although some of that land became national forests, the government designated some of the best rangeland as national grassland. Other land was transferred to the Bureau of Land Management and the Fish and Wildlife Service (Rowley, 1985). When the SCS had administered the grassland, its focus had been to induce better management on private land as a precondition for ranchers receiving leases on public grassland. The program called for private and public land to be managed together as a unit, and better overall range productivity probably resulted from this policy. After the transfer of this land to the Forest Service, SCS officials criticized Forest Service regulatory policies as being inferior to theirs. Rowley (1985) has argued that it is likely that SCS management philosophy influenced the Forest Service, and that the acquisition of the grassland was important in getting the Forest Service to return to its original mission of those promoting the health and economic welfare of those communities that depend on federal resources.

Rangeland policy underwent a major shift toward conservation during the 1960s (Dana and Fairfax, 1980). Congress passed the Multiple-Use, Sustained-Yield Act of 1960, which dictated the goal of using rangeland for its highest economic uses, but always with a view to maintain yield and the basic productivity of range resources. Agency planning procedures emphasized range improvements and cooperation with user groups (Rowley, 1985).

During the 1970s and 1980s, environmental groups, rather than the ranchers, became highly critical of the policies of federal rangeland management agencies. In several court cases, environmental and conservation groups argued that livestock grazing should be cut and that grazing fees be raised (Huffaker and Gardner, 1987). Mainly, but not entirely, in response to pressure from these groups, Congress passed the Federal Land Policy and Management Act of 1976, which provided funding for environmental impact statements on livestock grazing allotments, a new grazing-fee study, a range-betterment fund, and more secure tenure for livestock permittees.

> *During the 1970s and 1980s, environmental groups, rather than the ranchers, became highly critical of the policies of federal rangeland management agencies.*

Congress also initiated an "experimental stewardship program" through the Public Rangelands Improvement Act of 1978. This act led federal agencies to establish cooperative management agreements, which gave selected "exemplary" permittees more automony in setting stocking rates and managing their allotments. A federal court in California, however, ruled that the agreements violated earlier statutes, such as the Federal Land Policy and Management Act of 1976, and had to be abandoned (Huffaker and Gardner, 1987). Unless this ruling is overturned or new ways can be found to implement the goals of the experimental stewardship program, it appears that the program is moribund. The Public Rangelands Improvement Act of 1978 also described a formula for establishing grazing fees by requiring that the fees fluctuate around a designated base according to changes in beef prices, a cost-of-production index, and a factor that represents the market prices for comparable private forage (Clawson, 1983; Gardner, 1989).

Overall, government policies in the past have subsidized agricultural production, and the increase in cropland has tended to reduce the acreage in rangeland. On the other hand, price-support policies often have been accompanied by acreage set-asides from crop production that have increased acreage in fallow or other restricted uses, thus increasing the rangeland base. An excellent example is provided by the Food Security Act of 1985. In addition to the conventional acreage set-asides of 15 to 25 percent of base acreage (depending on the supported crop), the act made discretionary cropland removal available to the secretary of agriculture. Other programs in the act that have directly affected the acreage in rangeland are "sodbuster" and "swampbuster" provisions and the Conservation Reserve Program (CRP). If farmers grow crops on land designated as "wetland" (swampbusting) or plow soils that are designated as highly erodible (sodbusting), they are ineligible to receive the deficiency payments and other benefits as provided by law. The penalties are so severe that farmers are indeed complying with these provisions, thus impeding the conversion of highly erodible rangeland and wetland to crop production, and the provisions have become unpopular in the agricultural community. The Food, Agriculture, Conservation, and Trade Act of 1990 for the most part extends the provisions of the 1985 act, but gives more emphasis to the preservation of wetlands.

The Conservation Reserve Program, on the other hand, offers incentives for landowners to convert acreage of highly erodible cropland into grassland or forestland on a long-term basis. An important precursor to the Conservation Reserve Program was the Soil Bank, administered during the Dwight D. Eisenhower presidency in the 1950s. The Soil Bank took entire farms out of production of subsidized crops and placed them in conservation uses. The acreage in the Soil Bank program reached a peak during 1960, when the government placed approximately 5 percent of cropland (nearly 28.7 million acres) into the bank (U.S. Department of Agriculture, 1963). Creators of the CRP hope to enroll 40 million acres overall, with 4 million acres planted to trees (Joyce, 1989). Contracts are fashioned between the government and farmers who make a successful "rental" bid to place their land in the program. The government pays the rent if the bid is accepted and, in addition, pays half

the cost of the investment necessary to establish the plant cover in grass or trees. For ten years, the usual length of a contract, the farmers cannot graze permanent vegetative cover, except when authorized by the secretary of agriculture in a drought or emergency, such as occurred during the summer drought in 1988.

At present, the greatest acreage enrollment in the CRP is in the southern Great Plains region, which includes Colorado, New Mexico, Oklahoma, Kansas, and Texas. This region also is noted for great variability of forage production from year to year. That this region has such a large enrollment is apparently confirmation of the prevalent view that farmers will use the Conservation Reserve Program to take out of production the least efficient and most risky land rather than the land that is the most erodible, thus frustrating the real purpose of the program (Phipps, Crosson, and Price, 1986). The clear inference of this discussion is that the CRP and other programs have significantly affected the acreage in rangeland as well as its productivity.

Many public policy issues will continue to fester in the years and decades ahead. The public land states of the West will continue to feel cheated because of the perception that local economies do not benefit sufficiently from federal ownership of such a large fraction of the land in these states. In addition, they will continue to press for increased emoluments from the federal government in lieu of taxes that they believe would have been collected if land ownership were transferred to the states or privatized. Moreover, preservation and conservation organizations will continue to assert that the federal management agencies have been captured by commodity interests, and commodity organizations will counter that they are being run over by the environmentalists in agency decisions and court actions.

Many public policy issues will continue to fester in the years and decades ahead.

Land Ownership and Range Condition

Transferring land ownership from the federal government to the states or to private owners was the thrust of land policy in the United States for 150 years, and many people believe that the policy should have continued, thus stirring a lively controversy over the relationship between range condition and land ownership. Even the Taylor Grazing Act of 1934 implied that the time would come when the public domain would be disposed of, presumably to private owners (Dana and Fairfax, 1980).

Congress attempted to settle the ownership and management issue by passing the Federal Land Policy and Management Act of 1976. That act formally required the Bureau of Land Management to manage the public domain under the principles of multiple use and sustained yield. "It also granted [the bureau] new authorities and responsibilities, amended or repealed previous legislation, prescribed specific management techniques, and established BLM's California Desert Conservation Area. [The bureau] was now in the big leagues" (Muhn and Stuart, 1988, p. 158). However, the BLM and the nation were to learn that the issue was far from settled. The "sagebrush rebellion" of the late 1970s was a challenge to continuing federal ownership of land and energy resources (Muhn and Stuart, 1988). Led by Nevada, many western states proposed the transfer of federal land to the states (LeBaron and coauthors, 1980). Partly, the ownership issue was and remains a question of who captures the economic profits from natural resources, especially energy and mineral resources. The issue also is partly a question of who has the competence to manage resources most efficiently (Gardner, 1983). Is the federal government a less effective steward of rangeland than the states or private ranchers would be? Only a few comparative studies of range conditions under different ownership patterns have shed much light on the issue.

One such study, conducted by Loring and Workman (1987), sampled a representative county in Utah to evaluate range conditions on seven range sites comprising the majority of acreage within the sagebrush-grass ecosystem. The researchers used SCS climax composition guides as the basis for rating range condition. They found that land managed by the Forest Service had significantly higher range condition ratings than land managed by the BLM and the State of Utah. Private rangeland also was in higher condition than BLM land, and tended to be in higher condition than state land, but the differences were not statistically significant. In addition, expenditures for range improvement generally followed the rankings on range condition; that is, those in the best condition received more improvements. The researchers concluded that the level of management effort may be more important to producing a high level of range condition than who happens to hold the property rights to the land.

The "sagebrush rebellion" of the late 1970s was a challenge to continuing federal ownership of land and energy resources.

A study by Young and Sparks (1985) suggested that private landowners might be more effective. They cite as evidence two areas of Nevada—a block of land on Golliher Mountain and St. John's field, north of Battle Mountain. Since the nineteenth century, private landowners have managed both areas, which are "examples of near-pristine sagebrush/grasslands" (p. 233). However, Young and Sparks added that the condition of these ranges does not imply that private ownership would have improved the range condition of other regions as well. Clawson (personal communication to the author, May 1989), who also is familiar with the two areas, has observed that some federal ranges have been managed well but that other ranges also have been productive because they were privately owned. He suggests that in many cases "land disposal in large blocks at reasonable prices would have enabled the building of private landholdings on which economically efficient and environmentally conservative range management could have been practiced."

Among the most severe critics of public management of rangeland resources, Libecap (1981) has suggested that the current institutional arrangement for managing federal rangeland is flawed because its basis is bureaucratically assigned use rights. Such rights, he argues, encourage the government to use land inefficiently because bureaucrats do not hold property rights to the ranges; they do not pay the costs or receive the benefits. Thus the bureaucrats can ignore market signals and carry out socially wasteful land management policies. Moreover, the rights assigned to ranchers are tenuous because the government reallocates rangeland and changes use privileges to meet

Heavily utilized rangeland toward the end of the grazing season

changing political conditions. Evidence of this flawed management is in the decline, since the 1970s, of ranch sales prices, which include the appraisal values of BLM grazing permits. Government policies and uncertainty about future range conditions have caused prospective buyers to discount the value of BLM grazing land. Moreover, conflict between ranchers and BLM officials appears to have resulted in reduced investment in land improvements.

Bureaucrats and scientists who are in federal employment, according to Baden and Dana (1987), are subject to self-interest as well as to political pressures. "As bureaucrats, scientists who become policymakers lack the accountability for their decisions that is held by residual claimants in the private sector; they incur no direct costs or benefits from the policies they implement" (Baden and Dana, 1987, p. 6). In addition, government bureaucrats view the taxpayers' general fund as a common pool resource that they can exploit (Fort and Baden, 1981). Baden and Dana (1987) suggest that without accountability for costly decisions, few incentives in government will inspire sensitivity to economic efficiency. Clawson (1983) has suggested that some of the private users of federal land may practice better planning and more effective management for the long-run productivity of the land than do their federal agency counterparts. The ability of private corporations to commit funds is greater than the federal agencies' ability to guarantee long-run appropriations. "This fully offsets any greater devotion to the general welfare which agency personnel may have" (Clawson, 1983, p. 12).

For the time being at least, the sagebrush rebellion has died down, and continuing federal ownership of the public domain seems not to be a burning political issue.

Prospects for Range Improvement

A broad consensus seems to exist that western rangeland is producing at levels below its biological potential. Range condition data show that the great bulk of the acreage in rangeland is in less than excellent condition. Daugherty (1989) points out, however, that range condition classes are not measures of current productivity and probably cannot reveal much about improvement potential. For example, an area with a low proportion of natural climax vegetation (and thus a "low" class of range condition) may have a high proportion of an introduced forage species and may be quite productive. Nevertheless, if the potential of ecosystems in the Southwest could be realized, according to Herbel (1984), the area could support 450 percent of the AUMs of grazing now harvested.

New technology and management practices exist that could help increase rangeland productivity (Joyce, 1989). However, just because technology is available does not mean that it is economically feasible and should be implemented, as many observers recommend (among them, Box, 1984; Joyce, 1989; and U.S. General Accounting Office, 1988a, 1988b). Surely economic feasibility is an important if not the dominant factor determining whether ranges should be improved. After all, societal wealth will be diminished if the federal government uses scarce capital and labor resources to improve rangeland when this capital and labor have more productive uses elsewhere in the economy. It is true that Congress may make funds available for infeasible improvements (it happens all the time), but Americans will not be wealthier if these projects are implemented.

Critics of a benefit-cost test say that it may be inappropriate because many social values derived from range improvement cannot be evaluated in the economic or monetary terms required by the test. This point of view is of doubtful validity. True, some products from rangeland are not allocated in markets where values can be represented by market prices, but economists have been creative in finding evaluation techniques that enable monetization of so-called nonmarket "collective" goods, such as water and air quality, open space, and aesthetic beauty. Examples of such techniques are travel cost, hedonic price, and contingent valuation methods (Dyer, 1984; Bishop and Heberlein, 1979; Clawson 1959; Mitchell and Carson, 1989). Doing the best job possible to evaluate all relevant benefits and costs in a rigorous analysis, even if only rough estimates are possible, is likely to produce more efficient resource allocation than proceeding without the discipline of a benefit-cost test. Using political rather than economic criteria to allocate resources opens the door to special-interest pleading and pressure that will waste resources and lower average standards of living (Gardner, 1983).

TECHNIQUES FOR RANGE IMPROVEMENT

Several techniques exist to improve range condition. Among these are

(1) rehabilitation of range by seeding desirable species and controlling undesirable plants and shrubs, (2) construction of needed livestock control and handling facilities such as fences, (3) development of additional water supplies, (4) improvement of grazing systems and livestock management practices, and (5) decreased erosion (Darr, n.d., p. 82).

Through implementation of such techniques, productivity of private rangeland is expected to increase by 0.7 percent per year for the 1987–2040 period (Joyce 1989). Approximately 150 technological advancements exist that potentially could increase agricultural and livestock production. Examples of these technologies include better methods to control livestock pests and diseases, genetic engineering, gene splicing, superovulation, growth-inducing hormones, and improvements in animal nutrition. Assuming that market and other incentives will lead to the adoption of this technology by 2040, forage production per acre is projected to increase by 47 percent compared with 1985 levels (Joyce, 1989).

Such a projection is problematic, however. A lack of technology for improving ranges has not been a barrier

A broad consensus seems to exist that western rangeland is producing at levels below its biological potential.

to improvement for at least the past fifty years. Rather, the problem has been a lack of demonstrated economic feasibility; that is, an excess of benefits over costs.

ECONOMIC FEASIBILITY OF RANGE IMPROVEMENT

Evidence on the economic feasibility of range improvement must be appraised carefully (Workman, 1984). Gardner (1963) has shown that most of the differences in rates of return to range improvement investment reported in several studies of the West were attributable primarily to differences in the analytical techniques the researchers used rather than to real increases in forage output produced by the investment. Some studies (Gardner, 1962a) have shown improvement to be economically feasible, on both public and private land, but others, including more recent studies on public land (Nelson, 1984; Pope and Wagstaff, 1987; Ferguson and Ferguson, 1983), have suggested that such improvement would be infeasible.

FUNDING FOR RANGE IMPROVEMENT

The funding for range improvement on private land depends on the ranchers themselves and those who finance them. If the benefits expected from investment in range improvement can be shown by the landowner to be profitable, sufficient capital would appear to be available from the private capital markets, the farm credit system, and various conservation funds available in government programs. If, however, "public" benefits—such as for wildlife habitat—are produced by increased range productivity, and are not captured by the private landowner, a case can be made for public subsidy to encourage the optimal investment. The subsidy could be accomplished by tax relief or direct payments for specified improvement practices (Box, 1978). Often, however, government programs open the way for special-interest influence and inefficient and uncontrolled government spending.

Raising capital for range improvements on public land is a more complex problem. Until recently, federal agencies have been openly hostile to the use of private monies to finance improvements to grazing allotments on public land (Rowley, 1985). Even though private funds may have been needed to augment public funds to improve depleted allotments, officials apparently believed that such investment would give the permittees property rights that would interfere with government management and control (Gardner, 1984). Thus the federal public land agencies obtained their capital resources from user fees (such as grazing fees), sales of products (such as timber), or budget appropriations (Clawson and Held, 1957). A GAO (1988b) study found that under the experimental stewardship program federal funding for range improvements on grazing allotments has been significantly higher than federal funding for allotments not in the program, but that this funding increase has not been correspondingly matched by contributions from the permittee.

If public funds were sufficient to generate an "efficient" level of range improvements, private investment would not be required (Gardner, 1984). The Federal Land Policy and Management Act of 1976 dictated that one-half of all grazing fees collected by the government be earmarked for range improvements. Half of these "range betterment" funds are returned to the district or region where they were generated; the other half may be used anywhere on the public land for range rehabilitation, at the discretion of the secretaries of the Interior and Agriculture departments. In the absence of feasibility analyses, however, it is unclear whether such funds can generate the economically efficient level of range improvements.

Continuing Competition for Land Resources

Competition for use of rangeland is increasing. Over time, competing uses such as urban development, transportation, national defense, wildlife protection, wilderness, and recreation slowly but steadily reduce

The most rapid increase in nonagricultural uses of rangeland has been for rural parks and wildlife refuges.

the acreage in rangeland. The impacts from other competing uses fluctuate from year to year and decade to decade, as when rangeland moves in and out of cropland and forest as prices, costs, and public policies that influence land use change.

Historically, pasture and rangeland together have constituted the second largest use of land in the United States after cropland. Pasture and rangeland use declined only about 4 percent from 1954 to 1982 (Joyce, 1989). The most rapid increase in nonagricultural uses of rangeland has been for rural parks and wildlife refuges. In 1982, national and state parks and related areas included a total of 116 million acres of rangeland, and federal and state wildlife agencies administered an additional 95 million acres (Joyce, 1989). Cropland acreage used for pasture, however, was small compared with the pasture and rangeland total: 65 million versus 598 million acres (Frey and Hexem, 1985). Cropland used for pasture fluctuated from a low of 57 million acres in 1964 to a high of 88 million acres in 1969, but by 1982 only 65 million acres of cropland were used for pastures. These figures correlate closely with the governmental acreage set-asides implemented to cope with crop surpluses resulting from subsidized support prices.

What, then, are the prospects for American rangeland in the face of increasing competition? Rangeland acreage recently has declined for a number of reasons (Joyce, 1989). The profitable wheat industry has encouraged ranchers to diversify, in light of a depressed cattle industry, by including wheat production in their operations. Ranchers with cash flow problems have been forced to sell some or all of their grazing land. Because credit may be available for the purchase of cropland but not rangeland, lending institutions are pressuring ranchers to convert rangeland to cropland. The incentives of government farm programs, as well as income tax provisions, similarly encourage ranchers to convert their land. And advances in irrigation and other technology make it profitable to crop semiarid land (Joyce, 1989).

Nevertheless, the USDA Economic Research Service projects that pasture and rangeland areas will increase slightly up to the year 2040. Demand for cropland is expected to fall, primarily because of reduced agricultural exports, increased efficiencies in growing and producing feed grains, and increased efficiencies in feeding livestock (Joyce, 1989).

The widespread concern of the environmental community over the plowing of "fragile" rangeland

> *The USDA Economic Research Service projects that pasture and rangeland areas will increase slightly up to the year 2040.*

has prompted close monitoring of rangeland/cropland conversions. In the Great Plains, cropland in production in previous decades was found to be greater than cropland currently in production. Frey (1983) has suggested that if acreage control programs had not been in place, even more counties would have had record acres in crop production during the period of high farm prices in the 1970s. The conditions that were favorable to conversion to cropland during the 1975–1981 period, however, are not likely to recur in the immediate future because of less favorable cost/price relationships since 1981, the acreage set-asides mandated by recent farm legislation, and changes in the federal tax code that eliminate investment tax credits and capital gains exclusions and that alter land development cost deductions (Heimlich, 1985; Hexem and Krupa, 1987).

Beyond these factors, many scientists believe that the United States is on the threshold of a revolution in biotechnology that will greatly increase yields and thus reduce the demand for cropland and perhaps even for rangeland. The economic feasibility of this technology needs to be determined, and regulatory approval obtained. Obviously, any such projections are subject to significant margins of error because changes in any number of factors could radically affect the demand for cropland and thus the area remaining in range.

It is likely that the profitability of growing crops to feed and clothe Americans and the world will be the most important determinant of the acreage in rangeland in the decades ahead. The United States has become a significant trader in the world market for agricultural products since World War II, and is the dominant world trader in wheat, the feed grains, cotton, and rice. Because productivity per worker hour of labor in U.S. agriculture is among the highest in the world, the United States probably has a comparative advantage in producing agricultural goods. Therefore changes in a number of variables could reduce the demand for rangeland and increase the demand for cropland. An increase in cropland could be stimulated by demand for American farm products; higher rates of population growth worldwide than anticipated; loosening of trade barriers that currently limit American agricultural exports; abandonment of price and income support policies for food production in competitor nations; and, perhaps most important, changes in U.S. agricultural policies.

How much rangeland and pasture might be converted to cropland? A study of potential cropland done in 1975 indicated that "86 percent of nonfederal rangeland has little or no potential for conversion to cropland" (Pendleton, 1978, p. 486). Thus it appears certain that rangeland will continue to be an important resource in the United States for many decades. It is well to remember, however, that the uses of rangeland are constantly changing. As per capita income continues to increase, those uses that have high income elasticities particularly can be expected to increase. Foremost among these is recreational use: hunting, fishing, camping, picnicking, sightseeing, water sports, winter sports, and off-road vehicle travel.

Managers of public land are responding to these pressures by collecting data on land use. In Utah, the Bureau of Land Management collects data on recreational visits, estimated recreation visitor days, and estimated visitor hours on public land under its jurisdiction. These data show substantial interyear variation for most uses, but it is unclear how comparable the data are from one year to another because categorization of uses and enumeration procedures seem to be changing through time. It is significant, however, that agencies are building databases that will permit them to monitor and analyze a wide variety of public rangeland uses. Managers of public land appear to be increasingly conscious of the need to manage rangeland.

The Task Remaining: Evaluating Rangeland Condition and Improving Rangeland Management

In assessing rangeland condition, range professionals have turned only the conceptual corner. Range condition referred originally only to range produc-

tivity measured in terms of the principal use of range-land—livestock grazing. Today, nearly all government agencies that administer grazing base range condition on ecological status—the land's actual production of vegetation measured in terms of the quantity and quality of plants most suitable for the desired use of the range. But one large and costly task remains: collecting and evaluating data on ecological status.

Complicating this task in the question, What is "optimal" range condition or ecological status? Good reasons exist for believing that private owners will manage ranges wisely to maximize the net worth embodied in the land. But when society captures benefits that are unavailable or are of little interest to landowners, private management may not be socially optimal. At the same time, because of distorted incentives and a lack of improvement measures, little evidence exists that public management offers a panacea. It is not obvious that investment to improve the rangeland will yield positive net social benefits.

Range managers in the United States can no longer be sanguine concerning the state of knowledge about range condition and trends. Some range condition studies appear to have been politically motivated and thus cannot be trusted; others have been flawed because poor measurement and evaluation techniques were used. Much more needs to be done to evaluate the condition of U.S. rangeland as well as the economic feasibility of various practices intended to improve it. Environmentalists and public officials appear to be miles apart from private ranchers in judging range condition and trend. The result of this tension is that the courts have been asked to resolve by precedent or by legal argument important policy questions.

Management and administration of rangeland need improvement. The current permit systems that allocate grazing on public land are still inefficient because they prevent allowable AUMs of forage from moving to those ranchers who would value them most. Agency rules governing management control also reduce incentives for private investment on public rangeland. Recent legislation such as the Federal Land Policy and Management Act of 1976 and the Public Rangelands Improvement Act of 1978 has stabilized somewhat the institutional environment within which public rangeland is administered, but many significant policy questions remain unresolved.

Notes

The author gratefully acknowledges support from the Kennedy Center for International Studies at Brigham Young University, and owes a large debt to John Workman, Roger Sedjo, Ken Frederick, Marion Clawson, John Fedkiw, technical editor Samuel Allen, and three anonymous reviewers for helpful suggestions for improving earlier drafts. The caveat still applies that the author alone is finally responsible for the content of the paper. Student research assistants at Brigham Young University—Marshall Daneke, Suzanne Amos Hyland, and Melissa Grant—were also helpful in data acquisition and analysis.

1. Actually, historian Rowley believes that the letter was written by Gifford Pinchot, the utilitarian-conservationist guru of the Theodore Roosevelt administration.

Appendix 4

Table 4-A1. Major Uses of Land in the Contiguous Forty-eight States, 1880–1982 (in millions of acres)

Year	Cropland[a]	Grassland pasture and range[b]	Forestland[c]	Other land[d]	Total
1880	188	935	628	153	1,904
1890	248	892	604	160	1,904
1900	319	831	578	176	1,904
1920	402	750	567	185	1,904
1930	413	708	607	176	1,904
1940	399	723	602	180	1,904
1950	409	700	606	189	1,904
1959	392	696	614	200	1,902[e]
1969	384	689	603	221	1,897[e]
1978	394	661	583	259	1,897[e]
1982	404	659	567	266	1,896[e]

Source: Wooten (1953).

[a]Excludes cropland used only for pasture.

[b]Includes grassland and other nonforested pasture and range, including cropland used only for pasture.

[c]Excludes forestland in parks and other special uses.

[d]Includes urban areas; rural transportation systems; parks and wildlife areas; defense and industrial uses; miscellaneous uses not inventoried; and areas of little surface use such as swamps, bare rock areas, desert, and tundra.

[e]Changes in total area resulted from changes in methods and measures used to remeasure as well as from changes in surface area of reservoirs.

References

Axelrod, Daniel I. 1958. "Evolution of the Madro-Tertiary Geoflora." *Botanical Review* 24 (July):432–509.

———. 1979. "Desert Vegetation: Its Age and Origin." In *Aridland Plant Resources*, edited by F. R. Goodin and D. K. Northington, 1–720. Lubbock, Tex.: International Center for Arid and Semi-arid Land Studies, Texas Tech University.

Baden, John, and Andrew Dana. 1987. "Toward an Ideological Synthesis in Public Land Policy: The New Resource Economics." In *Federal Lands Policy*, edited by Phillip O. Foss, 1–20. New York: Greenwood Press.

Bahre, Conrad J. 1985. "Wildfire in Southeastern Arizona Between 1859 and 1890." *Desert Plants* 7, no. 4:190–194.

Bahre, Conrad J., and David E. Bradbury. 1978. "Vegetation Change Along the Arizona-Sonora Boundary." *Annals of the Association of American Geographers* 68 (June):145–165.

Bishop, R. C., and T. A. Heberlein. 1979. "Measured Values of Extramarket Goods: Are Indirect Measures Biased?" *American Journal of Agricultural Economics* 61 (December):926–931.

Box, Thadis W. 1978. "The Arid Lands Revisited." Paper presented at the 57th Annual Faculty Honor Lecture, Utah State University, Logan, February.

———. 1984. "Role of Land Treatments on Public and Private Lands." In *Developing Strategies for Rangeland Management*, 1397–1419. Report prepared by the Committee on Developing Strategies for Rangeland Management, National Research Council/National Academy of Sciences. Westview Special Studies in Agriculture Science and Policy. Boulder, Colo.: Westview Press.

———. 1990. "Rangelands." In *Natural Resources for the 21st Century*, edited by R. Neil Sampson and Dwight Hair, 101–120. Washington, D.C.: Island Press.

Box, Thadis W., D. D. Dwyer, and F. H. Wagner. n.d. "Report on the Condition of the Western Rangelands for the Council on Environmental Quality." National Archives, Washington, D.C.

Branson, Farrel A. 1985. *Vegetation Changes on Western Rangelands*. Range Monograph no. 2. Denver, Colo.: Society for Range Management.

Branson, Farrel A., and Reuben F. Miller. 1981. "Effects of Increased Precipitation and Grazing Management on Northeastern Mountain Rangelands." *Journal of Range Management* 34 (January):3–10.

Buffington, L. C., and C. H. Herbel. 1965. "Vegetational Changes on a Semidesert Grassland Range from 1858 to 1953." *Ecological Monograph* 35 (Spring):139–164.

Cholis, G. John. 1952. "Range Condition in Eastern Washington Fifty Years Ago and Now." *Journal of Range Management* 5 (May):129–134.

Clawson, Marion. 1959. *Methods of Measuring the Demand for and Value of Outdoor Recreation*. Reprint no. 10. Washington, D.C.: Resources for the Future.

———. 1983. *The Federal Lands Revisited*. Baltimore, Md.: The Johns Hopkins University Press for Resources for the Future.

Clawson, Marion, and Burnell Held. 1957. *The Federal Lands: Their Use and Management*. Lincoln, Neb.: University of Nebraska Press.

Comanor, Joan M. 1988. "Changing Times, Changing Values: New Directions for Range Management." *Journal of Forestry* 86 (November):29–32.

Comptroller General of the United States. 1977. *Report to Congress: Public Rangelands Continue to Deteriorate*. Report prepared for the U.S. Department of Agriculture, Bureau of Land Management. Washington, D.C.: GPO.

Culhane, Paul J. 1981. *Public Lands Politics*. Baltimore, Md.: The Johns Hopkins University Press for Resources for the Future.

Dana, Samuel T., and Sally K. Fairfax. 1980. *Forest and Range Policy: Its Development in the United States*. New York: McGraw-Hill.

Darr, David R. n.d. "The 1989 RPA Assessment of the Forest and Range Land Situation in the United States." U.S. Department of Agriculture, Forest Service. Typescript.

Daugherty, Arthur B. 1989. *U.S. Grazing Lands: 1950–82*. Statistical Bulletin no. 771, prepared for the Resources and Technology Division, Economic Research Service, U.S. Department of Agriculture. Washington, D.C.

Dix, R. L. 1964. "A History of Biotic and Climatic Changes within the North American Grassland." In *Grazing in Terrestrial and Marine Environments*, edited by D. J. Crisp, 71–88. British Ecology Society Symposium no. 4. Oxford, England: Blackwell Scientific Publications.

Donart, Gary B. 1984. "The History and Evolution of Western Rangelands in Relation to Woody Plant Communities." In *Developing Strategies for Rangeland Management*, 1235–1258. Report prepared by the Committee on Developing Strategies for Rangeland Management, National Research Council/National Academy of Sciences. Westview Special Studies in Agriculture Science and Policy. Boulder, Colo.: Westview Press.

Dunbar, C. O. 1960. *Historical Geology*. 2d ed. New York: John Wiley and Sons.

Dyer, A. A. 1984. "Public Natural Resource Management and Valuation of Nonmarket Outputs." In *Developing Strategies for Rangeland Management*, 1559–1596. Report prepared by the Committee on Developing Strategies for Rangeland Management, National Research Council/National Academy of Sciences. Westview Special Studies in Agriculture Science and Policy. Boulder, Colo.: Westview Press.

Dyksterhuis, E. J. 1949. "Condition and Measurement of Rangeland Based on Quantitative Ecology." *Journal of Range Management* 2 (July):104–115.

Fedkiw, John. 1989. *The Evolving Use and Management of the Nation's Forests, Grasslands, Croplands, and Related Resources. A Technical Document Supporting the 1989 USDA Forest Service RPA Assessment.* Fort Collins, Colo.: U.S. Department of Agriculture, Forest Service, Rocky Mountain Forest and Range Experiment Station.

Ferguson, Denzel, and Nancy Ferguson. 1983. *Sacred Cows at the Public Trough.* Bend, Oreg.: Maverick Publications.

Fort, Rodney D., and John Baden. 1981. "The Federal Treasury as a Common Pool Resource and the Development of a Predatory Bureaucracy." In *Bureaucracy vs. Environment*, edited by John Baden and Richard Stroup, 9–21. Ann Arbor, Mich.: University of Michigan Press.

Frey, H. Thomas. 1983. *Acreage Formerly Cropped in the Great Plains.* Staff Report no. AGE830404. Washington, D.C.: U.S. Department of Agriculture, Economic Research Service.

Frey, H. Thomas, and Roger W. Hexem. 1985. *Major Uses of Land in the United States.* Agricultural Economics Report no. 535. Washington, D.C.: U.S. Department of Agriculture, Economic Research Service.

Gardner, B. Delworth. 1962a. "Rates of Returns to Improvement Practices on Private and Public Range." *Land Economics* 38 (February):42–50.

———. 1962b. "Transfer Restrictions and Misallocation in Grazing Public Range." *Journal of Farm Economics* 43 (February):50–63.

———. 1963. "The Internal Rate of Return and Decisions to Improve the Range." In *Economic Research in the Use and Development of Range Resources*, 87–109. Report no. 5, *Development and Evolution of Research in Range Use and Development.* Laramie, Wyo.: Western Agricultural Economics Resources Council.

———. 1983. "Market Versus Political Allocations of Natural Resources in the 1980s." *Western Journal of Agricultural Economics* 8 (December):215–229.

———. 1984. "The Role of Economic Analysis in Public Range Management." In *Developing Strategies for Rangeland Management*, 1441–1466. Report prepared by the Committee on Developing Strategies for Rangeland Management, National Research Council/National Academy of Sciences. Westview Special Studies in Agriculture Science and Policy. Boulder, Colo.: Westview Press.

———. 1989. "A Proposal for Reallocation of Federal Grazing—Revisited." *Rangelands* 11 (June):107–111.

Gardner, B. Delworth, and N. K. Roberts. 1963. "Government Policy and the Beef Industry in the West." In *The Future for Beef*, 217–233. Report no. 15, prepared for the Center for Agricultural and Economic Adjustment. Ames, Iowa: Iowa State University Press.

Glendening, George E. 1952. "Some Quantitative Data on the Increase of Mesquite and Cactus on a Desert Grassland Range in Southern Arizona." *Ecology* 33:319–328.

Goldberg, Deborah E., and Raymond M. Turner. 1986. "Vegetation Change and Plant Demography in Permanent Plots in the Sonoran Desert." *Ecology* 67:695–712.

Hardin, Garrett. 1968. "The Tragedy of the Commons." *Science* 162 (13 December):1243–1248.

Hastings, J. R., and R. M. Turner. 1965. *The Changing Mile.* Tucson, Ariz.: University of Arizona Press.

Heimlich, Ralph. 1985. *Sodbusting: Land Use Change and Farm Programs.* Agricultural Economics Report no. 536. Washington, D.C.

Herbel, Carlton. 1984. "Successional Patterns and Productivity Potentials of the Range Vegetation in the Warm, Arid Portions of the Southwestern United States." In *Developing Strategies for Rangeland Management*, 1333–1363. Report prepared by the Committee on Developing Strategies for Rangeland Management, National Research Council/National Academy of Sciences. Westview Special Studies in Agriculture Science and Policy. Boulder, Colo.: Westview Press.

Hexem, Roger, and Kenneth S. Krupa. 1987. *Land Resources for Crop Production.* Agricultural Economics Report no. 572. Washington, D.C.

Huffaker, Ray, and B. Delworth Gardner. 1987. "Rancher Stewardship on Public Ranges: A Recent Court Decision." *Natural Resources Journal* 27 (Fall):889–898.

Humphrey, R. R., and L. A. Mehrhoff. 1958. "Vegetation Changes on a Southern Arizona Grassland Range." *Ecology* 39 (October):720–726.

Hurtt, L. C. 1950. "Northern Great Plains Range Problems." *Northwestern Science* 24 (August):126–131.

Johnson, Kendall L. 1987. *Rangeland Through Time—A Photographic Study of Vegetation Change in Wyoming 1870–1986.* Miscellaneous Publication no. 50. Laramie, Wyo.: University of Wyoming, Agricultural Experiment Station.

Johnson, L. E., Leslie R. Albee, R. O. Smith, and Alvin L. Moxon. 1951. *Cows, Calves, and Grass: Effects of Grazing Intensities on Beef Cow and Calf Production and on Mixed Prairie Vegetation on Western South Dakota Ranges.* South Dakota Agricultural Experiment Station Bulletin no. 412. Brookings, S. Dak.: South Dakota State University.

Johnston, Alex. 1978. "Panorama of the Rangelands of North America." In *Proceedings of the First International Rangeland Congress*, edited by Donald N. Hyder, 37–41. Denver, Colo.: Society for Range Management.

Johnston, Marshall C. 1963. "Past and Present Grasslands of Southern Texas and Northeastern Mexico." *Ecology* 44 (Summer):456–466.

Joyce, Linda A. 1989. *An Analysis of the Range Forage Situation in the United States: 1989–2040. A Technical Document Supporting the 1989 USDA Forest Service RPA*

Assessment. Fort Collins, Colo.: U.S. Department of Agriculture, Forest Service, Rocky Mountain Forest and Range Experiment Station.

Kendeigh, S. C. 1974. *Ecology.* Englewood Cliffs, N.J.: Prentice-Hall.

LeBaron, A., D. B. Nielson, J. P. Workman, and E. B. Godfrey. 1980. *An Economic Evaluation of the Transfer of Federal Lands in Utah to State Ownership.* Report submitted to the Four Corners Regional Commission for contract no. 501-400-015-4. Logan, Utah: Utah Agricultural Experiment Station.

Leopold, Luna B. 1951. "Rainfall Frequency: An Aspect of Climatic Variation." *Transactions of the American Geophysical Union* 32 (June):347–357.

Libecap, Gary D. 1981. *Locking Up the Range—Federal Land Controls and Grazing.* Cambridge, Mass.: Ballinger Publishing Co.

Loring, Michael W., and John P. Workman. 1987. "The Relationship Between Land Ownership and Range Condition in Rich County, Utah." *Journal of Range Management* 40 (July):290–293.

Martin, S. Clark, and Raymond M. Turner. 1977. "Vegetation Change in the Sonoran Desert Region, Arizona and Sonora." *Journal of the Arizona Academy of Science* 12 (June):59–69.

Mitchell, Robert Cameron, and Richard T. Carson. 1989. *Using Surveys to Value Public Goods: The Contingent Valuation Method.* Washington, D.C.: Resources for the Future.

Muhn, James Allan. 1987. "The Mizpah-Pumpkin Creek Grazing District: Its History and Influence on the Enactment of a Public Lands Grazing Polity." Master's thesis, Montana State University, Bozeman.

Muhn, James Allan, and Hanson R. Stuart. 1988. *Opportunity and Challenge: The Story of BLM.* Washington, D.C.: U.S. Department of the Interior, Bureau of Land Management.

Nelson, Robert H. 1984. "Economic Analysis in Public Rangeland Management." In *Western Public Lands: The Management of Natural Resources in a Time of Declining Federalism,* edited by John G. Francis and Richard Ganzel, 44–78. Totowa, N.J.: Rowman & Allanheld.

Pacific Consultants. 1970. *Public Land Study: The Forage Resource.* Report prepared for the Public Land Law Review Commission. Springfield, Va.: National Technical Information Service.

Pearson, Henry A., and Jack W. Thomas. 1984. "Adequacy of Inventory Data for Management Interpretations." In *Developing Strategies for Rangeland Management,* 745–763. Report prepared by the Committee on Developing Strategies for Rangeland Management, National Research Council/National Academy of Sciences. Westview Special Studies in Agriculture Science and Policy. Boulder, Colo.: Westview Press.

Pendleton, Donald T. 1978. "Nonfederal Rangelands of the United States—A Decade of Change: 1967–1977." In *Proceedings of the First International Rangeland Congress,* edited by Donald N. Hyder, 485–487. Denver, Colo.: Society for Range Management.

———. 1984. "Use of Inventory and Monitoring Data for Range Management Purposes: A Critique." In *Developing Strategies for Rangeland Management,* 855–865. Report prepared by the Committee on Developing Strategies for Rangeland Management, National Research Council/National Academy of Sciences. Westview Special Studies in Agriculture Science and Policy. Boulder, Colo.: Westview Press.

Phillips, W. S. 1963. *Vegetation Changes in the Northern Great Plains.* University of Arizona Agriculture Experiment Station report no. 214. Tucson, Ariz.: University of Arizona.

Phipps, Tim T., Pierre R. Crosson, and Kent A. Price, eds. 1986. *Agriculture and the Environment. Annual Policy Review 1986* from the National Center for Food and Agricultural Policy. Washington, D.C.: Resources for the Future.

Pope, C. Arden III, and Fred J. Wagstaff. 1987. "Economics of the Oak Creek Range Management Project." *Journal of Environmental Management* 25 (September):157–165.

Prouty, Mike. 1987. "A New Program for Riparian Research." *Forestry Research West* (April):7–10.

Rassmussen, Wayne D. 1974. *American Agriculture: A Short History.* Washington, D.C.: U.S. Department of Agriculture, Economic Research Service.

Renner, F. G. 1954. "The Future of Our Range Resource." *Journal of Range Management* 7 (March):55–56.

Ross, Robert L., and John E. Taylor. 1988. "Rangeland Resources of Montana." *Rangelands* 10 (October):207–209.

Rowley, William D. 1985. *U.S. Forest Service Grazing and Rangelands: A History.* College Station, Tex.: Texas A&M University Press.

Sampson, A. W. 1952. *Range Management Principles and Practices.* New York: John Wiley.

Schlatterer, Edward F., Linda A. Joyce, James T. Bones, and Ann E. Carey. n.d. "National Overview." In "An Analysis of the Land Situation in the United States: 1989–2040," edited by James T. Bones. A technical document supporting the 1989 RPA assessment. U.S. Department of Agriculture, Forest Service. Typescript.

Schlebecker, John T. 1963. *Cattle Raising on the Plains: 1900–1961.* Lincoln, Neb.: University of Nebraska Press.

Secrist, Glen. 1988. "Range Condition and Vegetation Management Status." U.S. Department of Agriculture, Bureau of Land Management. Mimeographed.

Smith, David A., and Ervin M. Schmutz. 1975. "Vegetative Changes on Protected Versus Grazed Desert Grassland

Ranges in Arizona." *Journal of Range Management* 28 (November):453–458.

Smith, E. Lamar. 1984. "Use of Inventory and Monitoring Data for Range Management Purposes." In *Developing Strategies for Rangeland Management*, 809–842. Report prepared by the Committee on Developing Strategies for Rangeland Management, National Research Council/National Academy of Sciences. Westview Special Studies in Agriculture Science and Policy. Boulder, Colo.: Westview Press.

Society for Range Management. 1989. *Assessment of Rangeland Condition and Trend of the United States, 1989*. Denver, Colo.: Public Affairs Committee.

U.S. Army Corps of Engineers. 1984. *Flood Control Study, Utah*. Washington, D.C.

U.S. Congress. House. 1897. *Annual Report of the Secretary of the Interior, 1897*. H. Doc. 1897, 55 Cong., 2 sess. (1897).

U.S. Congress. Senate. 1936. *A Report on the Western Range: A Great but Neglected Natural Resource*. S. Doc. 199, 74 Cong., 2 sess. (1936).

U.S. Department of Agriculture. Agricultural Stabilization and Conservation Service. 1963. *Conservation Reserve Program of the Soil Bank: Statistical Summaries*, 1961 and 1962. Washington, D.C.: GPO.

U.S. Department of Agriculture. Forest Service. 1972. *Forest Resource Report*. Report no. 19. Washington, D.C.: GPO.

———. 1987. *Changing Times, Changing Values . . . New Directions*. Report of the National Range Workshop, March 23–27. Washington, D.C.: GPO.

———. 1988a. "An Ecological Approach to Vegetation Analysis: Summary of Recommendations of the Forest Service Vegetation Analysis Task Group." Washington, D.C. Typescript.

———. 1988b. "Change on the Range, Caring for the Land . . . Serving People, Range Management." Washington, D.C.

———. 1988c. "New Measures for Range Management." Report of the Forest Service Range Management Task Group. Typescript.

U.S. Department of Agriculture. Soil Conservation Service and Iowa State University Statistical Laboratory. 1984. *Basic Statistics. 1982 National Resources Inventory*. SB-756. Washington, D.C.: GPO.

U.S. Department of Commerce. Bureau of the Census. 1975. *Historical Statistics of the United States—Colonial Times to 1970*. Part 1. Washington, D.C.: GPO.

U.S. Department of the Interior. n.d.a. Bureau of Land Management. *Public Land Statistics* (various years). Washington, D.C.

———. n.d.b. "Range Management Automation." Mimeographed.

———. 1975. *Range Condition Report*. Report prepared for the Senate Committee on Appropriations. Washington, D.C.

———. 1982a. "Final Grazing Management Policy." Instruction Memorandum no. 82-292. Washington, D.C.

———. 1982b. "Final Rangeland Improvement Policy." Instruction Memorandum no. 83-27. Washington, D.C.

U.S. General Accounting Office. 1988a. *Public Rangelands: Some Riparian Areas Restored by Widespread Improvement Will Be Slow*. Report no. GAO/RCED-88-105. Washington, D.C.

———. 1988b. *Rangeland Management: More Emphasis Needed on Declining and Overstocked Grazing Allotments*. Report no. GAO/RCED-88-80. Washington, D.C.

Vale, Thomas R. 1975. "Presettlement Vegetation in the Sagebrush-Grass Area of the Intermountain West." *Journal of Range Management* 28 (January):32–36.

Wagner, Frederic H. 1978. "Livestock Grazing and the Livestock Industry." In *Wildlife and America*, edited by Howard P. Brokaw, 121–145. Washington, D.C.: Council on Environmental Quality.

Weaver, J. E., and F. W. Albertson. 1956. *Grasslands of the Great Plains: Their Nature and Use*. Lincoln, Neb.: Johnson Publishing Co.

Whitman, W., H. T. Hanson, and R. Peterson. 1943. *Relation of Drought and Grazing to North Dakota Range Lands*. North Dakota Agricultural Experiment Station Bulletin no. 320. Fargo, N. Dak.

Wooten, H. H. 1953. *Supplement to Major Uses of Land in the United States—Basic Land Use Statistics, 1950*. Prepared for the U.S. Department of Agriculture, Bureau of Agricultural Economics. Washington, D.C.: GPO.

Workman, John P. 1984. "Criteria for Investment Feasibility and Selection." In *Developing Strategies for Rangeland Management*, 1475–1508. Report prepared by the Committee on Developing Strategies for Rangeland Management, National Research Council/National Academy of Sciences. Westview Special Studies in Agriculture Science and Policy. Boulder, Colo.: Westview Press.

———. 1986. *Range Economics*. New York: Macmillan.

York, J. C., and W. A. Dick-Peddie. 1969. "Vegetation Changes in Southern New Mexico During the Past Hundred Years." In *Arid Lands in Perspective*, edited by W. G. McGinnies and B. J. Goldman, 157–166. Tucson, Ariz.: University of Arizona Press.

Young, James A., and B. Abbott Sparks. 1985. *Cattle in the Cold Desert*. Logan, Utah: Utah State University Press.

5

Cropland and Soils:
Past Performance and
Policy Challenges

Pierre R. Crosson

The agricultural system in the United States is a great provider of food and fiber to its citizens as well as to a large portion of the world community. Of the existing total land area of 1.9 billion acres, about 600 million acres have physical characteristics favorable to crop production: sufficient rainfall, deep-to-adequate topsoil depth with good water-holding capacity, and gentle slopes. The Midwest, especially the states of Ohio, Indiana, Illinois, Iowa, most of Missouri, and the southern parts of Minnesota, Wisconsin, and Michigan, is favored in these respects. Soils in much of the Mississippi Delta region, along the Gulf Coast, and in the Tidewater region of the eastern states, also are rich and deep but generally require drainage to be most productive. More inland soils, stretching more or less continuously from New England down through Georgia and across eastern Texas, generally are thinner and less naturally fertile than the soils of the Midwest (Cochrane, 1979).

Nonetheless, much of the land in that area has been in crops for 100 years or more, indeed some of it since colonial times. West of the eastern Great Plains—except for parts of the Pacific Northwest—moisture, not soils, is the principal factor limiting crop production. However, when irrigated, much of that land is as productive as any in the country.

Yet the productivity of U.S. cropland and soils has raised questions about the economic and environmental values at stake. Some members of the environmental community suggest that the environmental damage has been pervasive and severe. In contrast, some members of the agricultural community do not see any reason for concern. This chapter examines the use of cropland and soils and the consequences of increased output of crops over three periods: from 1800 to 1910, from 1910 to 1940, and from 1940 to 1990. This selection of periods is based in part on data availability. For example, the data relevant to analysis of changing patterns of cropland use are much more abundant after 1910 than before that year. In addition, the division of periods before and after 1940 was made because, at about 1940, agricultural productivity began a sustained, sharp rise after showing essentially no change over the preceding seventy or eighty years. Therefore, 1940 is a useful reference point for examining the land-use implications of the change in productivity. The period after 1940 suggests what the future may hold for the capacity of the nation's land to produce crops and environmental services.

Changing Cropland Use Patterns and Their Effects: 1800–1910

The Land Resource

When the first European settlers arrived on the Atlantic Coast of the area composing the contiguous forty-eight states, approximately one-half of the land was in forests and about four-tenths in grass, from the tall abundant growth on the central Illinois prairie to the short and meager growth on the western edge of the Great Plains. The remaining one-tenth of the land was arid and unproductive (Cochrane, 1979).

Table 5-1. Cropland Used for Crops and Idle in the Contiguous United States, 1850–1910, and Land in Farms, 1880–1910

Year	Land in farms (millions of acres)	Cropland (millions of acres)	Cropland (%)
1850	NA	76	
1860	NA	109	
1870	NA	126	
1880	536	188	35
1890	623	248	40
1900	841	319	38
1910	881	347	39

Sources: U.S. Department of Commerce (1975) for land in farms; Fedkiw (1989) for cropland from 1850 to 1900; and U.S. Department of Agriculture (1982) for cropland in 1910.

Note: NA = not available.

Data on the amount of land in crops before the Civil War are scarce; Fedkiw (1989) estimated the land in crops to be less than 20 million acres in 1800. Subsequently, acreage in cropland rose from 76 million in 1850 to 109 million in 1860, and to 126 million in 1870. From 1880 to 1910, approximately 35 to 40 percent of the land in farms was cropland (table 5-1). The rest was mostly in pasture and forest, with a small amount in houses, other buildings, and wasteland. As is discussed later in this chapter, for the years after 1910 into the 1980s cropland consistently accounted for 35 to 40 percent of all farmland. The reasons for the long-term stability of this relationship are unclear, but it is evident that the cropland experience during the 1880–1910 period was consistent with that of the period after 1910.

At the beginning of the nineteenth century, most crop production still was concentrated in the original thirteen states. A key component of the nation's subsequent westward expansion was a shift in farmland and cropland first beyond the Allegheny Mountains into the midwestern prairies and through the South, then into the Great Plains, with a simultaneous leap across the intervening mountains and deserts (excepting the Mormon settlement of Utah in the later 1840s) to the Pacific Coast. Commenting on this development, Cochrane (1979, p. 91) has observed that

> the final settlement of the continental land mass and its linkage through a railroad network occurred in the period 1860–1897. Thus the specialization of agricultural production by areas which began in the 1820s and 1830s and which was in transition in the 1840s and 1850s, was

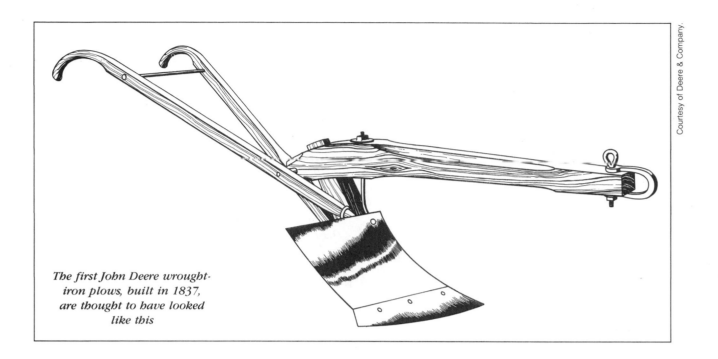

Courtesy of Deere & Company.

The first John Deere wrought-iron plows, built in 1837, are thought to have looked like this

largely completed in the period 1860–1897. The location of agricultural production in the United States has changed somewhat in the twentieth century but not to any important degree.

Technological Change

In 1800, farmers depended primarily on the ax and fire to clear the land; on a primitive plow drawn by oxen, mules, or horses to till it; on the hoe to control weeds; and on the scythe for harvest. The farmer's own labor, and that of the farm family, accounted for a vastly greater share of the total energy absorbed in agricultural production than it does today. Labor was scarce relative to the land in 1800, and it remained so throughout the course of the twentieth century. Accordingly, the history of agricultural technology in the 1800s is largely an account of the development of machines and implements to overcome the relative scarcity of labor by increasing its productivity relative to that of the land.

Eli Whitney's invention of the cotton gin at the end of the eighteenth century was an epochal early event in this history. By permitting the spread of cotton production, it transformed the agricultural economy of the South, with far-reaching ramifications for the social and political life of the region as well. Not long after Whitney's early success with the cotton gin, Charles Newhold patented the first cast-iron plow, all in one piece, in New Jersey in 1797. Improvements by others followed, and in 1837 John Deere developed a wrought-iron plow with a cutting edge of steel that was especially well adapted to breaking the heavy, sodded soils of the Midwest. Deere's new plow was both efficient and cheap, and by 1857 his plant in Moline, Illinois, was producing 10,000 wrought-iron plows annually (Cochrane, 1979).

A variety of other machines and implements also were developed in the first half of the century to aid the farmer in preparing the seed bed, planting the seed, and cultivating to control weeds. In addition, the first grain harvesters were patented in the 1830s and, by the 1850s, the McCormick harvester was widely used throughout the grain-producing regions of the country. Hiram and John Pitt patented a stationary grain-threshing machine in 1836, and such machines were widely used throughout the eastern part of the country and in much of the Midwest by the 1940s (Cochrane, 1979).

It probably was no accident that many of these machines were developed at about the same time (Cochrane, 1979). It would profit a farmer little to greatly increase crop output by more efficiently plowing the land, seeding the crop, and controlling weeds

From the sickle in the 1840s to the four-horse twine binder sixty years later, labor productivity in harvesting rose roughly thirty-five to fifty times relative to the land.

of modifying, improving, and enlarging machinery and equipment that had been developed in the first half of the century (Cochrane, 1979). The main exception to this proposition was the gasoline-engined tractor, which was developed in the 1880s and 1890s. This was a major innovation, with vast long-term implications not only for labor productivity but for the productivity of the land as well because it permitted the conversion of tens of millions of acres of land from production of feed for animals to more productive uses.[1] The first of these tractors were clumsy affairs, but by 1910 they had been much improved; several firms were mass-producing them, and farmers had begun to adopt them widely (Cochrane, 1979).

if the farmer had to continue to rely on traditional, labor-intensive techniques for harvesting and threshing his crop. The institutional and behavioral processes that in effect brought these multiple technical advances on line in a timely fashion are not well understood. Cochrane (1979) hints at an explanation: many of the advances were made by people such as village blacksmiths who were in intimate contact with farmers and who thus were in a position to recognize technical bottlenecks as they emerged. Of course, the expectation of an adequate economic return on the investment of time and other resources needed to remove the bottlenecks must have been part of the innovation process.

The Civil War increased the chronic labor shortages throughout the country, which gave added impetus to the development and adoption of labor-saving machinery. More advanced mowing machines, cultivators, and reapers came into wide use from the 1860s to the end of the nineteenth century, especially in the Midwest and eastern Great Plains, in California, and in the Pacific Northwest. In the South, where cotton remained the dominant crop, farmers continued to rely on more labor-intensive techniques—the hoe and a mule pulling a shallow plow typifying the crop production technology of that region. In the East, farmers had begun to concentrate on dairying and on specialty crops, which remained predominately labor-intensive activities (Cochrane, 1979).

The mechanization that took place from the Civil War to the end of the century was generally a process

Productivity Effects

The mechanization of American crop production that occurred in the nineteenth century did what it was intended to do: it increased the productivity of labor relative to the land. Hayami and Ruttan (1985) have described the changes over the century in the amount of land that one worker could harvest in one day. For example, with the sickle, which was in general use from the beginning of the century to the mid-1840s, a worker could harvest one-third to one-half of an acre per day; with the cradle, a hand-harvester more advanced that the sickle, the worker could harvest about one acre. With the McCormick reaper, in wide use from the 1850s to the 1880s, the worker could harvest two to two and one-half acres. By the end of the century, the twine binder, introduced by the McCormick Company in 1881, permitted the worker to harvest eight to eighteen acres in a day, depending on whether the two-horse or four-horse binder was used. From the sickle in the 1840s to the four-horse twine binder sixty years later, therefore, labor productivity in harvesting rose roughly thirty-five to fifty times relative to the land. Comparable data showing the labor productivity effects of the mechanization of other cropping operations are unavailable. However, the principle that the profitability of any technical innovation requires complementary technical advances in related processes suggests that labor productivity in all phases of crop production must have been substantially improved.

An implication of the rising productivity of labor relative to the land is that the ratio of cropland to labor must have risen, and indeed it did. With 1850

Table 5-2. Various Measures of Agricultural Output, 1870–1910

Year	Total output[a]	Crop output[a]	Corn (millions of bushels)	Wheat (millions of bushels)	Cotton (millions of bales)
1870	65	NA[b]	1,037	272	3.68
1880	100	100	1,625	495	6.20
1885	NA	112			
1890	115	130	2,020	514	7.94
1895	NA	139			
1900	154	161	2,467	669	9.96
1905	NA	177			
1910	165	182	2,762	641	12.60

Sources: U.S. Department of Agriculture (1982) for total output; Hayami and Ruttan (1985) for crop output; and U.S. Department of Commerce (1975) for corn, wheat, and cotton.

[a]Index of total and crop output for 1800 = 100.

[b]NA = not available.

(the first year with adequate cropland data) equal to 100, the cropland/labor ratio in 1910 was 190 (Fedkiw, 1989). The increases in the amounts of cropland, machinery, and labor (the number of people engaged in agricultural production increased more than five times from 1820 to 1910 [Fedkiw, 1989]) resulted in a substantial increase in production as well (table 5-2). The increase in the supply of output was a response to rising domestic and foreign demands. The population of the United States grew 91 percent from 1870 to 1900 and real per capita Gross National Product (GNP), which is nominal GNP adjusted for changes in the general price level using the Consumer Price Index (CPI), increased 95 percent in the 1870–1900 period (U.S. Department of Commerce, 1975).[2] Data showing what percentage of this increase in per capita income was spent on crops are unavailable. However, estimates for countries currently at about the same level of per capita income (about $500 in 1967 dollars) as characterized the United States in the latter part of the nineteenth century suggest that Americans would have spent some 20 percent of their per capita income increase on food. If this estimate is even approximately correct, then most of the increase in demand for crops implied by table 5-2 would have been domestic, reflecting the combined effect of rising population and per capita income.

A striking fact about the increases in production shown in table 5-2 is that they owed almost nothing to increasing productivity of cropland (measured by output per acre). Cropland productivity "barely increased" in the last thirty or so years of the nineteenth century (Cochrane, 1979, p. 92). Indeed, cropland productivity not only did not increase but may have declined during this period (table 5-3), even though the amount of inorganic fertilizer applied per acre of cropland quadrupled between 1880 and 1910 (Hayami and Ruttan, 1985). Two reasons might account

Table 5-3. Measures of the Productivity of Cropland and Shares of Main Crops in Total Cropland, 1870–1910

Year	All cropland (1880 = 100)[a]	Output per acre			Acres of land in the crop as % of all cropland			Total acres in cropland (%)
		Corn (bu.)	Wheat (bu.)	Cotton (bales)	Corn	Wheat	Cotton	
1870	NA[b]	27	13	.40	30	17	7	54
1880	100	26	13	.39	33	20	8	61
1890	98	27	14	.38	30	15	8	53
1900	95	26	14	.40	30	15	8	53
1910	96	27	14	.40	29	13	9	51[c]

Sources: Hayami and Ruttan (1985, p. 480), for indexes of crop production and cropland; and U.S. Department of Commerce (1975) for corn, wheat, cotton, and acres of cropland.

[a]The index of crop output (1880 = 100) was divided by arable land data and the results stated with 1880 = 100 (Hayami and Ruttan, 1985).

[b]NA = not available.

[c]In 1910, about 25 percent of the nation's cropland was in feed for work animals (U.S. Department of Agriculture, 1982).

for the anomaly of constant or even slightly declining crop yields and sharply increasing rates of fertilizer use. One is that the absolute amounts of fertilizer applied per acre still were small in 1910: 3.7 pounds compared with .9 pound in 1880. The other reason is that this fertilizer probably served primarily to replace the natural soil nutrients that were lost by the rapid oxidation of soil organic matter following the plowing of the virgin lands in the Midwest, Great Plains, and Mississippi Delta (Hayami and Ruttan, 1985).

The stagnation in land productivity from 1880 to 1910 was matched by slow growth in the productivity of all inputs combined. With the ratio of all outputs to all inputs (the total productivity ratio) in 1880 equal to 100, the ratio in 1910 was 102 (U.S. Department of Agriculture, 1982).[3]

Price Effects

Despite the failure of agricultural productivity to increase in the second half of the nineteenth century, the increase in the supply of output was sufficient to keep up with the rapid growth in demand. Consequently, real prices of agricultural commodities (the nominal price adjusted for changes in the general price level) generally did not rise (Cochrane, 1979). Real prices for individual crops varied, however: the real price of corn increased modestly from 1870 to 1900, that of wheat declined markedly, and that of cotton declined 12 percent from 1880 to 1900 (table 5-4).

In the first decade of the twentieth century, however, commodity prices generally rose sharply, and those of the three main crops followed suit (table 5-4). The reasons for this change in prices are not entirely clear, but analysis of the conditions underlying the supply of and demand for agricultural commodities suggests an explanation. On the demand side,

the combination of population and per capita income growth produced a faster rate of increase in real GNP from 1900 to 1910—5.4 percent annually—than from 1870 to 1900—4.6 percent annually (U.S. Department of Commerce, 1975). Apparently the rate of increase in domestic demand for agricultural output was not less than the rate of increase in the previous thirty years, and it may have been more. On the supply side, two situations weakened agricultural supply in the 1900–1910 period relative to the 1880–1900 period. First, and probably most important, total productivity, which had increased .6 percent annually from 1880 to 1900, declined at an annual rate of 1.0 percent from 1900 to 1910 (U.S. Department of Agriculture, 1982). The reasons for this decline are unclear. Cochrane (1979) suggests an explanation: by 1900, the nation's supply of good agricultural land was almost fully used, leaving only marginal land, such as the land in the Great Plains, to be brought into production. Economical development of much of that land awaited future technical advances in irrigation, drainage, and earth-moving machinery.

In any case, the annual increase in total farmland and cropland was much less from 1900 to 1910 than in the preceding thirty years (table 5-1), suggesting that constraints on land supply may have contributed to the decline in total productivity. The suggestion is inconsistent, however, with the fact that crop yields (output per acre) did not decline between 1900 and 1910 (table 5-3), which they should have if land constraints had contributed to the decline in total productivity.

Whatever the reasons for the performance of total productivity, the effect of its decline on agricultural supply was reinforced by adverse changes in input prices from 1900 to 1910, compared with the preceding two decades. For example, real wages of farm labor, which rose 1.3 percent annually from 1880 to 1900, accelerated to 1.9 percent annually from 1900 to 1910, and farm machinery prices, which declined 1.5 percent per year from 1880 to 1900, rose 0.4 percent annually from 1900 to 1910. Moreover, fertilizer prices fell 1.2 percent per year from 1900 to 1910, compared with an annual fall of 1.8 percent from 1880 to 1900.[4] The combination of substantially poorer productivity performance in the 1900–1910 period and distinctly less favorable input prices must have seriously constrained agricultural supply in that period relative to the 1880–1900 period. Given the increase in domestic demand for agricultural output, the sharp increase in prices is not surprising.

Table 5-4. Prices of Corn, Wheat, and Cotton, 1870–1910, Expressed in 1967 Dollars

Year	Corn ($/bu.)	Wheat ($/bu.)	Cotton ($/lb.)
1870	1.43	3.11	NA[a]
1880	1.50	3.39	.33
1890	1.41	2.90	.30
1900	1.55	2.44	.29
1910	2.16	3.25	.41

Source: U.S. Department of Commerce (1975).
[a]NA = not available.

This increase in output prices evidently increased farm profits in the first decade of the century compared with the previous twenty years. Profits are capitalized in land prices and these prices (adjusted for inflation) increased 5.8 percent annually between 1900 and 1910, compared with an annual rate of .9 percent from 1880 to 1900 (figures are adjusted using CPI to convert nominal GNP to real GNP; Hayami and Ruttan, 1985). Thus, agricultural land became more scarce economically in the first decade of the twentieth century than in the last two decades of the nineteenth century. This observation is consistent with Cochrane's comment (1979) that, by 1900, most of the nation's good agricultural land already was in production, suggesting that absent new land-saving technologies, increases in output after 1900 would push up land prices faster than in the 1880–1900 period.

Environmental Effects

Several writers in the late eighteenth and early nineteenth centuries expressed concern about the effects of prevailing crop production practices on soil erosion, noting the consequences both for soil productivity and for off-farm water quality (Fedkiw, 1989). The evidence these writers cited leaves little doubt that these effects were severe in some places, but the evidence is insufficient to form a judgment about the severity of the problem for major regions or for the nation as a whole. Information about the environmental effects of cropland management before 1910 is virtually nil. It is conceivable that the failure of crop yields to rise between 1870 and 1910 reflected, at least in part, the effect of erosion on soil productivity. However, given the lack of data on the amount of erosion and its productivity effects, this is merely speculation. It is at least as believable that yields failed to rise because farmers found it more economical to respond to rising crop demand by bringing more land under crops than by seeking to increase the per acre yield of the land. Land in crops increased 2.75 times between 1870 and 1910 (table 5-1).

It is unlikely that agricultural chemicals could have significantly harmed the environment before 1910 because the use of chemicals was minimal. The types of inorganic pesticides that would stimulate concern in the late twentieth century did not exist before 1910, and the amount of inorganic fertilizer that did exist was minuscule by current standards: .9 pounds per acre of nitrogen, potassium, and phosphorus in

> *Information about the environmental effects of cropland management before 1910 is virtually nil.*

1880, rising to 3.7 pounds in 1910 (Hayami and Ruttan, 1985), compared with about 85 pounds per acre in 1985. In addition, increasing soil salinity may have caused soil and water quality problems in some areas of the arid and semiarid West, but among the environmental problems of agriculture soil salinity was a second or third priority, as it is today (Crosson, 1986). The contribution of irrigation to total crop production was much less then than it is currently.

The expansion of crop production must also have contributed significantly to the decline in wildlife numbers. Cropland generally provides less hospitable animal habitat than forest; therefore, the conversion of several hundred million acres of forestland to crop production in the course of the nineteenth century must have tended to depress wildlife numbers. Moreover, the process of westward expansion severely depleted the numbers of many species of wildlife (see chapter 6). The killing of wildlife for food, commercial use, sport, and to control predators no doubt also was a major factor in the depletion of wildlife populations.

Policies

The general policy of the federal government to promote westward expansion must have been of key importance in the conversion of land to crop production in the nineteenth century. Measures to "privatize" most of the public land with potential for agriculture were principal instruments of this general policy, as were federal, state, and local investments in roads, canals, drainage, and other land improvements. Grants of land to the railroads also were instrumental in linking farmers moving into the Midwest and Great Plains with markets in the growing urban centers in the East and with the rapidly industrializing countries of Europe. However, the U.S. Department of Agriculture, which was established in 1862, had little to do with this general policy. Initially, USDA objectives were primarily to collect and disseminate data, test soils and agricultural implements, answer questions from farmers, introduce new plants and animals, and establish an agricultural library and museum (Cochrane, 1979). These objectives continued to guide the department into the first decade of the twentieth century, but with a sharpening focus on research in the agricultural sciences. Several decades later, this focus would have profound effects on crop production technologies and land use.

During the nineteenth and early twentieth centuries, conservation and environmental policies bearing on management of cropland were negligible. In 1894, the USDA published the bulletin *Washed Soils: How to Preserve and Reclaim Them*, in which it was stated that thousands of acres of good land were eroding annually and being abandoned by farmers. The USDA urged farmers to reclaim and reuse this land. In 1899, the department published its first soil survey, and in 1910 it published several bulletins on soil conservation in which it pointed out the dangers of soil erosion to farmers producing corn (Fedkiw, 1989). These activities were consistent with the USDA's mission, as it then was conceived, but hardly added up to a conservation or environmental policy.

During the last decade of the nineteenth century and into the first decade of the twentieth century, the federal government focused its conservation policies primarily on the management of forests on public land. Such policies held the attention of President Theodore Roosevelt and of Gifford Pinchot, appointed by Roosevelt as the first chief of the Forest Service. Concerns about conserving cropland and managing it to control environmental damages from crop production were not on the nation's policy agenda. Those issues would not emerge for several more decades.

Crop yields failed to increase in the 1910–1930 period despite substantial investments in cropland drainage.

The Transition from Stable to Increasing Productivity: 1910–1940

The nation continued to expand its land in farms and to bring more land under crops between 1910 and 1940, but at a much slower pace than in the thirty years preceding 1910. From 1880 to 1910, land in farms increased 345 million acres (64 percent) and land in crops increased 159 million acres (85 percent; tables 5-1 and 5-5). From 1910 to 1940, farmland increased 184 million acres (21 percent) and cropland used for crops and idle increased 52 million acres (15 percent). The amount of cropland in 1940 was actually less than in 1920 and 1930 (table 5-5).

The Pattern of Cropland Change

The slower growth of land in crops from 1910 to 1930 relative to the preceding thirty years is largely explained by two demand and supply conditions. Demand grew much more slowly from 1910 to 1930 than in the preceding period, and land productivity did not increase, as is evident in the index of crop yields (1967 = 100), which averaged 56 for the five years centered on 1912 and also for the five years centered on 1930 (U.S. Department of Agriculture, 1982). Thus, crop production grew precisely in step with the expansion of cropland harvested during the 1910–1930 period.

Crop yields failed to increase in the 1910–1930 period despite substantial investments in cropland drainage. According to Pavelis (1985), some 45 million acres of the nation's cropland were drained between 1900 and 1920, which was about 11 percent of the nation's cropland in the latter year (table 5-5). Drainage generally increases yields—that is why farmers invest in it. The amount of that land, however, and the yield effect of drainage were insufficient to increase national average yields.

Further evidence that the slow growth in crop production and land in crops from 1910 to 1930 reflected slow demand rather than supply constraints is the decline in real crop prices. The three-year average index of crop prices received by farmers (1967 = 100), adjusted for changes in the general price level, was 157 in 1910–1912 and 108 in 1929–1931.

Real prices of corn, wheat, and cotton fell 47 percent, 57 percent, and 45 percent, respectively (U.S. Department of Commerce, 1975). These price declines could not have occurred if the slow growth of production had reflected supply constraints. Additional evidence that supply was not the constraint was the decline from 1910 to 1930 in real farm wages and in real prices of fertilizer and farm machinery (Hayami and Ruttan, 1985; U.S. Department of Commerce, 1975).

The implication of this argument is that neither the quantity nor the quality of cropland limited the expansion of crop production between 1910 and 1930, despite the zero growth of cropland productivity during this period. Consistent with this argument is the 46 percent decline in the real price of agricultural land from 1910 to 1930 (Hayami and Ruttan, 1985; U.S. Department of Commerce, 1985). The increasing economic scarcity of land that emerged between 1900 and 1910 was reversed over the next twenty years.

Compared with the slow growth in land in crops during the 1910–1930 period, the decline in cropland acreage from 1930 to 1940 reflected a different set of underlying crop demand and supply conditions (table 5-5). By 1940 World War II had stimulated rising demand throughout the U.S. economy, even though the United States was not yet at war. In response to this demand, crop production in 1940 increased 14 percent over the production in 1930, a greater percentage increase in that single decade than from 1910 to 1930 (U.S. Department of Agriculture, 1982). However, the expansion of demand for crops from 1930 to 1940 encountered a more sluggish supply response than in the 1910–1930 period. The steep decline in real crop prices that occurred from 1910–1912 to 1929–1931 ended; real crop prices in 1939–1941 were slightly higher than in 1929–1931 (U.S. Department of Commerce, 1975). Rising real prices of farm machinery and fertilizer contributed to the higher crop prices, but the price of labor did not: real farm wages were less in 1940 than in 1930 (Hayami and Ruttan, 1985; nominal prices were adjusted for changes in the general price level).

The supply constraint on the growth of crop production from 1930 to 1940 was less than it otherwise might have been because, for the first time in recorded experience, crop yields began to rise in the 1930s. In the five years centered on 1940, the index of all crop yields was 12 percent higher than in the five years centered on 1930 (U.S. Department of Agriculture, 1982). Corn, wheat, cotton, and soybean yields were up 20 percent, 14 percent, 42 percent, and 36 percent, respectively, in 1940 from 1930 (U.S. Department of Commerce, 1975).

Technological Change

The increase in cropland productivity evident by 1940 began abruptly in the mid-1930s, and broke a period of stagnation in yields dating from the 1870s. In 1930–1936, the index of crop yields averaged 51 (1967 = 100). In 1937–1940, the index averaged 61, marking the beginning of a rising trend that, by the end of the 1980s, still showed no signs of ending.

The reasons for the abrupt shift to rising yields after at least six decades of stagnation and particularly why the shift occurred in the mid-thirties are not entirely clear. At the risk of some simplification, an argument runs along the following lines. The increasing economic scarcity of land that emerged in the first decade of the twentieth century was dissipated over the next twenty years, evidenced by a 30 percent decline in the real price of land from 1910 to 1930. The real

Table 5-5. Amounts of Farmland and Cropland, 1910–1940

Year	Cropland (millions of acres)[a] Used for crops and idle	Harvested	Farmland (millions of acres)	Cropland as a % of farmland[b]
1910	347	317	881	39
1920	402	351	959	42
1930	413	360	990	42
1940	399	331	1,065	37

Sources: U.S. Department of Agriculture (1976), except that cropland harvested is from U.S. Department of Agriculture (1982).
[a]Harvested cropland differs from that used for crops and idle not only by the amount that is idle, but also by the amount that is in fallow and that is not harvested because of crop failure.
[b]Refers to cropland used for crops and idle.

The number of tractors on U.S. farms increased from 1,000 in 1910 to 920,000 in 1930.

price of labor declined also, but not as much, and relative to the price of land it rose 26 percent (Hayami and Ruttan, 1985). The incentive to find ways of increasing the productivity of labor relative to productivity of the land remained strong, as it had been throughout the nineteenth century.

Mechanization was the key to increasing relative labor productivity, as it was before 1900. The development of the gasoline-engined tractor opened up vast new opportunities to pursue a mechanization strategy. Cochrane (1979, p. 108) asserted that the gasoline-engined tractor "was the most significant technological development" to emerge since 1900:

the tractor "provided an efficient and dependable source of power for operating the large soil preparation and harvesting machines that were being developed and sold to farmers." Although tractor prices for the period are unavailable, farm machinery prices generally fell almost 30 percent from 1910 to 1930.[5] In response to these economic advantages, the number of tractors on U.S. farms increased from 1,000 in 1910 to 920,000 in 1930 (Cochrane, 1979).

Although the main incentive for adopting the tractor and associated mechanical devices was to raise the productivity of labor relative to that of the land, adoption incidentally also diminished the economic scarcity of land by reducing the amount of cropland devoted to production of animal feed. In 1910, 88 million acres were used for animal feed, fully 27 percent of the land on which crops were harvested that year. By 1930, land producing animal feed had declined to 65 million acres—18 percent of the land from which a crop was taken (U.S. Department of Agriculture, 1982). The 23 million acres released by the tractor then were available for production of more valuable crops demanded for human consumption. The quantitative effect of this change in reducing cropland scarcity between 1910 and 1930 is unknown, but it may have weakened incentives for farmers to adopt land-saving (yield-increasing) technologies before 1930.

The scientific basis for such land-saving technologies was being laid, however, throughout the first decades of the century, with the USDA as the lead agency. Cochrane (1979) has asserted that, by the end of the nineteenth century, the institutional structure needed for research in plant breeding and nutrition, pest management, and other aspects of the agricultural sciences was in place at the USDA and the land grant colleges. Under the leadership of James Wilson, secretary of agriculture for what must have been a record sixteen years, from 1897 to 1913, "the Department of Agriculture became a great science producing institution . . ." (Cochrane, 1979, p. 104). Building on the rediscovery in 1900 of Mendel's laws of heredity and on the work on mutation and gene theory by European and U.S. institutions, the USDA Bureau of Plant Industries launched basic research on plant breeding and genetics. Moreover, the bureaus of entomology and of chemistry were formed and undertook comparable work in their respective fields. The USDA's research along these diverse lines was complemented and strengthened by research undertaken also in the state agricultural experiment stations attached to the land grant colleges. As knowledge relevant to improved farming practices began to emerge from these efforts, the federal-state extension service became engaged in a growing effort to communicate the knowledge to farmers. Spending on these research and extension activities increased from $14.6 million in 1915 to $52.9 million in 1930 (Cochrane, 1979). Adjusted for changes in the general price level, the increase was a little more than 100 percent in just fifteen years.

This research and the extension program began to pay off by the 1920s (Cochrane, 1979). The introduction of wheat varieties from abroad and the breeding of new domestic varieties made possible the development of varieties more resistant to drought and stem rust than the varieties in wide use. However, the most dramatic, and perhaps the most far-reaching, advance occurred with the development and introduction of hybrid corn. Indeed, hybrid corn generally typifies the shift in technical change in American agriculture from being primarily labor-saving to being primarily land-saving or yield-increasing. Scientific work to develop hybrid corn began in the late nineteenth century, and by the early 1920s hybrid corn breeding

programs were in place in many states (Hayami and Ruttan, 1985). Henry A. Wallace, a pioneering farmer in Iowa and subsequently secretary of agriculture under President Franklin D. Roosevelt in the 1930s, was one of the early leaders in commercial uses of hybrid corn. Farmers became immediately interested in the early hybrids because they could double or triple the yields obtained with the traditional varieties then in general use.

Despite this potential yield advantage, hybrid corn did not catch on widely with U.S. farmers until the mid-1930s (Hayami and Ruttan, 1985). The reasons for the lag between commercial introduction of the hybrid seeds in the 1920s and their widespread adoption by farmers in the 1930s are unclear. One factor may have been that the supply of the new hybrids could not be quickly expanded in response to the emerging demand for them. The relationship between the price of corn and the price of fertilizer also may provide a clue. Achieving the high yield potential of hybrid corn (and of high-yielding varieties of other crops) requires increasing per-acre applications of fertilizer. The more favorable the price of corn to the price of fertilizer, therefore, the stronger the incentive of farmers to capture the yield potential of the corn hybrids. With 1920 equal to 100, the corn/fertilizer price ratio was 112 in 1930. By 1940 it had risen to 154 (Hayami and Ruttan, 1985; U.S. Department of Commerce, 1975). Clearly, the incentives of farmers to adopt the corn hybrids were much stronger in 1940 than in 1930, and this may be a sufficient

Hybrid corn generally typifies the shift in technical change in American agriculture from being primarily labor-saving to being primarily land-saving or yield-increasing.

explanation for the delay between introduction and widespread adoption of the hybrids.

Fertilizer use between 1920 and 1940 is consistent with this explanation of the lag in adoption of hybrid corn. Between 1920 and 1930, fertilizer applied per acre of harvested cropland increased at an annual rate of 2.7 percent. Between 1935, when farmers began to widely adopt hybrid corn, and 1940, per-acre applications of fertilizer rose 8.1 percent annually. This comparison should not be pushed too far. The data are for fertilizer application to *all* harvested cropland, not just that in corn. Furthermore, economic conditions for farmers worsened in the 1920s, but improved from 1935 to the 1940s, although they rose from a very low level. Nonetheless, the generally brighter prospects after 1935 may have made farmers more willing to invest in fertilizers in the late 1930s than in the 1920s, apart from the fertilizer requirements of hybrid corn. Still, the much faster growth in per-acre use of fertilizer supports the argument that economic conditions for adopting the hybrids were more favorable after the mid-1930s than in the 1920s.

It would be incorrect to say that the introduction of hybrid corn (and other high-yielding crop varieties) in the 1930s marked an abrupt shift from labor-saving mechanical innovations to land-saving biological–chemical innovations because the number of tractors on American farms tripled between 1940 and their peak in 1965, and their horsepower increased seven times. Moreover, trucks, combines, and other farm machinery showed comparable increases over that period (Cochrane, 1979). Nevertheless, the emergence of biological–chemical innovations in the 1930s was a major event in development of U.S. agricultural technologies, with lasting implications for use of the nation's cropland. The abrupt increase in crop yields in the second half of the 1930s, after at least six decades of yield stagnation, was but a harbinger of even more profound changes to come.

Soil Conservation

Some observers (Bray and Watkins, 1964) have suggested that increases in corn production in the United States from the last third of the nineteenth through the first third of the twentieth centuries were achieved through operations that depleted soil fertility. Some loss of fertility would be the inevitable result of the oxidation of organic matter in the soil when virgin land is first plowed. Fertility could have been lost also because of soil erosion. No data exist on the amounts of cropland erosion before the 1930s, let alone its effects on crop yields. Nonetheless, concern about these effects began to mount sharply in the 1920s.

The leader in giving voice to that concern was a charismatic soil scientist, Hugh Hammond Bennett. Bennett began his career at the U.S. Department of Agriculture in the first decade of the twentieth century, and through his work and observations traveling the main agricultural regions of the country he became convinced that soil erosion was a major threat to the long-term productivity of the nation's soil resource and hence to its capacity to provide food for future generations of Americans. With colleague W. R. Chapline, Bennett gave powerful expression to his concern in the USDA publication *Soil Erosion—A National Menace* (Bennett and Chapline, 1928). He described the "menace" in dramatic, almost apocalyptic terms, referring to tens of millions of cropland acres "devastated" and "totally destroyed" throughout the South, Southwest, and Midwest. Although Bennett's evidence was anecdotal, much of it from visual observation of gullies, some of them immense, the force of his personality combined with the strength of his convictions and his well-earned credentials as a soil scientist got him a hearing in high places, and ultimately led to the establishment in 1935 of the Soil Conservation Service (SCS) as an arm of the USDA. Bennett was the first chief of the SCS.

No data exist on the amounts of cropland erosion before the 1930s, let alone its effects on crop yields. Nonetheless, concern about these effects began to mount sharply in the 1920s.

Although the SCS began its task without any comprehensive information about the amount of erosion actually occurring in the country or its effects on soil productivity, the agency was not without resources. Not the least of these was the support for soil conservation, not only in the federal government but also among the general public. Much of this support was owed to Bennett himself, but it was strengthened by the enormous dust storms then occurring in the Great Plains as a result of the drought of the mid-1930s and farming practices that left vast stretches of land without any vegetative cover between crops. Those storms made it easy to believe that erosion, in fact, was a serious threat not only to the land directly exposed to the blowing soil, but also to the long-term productivity of the land.

However, the SCS could also draw on more solidly based scientific work on the causes and consequences of erosion, much of it done by, or stimulated by,

Bennett in the 1920s. In support of this work, Congress in 1928 allocated $160,000 to the USDA to study soil erosion, and by mid-1932 the USDA had ten erosion experiment stations gathering information about the problem (Fedkiw, 1989). By early 1933 this work was sufficient to provide a scientific basis for an effective erosion control program (Swain, 1963). This information base was considerably broadened and deepened by the National Reconnaissance Erosion Survey initiated in 1934 by the U.S. Department of the Interior's Soil Erosion Service (forerunner of the SCS) under Bennett's direction. The survey gave the first comprehensive assessment of the erosion problem in the United States. Data collected at the county level were used to classify soils as not eroded, moderately eroded, or severely eroded. Data were not collected, however, on the annual amounts of erosion then occurring. Techniques for taking these measurements were not developed until some twenty

years later. On the basis of the 1934 survey, Bennett revised his 1928 estimate of cropland ruined or severely damaged by erosion from probably not less than 10 million acres to 100 million acres (Fedkiw, 1989).

The information gained from the 1934 survey provided a guide to the scale of the erosion problem, and the research undertaken in the late 1920s and early 1930s gave insights into solutions. Initially, the USDA became actively engaged with farmers in building terraces on the more sloping land and promoting a variety of vegetative management practices and contour plowing to reduce erosion on land not suitable for terracing. The USDA financed most of this work, with in-kind assistance from the Civilian Conservation Corps and from farmers themselves (Fedkiw, 1989). By 1936, the USDA had involved two agencies in soil conservation policy. The first, SCS under Bennett's leadership, engaged primarily in rendering technical assistance to farmers seeking measures to reduce erosion on their land. The second, the Agricultural Stabilization and Conservation Service (ASCS), provided financial assistance to fund these measures. The ASCS paid farmers to withdraw cropland from production, convert it to soil-conserving crops, or install soil-building practices (Fedkiw, 1989). The technical assistance of the SCS and the financial assistance of the ASCS were coordinated through county-level soil conservation districts. Local farmers controlled the districts, which were set up under state laws adopted specifically in response to federal soil conservation legislation. Participation by farmers in the various federal programs was strictly voluntary. Neither the SCS

The ASCS paid farmers to withdraw cropland from production, convert it to soil-conserving crops, or install soil-building practices.

nor the ASCS sought to identify the farmers whose land was most in need of protection against erosion; rather, the guiding criterion for participation was first come, first served.

Thus, by 1940 soil conservation was firmly established on the nation's policy agenda. The overriding policy objective was to reduce, if not eliminate, the threat of soil erosion to the productivity of the nation's soils, particularly its cropland soils. Pursuit of the objective was in no way deterred by the lack of comprehensive information about the amounts of erosion actually occurring or the resulting productivity losses.

Cropland and the Environment

Significant changes occurred in the management of the nation's cropland between 1910 and 1940, but there seems little reason to believe that the changes had major effects on the environment. Changes in the scale of the agricultural enterprise may affect the environment, but for crops changes in scale were modest. Crop production in 1940 was only 24 percent above the 1910 level, and the amount of cropland harvested was up only 4 percent. Crop production had become much more mechanized; but it is not obvious that increased mechanization would have increased environmental damage. Indeed, the effect of mechanization in reducing the number of work animals on farms from 24.9 million in 1910 to 14.5 million in 1940 (Hayami and Ruttan, 1985) may have contributed to improved groundwater and surface water quality in rural areas. Total inorganic fertilizers used doubled from 1910 to 1940 and nitrogen fertilizer tripled. However, the amounts in 1940 still were very small fractions of what they were in the 1970s when they began to excite environmental concern. Pesticides still were little used.

Average farm size increased from 138 acres in 1910 to 174 acres in 1940 (U.S. Department of Agriculture, 1976), which likely led to elimination of some fence-rows and hedgerows that provided habitats for animals. However, vegetative diversity on farms probably was not greatly different in 1940 than in 1910. Most crop farms still included an animal operation, so they kept some land in a forage crop and relied on a variety of vegetative rotational systems to control weeds and pests. Populations of most species of animals remained well below early nineteenth century levels,

Table 5-6. Percentage Distribution of the Nation's Cropland Among Ten USDA-Designated Producing Regions

Region	Year 1920	Year 1940
Northeast[a]	7	6
Appalachia[b]	8	7
Southeast[c]	7	7
Corn Belt[d]	22	19
Lake States[e]	10	10
Mississippi Delta[f]	5	5
Northern Plains[g]	20	23
Southern Plains[h]	11	12
Mountain[i]	5	7
Pacific[j]	4	5
Total	99[k]	101[k]

Source: Fedkiw (1989).

[a]Northeast includes New England and New York, Pennsylvania, New Jersey, Delaware, and Maryland.

[b]Appalachia includes Virginia, West Virginia, North Carolina, Tennessee, and Kentucky.

[c]Southeast includes South Carolina, Georgia, Florida, and Alabama.

[d]Corn Belt includes Ohio, Indiana, Illinois, Iowa, and Missouri.

[e]Lake States include Michigan, Wisconsin, and Minnesota.

[f]Mississippi Delta includes Arkansas, Mississippi, and Louisiana.

[g]Northern Plains include Kansas, Nebraska, South Dakota, and North Dakota.

[h]Southern Plains includes Oklahoma and Texas.

[i]Mountain States include all states between the Northern and Southern Plains and the Pacific states.

[j]Pacific States include California, Oregon, and Washington.

[k]Total may not equal 100 because of rounding.

but probably not much, if any, below the 1910 levels. The plight of these animals in the 1930s remained serious, but any change from the first decade of the century probably owed little to changes in patterns of cropland management.

Shifts in the regional distribution of crop production may affect the environment because, for example, the land in some regions is more erosive than in others and animal habitats that might be affected by crop production also are different. However, between 1910 and 1940 regional shares of crop production evidently did not change much (table 5-6). The principal changes were the loss of share in the Corn Belt and an equal gain in the Northern Plains. These changes may have resulted in somewhat less erosion by water in the Corn Belt, but somewhat more erosion by wind in the Northern Plains. Thus, it appeared that the shift in production did not have a major effect on the environment. Of course, these broad regional aggregates may conceal smaller-scale, but environmentally significant, intraregional shifts in production.

The most serious environmental consequence of cropland management in the years before 1940, however, may well have been the spread of malaria. In testimony before a congressional committee in the late 1930s, Bennett gave a persuasive account of the problems that sediment from eroded fields can cause when it produces large swampy areas by clogging natural drainage systems. He cited circumstances in many places in the South where such erosion had so improved mosquito habitat that it resulted in the spread of malaria in places where it had not previously existed.

Forces Affecting Cropland and Soils: 1940–1990

Cropland management during this period reflected the play of several deep-seated forces affecting the development of American agriculture. The growing importance and eventual dominance of the yield-increasing technologies based on biological and chemical innovations, which first emerged in the 1930s, was perhaps the most fundamental force. The cost-reducing effects of these technologies enabled American farmers to increasingly penetrate and eventually dominate world trade in grain and soybeans. As a result of these effects, the size of the agricultural establishment expanded greatly and dependence increased on world market and political forces, over which farmers had little control. Moreover, the reliance of the new technologies on vastly greater amounts of fertilizer and chemical pesticides evoked rising concerns about their environmental effects, concerns that in time would become a force in shaping the pace and direction of technological change.

Patterns of Land Use

Over a period of 100 years of vast changes in the economic, technical, and political conditions of American agriculture, the percentage of farm cropland used for crops and idle remained stable. The range from 35 percent in 1959 to 41 percent in 1982 is within the bounds existing between 1880 and 1930 (tables 5-1, 5-5, and 5-7). Variations within these

Table 5-7. Several Measures of Agricultural Land Use, 1940–1987

Year	Cropland used for crops and idle (millions of acres)	Cropland harvested (millions of acres)	Farmland (millions of acres)	Cropland as a % of farmland
1940	399	331	1,065	37
1950	409	336	1,161	35
1959[a]	392	317	1,124	35
1969	384	286	1,063	36
1978	395	330	1,015	39
1982	404	347	987	41
1987	NA[b]	293	964	NA[b]

Sources: U.S. Department of Agriculture (1989a) for cropland used for crops and idle and for farmland; U.S. Department of Agriculture (1987a; 1987c) for cropland harvested.

[a]Data include Alaska and Hawaii, but the effect is negligible.

[b]NA = not available.

bounds probably are explained by differences in the strength of crop markets. Crop production generally is the highest-value use of farmland, therefore it is plausible that when crop markets are strong farmers would put more of their land in crops. The cropland percentages for 1950 and 1959 (relatively low crop demand) and for 1982 (relatively high crop demand) are consistent with this argument (table 5-7).

Moreover, cropland used for crops and idle was much more stable than cropland harvested (table 5-7). The difference between the two, in addition to idle cropland, is that cropland used for crops includes land not harvested because of crop failure and land in fallow. When crop markets are strong, less land is left idle and more is planted, with intent to harvest; the contrary is true when markets are weak. The decision to put land in fallow also is partly motivated by short-term market conditions. Land is put in fallow primarily to restore soil moisture. (Virtually all such land in any given year is in the arid and semiarid Northern Plains and Mountain states.) However, if markets are strong, farmers may be willing to accept somewhat lower yields by reducing the amount of land in fallow to capture the higher prices available at that time. Between 1969, when crop markets were relatively weak, and 1982, when they were relatively strong, cropland used for crops and idle increased 20 million acres and cropland harvested increased 61 million acres (table 5-7). A decline in idle cropland from 51 million acres to 21 million accounted for 73 percent of the 41-million acre difference; a 10-million acre decline in land in fallow accounted for 24 percent of the difference; and a 1-million acre decline in

crop failure for the estimated remaining 2 percent. Markets were again weak in 1987 relative to 1982, and cropland harvested was down 54 million acres. Land on which crops failed and land in fallow were essentially unchanged from 1982 to 1987. Data for idle land in 1987 are not available at this writing, but when they become available it is virtually certain they will show a substantial increase from 1982.

The percentage distribution of cropland among regions also changed little from 1940 to 1987 and, overall, from 1920 to 1987 (tables 5-6 and 5-8). The data in tables 5-6 and 5-8 support Cochrane's (1979) assertion that the regional distribution of agricultural production in the United States that would prevail in the twentieth century was already established by the end of the nineteenth century. Some small westward and northward shift in cropland, which occurred between 1920 and 1940 (table 5-6), also continued from 1940 to 1987. In 1940 the Corn Belt, Northern Plains, Mountain, and Pacific states had 55 percent of the nation's cropland. In 1987 they had 65 percent. The decline in the shares of the eastern seaboard states and Appalachia accounted for half of this 10-percentage point gain, and the decline in the share of the Southern Plains accounted for the rest (table 5-8). The overall stability of the regional pattern, however, was more impressive than these changes.

Production and Productivity

Production of crops and other farm output increased far more than farmland and cropland from 1940 to 1987. The difference, of course, reflected the

Table 5-8. Percentage Distribution of Cropland Used for Crops Among Ten USDA-Designated Producing Regions

Region[a]	1940	1950	1960	1970	1980	1987
Northeast	5	5	4	4	3	4
Lake states	10	10	10	10	10	10
Corn Belt	20	20	22	22	23	22
Northern Plains	23	25	25	26	24	26
Appalachia	6	6	5	4	5	5
Southeast	6	5	4	4	4	3
Delta states	5	4	4	5	5	5
Southern Plains	13	11	10	10	9	8
Mountain	7	9	10	10	10	11
Pacific	5	5	6	6	6	6
Total	100	100	100	101[b]	99[b]	100

Sources: U.S. Department of Agriculture (1987a; 1987c).
[a]The regions listed in this column are defined according to notes in table 5-6.
[b]Total may not equal 100 because of rounding.

rising productivity of the land resulting from advances in technology. From 1939–1941 to 1969–1971 the percentage increase in total productivity was virtually the same as the percentage increase in total production (table 5-9). The implication is that over those years the quantity of farm inputs, taken in the aggregate, was unchanged, although there were substantial changes in the composition of aggregate inputs.

However, from 1969–1971 to 1979–1981 total production increased somewhat more than productivity, indicating that some of the additional output resulted from greater use of farm inputs. This trend reversed sharply, however, from 1979–1981 to 1985–1987. Total production hardly increased but total

productivity rose 19 percent (table 5-9), implying that the quantity of inputs declined, which it did, to the lowest level since 1935 (U.S. Department of Agriculture, 1987c). The quantity of inputs used in 1985–1987 was the smallest for any three consecutive years in the entire period from 1914 to 1987. The quantity of inputs used in 1987, the lowest in the three-year period, was 2 percent less than in the previous lowest year, 1934, in the depths of the Great Depression.

In addition, the relationship between crop production and crop productivity was similar to that between total production and total productivity. The main difference was that the quantity of cropland declined somewhat from 1939–1941 to 1969–1971

Table 5-9. Indexes of U.S. Farm Production and Productivity, 1940s to 1980s, and Average Annual Rates of Change (1967 = 100)

Period	Production		Average annual % production increase from previous period		Productivity		Average annual % productivity increase from previous period	
	Total	Crops	Total	Crops	Total	Crops	Total	Crops
1939–1941	60	66			60	62		
1959–1961	90	91	2.0	1.6	89	88	2.0	1.8
1969–1971	104	105	1.5	1.4	105	107	1.7	2.0
1979–1981	130	142	2.3	3.1	122	125	1.5	1.6
1985–1987	132	143	.3	.1	145	136	2.9	1.4

Sources: U.S. Department of Agriculture (1982) for 1939–1971; U.S. Department of Agriculture (1989b) for 1979–1987. The indexes in U.S. Department of Agriculture (1989b) were 1977 = 100. They were converted to 1967 = 100 using the ratios of the indices for 1979 and 1980 in U.S. Department of Agriculture (1982) 1967 = 100 to the indexes for those years in U.S. Department of Agriculture (1989b) 1977 = 100.
Note: For comparison, from 1910–1912 to 1939–1941 total production and crop production grew at average annual rates of 1.1 percent and .6 percent, respectively. Total productivity increased at an average annual rate of .6 percent from 1910–1912 to 1939–1941, and cropland productivity by .3 percent.

(tables 5-7 and 5-9). Increasing cropland accounted for some of the increase in crop production from 1969–1971 to 1979–1981, but for none of the rise in production from 1979–1981 to 1984–1987. Indeed the amount of cropland fell, but relatively not as much as total inputs.

Table 5-10 shows land in corn, wheat, soybeans, and cotton in various years from 1939–1941 to 1985–1987, as well as production and yields of these crops. It should be recalled that from the 1870s to the 1930s yields of corn, wheat, and cotton did not increase (soybean production was negligible in that period). The basis for the yield increases that occurred after 1939–1941 is discussed in more detail below. The increase after 1939–1941 in land in wheat, soybeans, and cotton as a percentage of all cropland harvested reflected the rising importance of exports in total crop production, with corn, wheat, soybeans, and cotton being the export leaders.

Technological Advances

The rising trends of total productivity and crop yields that began in the late 1930s and continued into the late 1980s reflected a shift from the land-using, labor-saving technologies that had prevailed from the beginning of the nineteenth century to more land-saving (and still labor-saving) technologies. An important reason for this shift in the technical base of American agriculture seems to have been the emerging economic scarcity of land, reflected in rising land prices. Signs of increasing land scarcity were evident by the late 1930s, although in that period real land prices still were well below those prevailing around 1910. Subsequently, land prices rose sharply. With 1936–1940 prices equal to 100, real land prices rose to 196 in 1968–1972 and to 342 in 1981–1985 (U.S. Department of Commerce, 1975; U.S. Department of Agriculture, 1976–1989a).[6]

Table 5-10. Corn, Wheat, Soybeans, and Cotton: Land Use, Production, and Yield (three-year averages)

Period	Corn	Wheat	Soybeans	Cotton	Percentage of total cropland harvested
1939–1941					
Land (millions of acres)	86.7	54.0	5.0	23.3	51
Production (millions of bu. or lb.)	2,563	832.6	92	5,855	
Yield (bu. or lb./acre)	29.6	15.4	18.4	251.3	
1969–1971					
Land (millions of acres)	58.7	46.1	42.1	11.2	54
Production (millions of bu. or lb.)	4,827	1,471	1,145	4.905	
Yield (bu. or lb./acre)	82.2	31.9	27.2	438.0	
1979–1981					
Land (millions of acres)	73.3	71.4	68.1	13.3	66
Production (millions of bu. or lb.)	7,562	2,433	2,016	6,624	
Yield (bu. or lb./acre)	103.2	34.1	29.6	498.0	
1985–1987					
Land (millions of acres)	67.9	60.5	59.0	9.6	63
Production (millions of bu. or lb.)	8,066	2,208	1,987	6,042	
Yield (bu. or lb./acre)	118.8	36.5	33.7	629.4	

Average annual yield increase (percentage)				
1939–1941 to 1969–1971	3.5	2.5	1.3	1.9
1969–1971 to 1979–1981	2.3	1.1	.8	1.3
1979–1981 to 1985–1987	2.4	1.1	2.2	4.0

Sources: U.S. Department of Agriculture (1972) for 1939–1941 to 1969–1971; U.S. Department of Agriculture (1983) for 1969–1971 and 1979–1981; U.S. Department of Agriculture (1989b) for 1985–1987.

The increase in land prices after 1940 primarily reflected the increasing economic scarcity of land, but policies of the federal government to support crop prices also played a role. These policies began in the depression years of the 1930s and have continued to the present. Although details have varied over the years, the policies generally required farmers participating in the price support programs to take a certain (varying) amount of their cropland out of production. The objective was to reduce production, thus easing the fiscal burden of the programs. A result of the land retirement provisions, however, was a policy-induced increase in cropland prices. How important this source of increasing land prices may have been relative to the effect of ordinary market forces is uncertain. However, Johnson (1985) has argued that land prices were measurably higher because of the programs.

Rising land prices gave farmers incentive to adopt more land-saving technologies. Farmers and the public institutions supporting them—most notably but not exclusively the U.S. Department of Agriculture and the U.S. Department of the Interior Bureau of Reclamation—responded along several lines. One response was to increase investments in drainage and irrigation, which are land-saving because they permit the same amount of output on a smaller land base or a larger output from a given land base—they raise yields. Between 1945 and 1980, drained land increased from 50 million acres to more than 105 million acres, about one-fourth of all cropland in 1980 (Pavelis, 1985). Irrigated acreage more than doubled from 1950 to 1977, surpassing 50 million acres (Frederick, 1988).

A result of the land retirement provisions was a policy-induced increase in cropland prices.

The contribution of drainage to national yield increases after 1940 is unknown, but it surely was positive. Irrigation contributed a small but significant amount to the increase in yields of major crops during the post–World War II period (table 5-11). For example, between 1950 and 1977 national average corn yields increased 145 percent; 8 percent of the increase was attributable to the growth of yields on irrigated corn land in the West. Frederick with Hanson (1982) indicated that the increased proportion of cornland irrigated contributed an additional 5 percent to the national average increase in corn yields, so the total irrigation contribution for corn was 13 percent (the 5 percent contribution is part of the 12 percent contributed to increased corn yields by the change in acreage mix; table 5-11). In similar fashion, irrigation contributed 16 percent of the national average increase of 150 percent in sorghum yields between 1950 and 1977, 7 percent of the 92 percent increase in wheat yields, and 44 percent of the 59 percent increase in cotton yields.

Table 5-11. Percentage of Changes in Total Crop Yields and the Sources of Changes, 1950 to 1977

| Crop | Percentage change in aggregate yield | Source of crop yield changes (percentages of total change in yield) | | | |
		Growth of yields in irrigated West	Growth of yields in dryland West	Growth of yields in East	Change in acreage mix[a]
Corn	145	8	6	74	12
Sorghum	150	12	74	8	6
Wheat	92	3	71	23	4
Cotton	59	7	22	45	27

Source: Frederick with Hanson (1982).

Note: Rows may not add to 100 because of rounding.

[a]The change in the acreage mix affects yield when crops shift among regions and between irrigated and nonirrigated land. For example, if the percentage of irrigated land increases (as it did from 1950 to 1977), this will tend to increase national average yields, even if yields on irrigated and nonirrigated land are constant, because yields are higher on irrigated than on nonirrigated land.

Clearly, most of the post–World War II increases in crop yield were on nonirrigated land. These increases reflected the other primary response to rising economic scarcity of land: the development and widespread adoption of higher-yielding, fertilizer-responsive crop varieties, and associated management practices. The role of public research and extension agencies in developing these varieties and practices continued and greatly strengthened after 1940. In that year, spending on research and extension by the USDA, the state agricultural experiment stations, and the federal-state extension services was $164 million (in 1967 dollars). By 1970, such spending by these agencies had risen to $712 million (in 1967 dollars).[7] By 1979, the amount (in 1967 dollars) had fallen to $552 million. This decline in spending reflected tightening federal government budgets and high inflation in the 1970s.[8]

The higher-yielding, fertilizer-responsive crop varieties developed by the USDA and other public agencies gave farmers incentive to adopt the varieties even at the fertilizer prices prevailing around 1940. The incentive was greatly strengthened after 1940, however, by steeply falling fertilizer prices relative to crop and land prices (table 5-12), reflecting technical improvements in the production and marketing of fertilizer (Hayami and Ruttan, 1985). So powerful was the combination of falling relative fertilizer prices and the high-yield responsiveness to fertilizer that the amount of fertilizer applied per acre roughly doubled each decade between 1940 and 1970 (table 5-12).

Table 5-12. Fertilizer Prices Relative to Crop and Land Prices, and Fertilizer Applied per Acre of Cropland, Various Years

| Year | Price of fertilizer relative to price of | | Fertilizer applied per acre of cropland (lb./acre) |
	Crops	Land	
1940	1.8	2.0	10.7
1950	.9	1.3	24.2
1960	.8	.7	47.1
1970	.7	.4	111.2
1980	.8 (1.07)[a]	.3 (.92)[a]	132.7
1985	(1.13)[a]	(1.05)[a]	130.3

Sources: Hayami and Ruttan (1985) for prices, which are five-year averages for the period ending in the year indicated, from 1940 to 1980 (excluding those prices in parentheses; and U.S. Department of Agriculture (1982, 1987b) for fertilizer per acre of cropland.

[a]Numbers in parentheses are derived from indexes of prices in U.S. Department of Agriculture (1987b).

The price of fertilizer rose relative to crop prices from 1970 to 1980, and the decline in the fertilizer-to-land price slowed during this period. On both counts, farmers' incentives to increase per acre applications of fertilizer were weaker than they had been before 1970. In addition, it is likely that by the 1970s the per-acre amounts of fertilizer were so high that the crop yield response to additional amounts was less than it had been earlier. This, too, would have weakened farmers' incentive to increase per-acre applications. The combination of less favorable price relations and lower yield response likely accounts for the slower increase in fertilizer use per acre after 1970 and the slight decline from 1980 to 1985.

The biologically based innovations-cum-fertilizer were not the only sources of the yield increases achieved after 1940. From 1920–1924 through 1946–1954, increases in corn yields resulted about equally from improved seeds, greater use of fertilizer, and increased mechanization (Johnson and Gustafson, 1962). From the mid-1950s to 1980, improved varieties accounted for slightly less than half of corn yield increases, the rest being attributable to more fertilizers and pesticides and improved management (Sundquist, Menz, and Neumeyer, 1982).

The private sector contributed little to the early development of the yield-increasing technologies introduced after the late 1930s (Hayami and Ruttan, 1985), concentrating instead on innovations in farm machinery and equipment. Difficulties in securing patents on biologically based technologies evidently inhibited private research and development in this area. This began to change in the 1970s and 1980s. The federal Plant Variety Protection Act of 1970 and the 1980 U.S. Supreme Court decision in *Diamond v. Chakravarty* (U.S. Supreme Court, 1980) on the patentability of microorganisms made it easier to establish private property rights in biological innovations. Feller and coauthors (1984) regard this as a major reason for the proliferation in the 1980s of firms engaged in research on biotechnologies. Thus the private sector likely will make important contributions to future development of such technologies.

Crop Prices and Exports

The improvements in total productivity after 1940 led to declining unit production costs, which permitted American farmers to greatly increase their penetration of world agricultural markets. The decline in production costs is evident in the decline in real prices of crops since 1940, and is especially impressive because demand for agricultural output evidently grew faster after 1940 than in the preceding three decades (tables 5-9 and 5-13). Between 1939–1941 and 1979–1981, total output grew an average of 2.0 percent per year and crop output an average of 1.9 percent (table 5-9). The acceleration in output growth from 1939–1941 to 1979–1981 and its failure to grow after that primarily reflect the expansion, then collapse, of crop exports. In 1939–1941, 4.2 percent of the land on which crops were harvested was devoted to exports, with the rest given to domestic uses (12.6 percent to feed work animals and 83.2 percent for the rest of the domestic market) (U.S. Department of Agriculture, 1982). By 1969–1971 the export share of the land harvested had risen to 21.9 percent, land to feed work animals had fallen to zero, and the rest of the domestic market accounted for 78.1 percent. In 1979–1981 the export share was 37.5 percent, and the domestic share had fallen to 62.5 percent. Over the period as a whole from 1939–1941 to 1979–1981, land harvested for exports increased from an annual average of 14 million acres to 130 million acres. Land devoted to production for the domestic market for all purposes decreased from an annual average of 324 million acres to 225 million acres (U.S. Department of Agriculture, 1987b).

After 1982, the growth of the world economy slowed drastically and the value of the dollar began to rise relative to foreign currencies. The combination resulted in a drastic fall in crop exports from 1979–1981 to 1985–1987. The U.S. boycott of grain exports to the Soviet Union in 1980, following that country's invasion of Afghanistan, contributed to this decline by encouraging the USSR to seek other sources

It is likely that by the 1970s the per-acre amounts of fertilizer were so high that the crop yield response to additional amounts was less that it had been earlier.

of supply. As a consequence, land harvested for exports fell from an average of 130 million acres in 1979–1981 to 87 million in 1985–1986. The percentage of land devoted to exports fell from 37.5 percent to 26.1 percent.

To summarize, crop production in the United States shifted to a strongly land-saving mode after 1940, a mode that persists today. The shift was made possible initially by research done in the four preceding decades by USDA scientists and university scientists supported by the USDA on biologically based technologies, such as hybrid corn. Although the connection is not entirely clear, this research seems to have been motivated, at least in part, by the emerging economic scarcity of good cropland that already had been evident early in the twentieth century. The research was supported at an increasing level of public spending throughout most of the period covered here, leveling off in the 1980s under the force of increasingly tight federal budgets. Private research contributed

Table 5-13. Real Prices of Agricultural Output

Period	Total output[a]	Crops[a]	Corn ($/bu.)	Wheat ($/bu.)	Soybeans ($/bu.)	Cotton ($/lb.)
1939–1941	98	110	1.53	1.81	2.56	.28
1959–1961	107	112	1.19	2.01	2.40	.36
1969–1971	95	87	1.02	1.12	2.35	.21
1979–1981	100	98	1.10	1.54	2.70	.26
1985–1987	70	64	.57	.82	1.61	.18

Sources: U.S. Department of Commerce (1975), for 1939–1941; U.S. Department of Agriculture (1972) for 1959–1961 and 1969–1971; U.S. Department of Agriculture (1983) for 1970–1981; and U.S. Department of Agriculture (1989a) for 1985–1987.

[a]Nominal prices (or indexes) are deflated by the Consumer Price Index; 1967 = 100.

*Total production
and crop
production grew
at much faster
rates from 1940 to
the 1980s than at
any time in the
seventy years
preceding 1940.*

relatively little to development of the new technologies, although this began to increase in the 1970s.

A characteristic of the new technologies was relatively high crop responsiveness to fertilizer. This feature made the new varieties attractive to farmers in an environment of increasing economic scarcity of land, but the attractiveness was greatly enhanced by a long-term decline in the price of fertilizer relative to prices of land and crops.

The new technologies led to rising trends in total productivity and crop yields, ending seventy years of stagnation in these indicators of performance. The increases in productivity reduced crop production costs, making it possible for American farmers to expand exports at an unprecedented rate. Thus total production and crop production grew at much faster rates from 1940 to the 1980s than at any time in the seventy years preceding 1940. Despite the long-term decline in crop prices, real land prices rose sharply from 1940 to the 1980s, reflecting the increasing economic scarcity of land. Land prices fell precipitously after 1982 because of growing weakness in foreign markets for U.S. crop production, but nevertheless remained well above pre-1970 levels.

Soil Erosion

Whatever the effects of soil erosion on soil productivity before and after 1940, they were not incompatible with the successful deployment of the new technologies after 1940, nor were they sufficient to impede the substantial increases in crop yield resulting from the technologies. The success of the technologies depended heavily on the strong yield response of the new crop varieties to fertilizer; moreover, it is well established that this response is suppressed on soils whose water-holding capacity has been impaired by erosion. Consequently, the success of the new technologies strongly suggests that erosion damage to soils in the main crop-producing regions of the country was not and is not as severe as is sometimes claimed.

This conclusion applies to the strong claims of severe erosion damage made by Bennett. In one study (Bennett and Chapline, 1928), Bennett described in vivid detail the erosion damages in the southern Piedmont and across the lower South, in the rolling Blacklands of central Texas, and in the region of loess soils that covers the uplands bordering on the Mississippi River. Subsequently, Bennett cited various soil and erosion surveys as indicating that the nation had lost at least 17.5 million acres of formerly tilled land to gullying and related deep sheet erosion (Bennett, 1931). As in the 1928 study with Chapline, he singled out the Piedmont region as an area where erosion damage was especially severe, but noted that other regions (such as the rolling Blacklands of Texas) had suffered even greater damage, amounting to "almost complete devastation" from the standpoint of crop production (Bennett, 1931, p. 155). Bennett also reported a 1931 survey by the USDA Agricultural Experiment Station in Oklahoma that revealed that 13.2 million of the state's 15.8 million acres of cropland were severely eroded.

Bennett also claimed that similar conditions prevailed in the sloping areas of northern Missouri and southern Iowa, where highly productive glacial soils had been so severely eroded that the subsoil was exposed across wide areas, and gullies were common. Most of 9 million acres of low-grade farmland in Illinois, he reported, were "tremendously impoverished" by erosion, and another 12 million acres of high-grade land were "suffering severely" from erosion. He said that nearly half of the 12 million acres were approaching a condition of gullying. In other Corn Belt states, in the Great Plains, in Tennessee and Kentucky, and in the deep South, larger areas, according to Bennett, had been virtually destroyed "in the practical crop producing sense" (Bennett, 1931, p. 160).

In a later publication, Bennett (1939) asserted that about 50 million acres of the nation's cropland had been ruined for cultivation, another 50 million acres were bordering on the same condition, and 100 million acres were severely damaged by having lost half to all their topsoil. By Bennett's standard, almost half of the nation's 415 million acres of cropland had suffered severe erosion damage.

The nationwide productivity performance and that of many of the areas Bennett cited as suffering severe erosion damage suggest that he overestimated either the degree of damage, or its permanence, or both. Crosson and Stout (1983) collected data on yields of corn, wheat, soybeans, and cotton for states, and areas within states, which according to Bennett had been severely eroded in the 1930s. The data were average yields in 1950–1954 and 1976–1980. The data showed that, over the period, yield growth in those areas for the various crops were comparable with the high national rates of increase.

Crosson and Stout (1983) also calculated the cumulative effect of erosion between 1950 and 1980 on intercounty differences in the growth of corn, soybean, and wheat yields in parts of the Corn Belt (for corn and soybeans) and the Northern Plains (for wheat). The hypothesis was that intercounty differences in cropland erosion in 1977 (the only year for which actual erosion data then existed) were proportional to intercounty differences in cumulative erosion over the 1950–1980 period. Trends in county yields of each crop for that period were then regressed against county erosion on land in each crop (as well as against certain other variables believed to help explain intercounty differences in yield growth). The effects of erosion on intercounty differences in growth of wheat yields were not statistically significant. They were significant for corn and soybeans, but small. The results showed that, because of erosion, average corn yields among all counties studied were 2 percent less in 1980 than they would have been otherwise. Soybean yields were 1.5 percent less in 1980 because of erosion.

Statements in the 1930s and subsequently about the threat of erosion to soil productivity thus appear to have been exaggerated. Two elements bearing on the interpretation of erosion and its consequences for productivity may help to explain this tendency for overstatement. One is the tendency to underestimate the capacity of people to restore the productivity of even severely eroded soil. The other is the tendency to regard estimates of soil erosion as soil forever lost to future agricultural production.

Soil scientists have acknowledged that even severely eroded soil can be restored to high productivity with investments of human skill and other resources, even though they may seem to forget this when they make pronouncements about the erosion threat. Even Bennett (1931, pp. 161–162) observed that with "good tillage and liberal additions of organic matter and plant food . . . the yields [of severely eroded land] can largely be increased," and he noted that sometimes pre-erosion yields may be exceeded. However, he argued that the technical feasibility of restoring severely eroded land was more limited than commonly supposed and that the economic cost of restoring the land "should not be forgotten" (p. 162).

Bennett's point about economic cost is crucial because it implies that on many severely eroded soils the loss of productivity is not permanent, but can be restored at a cost. Thus the issue of erosion management falls within the purview of the management of all other agricultural resources. In deciding what to do about erosion, the farmer (as in all his or her management decisions) will calculate the costs and returns of the alternatives. If the cost in lost productivity of current rates of erosion is higher than the costs of erosion control, the farmer will opt for control. If the costs of control are higher than the cost of lost productivity, the farmer will not opt for control. Of course, to make this decision wisely, the farmer must know how much productivity is likely to be lost and when it will be lost—knowledge not generally available. Thus publicly funded research plays an important role: it provides farmers with the information they need about erosion/productivity relationships. If the farmer does not have this knowledge, erosion on many soils may proceed to the point where the cost of halting it and restoring soil productivity is greater

Statements in the 1930s and subsequently about the threat of erosion to soil productivity appear to have been greatly overstated.

Natural regeneration of loblolly pine on eroded slopes, Mississippi

than if corrective action had been taken sooner. However, this is an economic problem in the optimal allocation of resources over time in the presence of uncertainty. It generally is not a problem of preserving soil productivity now or losing it forever.

One important means for restoring the productivity of eroded land is by adding organic matter to the soil. Organic matter not only stores plant nutrients, but also improves soil structure by binding mineral particles in the soil into larger aggregates, thus promoting aeration, increasing infiltration of water, and making "heavy" soils easier to work (Broadbent, 1957; Thompson and Troeh, 1973). According to Bartelli (1980), plant roots are the main source of organic matter in cultivated soils, and the quantity of roots per acre is positively correlated with crop yields. Crop residues, also positively correlated to yields, also are a potentially important source of organic matter when plowed into the soil. It is a plausible inference, therefore, that the growth of crop yields after the 1930s may have contributed to the partial restoration of organic matter to many of the badly eroded soils observed by Bennett in the 1930s.

It is not clear how important the soil-building processes may have been in restoring the productivity of eroded land over the past several decades. Where the processes occur, rates of soil regeneration may be considerably faster than commonly supposed. In a review of the literature, Bartelli (1980) found that on permeable, unconsolidated material, the A horizon (roughly the topsoil, and usually the most productive soil layer because it contains most of the organic matter) may develop at the rate of about 1 centimeter (.4 inch) per year. This rate would be about 60 tons per acre per year, far more than the 5 tons per acre per year rate of topsoil regeneration used by the Soil Conservation Service to set standards of maximum "tolerable" erosion. Where the underlying material is hard rock, the rate of regeneration is much less than where it is unconsolidated material. A key issue, therefore, in judging the extent to which soil regeneration may have restored the eroded soils observed by Bennett concerns the nature of the parent material underlying the soils. Bartelli (1980) believes that on the Tama, Decatur, and Davidson soils found in much of Illinois, the rate of formation of an A horizon with modern farming techniques is not less than 12 tons per acre per year, almost two-and-a-half times the SCS maximum for "tolerable" erosion. Bennett had singled out Illinois as an erosion disaster area; apparently he underrated the ability of the soil to regenerate quickly. Corn and soybeans in Illinois, the state's leading crops, fully shared in the rapid national growth of yields for these crops.

Bennett may have underestimated the extent to which gullied land could be restored. In the 1940s and 1950s, farmers reclaimed badly eroded and gullied land on loess soils in Mississippi and western Tennessee by using then-modern earth-moving machinery (Bartelli, 1980). Yet, Bennett in the 1930s had identified gullying in those areas as one of the prime indicators of the severity of the erosion problem.

The restoration of badly gullied land illustrates a key point. The extent of erosion damage to soil productivity depends in large part on economic and technical conditions. The large earth-moving machinery available in the 1950s was technically more advanced and efficient than equipment available in the 1930s. Similarly, the economic conditions for crop production in the 1940s and 1950s were much more favorable than in the severely depressed 1930s. Consequently, in the later decades farmers had both the technical means and the economic incentive to restore badly gullied land. It is easy to understand why, lacking this knowledge about future technical and economic conditions, Bennett and others in the 1930s might have mistaken land temporarily rendered unproductive by erosion for land permanently lost to crop production.

IS SOIL LOST OR MOVED?

The tendency to mistake temporarily unproductive land for permanently lost land is evident in the widely accepted, popular notion that when soil is eroded from fields it is forever after "lost," therefore unavailable to support future crop production. For example, one report by the Conservation Foundation (1982, p. 234), referring to data from the 1977 National Resources Inventory taken by the Soil Conservation Service, stated that "nationally, over 6.4 billion tons of soil a year are lost in wind and water erosion." This notion of soil "lost" is found throughout the popular literature on soil erosion. However, a committee of the National Research Council (1986) has asserted that referring to erosion estimates as measures of "soil loss" is a misnomer, and that "movement" or "displacement" are better terms. The committee noted that often the soil is merely moved from one part of a field to another to be deposited in a low-lying place.

The Universal Soil Loss Equation and the Wind Erosion Equation, as used in the National Resource Inventories of 1977 and 1982, estimated the amount of soil moved on an acre of land. The equations tell nothing about the fate of the soil so moved. The evidence is clear, though, that most of the soil is not permanently lost to agriculture. Although the famous dust storm of 1935 in the Great Plains carried soil across the eastern portion of the country and deposited some of it in the Atlantic Ocean, the heavier soil particles, which may account for about half of wind-eroded soil, move short distances by processes described as "saltation" and "creep" (Gillette, 1986). Gillette argued that finer-grained particles (which generally are richer in nutrients than coarser grains) are picked up by the wind and may be moved great distances. It is known that some wind-eroded soil is deposited in the Great Lakes, which makes it truly "lost." However, it seems likely that much of even the fine-grained particles is deposited in a place not

The tendency to mistake temporarily unproductive land for permanently lost land is evident in the widely accepted notion that when soil is eroded from fields it is forever after "lost" to crop production.

too unlike the place of origin. The Great Plains, where most wind erosion occurs, is a vast region, with the greater part of the land in crops, pasture, and range. Much of the fine-grained soil picked up in one part of the region must be deposited on land in much the same actual or potential use somewhere else in the region.

Most studies of soil transport, however, have focused on soil eroded from the land by water. How much of this soil is permanently lost to agriculture? Not much. The strongest case for permanent loss perhaps can be made for soil carried to the two oceans and the Gulf of Mexico. Recent estimates are that the proportion making the trip is 5 to 10 percent. Trimble (1975) studied erosion and sedimentation in ten large river basins in the southern Piedmont from colonial times to the 1970s, and concluded that of the material eroded from upland slopes since European settlement, only about 5 percent had been delivered to the fall line of rivers in the region. Meade and Parker (1985) also commented that, in the country as a whole, only about 10 percent of the soil eroded from upland areas is delivered to the oceans (and the Gulf of Mexico) by rivers.

What of the 90 percent not deposited in the oceans? Meade and Parker have asserted that a fraction of it is captured by reservoirs, "but most of it is stored in other places, such as on hill slopes, floodplains, and other parts of stream valleys" (1985, p. 55). Foster and Hakonson (1983) have observed that much sediment is deposited on the landscape near the point of origin, frequently at the toe of concave slopes, in marshes, shallow channels, road ditches, fencerows,

In the country as a whole, only about 10 percent of the soil eroded from upland areas is delivered to the oceans (and the Gulf of Mexico) by rivers.

and dense vegetative strips along the edge of fields and streams. Deposition also occurs in channels, on floodplains, and in reservoirs downstream from the erosion site and remote from it.

Larsen, Pierce, and Dowdy (1983) in a study of five watersheds in Minnesota varying in size from 1,270 to 440 square miles, found that only .8 percent to 26.9 percent of the soil eroded in the watersheds entered stream channels. The rest was deposited on cropland, wasteland, pasture, or forestland. Much of the soil eroded from cropland probably was deposited on other cropland. In addition to his work on the southern Piedmont, Trimble (1981; Trimble and Lund, 1982) studied erosion and sedimentation occurring from 1853 to 1975 in the 139-square mile Coon Creek basin of southwestern Wisconsin. The basin was first opened to agriculture in the early 1850s. In the 122 years, only 6 to 7 percent of the soil eroded from upland areas and valleys tributary to Coon Creek was exported from the basin to the Mississippi River. The rest was deposited within the region. Of that, the greater part—more than half between 1938 and 1975—was deposited on lower slopes or at the bottom of hills. About 75 percent of the rest was deposited in the upper and lower main valleys (Trimble, 1981). By the 1930s, floodplains in the basin were accumulating deposited soil at a rate of about 6 inches per year.

This review leaves little doubt that only a small percentage of the soil eroded from farmers' fields is permanently lost to agriculture. To be sure, sediment that ends up in ditches, against fences, or in other unfarmable places cannot be turned to crop production unless it is moved to a more favorable location (or the fences are taken down). Such an effort is not without an economic cost. However, the issue for the farmer, and for society, is one of the economic gains and losses of holding the soil in place; letting it go and forgetting about it (recognizing that little of it will be permanently lost); or letting it go for now with the prospect of recovering it later when economic and technical conditions make that worthwhile. Some portion of the soil moved from farmers' fields is always in stream channels, and that portion obviously is unavailable for farming. However, if the erosion threat to soil productivity became so serious that major efforts to hold the soil on the land were justified, then the amount of soil delivered to streams would be greatly reduced. Stream dynamics are such that the water would then begin to scour the stream channel, and much of the soil stored there would be moved downstream, ultimately to be deposited in some potentially (at a cost) farmable place.

Even the soil deposited in reservoirs is not forever lost. Reservoirs are designed with the expectation that they eventually will fill up, although the filling time typically is measured in decades to a century or more. Of course, sedimentation of reservoirs may impose high costs in lost power generation capacity, increased flooding hazard, and damage to recreational values, but this is a different set of problems. As far as the effect of erosion on soil productivity is concerned, the soil deposited in the reservoirs will in time be available to once again support agricultural production.

FUTURE PRODUCTIVITY EFFECTS OF EROSION

It may be accepted that over the past fifty years the threat of erosion to permanent losses of soil productivity was never as great as many people had claimed. However, what about the present and future effects of erosion on productivity?

Cropland erosion in the late 1970s was almost surely less than it was in the 1930s, when it excited greatest concern about its effects on productivity. Although no data on the amount of annually occurring erosion were available before the SCS 1977 National Resources Inventory, analysis supports the inference that cropland erosion was less in the late 1970s than in the 1930s. That analysis, reported in Crosson and Stout (1983), has suggested that because the amount of cropland in the 1930s was almost exactly the same as in the late 1970s, erosion differences between the two periods would reflect only changes in erosion per acre. Crosson and Stout considered five factors affecting erosion per acre: shifts in crop production among regions with different amounts of per-acre erosion; changing amounts of land in crops with different erosion rates; per-acre erosion effect of changes in technology; changes in the percentages of cropland farmed by tenants and owner-operators (tenants generally being regarded as having weaker incentives to control erosion); and soil conservation policies. They found the effects of changes in the regional distribution of crop production to be neutral, as was the tenant and owner-operator factor. Changes in the crop mix (the increasing importance of soybeans, a highly erosive crop) were judged to have increased per-acre

erosion, but changes in technology—the increasing yield effect and also the widespread adoption of conservation tillage techniques after 1970—almost surely decreased per-acre erosion more. Furthermore, the soil conservation policies launched in the 1930s and sustained ever since must have had some effect in reducing per acre erosion, although the effect has not been measured. These policies combined financial incentives to farmers to adopt terracing and other erosion control measures with technical assistance and a broad program to educate farmers and the larger community about soil erosion and how to control it. Although uncertain, the "consciousness-raising" effects of these policies may have been at least as important as any other aspect in reducing erosion.

Other evidence concerning future productivity effects of erosion suggests that after another 100 years of cropland erosion at present rates, crop yields would be only 3 to 10 percent less than they would be without any erosion effect. Three separate studies support this conclusion. One was done by soil scientists, economists, and others at the USDA facility at Temple, Texas, to develop the Erosion Productivity Impact Calculator (EPIC). Using EPIC, Alt, Osborn, and Colacicco (1989), agricultural economists at the USDA Economic Research Service, projected that after 100 years of cropland erosion at the annual rates found in the SCS 1982 National Resources Inventory (U.S. Department of Agriculture, Soil Conservation Service, 1984), national average yields would be 3 percent less than they would be without an erosion effect.

In another study, soil scientists at the University of Minnesota, working under the leadership of William Larsen, developed the Productivity Index (PI) model to measure long-term effects of erosion on crop yields. Using the model to study the effects on 98 million cropland acres in the Corn Belt, they found that after fifty years of erosion on this land at the 1977 rate (taken from the 1977 National Resources Inventory and not much different from the rate found in the 1982 inventory), yields would be 2 percent less than they would be without an erosion effect (Pierce and coauthors, 1984). After 100 years, yields would be 4 percent less.

In another study, Crosson (1986) examined erosion-yield relationships in the Corn Belt and Great Plains following research reported in Crosson and Stout (1983). Using erosion data from the SCS 1982 National Resources Inventory and a more advanced regression model than that used in Crosson and Stout, Crosson (1986) found that continuation of erosion at the 1982 rate for 100 years would not significantly affect wheat yields in the region studied. Corn and soybean yields would be down 5 percent and 10 percent, respectively, relative to what they would be without an erosion effect.

Considering the quite different analytical approaches taken by these three studies, the similarities in their results are strong evidence that continuation of present rates of erosion throughout most of the next century would pose no serious threat to the productivity of the nation's soils. This, of course, does not imply that the nation can now safely relax its soil conservation efforts. Such inaction surely would lead to an increase in erosion, at least as long as the amount of land in crops remains the same. Consequently, the erosion threat, now minor, might become more se-

rious. The current situation undoubtedly reflects to some extent the success of the USDA soil conservation policies sustained over the past fifty years. Arguments have been made (see, for example, Crosson, 1986) that the USDA ought to redirect the policies to give less attention to the (minor) threat of erosion to soil productivity and more to the (much bigger) threat of off-farm sediment damages to water quality. Properly managed, such policy redirection could be done without increasing the threat of erosion to long-term soil productivity.

Conversion of Agricultural Land

The conversion of agricultural land to urban uses emerged as a major issue in the 1970s. Three events combined to spark concern. First, exports of grains and soybeans accelerated after 1972, and farmers responded by bringing into crop production some 60 million acres of land previously idle or in pasture or woodland. This response reversed the declining trend in cropland that began about 1950 (table 5-7). The belief was widespread that export demand would continue to increase rapidly. The second event was that the sharp rise in crop yields which began in the 1940s tapered off in the 1970s (table 5-8). This event raised questions about the nation's ability over the long-term future to continue substituting technology for land in response to rising demand for agricultural output. The third event was a USDA survey in 1975 which showed that the annual rate of conversion of rural land to urban, transportation, and other "built-up" uses increased from about 1 million acres to 2

Continuation of present rates of erosion throughout most of the next century would pose no serious threat to the productivity of the nation's soils.

million acres from 1967 to 1975 (Dideriksen, Hidlebaugh, and Schmude, 1977). The 1977 National Resources Inventory indicated an even higher rate of conversion: 2.9 million acres annually from 1967 to 1977.

Taken together, these three events suggested the possibility of sharply increasing economic scarcity of agricultural land, particularly cropland. In response to the perceived threat, the Congress mandated that the USDA, jointly with the federal Council on Environmental Quality, should undertake a study of the long-term demand-supply conditions for agricultural land. The resulting study, the National Agricultural Lands Study, concluded that the emerging supply-demand conditions for agricultural land posed a long-term threat of rising economic costs of food and fiber (U.S. Department of Agriculture and Council on Environmental Quality, 1981). Although the threat was not viewed as immediate, by the 1990s, the report stated, it could be of the same order as the threat of rising energy costs, thought to be immediate and severe at the time the study was done. The study urged that the federal government should take explicit account of the impact of its operations on conversion of agricultural land and that it encourage and assist the states to adopt programs for slowing conversion

and diverting it away from prime agricultural land. Some of these recommendations were written into the 1981 farm bill (see the section on Effects on the Environment, below).

By the mid-1980s, the conversion of agricultural land as a threat to the nation's long-term capacity to produce food and fiber had disappeared from the nation's policy agenda. This occurred in part because the National Resources Inventory taken in 1982 by the SCS indicated that the 1977 inventory estimate of urban land was substantially too high, and that the annual rate of urban land growth was about the same in the 1970s as in the 1960s. Analysis of population census data supported this conclusion (Frey, 1983). In addition, the decline in land in crops and collapse of farmland prices following the sharp reduction in export demand for corn, wheat, and cotton in the early 1980s made it difficult to maintain the earlier concern about losses of agricultural land to urban uses.

By the late 1980s, foreign demand for U.S. crops had begun to recover, and the likelihood is strong that it will continue to grow over the long term (Crosson, forthcoming). However, if crop yields continue to increase at the relatively slow 1980s rate, increases in crop demand are unlikely to put much pressure on the nation's supply of cropland (Crosson, forthcoming). Rural land will continue to be converted to urban uses—the USDA projects conversion of 50 million to 75 million acres between 1980 and 2030—but probably no more than half of this acreage will be present or potential cropland. Given the nation's current supply of some 570 million acres of such land (420 million acres of cropland and 150 million acres of pasture and forestland with high-to-medium potential for conversion to crops, according to the 1982 National Resources Inventory), the threat of future conversions to crop production capacity appears small.

Effects on the Environment

The new technologies that emerged after 1940 resulted in a number of practices which, by the 1960s, generated concern about the consequences of the technologies for the environment. The vast increase in fertilizers inevitably resulted in increased delivery of nutrients to lakes and reservoirs, where they were believed to accelerate the eutrophication of these waters. In addition, an increasing number of aquifers and rural wells were found to have nitrate concentrations above the U.S. Public Health Service standard of ten parts per million. Pesticides came into common use in the 1950s, with DDT in the lead; within a decade pesticides became the main focus of concern because of their potential for injury to nontarget plants and animals, as well as to humans. Rachel Carson's (1962) *Silent Spring* gave powerful voice to these concerns and an impetus to the environmental movement, which continues today.

The increasing use of fertilizers for nutrients and pesticides for weed and insect control freed farmers from the need to maintain mixed systems (that is, animals to provide nutrient in crop enterprises and legume-cash crop rotations for both nutrient supply and pest control). Thus farmers were able to shift to systems of continuous row cropping, either continuous corn or soybeans, or a corn-soybeans rotation. The result was less vegetative variety on the farm, with unfavorable consequences for animal habitat. At the same time, average farm size increased to make more efficient use of the seemingly endlessly larger

tractors and other farm machinery that were developed in the last several decades. Making farms larger entailed the removal of fencerows and hedgerows, which had provided habitat for a wide variety of birds and other small animals. The new technologies thus put habitat at a double disadvantage. Concern about damage to water quality from sediment from eroded sites did not emerge as a significant issue until the 1980s. The pivotal event was a study published by the Conservation Foundation, which showed that the cost of water-quality damage ranges between $3 billion and $13 billion annually (Clark, Haverkamp, and Chapman, 1985).

Assessing the severity of the various environmental damages of the biologically based technologies that emerged after 1940 is difficult because, with the exception of sediment damages, comprehensive estimates of the costs of the damages do not exist. The reasons are complex, relating to technical and institutional obstacles preventing the establishment of transactions among people using and enjoying the environment in various ways, or suffering the consequences of the way others use it. People contracting cancer or suffering birth defects because of pesticides typically have no way of identifying the responsible party. Even if they could do so, their most likely recourse would be a lawsuit, which is not a clear-cut

or reliable way of registering the costs of the damage. Other people value the mere knowledge that certain species of wild animals exist, but they have no easy way to register this value with the farmers who may provide the necessary habitat. Consequently, farmers' decisions about whether to maintain the habitat or convert it to some other use will give insufficient weight to the social value the habitat provides.

These examples are only suggestive of the complex conditions that impede the emergence of clear signals of the costs of the environmental damages imposed by modern agricultural technologies. Because these conditions make it difficult for individuals to deal with one another through private markets in environmental services, public institutions have been devised to provide the mediating mechanisms. The absence of clear measures of environmental costs is a major difficulty for these institutions in setting priorities among the various problems demanding their attention, but act they must—and do.

The U.S. Environmental Protection Agency (EPA) probably is the most significant such institution for agriculture because of its role in regulating the pesticides that farmers may use. One of the EPA's earliest actions in this area was the banning of DDT from farm use in 1972. The EPA subsequently took the same action against other pesticides of the same class—the chlorinated hydrocarbons. The agency considered these materials particularly dangerous because they are persistent in the environment and are suspected of causing cancer, genetic damage, and birth defects. The regulatory procedures the agency uses also increase the costs of developing new pesticides, another feature of some importance to farmers.

Under the Clean Water Act Amendments of 1987, the EPA has broad responsibilities for dealing with other sources of water pollution from agriculture, including sediment and fertilizers. However, the EPA has delegated action in dealing with these problems to the states, each of which is obliged to develop plans for doing so. The plans in place in the late 1980s relied in large measure on erosion control practices originally developed by the SCS and on education and economic incentives to induce farmers to voluntarily adopt the practices.

The U.S. Department of Agriculture was also given new responsibilities for environmental protection under the Farm Security Act of 1985 (the 1985 farm bill). Under the act, farmers who drain wetlands—a major resource for waterfowl and other animals and a resource that provides other environmental services such as flood control—may be denied participation in commodity price support and other federal programs. Farmers who break fragile land to the plow are subject to the same penalties. By 1995, all farmers whose land is subject to erosion above the "tolerable" level will be required to install SCS-approved control measures or forfeit the benefits of program participation. These provisions were carried foreward in the 1990 farm bill.

The key policy issue is how to identify the public interest and how to devise modes of public intervention that most effectively serve that interest.

A Perspective on the Future

By the early 1990s, concerns about the environmental consequences of modern agricultural technologies had resulted in a variety of constraints on farmers' management of their cropland (and other land). Although the empirical evidence of damage cited as the basis for some of these constraints is weak, the principle underlying the constraints is not in serious question in the mainstream of U.S. political life. Because some of the environmental consequences of agricultural technology and land use impose real social costs, which farmers have little incentive to control, the public interest justifies control by public intervention through incentive and regulatory programs.

The key policy issue is how to identify the public interest and how to devise modes of public intervention that most effectively serve that interest. Maintaining the capacity to produce food and fiber at reasonable economic cost is clearly an important part of that interest. It is imperative to recognize that the public interest cannot be served without continued technological advances in agriculture. Without a continuing stream of new technology, the nation's farmers inevitably will run up against limits of land and other natural resources that will block additional production except at steeply rising economic costs. Increasing water scarcity (see chapter 2) is particularly relevant because it suggests that in the future irrigation is unlikely to contribute as much to increasing yields of the land as it did between the 1940s and the 1980s (table 5-11). Indeed, increasing water scarcity may make it uneconomical to maintain the 1980s base of irrigated land. Future patterns of technical change, therefore, will have to reflect increasing scarcity of both land and water.

In considering policies to deal with the environmental problems of agriculture, it is difficult to keep perspective because of the great uncertainty about the scale and severity of the problems. Because of the uncertainty, achieving consensus among contending interests about what to do is more difficult than for better-understood issues of public policy. Arguments range from those of some members (but not all) in the environmental community who assess present environmental damage as pervasive and severe, if not catastrophic, to those of others (but not all) in the agricultural community who see no reason for serious concern. However, the documented damages of sediment and related chemical pollutants to surface-water quality, the losses of habitat from wetland drainage, and the known actual and potential damages of pesticides to human health and ecological systems appear sufficient to merit sustained public efforts to deal with these problems. In doing this, however, it is essential to consider that the agricultural production system is the great provider of food and fiber to the nation and a sizable portion of the rest of the world. The task is to find ways to deal with the environmental problems of agriculture that do not dangerously impair the capacity of that system to produce food and fiber.

The policy problem can be thought of as one of finding the socially optimal balance between the various economic and environmental values at stake in development of agricultural technology. Economists see the problem as one of establishing tradeoffs among the values, and they offer relative prices as measures of the tradeoffs among the marketable values. Environmental groups respond that this is insufficient because many of the values at stake do not reflect market transactions and hence are not priced.

Environmental economists have recognized the legitimacy of this criticism and have begun to develop techniques for measuring some of these unpriced values. The techniques have been used in empirical studies, with promising results (see, for example, Mitchell and Carson, 1989). Pursuit of this line of research should in time help to reduce the conflicts over the socially optimal path for agricultural technology. However, no matter how much tradeoff-relevant information is brought to bear on the issue, some bedrock differences of view will remain: not everyone will be persuaded about the proper course of change. Fortunately, in a democratic society it is unnecessary that everyone be persuaded. The essential condition is that the institutions that govern choices about development of agricultural technology should generate abundant tradeoff-relevant information, assure that the

information is easily available to all who may have an interest in it, and provide high probability that the choices made reflect a consensus view of the relative weights to be given the economic and environmental values at stake.

Those holding religious views about the sacredness of some of these values—and some people do—will be offended by some of the choices made under institutional processes, if not by the processes themselves. Still, these are the processes by which, in principle, choices touching the public interest are made in democratic societies. In a long-term perspective on alternative paths of technological change, the fundamental policy issue is how to continuously validate that principle, not whether specific measures of control are exactly right or clearly wrong.

The policy issue is challenging, but manageable. Arguably, the U.S. legislative, administrative, and judicial processes now in place for dealing with conflicts about technological change in agriculture already meet, however imperfectly, the key conditions specified: they provide for the collection and dissemination of tradeoff-relevant information, skimpy though that information currently is; they allow for wide public discussion of the information; and the choices made appear to reflect some rough consensus, although here the picture is less clear. The policy challenge, therefore, is not to construct a whole new set of institutions but to improve the ones already existing. More fundamentally, the challenge is to maintain and strengthen the openness of these institutional processes. The processes will always be exposed to capture by special interests on various sides of the conflict about agricultural technology. Preventing this capture will require the "eternal vigilance" that John Stuart Mill saw as the price of liberty. The nation's liberty is not at stake in the present case. However, finding and hewing to a socially optimal path for future agricultural technology is at stake. It is no small challenge. If the country fails to meet it, then the nation's agricultural land resources will come under mounting pressure, and the ability to meet rising demands for commodity and environmental values of the land at socially acceptable costs will be put at increasing risk.

Notes

1. In 1910, 88 million acres of cropland were devoted to production of feed for animals. By 1950 this had declined to 19 million acres, and by the 1960s the amount was so small that the U.S. Department of Agriculture no longer collected data on such acreage (U.S. Department of Agriculture, 1982).

2. The nominal GNP from the U.S. Department of Commerce (1975) as deflated by the Consumer Price Index (CPI), for which the base year 1967 = 100.

3. Total productivity is measured by the ratio of indices of total output—crops and animal products—to total measured inputs—land, labor, farm machinery, fertilizers, and so on. Total productivity increases when improvements in technology and management cause the output index to rise more than the input index.

4. All figures in this paragraph are based on Hayami and Ruttan (1985), pp. 480–481, as adjusted by the Consumer Price Index to convert their nominal price data to real prices.

5. Nominal machinery prices are from Hayami and Ruttan (1985), deflated by the Consumer Price Index.

6. Indexes of average per-acre value of farm real estate were deflated by the Consumer Price Index.

7. Nominal spending each year is from Cochrane (1979), deflated by the Consumer Price Index; 1967 = 100.

8. Ruttan (1982) gives the nominal federal and state spending on agricultural research of $1.2 billion in 1979. This was adjusted to 1967 prices using the Consumer Price Index; 1967 = 100.

References

Alt, K., C. Osborn, and D. Colacicco. 1989. *Soil Erosion: What Effect on Agricultural Productivity?* Agriculture Information Bulletin no. 556. Washington, D.C.: U.S. Department of Agriculture, Economic Research Service.

Bartelli, L. 1980. "Soil Development, Deterioration and Regeneration." Paper presented at the National Research Council Soil Transformation and Productivity Workshop, Washington, D.C., October 16–17, 1980.

Bennett, H. 1931. "The Problem of Soil Erosion in the United States." *Annals of the Association of American Geographers* 21, no. 3:147–170.

———. 1939. *Soil Conservation*. New York: McGraw-Hill Publishing Co.

Bennett, H., and W. Chapline. 1928. *Soil Erosion—A National Menace*. Circular no. 33. Washington, D.C.: U.S. Department of Agriculture.

Bray, J., and P. Watkins. 1964. "Technical Change in Corn Production in the United States, 1870–1960." *Journal of Farm Economics* 46 (November):751–765.

Broadbent, F. 1957. "Organic Matter." In *Soils: The Yearbook of Agriculture* by U.S. Department of Agriculture, 151–156. Washington, D.C.: GPO.

Carson, R. 1962. *Silent Spring*. Boston: Houghton-Mifflin.

Clark, E. II, J. Haverkamp, and W. Chapman. 1985. *Eroding Soils: The Off-Farm Impacts*. Washington, D.C.: The Conservation Foundation.

Cochrane, W. 1979. *The Development of American Agriculture: A Historical Analysis*. Minneapolis: University of Minnesota Press.

Conservation Foundation. 1982. *State of the Environment 1982*. Washington, D.C.

Crosson, P. 1986. "Soil Erosion and Policy Issues." In *Agriculture and the Environment*, edited by T. Phipps, P. Crosson, and K. Price, 35–73. Washington, D.C.: Resources for the Future.

———. Forthcoming. *The Long-Term Adequacy of Agricultural Land in the United States: Economic and Environmental Issues*. Washington, D.C.: Resources for the Future.

Crosson, P., and A. Stout. 1983. *Productivity Effects of Cropland Erosion in the United States*. Washington, D.C.: Resources for the Future.

Dideriksen, R., A. Hidlebaugh, and K. Schmude. 1977. *Potential Cropland Study*. Statistical Bulletin no. 578. Washington, D.C.: U.S. Department of Agriculture.

Fedkiw, J. 1989. *The Evolving Use and Management of the Nation's Forests, Grasslands, Croplands, and Related Resources. A Technical Document Supporting the 1989 USDA Forest Service RPA Assessment*. Fort Collins, Colo.: U.S. Department of Agriculture, Forest Service, Rocky Mountain Forest and Range Experiment Station.

Feller, I., L. Kaltreider, P. Madden, D. Moore, and L. Sims. 1984. *The Agricultural Technology Delivery System*. Vol. 5, *Overall Study Report: Findings and Recommendations*. State College, Pa.: Pennsylvania State University, Institute for Policy Research and Evaluation.

Foster, G., and T. Hakonson. 1983. "Erosional Losses of Fallout Plutonium." Los Alamos, N.M.: Group LS-6 Environmental Science, Los Alamos National Laboratory.

Frederick, K. D. 1988. "The Future of Irrigated Agriculture." *Forum* (Summer):80–89.

Frederick, K. D., with J. C. Hanson. 1982. *Water for Western Agriculture*. Washington, D.C.: Resources for the Future.

Frey, H. (1983). *Expansion of Urban Area in the United States: 1960–1980*. ERS Staff Report no. AGES 830615. Washington, D.C.: U.S. Department of Agriculture.

Gillette, D. 1986. "Wind Erosion." In *Soil Conservation: Assessing the National Resources Inventory*, vol. 2, 129–158. Washington, D.C.: National Research Council, National Academy Press.

Hayami, Y., and V. Ruttan. 1985. *Agricultural Development*.

Baltimore, Md.: The Johns Hopkins University Press.

Johnson, D. 1985. "The Performance of Past Policies: A Critique." In *Alternative Agricultural and Food Policies and the 1985 Farm Bill*, edited by K. Farrell and G. Rausser, 11–36. Berkeley, Calif.: Giannini Foundation, University of California, and Washington, D.C.: Resources for the Future.

Johnson, D., and R. Gustafson. 1962. *Grain Yields and the American Food Supply: An Analysis of Yield Changes and Possibilities*. Chicago: University of Chicago Press.

Larsen, W., F. Pierce, and R. Dowdy. 1983. "The Threat of Soil Erosion to Long-Term Crop Production." *Science* 219, no. 4584:458–465.

Meade, R., and R. Parker. 1985. "Sediment in Rivers in the United States." In *National Water Summary 1984*, Geological Survey Water Supply Paper no. 2275, 49–60. Washington, D.C.: GPO.

Mitchell, R. C., and R. T. Carson. 1989. *Using Surveys to Value Public Goods: The Contingent Valuation Method*. Washington, D.C.: Resources for the Future.

National Research Council. 1986. *Soil Conservation: Assessing The National Resources Inventory*, vol. 1. Washington D.C.: National Academy Press.

Pavelis, G. 1985. *Natural Resource Capital Formation in American Agriculture—Irrigation, Drainage and Conservation 1955–1980*. Washington, D.C.: U.S. Department of Agriculture, Economic Research Service.

Pierce, F., R. Dowdy, W. Larsen, and W. Graham. 1984. "Soil Productivity in the Corn Belt: An Assessment of Erosion's Long-Term Effects." *Journal of Soil and Water Conservation* 39 (March):131–136.

Ruttan, V. 1982. *Agricultural Research Policy*. Minneapolis: University of Minnesota Press.

Sundquist, W., K. Menz, and C. Neumeyer. 1982. *A Technology Assessment of Corn Production in the United States*. Agricultural Experiment Station Bulletin no. 546. St. Paul, Minn.: University of Minnesota.

Swain, D. 1963. *The Beginning of Soil Conservation, 1921–1933*. University of California Publications in History, vol. 7. Berkeley, Calif.: University of California Press.

Thompson, L., and F. Troeh. 1973. *Soils and Soil Fertility*. 3d ed. New York: McGraw-Hill Publishing Co.

Trimble, S. 1975. "Denudation Studies: Can We Assume Stream Steady State?" *Science* 188, no. 4194:1207–1208.

————. 1981. "Changes in Sediment Storage in the Coon Creek Basin, Driftless Area, Wisconsin, 1853–1975." *Science* 219, no. 4517:181–183.

Trimble, S., and S. Lund. 1982. *Soil Conservation and the Reduction of Erosion and Sedimentation in the Coon Creek Basin, Wisconsin*. U.S. Geological Survey Professional Paper no. 1234. Washington D.C.: GPO.

U.S. Department of Agriculture. 1972. *Agricultural Statistics 1972*. Washington, D.C.: GPO.

————. 1976. *Agricultural Statistics 1976*. Washington, D.C.: GPO.

————. 1982. *Economic Indicators of the Farm Sector Production and Efficiency Statistics 1980*. Statistical Bulletin no. 679, Economic Research Service. Washington, D.C.

————. 1983. *Agricultural Statistics 1983*. Washington, D.C.: GPO.

————. 1987a. *Agricultural Resources, Cropland, Water and Conservation Situation and Outlook Report*. Report no. AR-8, Economic Research Service. Washington, D.C.

————. 1987b. *Economic Indicators of the Farm Sector Production and Efficiency Statistics 1985*. ECIFS-5-5, Economic Research Service. Washington, D.C.

————. 1987c. "The Second RCA Appraisal." Typescript.

————. 1988. *Economic Indicators of the Farm Sector Production and Efficiency Statistics 1987*. ECIFS-7-5, Economic Research Service. Washington, D.C.

————. 1989a. *Agricultural Statistics*. Washington, D.C.: GPO.

————. 1989b. *Agricultural Outlook*. Report no. AO-150, Economic Research Service. Washington, D.C.

U.S. Department of Agriculture and Council on Environmental Quality. 1981. *The National Agricultural Lands Study, Final Report*. Washington, D.C.: GPO.

U.S. Department of Commerce, Bureau of the Census. 1975. *Historical Statistics of the United States, Colonial Times to 1970*. Bicentennial Edition, Parts 1 and 2. Washington, D.C.: GPO.

U.S. Supreme Court. 1980. *Diamond vs. Chakravarty*. In *U.S. Reports* 477:303–322. Washington, D.C..

6

Wildlife: Severe Decline and Partial Recovery

Winston Harrington

Wildlife in America Before 1900

The first settlers were amazed by many findings in the New World, but none more than the abundance and variety of wildlife. Having come from a continent where meat was already becoming scarce and game was the exclusive preserve of the king, they arrived at a continent where game of every variety was so plentiful that hardly any effort was required to secure it. The native inhabitants of the southeast coast apparently had not developed a method of drying meat or fish because fresh game was always so easy to get (Kimball and Johnson, 1978).

Americans today have a difficult time appreciating not only the abundance but the variety of wildlife found by the earliest settlers. Animals associated with the West, such as bison and elk, actually were found along the Atlantic seaboard from New York to Georgia. Their presence in the East today is signaled only by a few place names. The last bison east of the Appalachians was killed at Buffalo Cross Roads (near Lewisburg), Pennsylvania, in 1801. Elk survived in

Although some outright antagonism toward wildlife and wilderness existed, the prevailing attitude was utilitarian. The growing population required the wilderness to be pushed back and the land converted to agriculture.

Pennsylvania until 1867, although some have recently been reintroduced in a few spots in the East (Matthiessen, 1987). The settlers occasionally found even more surprising species. The jaguar, considered by most Americans to be a denizen of the jungles of Central and South America, inhabited the southwestern desert and the Mississippi Valley until the nineteenth century; as late as 1737 the jaguar's range extended as far north and east as the mountains of North Carolina (Matthiessen, 1987). The great mammals once found in abundance along the eastern coast of North America included black bears, grizzly bears, mountain lions, bobcats, wolves, and, in the northern reaches, the important furbearers, including martens, fishers, river otters, and lynxes. The Great Plains contained enormous herds of bison and nearly as many pronghorn antelope. Lesser animals, such as the prairie dog and prairie chicken, also were extremely numerous.

By 1900 the stock of native American wildlife had been severely reduced. The ultimate cause of its near disappearance was the arrival of millions of immigrants—mostly European. At the turn of the century the U.S. population was 100 million people; in contrast, the population of pre–Columbian America north of the Rio Grande did not exceed 12 million (Farb, 1978). This estimate is considerably higher than the

concensus estimate, which is usually given as 1 to 3 million (Merk, 1978). Nevertheless, the Native American human population did not fare any better than the native wildlife. By 1900, the first census in which Native American populations were tabulated separately, the total population of Native Americans had dwindled to 235,000 (Farb, 1978).

The peopling of the continent, together with the development of a modern industrial economy, meant that a large part of the land and water resources previously made available to wildlife was being devoted to human uses. Although some of these uses may have been compatible with large wildlife populations, most were not. Thus, even if the European settlers had taken all possible steps to minimize the impact of settlement on wildlife habitat, severe impacts would have been unavoidable.

Settlers usually did not take such steps; they generally had ambivalent attitudes about the wilderness and its wildlife and Native American inhabitants. At first, the wilderness represented a sanctuary from the corruption of Old World civilization. However, any romantic notions of a paradise did not survive the first contact with such a hostile environment: "The wilderness of the New World was not a paradise; it would become one only if man so transformed it" (Stankey, 1989, p. 17). Although some outright antagonism toward wildlife and wilderness existed, the prevailing attitude was utilitarian. The growing population required the wilderness to be pushed back and the land converted to agriculture. Attitudes toward the wildlife also were utilitarian: wildlife was variously a source of food and clothing, a competitor for resources, and, sometimes, a source of danger. These utilitarian attitudes contributed to the reduction of wildlife populations and the conversion of their habitats.

The impacts of European settlement on wildlife were aggravated by the peculiar nature of wildlife as an open-access resource. Because fish and wildlife do not in their peregrinations respect property lines, private ownership of wildlife resources generally is impossible. Whereas an individual may elect to save a privately owned resource for use at a later time, an open-access resource is available for taking by anyone. Such resources are destined to be overexploited in the absence of social institutions designed to prevent it. Over time, societies generally do develop institutional mechanisms for controlling such excess, and such mechanisms had evolved in Europe to protect game animals. For example, in the Middle Ages the vast royal forests in England were open only to the nobility, with all wildlife considered the property of the king, and any common person caught taking game was severely punished. When enforcement of the forest laws declined after the English revolution in the 1640s, wholesale slaughter followed, permanently diminishing English wildlife in a short time (Johnson, 1974).

In the New World, the great abundance of wildlife meant, initially at least, that development of corresponding institutions was unnecessary. The legal doctrine of royal ownership of wildlife did cross the Atlantic to reappear as the doctrine of state ownership (Bean, 1983), but nominal state ownership of the wildlife resource did not usually interfere with the unregulated private taking of wildlife specimens. The small human population (at that time) and great size of North America meant that it would take far longer to make serious inroads into total wildlife populations than in England, but effects of settlement on local wildlife populations began to be noticed even during the colonial period.

In response to these effects, legislators attempted to introduce laws to protect valued wildlife, beginning in the colonial period. As early as 1694 Massachusetts instituted a closed hunting season for deer. Over the next two hundred years, other states enacted wildlife-related legislation as well to protect a variety of animals, including heath hen, grouse, quail, and turkey (enacted in New York, 1708); larks and robins (Massachusetts, 1818); moose (Maine, 1830); and antelope and elk (California, 1852). By 1880 every state had enacted laws for the protection of game (Lewis, 1987). These regulations were chiefly bag limits and designated open and closed seasons for hunting, although by modern standards they were incredibly lax. For example, Oregon's first trout limit allowed 125 to be taken per day, although the limit for ducks was the lesser of 50 per day or 100 per week (Balenger, 1988).

Besides the lack of stringency, these state wildlife laws were largely ineffectual for other reasons. States were somewhat ambivalent about protecting wildlife. State and local governments were equally active, and certainly more effective, in taking measures having adverse effects on wildlife populations, such as encouraging control of predator wildlife and introducing exotic plant and animal species. Wildlife losses often had to become severe for a consensus on wild-

life protection to develop. Moreover, to some extent the incentive of states and localities to write and enforce laws to protect wildlife was limited by the fugacity of the resource. Furthermore, hunters as well as wildlife crossed state lines. Thus violators of state game laws could often claim that game was taken in other states and therefore was not a violation of that state's game laws. The fugacity of wildlife resources also meant that landowners had insufficient incentives for providing wildlife habitat without government encouragement. Overcoming this failure and encouraging private provision of habitat has become an important issue in modern wildlife policy.

Overall, the drastic decline in wildlife populations before 1900 resulted from several causes: loss of habitat, systematic destruction of predators that were viewed as vermin, introduction of harmful exotic species, and perhaps most important, overexploitation of the wildlife commons.

Loss of Habitat

Before 1900, settlement profoundly affected three important classes of wildlife habitat: forest, wetlands, and prairie, especially east of the Rocky Mountains. The most pronounced, and obvious, change in land use over this period was the large-scale conversion of the primeval forest into cropland. In 1500, the area of forest in what is now the continental United States was about 1 billion acres, nearly half the total land area. Although the Native Americans practiced agriculture, the acreage affected was negligible when compared with what came later. Almost the entire area east of the Mississippi River was covered by forest, as were large areas in the Rocky Mountains, the Sierras, and the Pacific Coast. Most of the eastern forest was converted at one time or another to agricultural land, although a considerable amount of cropland has since been allowed to return to forest (see chapter 5). The area of forest land is no longer declining; it reached its nadir about 1920 at about 465 million acres and since has slowly expanded to more than 700 million acres (see chapter 3).

Another major change in land use was the loss of a substantial part of the nation's original endowment of wetlands, from an estimated pre–Columbian area of 215 million acres (in the continental United States) to 108 million acres in 1954 (Tiner, 1984), to 99 million acres in the mid-1970s. Unlike forestland, wetlands are still in decline. Because wetlands are often highly productive as wildlife habitat, this continuing decline remains a matter of concern.

FOREST

In the East, wildlife abundance and diversity depended to a considerable degree on the great eastern forest, of which it was said that a squirrel could travel from New England to Texas without ever touching the ground. The edge of the forest marked the edge of the frontier. As settlers poured into the colonies, they cleared land for agricultural production, with newer settlers pushing westward past the land already cleared. The general pattern of resource use was for settlers to move into an area, clear and cultivate the land for a few decades, and then, as soil productivity declined, move farther west to newly available land. The Appalachians posed a significant barrier to the western settlement, but by 1776 the mountains had been breached—by Daniel Boone among others, at the Cumberland Gap in Kentucky. New immigrants poured into the interior, so that on the eve of the Civil War less than half the U.S. population of 31.5 million lived in the Atlantic seaboard states (U.S. Department of Commerce, 1960). Except for Oklahoma, which was still Native American country, by the 1870s the entire continental U.S. had been organized into states and territories.

Although the settlement of this acquired land, together with the attendant effects on native wildlife, was an inevitable consequence of population and economic growth, the federal government consistently acted to encourage and assist settlement, especially before 1900. Among the policies contributing to this end were generally successful attempts to confine Native American tribes to small reservations, by pur-

It was said that a squirrel could travel from New England to Texas without ever touching the ground.

chase of tribal land or, when purchase did not work, by making war on Native Americans. The way of life among most of the Native American tribes was seen as incompatible with dense settlement, and those tribes had to be removed for settlement to occur.

From the earliest days, it was also the policy of the federal government to dispose of the newly acquired land to private citizens as rapidly as possible. Before the Civil War, this disposal was a practical necessity, because, frequently, settlers has already seized the land anyway. The settling of the interior often was a struggle between the squatters and the speculators. Many of the early land laws were simply designed to make legal the status quo, because the federal government had no practical way of evicting squatters from the land (Robbins, 1942). However, government land policy went beyond the recognition of land seizures. When territories became states, large blocks of land were turned over to the new state governments, which then sold them cheaply. There were times in U.S. history when states attempting to sell land could not compete with federal land giveaways (or with land seizures by squatters) farther west (Robbins, 1942). In addition, land policy in the nineteenth century was used to stimulate the economy. Major liberalizations in land policy occurred in the years following the economic panics of the late 1790s, 1819, 1837, 1861, 1873, and 1893 (Merk, 1978).

Private disposal of public land was still the prevailing policy toward the end of the nineteenth century, but a few land parcels of outstanding amenity value were reserved, later to become national parks. The first national park to be established was Yellowstone, in 1872. Not only the federal government but the states as well became more interested in retaining land in public ownership. In 1883, New York prohibited the continued sale of state land in certain parts of the state. Two years later the state legislature created, out of a patchwork of tracts of undistributed state land, the Adirondack and Catskill Forest Preserve, one of the largest publicly owned holdings in the eastern United States. The revision of the state constitution in 1894 provided that the land in the preserve would remain in a wild state (Outdoor Recreation Resources Review Commission, 1962). This shift away from privatization is associated with the conservation movement, discussed in the section on The Conservation Era, below.

The conversion of forest to agricultural land during the nineteenth century was not uniformly detrimental to wildlife. Rather than requiring all land to be cleared, agricultural development usually produced a mixture of cleared and forested land. Although this land-use pattern was unfavorable to the many species that preferred unbroken woodland, it was favorable to some others. Agricultural clearing increased the amount of forest edge—the boundary region between forest and field—and species preferring edge habitat, such as the bobwhite quail, cottontail rabbit, fox squirrel, and opossum, became more numerous. These and other animals with similar habitat preference became known as "farm wildlife" (National Research Council, 1982), and they prospered at the expense of interior forest and human-intolerant species.

WETLANDS

Wetlands—land that is under water part of the time or that supports plant life adapted to saturated soil conditions—are among the most productive habitats for wildlife. They are predominantly of two types: *estuarine* wetlands, associated with estuaries or brackish tidal waters, and *palustrine* wetlands, mostly freshwater wetlands found in the interior of the continent. Although wetlands are found scattered throughout the continental United States, they are particularly prominent in the Atlantic and Gulf coastal zones, the coastal flats in Florida and east Texas, the alluvial plains of the Mississippi River, the lakes region of Minnesota, and the Dakotas. About 95 percent of all wetlands are palustrine wetlands, and about half of that is bottomland forest. About half the original endowment of wetlands had disappeared by 1954, but in some areas the decline was much more extreme. For example, 99 percent of Iowa's original wetlands (2.3 million acres) and 91 percent of California's orginal 5 million wetland acres have disappeared. The wetlands of the Mississippi alluvial plain, originally 24 million acres, now cover only 5 million acres (Tiner, 1984).

The bulk of these wetlands losses occurred in the nineteenth century, mostly through conversion to agricultural land. At the time, swampland was almost universally regarded as worthless and could be made productive only by reclamation. To be agriculturally productive, the swamps and marshes had to be drained, diked, or filled. Once drained, wetlands were often extremely fertile, especially the freshwater wetlands along the Mississippi and other rivers, because of the alluvial deposits left by intermittent floods. Despite

No federal funds were available for wetlands conversion ... Federal support for "internal improvements" of such local benefit was widely considered unconstitutional at the time.

their greater fertility, such land required protection from subsequent floods to permit settlement. At that time, no federal funds were available for wetlands conversion; the primary sources of funds were private landowners and state governments. Federal support for "internal improvements" of such local benefit was widely considered unconstitutional at the time. Most states allocated monies for internal improvements, and most such improvements were jointly financed by the state and the private sector (Degler, 1970). However, the federal government did provide indirect assistance to the financing of internal improvements by turning over to the states public domain land that could be sold to help finance internal improvements (Smith, 1971).

Some of the lands thus converted were wetlands. The Swamp Land Act, first passed in 1847 and amended in 1850 and 1860, made it attractive to purchase and convert wetlands, and during the 1850s more than 20 million acres of wetlands were disposed of in this way, mostly along the Mississippi River. (Actually, more than 60 million acres were disposed of under the Swamp Land acts, but most were perfectly dry, a reflection of the prevalence of corruption and scandal in the nation's land disposal policies.) Without these laws, this otherwise unattractive land might have remained in the public domain until federal policy began to shift, late in the 1800s, toward public land retention. Even if this land had been thus retained, though, it is far from clear that it would have remained as wetlands.

PRAIRIE

Between 1840 and 1900, the land between the Mississippi River and the Rocky Mountains underwent rapid population growth as the fertile lands were given over to agriculture. Settlement of the plains also resulted in loss of wildlife habitat, although, in this instance, not of forest so much as of prairie and prairie wetlands. The conversion of prairie into farmland meant that the native plants were replaced by exotic cultivated grains and that the bison and pronghorn antelope were replaced by domestic livestock. The great western cattle industry got its start in the period following the Civil War. Cattle ranchers who raised immense herds in Texas drove their herds north to "cow towns" such as Abilene and Dodge City, Kansas, where they shipped the cattle by rail to slaughterhouses in Kansas City and Chicago. Texas cattle were also driven north to stock the ranges of Nebraska, Wyoming, Montana, and the other northern territories (Dale, 1930).

The settlement of the plains meant the slow, but nearly complete, decline of the prairie dog. Originally found in "towns" often miles across in extent in the shortgrass prairie from Saskatchewan to Arizona and Texas, the prairie dog is found today in far fewer numbers. Because prairie dogs competed with cattle for grasses, ranchers systematically exterminated them throughout the prairie dog's range. Moreover, the decline of the prairie dog had even more serious consequences for two species that preyed on prairie dogs: the black-footed ferret and the burrowing owl. The black-footed ferret had long been thought to be extinct, but in 1981 a small popluation of 100 ferrets was found in Wyoming. This small colony grew in number to 129 in 1984 and was then struck by an epidemic of canine distemper that nearly wiped it out. The ferret currently is considered extinct in the wild, although 57 survive in captivity. Reintroduction of that species into the wild is under consideration (Weinberg, 1989).

Destruction of "Undesirable" Wildlife

Even as the early settlers were awed by the wildlife they found, they also brought from Europe ambivalent attitudes about wildlife, attitudes that were remarkably similar to their attitudes toward the native human inhabitants. Although an object of fascination, wildlife also was a resource to be exploited—and often a pest, a threat to crops and livestock. Feelings of enmity were particularly pronounced regarding one ancient adversary—the wolf. Fear and hatred of wolves, so prevalent in folklore and fairy tales, were based on a germ of fact. In medieval Europe, wolves were common, seeming to vary in number and ferocity inversely to local economic conditions. In 1420 and again in 1438 wolf packs entered Paris through a breach in the walls of the city, and as late as the 1770s French officials discussed rounding up a large number of wolves, transporting them to England, and unleashing them on the people (Braudel, 1981).

Campaigns against wolves are almost as old as the American colonies. Matthiessen (1987) reported that the Massachusetts Bay Company established a wolf bounty in 1630, with a payment of one penny per wolf, a rate that suggests a remarkable abundance of the species. Other colonies followed suit, with such success that by 1800 the wolf had virtually disappeared from New England. Many other animals also faced bounties in the New World. Black bears were bountied in several states until well into the twentieth century, as were other predators, including the mountain lion. It is ironic that these large predators, so despised in the past, are now among the most highly prized of all forms of wildlife, not for their fur or meat but as endangered species and perhaps also as symbols of wilderness.

The needs of the developing western livestock industry also resulted in declared war against predators, including wolves, coyotes, mountain lions, and bald and golden eagles. Most prominent was, again, the wolf, whose alleged depredations were prodigious. Around 1900 it was estimated that 500,000 head of cattle were lost to wolves each year (Matthiessen, 1987). After years of unsuccessful attempts at control at the state level, the federal government coordinated an interstate campaign that virtually eliminated wolves from the American West, just as they had been eliminated from the East. In the lower forty-eight states, wolves survive today only in small bands in northern Minnesota. Other prairie species also retreated into

the mountains or faded into insignificance, including the pronghorn antelope, the prairie chicken, and the sharp-tailed chicken (Burger, 1978).

Introduction of Exotic Species

Besides taking fish and furbearing animals, destroying predators, and incidentally altering habitat, European settlers greatly changed American wildlife in yet another way by introducing exotic species—the plants and animals of cultivated agriculture. The settlers made habitat conversions to devote land to these exotic species. However, exotic species introductions other than cultivated plants and animals also were prominent from the beginning of the European settlement of the New World. Two early arrivals, the Norway rat and house mouse, were probably stowaways on sailing vessels crossing the Atlantic (Courtenay, 1978).

Many such unintentional introductions resulted from the escape of domestic or captive species. The wild mustangs of the Southwest and the razorback hogs of the Southeast and the Mississippi Valley are said to be descendants of horses and pigs that escaped from Spanish explorers (Matthiessen, 1987). Another is the gypsy moth, introduced into Massachusetts from Europe in 1869 to develop a silkworm industry. A few escaped and spread slowly across Massachusetts during the latter part of the nineteenth century. The moth has since spread throughout the Northeast, most recently into Pennsylvania and Maryland, and is also now found in isolated areas in a number of other states (Doane and McManus, 1981). Its spread has been accompanied by the defoliation of millions of acres of forest, residential property, and recreation areas. A major outbreak between 1980 and 1984 resulted in the defoliation of more than 29 million acres, making the gypsy moth a major public nuisance (U.S. Department of Agriculture, 1985).

Intentional introductions also were prevalent, beginning even in the colonial period. Two nuisance birds, the house sparrow and the starling, were introduced in the 1850s and 1890, respectively. The starling was apparently brought over as part of a project to introduce to the New World all the birds mentioned in Shakespeare (Courtenay, 1978). The starling and sparrow were introduced even though it had long been known that both birds caused agricultural damage. Both also had detrimental effects on native species, including martins, swallows, wrens, and bluebirds.

Most intentional introductions during this period were made for nonsentimental reasons, including improvement of recreational opportunities, control of previously introduced exotics, and as articles of commerce. For example, the ring-necked pheasant and the European brown trout were introduced as game animals as early as the 1750s (Courtenay, 1978). These two species are now counted among the few successful introductions of exotics (Dahlgren, 1987), providing recreational opportunities without interfering with native species. Even though they do not now appear to be displacing native species, some authorities believe that they did interfere in the nineteenth and early twentieth centuries. The pheasant's arrival may have hastened the extinction of the heath hen, and the brown trout is said to have contributed to the decline of several species of native trout (Matthiessen, 1987).

Overexploitation

Some of the New World products most desired by the Old World were derived from wildlife resources, mainly fish and furbearing mammals. The first recorded fur trade in North America took place in 1534, and by 1700 French and English traders and trappers had established trading posts throughout eastern Canada and the Great Lakes region. By 1821 the previously highly competitive fur trade had come to be dominated by the Hudson Bay Company, which by dint of its market power was able to exert some control of the taking of furs. Despite the company's efforts

> *Two early arrivals, the Norway rat and house mouse, were probably stowaways on sailing vessels crossing the Atlantic.*

to control the harvests of beaver, the principal fur-bearer, those harvests had begun to decline by 1840 (Innis, 1970). These declines reflected population declines except in the more remote areas of northern Canada and the Rocky Mountains.

The fate of the beaver was repeated for many other commercially valuable American species during the last third of the nineteenth century. During this period, and possibly in earlier periods as well, habitat alteration was probably of less importance to the decline of wildlife than excessive exploitation of wildlife resources. What distinguished the late nineteenth century from earlier periods was the appearance of new technologies that made wildlife harvesting easier and more profitable than ever. In particular, the invention of the repeating rifle and the refrigerated railroad car made it possible to deliver fresh game to cities all year. The market in these highly desired food items was large. In addition, there was an enormous demand for feathers for the millinery trade.

Thus came the advent of market hunting, an occupation that finds no modern counterpart in the wake of more effective regulation and the rapid decline of wildlife late in the nineteenth century. Professional hunters, bringing weapons of unprecedented efficiency to the wildlife commons, reduced many populations to low levels compared with the presettlement period. A few species, such as the passenger pigeon, were extirpated, and many others nearly so, including beaver, elk, bison, black bear, wolf, mule deer, white-tailed deer, pronghorn antelope, and many waterfowl species. In 1904, naturalist Madison Grant commented, "It may confidently be asserted that twenty-five years hence, . . . game in North America in a wild state will have ceased to exist" (Williamson, 1987, p. 1). Likewise, William Hornaday, preservationist and director of the New York Zoological Park, lamented, "It seems as if all the killable game of North America, except rabbits, is now being crushed to death between the upper millstone of industries and trade, and the conglomerate lower millstone made of by the killers of wildlife" (Williamson, 1987, pp. 1–2).

Among the earliest groups to perceive the growing threat to wildlife from market hunting were the small but growing band of recreational hunters. Not only did they wish to end the overexploitation of wildlife, but they also wished to drive out a major competitor, the commercial hunters, and preserve wildlife for recreational use only. Taking as their model the European aristocracy, this group of (mostly) men developed

Habitat alteration was probably of less importance to the decline of wildlife than excessive exploitation of wildlife resources. . . . new technologies made wildlife harvesting easier and more profitable than ever.

a sport of taking wildlife, but only according to a set of rules, a sportman's "code" (Rieger, 1986). The code was contemptuous of "pot-hunters" who would shoot birds on the ground or water rather than in the air; the "meat hunter," who killed only for food; the poacher, who had no respect for property and hunted regardless of season or sport; and most of all, the market hunter. During the 1870s numerous sporting journals were founded, including *The American Sportsman* and *Forest and Stream*. Such magazines kept up a steady stream of articles and editorials advocating more effective regulation of hunting and better enforcement of antipoaching measures in Yellowstone Park.

One of the most influential of these "gentlemen sportsmen" was George Grinnell, editor of *Forest and Stream*. In an editorial in 1884, Grinnell advocated establishment of an interest group to lobby Congress and state legislatures on behalf of wildlife protection (Rieger, 1986). Grinnell was later to take his own advice, founding the National Audubon Society in 1886 to deal with matters pertaining to birds and the Boone and Crockett Club in 1887 to deal with large game mammals. Most sportsmen and wildlife conservationists at the time belonged to one or the other of these two groups, which were later to play an instrumental role in the enactment of landmark wildlife protection legislation early in the twentieth century.

Overexploitation also may have adversely affected many of the major U.S. fisheries before 1900. In Lake Michigan, for example, it was noticed as early as 1860 that greater and greater effort was being required to harvest whitefish, the most desired food fish at the time. In 1879 the total commercial whitefish catch was estimated to be 12 million pounds; in 1889, 5.5 million; and the average for the 1892–1908 period, 2.4 million (Wells and McLain, 1973). As the whitefish declined, it was replaced as the preeminent commercial species by the lake trout, for which the average catch was 8.2 million pounds between 1890 and 1910, dropping to 5.3 million by the 1927–1939 period (Wells and McLain, 1973).

Simultaneously, overfishing began to have an effect on the fish stocks of the Columbia River. Predevelopment runs of salmon and steelhead trout in the Columbia River have been estimated variously at 7.5 million to 16 million fish (Chapman, 1986; Northwest Power Planning Council, 1986), a degree of abundance that attracted a large canning industry to the Pacific Northwest around the turn of the century. The peak year of commercial landings was 1918, when 3.6 million fish were landed, but some species peaked long before then: Chinook salmon in 1883, sockeye in 1898, and steelhead trout in 1892 (Northwest Power Planning Council, 1986). After 1918 commercial landings at the mouth of the Columbia River declined erratically but unmistakably, in part because of a decline in the resource and in part because the fish were being taken in the ocean before they ever made it back to the Columbia River. These declines have continued almost to the present day, but the role of overfishing is now confounded with the role of river development, discussed later in this chapter.

The Conservation Era: 1890–1940

In the years just before 1900 Americans began to realize that the resources of the continent, vast as they were, were not inexhaustible. As the century came to a close, the conservation of natural resources was recognized as a desirable goal, and one that would require public intervention.

Several dramatic events in the wildlife sphere helped call attention to the limits of natural resources. Unlike the wildlife losses before the Civil War, these events involved the rapid decline of previously numerous species. One of the more familiar examples is the fate of the bison, which once ruled the plains from the Mississippi River to the Rockies. With the advance of the railroads across the plains, millions of bison were killed for food for the railroad workers and for sport. Millions more were casualties of the Native American wars of the late nineteenth century, part of a U.S. policy designed to deprive Native Americans of their livelihood and force them onto the reservations established by the government. As late as 1870, millions of animals still could be found on the plains; by 1884, the bison was gone, except for the tiny herds in Yellowstone Park and in Alberta, Canada (Dale, 1930).

Even more startling were the extinctions of the heath hen and passenger pigeon, at one time extraordinarily numerous birds. These extinctions were especially noticed because they involved eastern birds, providing the majority of the people with first-hand evidence of wildlife losses. The heath hen, a subspecies of the prairie chicken, was found throughout the Midwest and Atlantic Coast states as far south as Virginia, and was a major dietary staple of the first settlers. By 1876 none remained but a small flock on Martha's Vineyard (Matthiessen, 1987). Despite strenuous efforts by the state of Massachusetts, including protection against hunters and elimination of other predators, the last heath hen died in 1927. A similar fate befell the passenger pigeon, probably the most numerous American bird until the late nineteenth century. Contemporary estimates of its population appear astounding to modern eyes. For example, in 1871 a nesting of passenger pigeons covered 750 square miles at an estimated density of 250 birds per acre, well over 100 million birds (Matthiessen, 1987). The last wild pigeon is believed to have been taken in 1900, though one survived in captivity until 1914.

The spectacular extinctions and near-extinctions signaled the increasingly desperate condition of wildlife resources as the nineteenth century ended. Reaction to the excesses of the post–Reconstruction period led to the rise of the conservation movement, which campaigned to put an end to the unbridled resource exploitation that characterized this period.

Two strands of thought contributed to the conservation movement—conservation and preservation. Gifford Pinchot, regarded by many historians as the founder of the conservation movement, defined conservation as "the use of natural resources for the greatest good of the greatest number for the longest time" (Pinchot, 1947, p. 326). This definition highlights two important characteristics of the conservationist outlook: sustainability, the protection of a resource so that it would continue to generate a stream of benefits into the indefinite future, and utilitarianism. The conservationists' utilitarian outlook was no break with the past, but they were different from earlier generations in their perception of the scarcity of natural resources; in their greater experience, having seen the effects of previous overexploitation on existing resource stocks; and in their predilection for taking the long view.

The preservationist view subscribed to the first of these positions, but it was not utilitarian. Among the philosophical antecedents in the United States was Thoreau, who expressed a preservationist ethic in *Walden*: "At the same time that we are earnest to explore and learn all things, we require that all things

As late as 1870, millions of animals still could be found on the plains; by 1884, the bison was gone, except for the tiny herds in Yellowstone Park and in Alberta, Canada.

be mysterious and unexplorable, that land and sea be infinitely wild, unsurveyed and unfathomed by us because unfathomable" (1947, p. 557). The preservationists wanted to see the remaining wilderness, together with the wildlife inhabitants, left as it was.

In the wildlife sphere, the conservation movement was a coalition of sports hunters and those in opposition to all hunting. These categories, however, do not parallel the division of the larger movement into conservationists and preservationists, because many prominent preservationists, such as Aldo Leopold, also were ardent hunters (Rieger, 1986).

In the late 1800s, both proponents and opponents of hunting generally agreed that efforts were needed to bring natural resource use under control and stop what was viewed on the one hand as excessive and wasteful use and on the other as immoral behavior. However, the interests of the two factions would diverge when it came to the provision of wildlife refuges, and especially whether hunting on them would be allowed. This conflict would help delay by a decade the establishment of a national wildlife refuge system. In the mid-twentieth century, there would be even more acute conflicts between these two points of view, and by 1970 sportsmen and "animal rights" groups would be in open warfare.

The growing level of concern about the state of wildlife, as well as other natural resources on which wildlife depend, led to the establishment of numerous government bodies specifically concerned with wildlife protection. Besides state fish and game departments, established in every state before 1880, wildlife protection and management became a concern of the federal government with the establishment of the Fish and Wildlife Service in 1885 (originally called the Bureau of Biological Survey). Concerned individuals also founded a large number of private advocacy and professional organizations, including the Sierra Club in 1892; the Izaak Walton League in 1923; Defenders of Wildlife, begun in 1926 as the Anti-Steel Trap League; the National Wildlife Federation in 1934; the Wildlife Management Institute in 1936; and the International Association of Fish and Wildlife Agencies in 1902, an umbrella organization whose members are mostly state and provincial (Canadian) wildlife agencies. Concern about wildlife also led to the development of modern wildlife science and policy, largely through the efforts of individuals in these agencies and advocacy groups.

By 1940, few authorities were predicting the imminent disappearance of prominent wildlife species, which many had predicted at the turn of the century. Most important wildlife species had at least stopped declining, and the populations of some species in some locations had improved somewhat. In addition, much of the legal and institutional structure that currently underlies wildlife restoration and protection was established, laying the groundwork for the remarkable increase in wildlife populations after World War II. Achieving these results required three problems to be addressed. First, excessive killing of wildlife associated with market hunting and predator control had to be stopped; second, the remnants of land providing suitable habitat had to be conserved; and third, to the extent possible species had to be restored to the land that had been part of their original range.

Controlling the Taking of Wildlife

The overexploitation of wildlife in the late nineteenth century had dramatized the near-total impotence of state and local governments in controlling wildlife harvests. Until that time, all matters pertaining to wildlife were under the jurisdiction of the states. Unlike land, which originally was owned by the federal government before being distributed to the states or individuals, in the common law the ownership of wildlife was lodged in the states, not the federal government. The development of effective institutions for the management of wildlife was another chapter

Wildlife protection and management became a concern of the federal government with the establishment of the Fish and Wildlife Service in 1885.

in the expansion of the role of the federal government in American life, but this expansion did not come at the expense of the states, at least not at first. Both states and the federal government were stepping into a sphere of national life that had previously been subjected to minimal regulation. Indeed, one of the main purposes and outcomes of federal intervention was to make state regulation of wildlife work better.

The increasingly evident threats to wildlife resources and the apparent inability of states to do much about it finally led to the enactment of federal legislation specifically designed to protect wildlife, beginning with enactment of the Lacey Act of 1900. The act, designed to help make state wildlife protection more effective, made it a federal crime to cross state lines with wildlife killed in violation of a state law. It also made any dead wildlife brought into a state subject to the laws of the state just as if it had been killed there (Bean, 1983). Thus the Lacey Act of 1900 struck directly at the difficulty of enforcing state wildlife laws by embargoing interstate shipping of wildlife taken in violation of state law.

However, the Lacey Act did not directly regulate the taking of wildlife and therefore did not collide with the state ownership doctrine, which had been reaffirmed in 1896 by the U.S. Supreme Court decision in *Geer v. Connecticut*. That collision did not occur until 1913, when the Weeks-McLean Act placed migratory birds under federal custody. This act was declared unconstitutional in federal district courts in Arkansas and Kansas and was appealed by the government to the Supreme Court. By 1916 the U.S. Department of Agriculture, apparently anticipating defeat, urged the Department of State to sign a treaty with Great Britain (on behalf of Canada) to protect migratory birds. Legislation for implementing this treaty was contained in the Migratory Bird Treaty Act of 1918, which also repealed the Weeks-McLean Act of 1913 and rendered moot the federal government's appeal before the Supreme Court. A new constitutional weapon was now available, namely the supremacy clause, which gave all treaties and implementing legislation precedence over state law. Shortly thereafter, in 1920, the Supreme Court in *Missouri v. Holland* upheld the 1918 act and affirmed the treaty-making power as a basis for federal wildlife regulation. It also "forcefully rejected the contention that the doctrine of state wildlife regulation functioned to bar federal wildlife regulation, and invited the question of what further sources of federal power might be utilized in the development of federal wildlife law" (Bean, 1983, p. 21).

Other bases of federal intervention soon materialized. Beginning in 1928, the Supreme Court affirmed the property clause, which gave Congress power to make rules on property belonging to the United States, as a basis of wildlife regulation on federal land irrespective of state law. This argument had been explicitly rejected by lower federal courts in 1916. In view of the extensive landholdings the federal government was in the process of accumulating, the new interpretation of the property clause was an important vehicle for the regulation of wildlife. In addition, the commerce clause has been asserted as a basis for federal wildlife regulation, but its use is more uncertain than either the treaty clause or the property clause (Bean, 1983). These additional bases of federal authority over wildlife are sufficiently broad that, by 1973 when the Endangered Species Act first prohibited the taking of protected wildlife species, the doctrine of state ownership of wildlife was not seriously raised as a legal impediment to federal regulation of taking.

The combined effect of federal and state regulations on hunting finally brought overexploitation of wildlife under control. However, action of a different sort was needed to ensure that land would remain available for wildlife habitat even as population and economic growth continued. Also, by the time the public awakened to the truncated condition of wildlife resources, many valuable species had disappeared altogether from much or most of their historical ranges.

Habitat Protection and Preservation

Around 1900, certain developments occurred that tended to reduce the pressure to convert land from wildlife habitat to other uses. To some extent these developments resulted from changing economic conditions. By the turn of the century, most of the land most suitable for cropland had already been converted to that purpose. In addition, the rate of conversion of forest to agricultural land began to slow down, and by 1930 the trend reversed direction. Although new ground continued to be converted to agricultural use in the West, even more acreage in the East was abandoned and allowed to return to forest. Abandonment of agricultural land and reversion to forest continued into the 1960s. The revolution in agricultural productivity permitted the percentage of the U.S. population engaged in farming to drop substantially and spurred a corresponding movement of Americans into the cities. Between 1880 and 1940 the fraction of the population living in "urban places" (2,500 people or more) increased from under 30 percent to about 60 percent (U.S. Department of Commerce, 1960).

The effect of these changes on wildlife was probably beneficial. Certainly this was true of the reforestation. Although the abandoned land often was poor-quality scrubland initially, in time the quality and quantity of eastern forest has slowly improved, especially in the Southeast and New England. Moreover, the decline in farm population may have reduced hunting pressure on wildlife resources.

Both states and the federal government were stepping into a sphere of national life that had previously been subjected to minimal regulation.

The period before 1900 also saw a modification of a century-old policy of transferring ownership of public land to private individuals as rapidly as possible, with the retention of substantial parcels of public land remaining in the public domain. One objective was to keep in the public domain areas of outstanding amenity value. The earliest legislative expression of this objective was the establishment of the first national park at Yellowstone in 1872. In the park, a small bison herd was protected from hunters. Other such areas were soon set aside as national parks: Mackinac Island in 1875 (ceded to Michigan in 1895) and Sequoia, Yosemite, and General Grant in 1890 (Foresta, 1984). These years did not mark the end of public land disposal, however. In terms of acreage the height of land disposal did not occur until 1910.

The first bill providing for the systematic reservation of public land from private ownership was introduced in 1876; in 1878 a report to Congress proposed setting aside forest "reserves." The Forest Reserve Act, which ultimately was passed in 1891, allowed the president to set aside forested land. Nearly 40 million acres were set aside by presidents Harrison and Cleveland under this act, and Theodore Roosevelt added 132 million more acres by 1909. These forest reserves became the nucleus of the national forest system.

Except for certain cases (such as the preservation of the bison herd in Yellowstone Park), these public land reservations probably had only a minimal short-run effect on wildlife. They were not established for the purpose of wildlife protection. The reserved land was almost exclusively located in the West, and the timber production and grazing permitted on the land might have occurred if the land was in private hands. The long-run impact was probably quite significant. When public sentiment later shifted away from a predominantly utilitarian approach to the public land toward a more preservationist stance, these lands could be designated as wilderness or wildlife refuge with comparative ease.

East of the Rockies nearly all land was already in private ownership; the reversal in national land policy came too late to permit the reservation of much public land in the East. Still, the slowdown in the conversion of land for agriculture probably slowed the continuing decline in most wildlife species. The federal reacquisition of private land was made possible by the Weeks Act of 1911, which allowed purchase by the federal government of land—usually abandoned farmland and cutover woodland—for the national forest system, and authorized appropriations for this purpose. The national forests of the East, totaling 24 million acres, were acquired in this manner before the outbreak of World War II. At that time, much of the derelict land had low value for any use as a result of soil exhaustion and depressed markets,

American kestrel

but the quality would improve with time. The small size of the eastern national forests relative to those of the West attest to the difficulty of assembling national forests from previously private land holdings.

National wildlife refuges, the only federal land managed primarily for wildlife, also were created around the turn of the century. The Penguin Island Refuge in Florida was the first to be established, by presidential proclamation, in 1903. Shortly thereafter other wildlife refuges were established by congressional resolution, including a National Bison Range in Montana and the Grand Canyon National Game Preserve in northern Arizona (primarily set aside for mule deer). The earliest wildlife refuges were carved out of existing federal landholdings and therefore did not require any appropriations of funds. The principal concern of wildlife preservation interests at the time, and therefore the principal focus of efforts to provide wildlife refuges, was the plight of waterfowl. Despite the Migratory Bird Treaty with Canada in 1916 and the Migratory Bird Treaty Act of 1918, waterfowl continued to decline, mainly because of disappearing habitat. Two particularly depressing losses were Malheur and Klamath lakes in Oregon, which were excellent habitat for waterfowl. Farmers there drained the lakes to provide irrigation water and additional agricultural

land; once drained, they turned out to be alkali flats (Balenger, 1988).

Apparently the control of excessive taking of waterfowl was insufficient to stop or reverse their decline, and refuges for waterfowl would be necessary for the United States to live up to its Canadian treaty obligations. These refuges would not be found in the existing federal landholdings, because, with few exceptions, the important waterfowl habitat was located not in the forests but generally along the coasts, in the Mississippi Valley, and in the pothole wetlands of the northern Great Plains, where hardly any land was owned by the federal government. Securing waterfowl habitat, then, necessarily meant the acquisition of wetlands in nonfederal ownership.

Throughout the 1920s legislators made efforts to secure wildlife refuges, especially for waterfowl, usually in a combined package that included provision for public shooting grounds and federal game wardens, all supported by the sale of federal hunting stamps to hunters. Although such legislation had broad support, it also had many enemies, including people who were suspicious of more federal intrusion, and even some within the conservation movement. The coalition of hunters and wildlife preservationists had always been an uneasy one. Wildlife preservationists, led by the redoubtable William Hornaday, bitterly opposed the sale of hunting stamps because it necessarily meant the continuation of hunting within the refuges. Besides any moral repugnance they may have felt, Hornaday and his followers also believed that depleted wildlife stocks could hardly endure the additional stress that hunting would cause. A compromise was eventually proposed consisting only of a provision authorizing land acquisition for waterfowl refuges, and stripped of any other provisions. This became the Migratory Bird Conservation Act of 1929. Except for the relatively small system of refuges carved out of existing federal landholdings, this legislation marked the beginning of the national wildlife refuge system.

A problem remained: How were these federal purchases of private land to be financed? The Migratory Bird Conservation Act of 1929 contemplated funding by means of direct congressional appropriation, not a reliable source of funding at any time and particularly not in the middle of the depression. At that time, the waterfowl stamp idea was resurrected. In 1934, with the enactment of the Migratory Bird Hunting Stamp Act, waterfowl stamps became the funding mechanism. This legislation required every adult hunter of migratory waterfowl to buy migratory bird hunting stamps, or "duck stamps," with the proceeds to go to the operation and acquisition of waterfowl refuges. This funding mechanism led the national wildlife refuge system to acquire a waterfowl orientation that it retains to this day (Bean, 1983). The number of waterfowl stamps sold grew rapidly between 1935 and 1950, but since 1950 the number of stamps sold and inflation-adjusted revenues have not increased. In addition, the area of national wildlife refuges at the beginning was quite small, and grew slowly until 1935. Since then, significant areas have been added during every decade except the World War II period of the 1940s (table 6-1). Since 1935, a substantial portion of the acquisition costs of the land has been paid for by tax receipts from the duck stamp program.

Wildlife Restoration and Management

At the beginning of the twentieth century people knew that it was going to take more to restore depleted wildlife populations than ending the exploitation of the resource and providing suitable habitat. Many species of wildlife had been completely elimi-

Table 6-1. Acreage of Refuge Land Under Jurisdiction of the U.S. Fish and Wildlife Service, 1910 to 1975 (in thousands of acres)

Year	Alaska	Continental United States	Total
1910	51	384	435
1915	2,954	430	3,384
1920	2,954	441	3,395
1925	2,954	452	3,406
1930	4,078	744	4,822
1935	4,078	2,013	6,091
1940	4,294	9,341	13,635
1945	7,941	9,355	17,296
1950	7,985	9,195	17,180
1955	7,837	16,042	23,879
1960	18,684	27,104	45,788
1965	19,906	27,970	47,876
1970	22,236	30,281	52,517
1975	33,479	43,051	76,530

Source: Clawson and Van Doren (1984).

nated from some areas and would not come back unless reintroduced. Furthermore, wildlife would largely be reintroduced on land that also served other purposes, among them recreation, timber production, and agriculture. Management of land for multiple use requires scientific knowledge of wildlife and its relationship with its environment, but little wildlife science existed at the turn of the century beyond the observations of naturalists. The infant science of wildlife management, such as it was, centered almost exclusively on the animals to be restored. This preoccupation seriously limited the restoration options available for elimination of a species' predators, the regulation of the species' harvest by hunters, or the release of more transplanted animals. Without an understanding of the species' relation to its environment, it was impossible to predict the outcome of a restoration attempt (Poole and Trefethen, 1978).

The idea of deliberate introduction of species into an area was not new. Numerous attempts to introduce exotic species had been made in colonial times and in the nineteenth century. These attempts usually were unsuccessful. Even when they were successful, the results often were detrimental to native wildlife. In addition, many fish hatcheries had been established during the nineteenth century, typically with the objective of restocking rather than restoration.

As the depletion of wildlife became more evident late in the nineteenth century, many trial-and-error attempts were made to reintroduce wildlife species that had disappeared (Peterle, 1987). Numerous game farms were established to raise wild or semidomesticated animals in captivity for later release in the wild. Often these early projects simply rounded up some wild animals in one part of the country and transported them to another without paying much attention to whether the destination area had ever even been part of the species' range. For example, the wild turkey, originally found throughout the forested areas of the lower forty-eight states, had all but disappeared by the late nineteenth century mainly because of the loss of the mature upland hardwood forest habitat to agriculture and timber production. The earliest efforts to restock the wild turkey used semidomesticated turkeys that turned out to be inappropriate for reintroduction into the wild. Not only

did these turkeys not survive long in the wild, making their introduction a waste of resources, they had adverse effects on the target environment. It was demonstrated in the 1940s that these turkeys had affected the gene pool of the remnant population of wild turkeys in southeastern Virginia (Lewis, 1987).

Other problems caused by ineffective or inappropriate wildlife management often arose, as when one species in an area became overabundant relative to others. Most commonly this occurred when the destruction of predator species allowed a glut of prey. (Until fairly recently wildlife managers and even wildlife preservationists thought of predators as vermin.) A famous example was the explosion of mule deer populations in the Grand Canyon National Game Preserve during the 1920s, following the systematic destruction of wolves and mountain lions (Balenger,

Quail feeder at a wildlife study area, Louisiana

1988). Subsequent overgrazing by deer so damaged the forests of the Kaibab Plateau that it is only now recovering.

The early failures of wildlife restoration and management made clear the need for systematic study of wildlife populations. In the United States such study was begun around 1920 by Aldo Leopold, a forester from New Mexico. Leopold's field experience, including study of the Kaibab deer overpopulation problem, persuaded him of the importance of ecological interrelationships among plant and animal species. He showed that the successful introduction of the ring-necked pheasant in the Midwest was attributable to its ability to exploit an unoccupied ecological niche. Unlike any native American bird, the pheasant had evolved in the Orient to take advantage of land cleared for agriculture. The concomitant decline in the prairie chicken resulted in part from the replacement of the native grasses by domestic crops. Another contribution of Leopold was the notion of carrying capacity—the idea that an ecosystem can only support a limited number of a single species (Poole and Trefethen, 1978).

Leopold's new approach to wildlife management greatly increased in number and subtlety the potential approaches to introduction and restoration of wild-

life. In so doing, it also increased the opportunities for and practical potential of scientific research. To this end, the Bureau of Biological Survey (forerunner of the U.S. Fish and Wildlife Service) in the U.S. Department of Agriculture established in 1935 a network of cooperative wildlife research units at land-grant universities. These university programs provided a means of carrying out the necessary scientific investigations and encouraged the development of wildlife biology as a scientific discipline, and wildlife management as a profession (Balenger, 1988).

By the outbreak of World War II, efforts to save wildlife encompassed numerous tasks: acquiring and protecting habitat, restocking, conducting scientific research, and providing education. These efforts required a lot of money; part of the funding problem was addressed by the Migratory Bird Hunting Stamp Act of 1934. A much more extensive funding effort was made possible by the Federal Aid in Wildlife Restoration Act of 1937, commonly called the Pittman-Robertson Act after its congressional sponsors.

The Pittman-Robertson Act levied an 11-percent excise tax on sales of firearms and ammunition; these funds were made available to state programs for wildlife restoration. The arms and ammunition tax had already existed for general revenue collections, but like other excise taxes was being phased out. Wildlife interests persuaded Congress to retain the tax and dedicate it to wildlife preservation (Balenger, 1988). In the original Pittman-Robertson Act, Congress had to appropriate the revenues collected and occasionally impounded them in an effort to reduce federal expenditures. However, in 1951 Congress gave Pittman-Robertson funds "permanent-indefinite" status, meaning that revenues were automatically transferred to the U.S. Fish and Wildlife Service (Williamson, 1987). Later amendments, in 1972, made sales of archery equipment and handguns subject to the tax.

Funds were allocated to eligible states according to a formula giving equal weight to a state's area and its hunter population, as estimated by duck stamp sales, with a maximum grant of $150,000 per year per state. To be eligible, a state had to pass enabling legislation to ensure that hunting license fees would not be used for any purpose but to administer wildlife programs. Acceptable uses of Pittman-Robertson Act funds included the acquisition of wildlife habitat, hiring of personnel, and research that would aid in wildlife restoration. Any management personnel hired under the act's funds had to be professionally qualified. This provision was helpful in developing a sense of professionalism in state wildlife programs, which had in many states been repositories for political hacks (Williamson, 1987). The Pittman-Robertson Act would provide 75 percent of the funds for any approved state project, with the state providing the other 25 percent. Revenues from firearms and ammunition grew rapidly until 1975. Between 1970 and 1975 the excise tax also was levied against pistols and bows and arrows; the broadening of the base provided a jump in revenues in 1975. Receipts in real terms have been essentially constant since 1970.

Pittman-Robertson grants allowed extensive purchases of land for habitat preservation (see appendix 6). In addition, wildlife management funds were provided for a much larger area. One oddity is the frequency with which state wildlife agencies cited two species—the wild turkey and the white-tailed deer—as examples of the accomplishments of Pittman-Robertson projects. This does not necessarily mean that these two species have received disproportionate attention from state wildlife authorities, but that state wildlife authorities tend to focus on their biggest successes. In general, it appears from the testimony of the states that the Pittman-Robertson program has

been a boon to state efforts in the restoration of some wild game.

The Pittman-Robertson approach has been imitated in other legislation. In 1950 the Dingell-Johnson bill was enacted to provide grants to the states for enhancement and restoration of fish populations, with funding to be provided by an excise tax on fishing tackle. The Dingell-Johnson Act was amended in 1984 to extend the tax to include boats. The Fish and Wildlife Conservation Act of 1980 (commonly called the Nongame Act) makes grants to state wildlife authorities for restoration of nongame species. So far no funding mechanism has been designated, although a tax on camping and backpacking equipment has been proposed. The Nongame Act attempts to fill a gap in the coverage of the original Pittman-Robertson Act, which was limited by law to restoration of birds and mammals used for game. Given the source of funding, this limitation is not surprising.

These federal efforts were accompanied by extensive efforts on the part of states, all of which had game management agencies before the turn of the century. In fact, in terms of budgets, the aggregate effort of the states was larger than the federal programs. Hunting and fishing license revenues have always been much larger than either the federal waterfowl stamp revenue or the Pittman-Robertson funds.

The outbreak of World War II marked the end of a half-century of legislative and institutional experimentation. A remarkable turnaround in the fortunes of wildlife had been effected, although its full implications were yet to be revealed.

The Modern Period: 1940–1988

The story of wildlife since 1940 has been dominated by three interrelated themes. First, this period has seen continued improvement in the numbers and distribution of many species, especially game species requiring forest or rangeland habitat. The excessive harvest of game apparently has been successfully regulated by state and federal governments, and thanks to restoration efforts many game species have been successfully reintroduced into areas where they had been extirpated. Accompanying this wildlife recovery has been the slow but steady growth in the area of forestland, especially in the eastern United States. Over the most recent two decades, however, population trends have been mixed.

Second, although forestland has expanded substantially from the historic lows of the late nineteenth century, development pressures have increased on water resoures and the lands associated with them. These pressures have come from many sources and have profoundly altered the configuration of water resources in the United States. The wildlife species dependent on these water resources naturally have been affected.

Third, a major change has occurred in the uses of and attitudes toward wildlife. Unlike earlier periods in U.S. history, the principal uses of wildlife today are not for the commercial production of food or furs but to provide recreational experiences. These recreational uses may be consumptive (such as hunting and fishing) or nonconsumptive (such as birdwatching or nature study). Moreover, "use" no longer captures entirely the public's interest in wildlife resources. The utilitarian attitudes that were dominant in an earlier age have been supplemented by a regard for the existence of wildlife species as an end in itself (existence value). This change is seen most clearly in the adoption of a policy and a willingness to commit resources to protect endangered species both at home and abroad.

Recent Trends in Wildlife Populations

Data on bird populations are routinely collected by the U.S. Fish and Wildlife Service (the annual breeding bird and migratory waterfowl surveys). These data, together with two recent wildlife trend assessments conducted by the U.S. Forest Service, provide information for examining recent trends in wildlife populations. The first Forest Service assessment was to support the 1989 Resources Planning Act (RPA) assessment required by the Forest and Rangeland Renewable Resources Planning Act of 1974 (Flather and Hoekstra, 1988). The second involved a survey of wildlife trends by a number of regional wildlife biologists (Thomas and coauthors, 1988). For the RPA assessment, the Forest Service divided the country into four sections: the North (states of the Northeast as far south as Maryland and the Ohio River and as far west as Missouri, Iowa, and Minnesota); the South

(those states in the Southeast as far west as Texas and Oklahoma); the Pacific (Washington, Oregon, California, Alaska, and Hawaii); and the Rocky Mountain and Great Plains states. Although the second Forest Service assessment draws on the RPA assessment document, it also contains additional information. Game birds and mammals have received the most attention from wildlife researchers, although some attention has also been given to nongame species.

BIRDS

Nongame birds. Since 1968 the U.S. Fish and Wildlife Service has conducted an annual breeding bird survey, consisting of counts of various bird species observed at randomly selected sites throughout the country. Population trends for the years 1968–1981 for the 552 bird species in the survey show the following (Flather and Hoekstra, 1988): 66 species have significantly increased; 46 have significantly decreased; 298 show no significant change; and for 142 species the sample was too small for trends to be constructed.[1]

The reason for the observed population increases and decreases in most bird species is unknown. In some cases, increasing population was associated with increases in habitat. Restrictions on the use of DDT and other chlorinated hydrocarbon pesticides over the previous two decades were also a factor. Among the causes for decreasing population trends were the severe winters during the late 1970s, habitat degradation, and competition from starlings.

Raptors. Raptors are an important class of birds not well covered by the breeding bird survey. Evans (1982) examined the status of twelve raptors thought to be of concern and found that six were recovering from low population levels of the 1960s. These were the bald eagle, Cooper's hawk, osprey, peregrine falcon, merlin, and sharp-shinned hawk. Because raptors are at the top of the food chain, they are particularly vulnerable to accumulations of DDT; restrictions on its use have allowed the populations of these six species to recover. Of the remaining six, three (the ferruginous hawk, marsh hawk, and prairie falcon) have stable population trends and three (the caracara, burrowing owl, and northern aplomado falcon) appear to be declining.

Migratory waterfowl. The U.S. Fish and Wildlife Service conducts annual surveys of waterfowl in both their wintering grounds and breeding grounds (see U.S. Department of the Interior, Fish and Wildlife Service, *Waterfowl Status Report*, various years). For ducks, the total breeding population showed a rapid increase from 29 million in 1969 to 44 million in 1972, followed by a slow decline to about 28 million in 1985. Interestingly, the number of waterfowl hunters has closely tracked the breeding population, rising from 1.2 million to 2.0 million between 1965 and 1971 and then falling back to 1.3 million by 1986. The recent decline in duck populations has been attributed to the succession of summer drought and cold winters experienced during the late 1970s, made worse by the steady decline in wetland acreage, especially in the Mississippi and central flyways. The decline also is related to the decrease in nesting habitat as cropland acreage has expanded.

In contrast to ducks, nationwide goose populations have more than doubled since 1966, although there has been a slight decline in populations in the Pacific flyway generally and for some specific species of geese. Like ducks, goose populations have been adversely affected by wetlands losses, but expansion of cropland acreage apparently favors production of geese.

Swan populations also have increased substantially, with population trends showing a slow but consistently upward pattern. The once-endangered trumpeter swan has increased in population from about 66 known birds in 1933 to 10,000 to 1990.

Other game birds. Among the few game birds that are not waterfowl are the mourning dove, wild turkey, pheasant, and grouse. The mourning dove is also one of the most numerous American birds. However, mourning dove populations apparently declined about 25 percent between 1966 and 1984, to about 500 million. Based on call-count indices, the decline has been greatest in the West, where the index fell from 18.4 in 1967 to 10.6 in 1985 (Flather and Hoekstra, 1988).

The wild turkey, one of the major success stories of wildlife restoration, is now found—and hunted—

in nearly every state, although most predominantly in the East. Its growth in the past two decades has been impressive. In the North, the population of wild turkeys increased from 60,000 in 1965 to 225,000 in 1980; in the South, the increase was from 600,000 to 1,400,000 over the same period. Paralleling this population increase has been an increase in harvests; annual wild turkey harvests between 1965 and 1985 grew from 20,000 to 85,000 in the North and from 100,000 to 225,000 in the South.

For other game birds, population data in the surveys are incomplete, but harvests have shown pronounced declines. To the extent that harvests track populations, the populations are probably declining as well. In the North, pheasant and quail harvests have dropped by 50 percent in the past two decades, to 1.6 million and 2 million, respectively. The grouse harvest has remained constant at about 900,000 per year. In the South, quail harvests also have dropped by 50 percent, to about 8 million. Although grouse harvests have remained about constant and pheasant harvests have increased, these birds are relatively unimportant in the South.

MAMMALS

Data on wild mammal populations are less comprehensive than the data are for bird populations, because mammals are not similarly surveyed. Most of the available population information on wild mammals is for game species, although some information exists for bats, a mammalian order that appears to be in particular jeopardy.

Big game. Some of the biggest success stories of wildlife management in the earlier part of the twentieth century concerned big game mammals. Those successes have continued to the present for selected species. The western states have a considerable variety of big game. In the East, big game hunting essentially means deer hunting, although some bears are hunted in the northern states. Western states, in addition to deer, offer elk, bear, and pronghorn, as well as bighorn sheep, mountain goat, and moose.

By far the most numerous big game species nationwide is the white-tailed deer, numbering about 20 million. Almost all states report healthy increases in both white-tailed and mule deer populations in recent decades, with total population increasing by more than 100 percent since 1965. In the Rockies,

the reported number of elk has also doubled, and the estimated pronghorn population has increased by more than 300 percent. Only in the Pacific region have big game failed to show substantial increases, with deer populations declining since 1965 and elk and bear remaining about the same.

Furbearers. In terms of total revenues, the most valuable American furbearers are the raccoon, muskrat, opossum, beaver, and nutria, none of which is in any danger in any part of its range. Since 1975 the muskrat has been the only one of the five furbearers with a declining population in any part of its range (the Rocky Mountains), although it is still abundant everywhere. Beaver populations, driven nearly to zero at the turn of the century, have since recovered thanks to extensive reintroductions in areas where it had been eliminated. It is now thought that the beaver is more numerous than ever before. Raccoons, of course, have prospered through their association with people, as they tolerate and indeed thrive in areas of high human activity. The nutria, since its introduction from South America, has become a nuisance in places. The opossum steadily expands its range northward. In short, these five species are doing well.

Among other valuable furbearers, such as the red fox, bobcat, mink, and Canada lynx, the population trends are less favorable. Both the red fox and mink are declining in parts of their range.

Small mammals. This group includes some of the most familiar woodland animals, including rabbits, squirrels, field mice, chipmunks, and many others equally familiar and others less well known. Because these mammals are small, inconspicuous, and often nocturnal, their populations are rarely monitored, and it is difficult to determine population trends. Generally, those species that are adaptable to a variety of habitat conditions have been successful, and animals with more stringent habitat requirements have not adapted. For example, several subspecies of beach mouse, which live only in natural coastal dunes in Florida and California, are now considered endangered because their habitat is increasingly subjected to second-home development ("Listing Protection Proposed for Seven Species," 1988). According to Thomas and coauthors (1988), of 32 small mammal species in California identified as declining in population, loss of habitat was a factor for 28.

Of the small mammals, bats are in special difficulty. Of 37 American bat species, 5 are listed as endan-

gered. The vast number of bats at Carlsbad Caverns, New Mexico, have declined by 98 percent in the past fifty years. A similar decline has occurred at Eagle Creek Cave, Arizona (Thomas and coauthors, 1988). These declines are primarily the result of habitat losses.

Water Resources and Wetlands

Fishes have faced the same kinds of pressures from economic development and population growth that terrestrial wildlife have faced, including habitat alteration, overexploitation, and exotic species introduction, but generally have experienced these pressures later. Overexploitation of fishery resources had begun in the late nineteenth century. The major habitat alterations and exotic species introductions were to come somewhat later, and to a large extent they were the direct or indirect result of water resource development, the pace of which accelerated tremendously after 1935.

WATER RESOURCE DEVELOPMENT

Before 1900 the development of water resources in the United States was for the most part limited to navigational improvements. The period between 1820 and 1850 was the golden age of canal and river travel in the United States. Both federal and state governments, as well as the private sector, were involved in these efforts. Federal involvement with water resources began as early as 1802 when the U.S. Army Corps of Engineers was established, although the first federally financed water resource project was not begun until 1824 (Haveman, 1965). By the late nineteenth century, Congress was routinely passing "rivers and harbors" bills to make navigational improvements: the dredging of rivers and harbors, the clearing of channels, the removal of snags, and the building of canals. These "run-of-the-river" navigational improvements have often disturbed riparian habitats along the major rivers, but compared with other kinds of water resource development the consequences of navigational improvements for fish and wildlife have usually—but not always—been minor.

A navigation improvement that joined two previously isolated water bodies could have major ecological consequences. A dramatic example is provided by the invasion of the upper Great Lakes by the sea lamprey, a parasitic fish that attaches itself to its prey by suction. The lamprey is indigenous to the Atlantic Ocean and also, possibly, to the St. Lawrence River and Lake Ontario. Its spread into the upper Great Lakes was made possible by the deepening (in 1932) of the Welland Canal, which joins Lakes Erie and Ontario, together with the replacement of wooden-hulled vessels by steel-hulled vessels. The lamprey actually made its way into Lake

*The replacement of
a freeflowing river
by a reservoir
often had profound
ecological
consequences,
because the flora
and fauna
characteristic of
one environment
were often
unsuited to the
other.*

Erie by attaching itself to the steel hulls; it had been unable to attach itself to wooden ones (Douglas Jester, Great Lakes Regional Commission, personal communication, July 27, 1989). The lamprey's earliest victim in the Great Lakes was the lake trout. Overfishing in Lake Michigan had reduced the annual harvest of lake trout from 8 million to 5 million pounds by the late 1930s. During World War II, the catch was again above 6 million pounds, but afterward the lake trout suffered a sudden catastrophic decline, so that by 1955 the fish could no longer be found in Lake Michigan (Wells and McLain, 1973). Lake trout also were eliminated from Lake Huron by about 1960, and driven to extremely low levels in Lake Superior (U.S. Council on Environmental Quality, 1973). This precipitous decline in the lake trout after World War II has been attributed to the lamprey. As the lake trout declined, the lamprey began to attack whitefish, production of which declined from its postwar peak of about 6 million pounds in 1949 to near zero in 1960 (Wells and McLain, 1973).

The decline of the lake trout and the whitefish, two important predators, opened the way for the alewife, a small herring-like fish that also entered the upper Great Lakes through the Welland Canal (U.S. Council on Environmental Quality, 1973). The alewife has become one of the major commercial species of the Great Lakes (production grew from 5 million to 42 million tons per year between 1962 and 1967), but has had an adverse effect on native fishes through predation of their young

and competition for plankton. It is also a considerable nuisance at times. An enormous die-off of alewives in 1967, estimated to involve billions of fish (Wells and McLain, 1973), caused sufficient inconvenience to attract the attention of the national news media.

Late in the nineteenth century, the federal government began to contemplate water resource development for purposes other than navigation, but it was not until the coming of the New Deal that multipurpose development of water resources was instituted on a large scale. These additional purposes included flood control, hydropower generation, irrigation, and flatwater recreation. Environmentally, these developments were much more intrusive than the earlier improvements designed solely for navigation. Most involved the construction of large dams, which replaced freeflowing river reaches with large artificial lakes. Most of the major rivers in the United States, and many smaller ones as well, had one or more dams placed across them, including the Missouri, Tennessee, Columbia, and Colorado. Although no dam was placed on the main stem of the Mississippi River, flood control in the Mississippi delta region was brought about by construction of dams on its major tributaries.

The replacement of a freeflowing river by a reservoir often had profound ecological consequences, because the flora and fauna characteristic of one environment were often unsuited to the other. For example, the Flaming Gorge, Glen Canyon, and Boulder dams in the Colorado River system have greatly reduced the habitat suitable for the native fishes of the Colorado basin. These fish require warm, silty water found historically in the freeflowing Colorado. Because of the dams the native fish now are being replaced by a number of fishes that have been introduced, either deliberately or accidentally, into the Colorado River reservoirs. Many of these fish species are more suited to the cold, clear waters of the impoundments created by the dams. As a result, several of the native fishes in the Colorado are in decline and at least two, the humpbacked chub and Colorado squawfish, are now considered endangered (Behnke, 1980). This particular example also illustrates the occasional conflicts between the recreational use of wildlife and endangered species prevention. The deliberately introduced species include those, such as the rainbow trout, that are more highly prized by fishermen than the "trash fish" supplanted.

Water resource development also has had an adverse effect on fish habitat in the Pacific Northwest, where dams built for power production and other purposes interfere with the spawning runs of anadromous fish such as Chinook, coho, and sockeye salmon and steelhead trout. The Columbia River drainage basin is one of the most heavily developed in the world, with more than 500 dams across the Columbia and its tributaries, although the effect of these dams on the spawning runs of anadromous fish is mitigated to some extent by fish-passage devices at many of the dams (Northwest Power Planning Council, 1986). Before development, an estimated 13,000 stream-miles of salmon and steelhead habitat existed in the Columbia River basin. Dam construction has reduced the available habitat to about 9,000 stream-miles (Northwest Power Planning Council, 1986). However, it has been difficult to show quantitatively the extent to which dam construction and operations have contributed to declines in anadromous fish runs. Salmon runs at Bonneville Dam, the furthest-downstream and earliest-constructed of the major dams on the Columbia itself, have either exhibited no trend (as with the Chinook salmon) or have substantially declined and then recovered (as with the coho salmon); see table 6-2. Since 1938, when the Bonneville Dam was built, water resource development has been considerable. However, fish populations have been affected by other factors as well, including the release of large numbers of hatchery fish (accounting for perhaps two-thirds of the commercial fish catch); great changes in the commercial fishing industry; enormous postwar expansion of recreational fishing; and the exertion of historic fishing rights by the Native American tribes of the basin. Untangling the effects of these causes on fish populations has proven to be a highly contentious and as yet unresolved problem.

WETLANDS

The U.S. Fish and Wildlife Service recently completed a study to determine wetlands trends between the mid-1950s and the mid-1970s (Tiner, 1984). The study showed that total wetlands acreage declined from 108 million acres in 1954 to 99 million acres in 1975, which represents a loss of 4.3 percent of the remaining wetlands per decade. It is difficult to compare this rate of loss with earlier periods, but if it is assumed that wetlands losses began on a large scale around 1850, about the time the Swamp Land acts were passed, then the loss rate between 1850 and 1950 was 6.9 percent per decade. Taking 1800 as the starting point, the loss rate is 4.6 percent per decade. Thus it is possible that the recent wetlands conversion rate is not much different from the historical rate, but at all events the 4.3-percent loss rate is alarming enough. If it were to continue for another century, only 65 million acres of wetlands would be left.

Table 6-2. Average Annual Fish Counts over Bonneville Dam (in thousands of fish)

Period	Chinook salmon	Steelhead trout	Sockeye salmon	Coho salmon
1938–1940	317	138	74	14
1941–1945	343	117	37	8
1946–1950	396	130	101	6
1951–1955	353	200	191	7
1956–1960	346	129	101	4
1961–1965	302	143	52	32
1966–1970	388	126	108	72
1971–1975	398	152	61	63
1976–1980	358	133	55	38
1981–1985	326	235	105	41

Source: Northwest Power Planning Council (1986).

These totals mask significant variations in the losses for different kinds of wetlands (table 6-3). Two types of wetlands actually gained area during these two decades. The near-doubling of palustrine open-water wetlands indicates the large increase in the area of farm ponds. Although most of these ponds were located on upland sites, 25 percent were previously different kinds of wetlands (Tiner, 1984). By far, the bulk of wetlands losses by area are palustrine, not an unexpected result considering that only a small portion of total wetlands are estuarine. Yet even on a relative basis the rate of palustrine wetlands loss is considerably greater than the loss of estuarine wetlands. Palustrine wetlands declined 8.6 percent between 1954 and 1975, compared with 6.5 percent for estuarine wetlands.

The difference in the rate of wetlands conversion between these two types of wetlands is all the more striking considering the recent trends in population growth and economic development. For some time now, the rate of population growth in coastal counties along the Atlantic and Gulf coasts, where most of the estuarine wetlands are located, has been much faster than in inland areas. Between 1940 and 1960 the coastal counties increased their population by 79 percent, while the population in the coastal states overall (from Maine to Texas) increased by only 36 percent. Between 1960 and 1980 the corresponding increases were 35 percent and 25 percent. Population growth in the nation as a whole in these two intervals was 35 percent and 26 percent, respectively. That is, despite relatively rapid population growth in the vicinity of estuarine wetlands, their conversion rate has been less than the average for all wetlands. Moreover, it is likely that the rate of estuarine wetland losses has slowed

even further since 1974 because most states have enacted laws to protect coastal wetlands. After passage of such laws, wetlands losses in Maryland were reduced from 1,000 acres to 20 acres per year, and in Delaware from 444 acres to 20 acres per year (Tiner, 1984). Nonetheless, urban development was locally important in estuarine wetlands conversion.

In the palustrine wetlands, the reverse situation is observed. For example, in 36 counties studied by the U.S. Department of the Interior in the Mississippi delta region, population actually declined during the years between 1940 and 1980, even as land in cultivation expanded. In the 36-county study region, forest wetlands acreage dropped from 6.3 million acres to 2.6 million acres between 1934 and 1984, and agricultural acreage increased from 3.6 million to 6.8 million acres. An econometric analysis of wetlands conversion in this region concluded that the levee system built mostly before 1935, together with the natural topography of the region, accounted for 25 percent of wetlands depletion between 1935 and 1984. Federal flood control and drainage projects built since 1935 accounted for another 25 percent. Agricultural price supports and tax code provisions favorable to conversion investments were found to increase the profitability and reduce the risk of land conversion.

As these figures suggest, the recent losses of wetlands are attributable overwhelmingly to increased agricultural production, not to urbanization or other development. Furthermore, a recent study by the U.S. Department of the Interior (1988) concludes that various federal programs have played a major role since 1935 in encouraging wetlands conversion in both the Mississippi delta and prairie pothole regions. Current market conditions, however, no longer favor wetlands conversion even with agricultural subsidies in place, although that could change with an increase in agricultural prices.

Wildlife and Recreation

The massive growth in outdoor recreation in the United States in the twentieth century is described in chapter 7. Much of that recreation has involved the direct consumptive use of wildlife (hunting, fishing, and, to a much smaller extent, trapping).

Hunting for sport increased rapidly after the Civil War and may have contributed to the serious decline in game populations in the late nineteenth century

Table 6-3. Wetland Area in the Continental United States, 1954 and 1974 (in thousands of acres)

Wetland area	Year		Change	
	1954	1974	Absolute	Percentage
Estuarine wetlands	5,609	5,242	−367	−6.5
Palustrine wetlands	102,522	93,736	−8,786	−8.6
Open water	2,320	4,393	+2,073	+89.4
Flat	384	577	+193	+50.3
Emergent	33,113	28,442	−4,671	−14.1
Scrub-shrub	10,998	10,661	−387	−3.5
Forest	55,707	49,713	−5,994	−10.8

Source: Tiner (1984).

(although the main cause was market hunting). On the other hand, much of the success in protecting and restoring wildlife populations in the twentieth century is attributable to sportsmen and sports organizations. These groups were at the forefront of efforts to enact the landmark wildlife protection, and it was the revenues from hunting licenses and hunting equipment purchases that financed the restoration effort. The growth of hunting since World War II has been more moderate, and in relative terms much slower than many other outdoor recreational activities. However, in absolute terms the increase in both hunting and fishing between 1955 and 1980 was substantial. The number of hunting participants of age 16 and older grew from 10.7 million to 17.4 million (63 percent), considerably faster than the population growth rate over the same period (37 percent). The growth rate for fishing was even higher, with the number of people fishing approximately doubling from 19 million to 42 million during the same period (Clawson and Van Doren, 1984; U.S. Department of the Interior, Fish and Wildlife Service, 1982). Between 1980 and 1985 fishing participation continued to increase—to 46.4 million; hunting participation actually declined to 16.7 million.

In recent years, the nonconsumptive use of wildlife, including such activities as birdwatching, wildlife feeding, and nature photography, may have come to rival consumptive use as a generator of recreational enjoyment. In recognition of this trend, the fishing and hunting surveys conducted in 1980 and 1985 by the Fish and Wildlife Service (U.S. Department of the Interior, Fish and Wildlife Service, 1982, 1988) also collected data on nonconsumptive wildlife use. In these surveys, activities were classified according to two criteria: Was involvement with wildlife the main purpose of the activity, or was it a secondary or unintended outcome? Did the activity take place around the home, or did the participants have to travel to enjoy the activity? Together, the two criteria define four categories of nonconsumptive use: primary nonresidential, primary residential, secondary nonresidential, and secondary residential.

Estimated participation under each of these categories substantially outnumbers participation in hunting. Participants under the primary nonresidential user category are those who travel from their homes with the intention of interacting with wildlife; this is the most restrictive category. Survey results reveal that more than 29.3 million people of age 16 and older

It was the revenues from hunting licenses and hunting equipment purchases that financed the restoration effort.

are estimated to have participated in this sort of activity in 1985. This total is up slightly from 1980, when participation was estimated to be 28.8 million. Participation under the other categories was both larger in absolute terms and has been growing faster: secondary nonresidential users rose from 69.4 million in 1980 to 89.5 million in 1985; primary residential users rose from 79.6 million to 94.8 million; and secondary residential users rose from 80.4 million to 117.4 million. Clearly, nonconsumptive enjoyment of wildlife is growing rapidly, especially around the home. Although participation in nonconsumptive activities dwarfs participation in hunting and fishing, it is also true that most hunters and fishermen—89 percent— also report nonconsumptive use, and thus are included in the survey totals.

The extent of residential nonconsumptive use is perhaps surprising. The most common of these activities is wildlife observation, with 56 million participants in 1980, and wild bird feeding, with 62 million participants. (The 1980 survey provided somewhat more detail on the kinds of activities and the wildlife involved in these activities.) The most common wildlife observed were songbirds (90 percent of survey respondents), squirrels or chipmunks (70 percent), and rabbits (52 percent). In addition, 19 percent of the respondents reported observing deer and 31 percent, birds of prey. That a fifth of the population reported observing deer near their home is a reflection of both the high degree of postwar suburbanization and the increase in deer population. It is highly doubtful, for instance, that 20 percent of Americans would have observed deer near their homes in 1950.

Although nonconsumptive participants are much more numerous than sportsmen, the revenues necessary to support wildlife management programs are mostly generated by the latter, through their payments for licenses and the excise taxes on equipment (which support the Pittman-Robertson and Dingell-Johnson programs). To some extent, nonconsumptive wildlife recreation is being subsidized by wildlife consumers, and as long as wildlife management funds are raised by the existing funding mechanisms both consumptive and nonconsumptive users of wildlife have an interest in protecting and promoting hunting and fishing opportunities. For the same reason, hunting and fishing remain the central concern of state wildlife management agencies, despite the much greater number of nonconsumptive users.

One of the major differences between hunting and many other forms of outdoor recreation is that so much hunting takes place on private land. About 72 percent of all hunting days reported in the 1985 survey were enjoyed exclusively on private land, and another 5 percent were spent in part there. For big game and waterfowl hunters, the percentages of hunting days enjoyed wholly or partly on private land is 68 percent; the smaller figure reflects the somewhat greater importance of big game hunting in the West, where public land is more common, as well as the extent of public land devoted to waterfowl management. Private land is unlikely to be as important for most other forms of outdoor recreation, especially wildland recreation. Although comparable figures are hard to find, it is difficult to believe that, for example, two-thirds of all camping days are spent on private land.

Private land is important to hunters in part because most land east of the Rocky Mountains, where the preponderance of people live, is in private hands. Furthermore, on much of the public land set aside for outdoor recreation hunting is either restricted or not permitted. Campgrounds, hiking trails, ski areas, and other important types of recreation facilities permit a density of participation that simply would not be safe with hunting.

The continuing availability of hunting opportunities on private land depends on two conditions. First, wildlife habitat and populations now found on private land must not decline. As suggested by the available trend data, this condition is generally being satisfied; the populations of most game species are remaining constant or are increasing. The second condition is that landowners must permit access to the wildlife on their lands. Traditionally, private rural land in the

On much of the public land set aside for outdoor recreation hunting is either restricted or not permitted.

United States has been widely available to hunters, and in general farmers and other landowners were not harmed by trespass and were generous in giving permission to hunt. At mid-century, with the scarcity of game and the growing number of hunters, landowners were becoming increasingly reluctant to keep their land open for public hunting. By 1960, the reduction in private land available for public hunting had become quite noticeable. For example, a 1961 survey of privately owned rural land in central Michigan revealed that posted or fenced acreage increased from 339,000 acres in 1939 (4 percent of the total) to 1.4 million acres in 1960 (18 percent) (Outdoor Recreation Resources Review Commission, 1962). Moreover, in some situations denial of entry onto private land also restricts use of public land that may only be accessible from the private land. The Outdoor Recreation Resources Review Commission found that in some Colorado counties as much as 98 percent of public land was unavailable to sportspersons in 1958.

Public access to private hunting land continues to be an issue today. Lassiter (1985), in a survey of timber companies with large forestland holdings in four southeastern states (Alabama, Florida, Georgia, and Tennessee), found that of 17.2 million acres of forest owned or leased by these firms, 9.8 million acres were open to the public in 1983. Three million of these acres were in state "wildlife management areas," the result of cooperative agreements between the state and landowner whereby an individual gains access by obtaining a permit from the state or from the landowner. The remainder were open to hunters without fee or upon payment of a nominal fee. The firms anticipated that by 1988 open acreage would be reduced to 8.1 million acres, a 17-percent reduction in five years. The principal reasons given for withdrawal of land from the "open" category are the growing damage to property experienced in these areas, and the realization that the land often can bring in substantial income if access rights are leased to hunting groups. In addition, these firms say that leasing of access rights allows greater control of property damage. Thus, between 1983 and 1985 the acreage of forestland controlled by these firms with access rights leased was expected to grow from 5.6 million acres to 7.8 million acres.

The closure of the private land to public hunting is usually a rational response by private landowners to the incentives they face. Unless land is leased or an access fee charged, landowners receive no benefit from allowing access, yet they may suffer damage to forest resources or livestock. Requiring payments from sportspersons, on the other hand, often increases the landowner's exposure to liability, and enforcement of payment arrangements is often more difficult than outright exclusion. Many states have developed programs that attempt to change the structure of incentives facing private landowners. A recent survey found that at least 20 states (out of 41 responding) had such programs (Montana Department of Fish, Wildlife and Parks, 1987). Of the positively responding states, 2 have programs to encourage habitat enhancement only, 8 to encourage landowners to provide access, and 10 to do both. A variety of incentives are used, including provisions for tax benefits, lease payments, limitation or elimination of injury liability, and enforcement assistance.

Endangered Species

With the emergence of the environmental movement about 1970, a welter of legislation was conceived and enacted at both the federal and state levels to deal with what were perceived to be serious environmental problems. The implementation of such legislation had beneficial consequences for wildlife generally. The rising concern with the environment also brought into sharp relief the conflict between economic development and the protection of wildlife habitat, a conflict that was not so much in evidence during the conservation era. Numerous statutes were enacted to ensure that environmental considerations were fully reflected in development decisions. For example, the National Environmental Policy Act of 1969 required preparation of an environmental impact statement (EIS) for any project having significant federal involvement (such as use of federal funds,

need for a federal permit, or implementation by a federal agency). Environmental advocacy organizations became adept at using these statutes to halt or modify environmentally damaging projects.

Other actions that had important implications for wildlife were the ban on DDT and the gradual phasing out of other organochloride pesticides. Such actions were taken in 1970 pursuant to the Federal Insecti-

California condor

cide, Fungicide, and Rodenticide Act (FIFRA) and were a response to concerns about the effects of the accumulation of these persistent pesticides in the higher trophic levels of ecosystems, and in particular on birds of prey. These concerns were elevated by the publication in 1962 of Rachel Carson's *Silent Spring*, which led to fears that DDT accumulation was interfering with the reproduction of raptors by causing eggshells to thin to the point of breaking.

The great innovation of the postwar period was the emergence of a policy to protect and enhance all varieties of wildlife, not just those of value to hunters or fishermen. Support for such a policy grew throughout the twentieth century with the gradual shift in public sentiment away from utilitarian and toward preservationist attitudes (at least with respect to wildlife). The need for such a change was passionately argued at the Thirteenth North American Wildlife Conference in 1948 by William Vogt, chief of the conservation section of the Pan American Union:

> It is an eloquent commentary on our sense of values and our very human egotism, that over the years we have given the preponderance of attention in the North American Wildlife Conferences to species of animals that are among those which, through these years, have least needed attention! We have devoted hundreds of hours and scores of papers to discussing waterfowl, pheasants, rabbits, quail, etc., which exist in scores of millions. It is, I think, a fair conclusion that we have been more interested in ourselves than in the wildlife. (Vogt, 1948, p. 107)

Whether this change in attitudes is attributable to the growing acceptance of the idea that animals have "rights" or to a conception of enlightened self-interest that appreciates preservation of species for its own sake is beyond the scope of this analysis. Either way, the growth in concern for wildlife has given impetus to a policy to protect particular species in jeopardy of becoming extinct.

Extinction is a natural evolutionary process, but many biologists believe that human population growth and economic activity have speeded it up enormously. In North America, more than 500 species are known to have become extinct since the year 1600, an average of one to two species per year. Almost all the extinctions that have occurred in the United States have come about through conversion of natural habitat. Some habitats, moreover, have been much more heavily damaged than others. Two-thirds of the extinctions that have been verified in the United States have taken place in Hawaii, and the arid Southwest

has accounted for another 17 percent (Opler, 1971). The heavy losses in Hawaii are mostly attributable to the clearing of native forests and the introduction of exotic species, including domestic animals. Both the Southwest and Hawaii can be considered "island" habitats, biologically isolated from the outside world. Such habitats are often particularly vulnerable to invasion or disruption by exotic wildlife (Molles, 1980).

Elsewhere in the United States extinctions have been less common, although the populations and genetic ranges of many, perhaps most, other species have declined markedly. Because the genetic composition of geographically separated populations of a species are often different—a result of adaptation to specific local conditions—restriction of the range of a species may reduce genetic variability even when it does not result in extinction.

Vogt's (1948) concerns about extinction were not totally new. The demise of the passenger pigeon and the heath hen, together with the near-extinction of the bison, were among the events that aroused public concern about natural resources in the late nineteenth century. The new development after World War II was a desire to systematically seek out those species in the most trouble and to protect them. In 1945 the Smithsonian Institution published a list of endangered species containing about 40 animals (Vogt, 1948), including some of today's most prominent endangered species—among them the black-footed ferret, timber wolf, Florida puma, California condor, Everglade kite, whooping crane, and Bachman's warbler.

The most prominent of these was the whooping crane, a bird that became an effective symbol of efforts to save endangered species throughout the world.

The first federal law designed to protect endangered species was the Endangered Species Preservation Act of 1966.

Standing five feet tall when mature and weighing up to sixty pounds, the whooping crane is one of only two species of crane found in the United States (the other is the far more abundant sandhill crane). Never numerous, the whooping crane population declined until by 1941 only one whooper flock was left, numbering only 13 birds. This flock spent its winters on the Texas Gulf Coast just north of Corpus Christi, an area that was designated as the Aransas National Wildlife Refuge in 1938 in an effort to save the crane. (Its summer home, not discovered until 1954, is the Wood Buffalo National Park in northern Canada.) The recovery of this species is discussed below.

Until the mid-1960s, efforts to protect endangered species had to be conducted within the limits of federal and state statutes designed to aid game species, and implemented in programs primarily funded by hunting revenues. Not surprisingly, endangered species protection was not a high priority with either the states or the federal government. The first federal efforts to systematically study endangered species were undertaken by the Endangered Wildlife Research Station, established in 1965 at the Patuxent Wildlife Research Center near Laurel, Maryland.

The first federal law designed to protect endangered species was the Endangered Species Preservation Act of 1966, which directed the secretary of the interior to carry out a program of endangered species protection and authorized the use of up to $15 million from the Land and Water Conservation Fund specifically to provide endangered species habitat. This act, regarded as a weak tool because it contained no mechanism for controlling the taking of species, was superseded by the Endangered Species Act of 1973. The 1973 act marked a significant change in the strategy of endangered species protection, from the use of public funds to acquire and maintain habitat to the direct regulation of activities on privately owned land. It was made unlawful to "take" an individual member of an endangered species. Thus the killing of endangered species was prohibited everywhere in the United States.

In the 1973 act an attempt also was made to control indirect threats to the survival of endangered species. Section 7 authorized the secretary of the interior (through the Fish and Wildlife Service) to identify areas as "critical habitat" for particular species. All other federal agencies are required by the act to ensure that their activities do not jeopardize the "continued existence" of endangered species or modify their critical habitat. If officials of other agencies are uncertain, they must consult the Fish and Wildlife Service. Section 7 does not allow for the regulation of all activities to protect endangered species—only those with some federal agency presence. This is a large class of activities, because it includes not only all federally funded projects but also those for which a federal permit is required. For such projects, the Fish and Wildlife Service issues "biological opinions" on the effects of activities on endangered wildlife. The agency involved is not bound to accept these opinions, but if it does not the agency's position becomes more vulnerable should there be a subsequent court action.

At the time of passage and for a few years thereafter, the Endangered Species Act of 1973 aroused strenuous opposition. Not only did the consultation process raise the possibility of costly alterations of development projects, it also inspired fears of costly

Fears were expressed in some quarters that the Endangered Species Act provided a "hunting license" for environmental groups to stop any project by discovering some obscure species or subspecies in the area affected by the project.

---

delays of construction projects while biological studies were completed. Because so much economic activity requires a federal permit of some kind, especially in the West, a critical habitat designation could cause a potentially serious restriction on the use of private property. Although these regulations are applicable only to listed species, fears were also expressed in some quarters that the Endangered Species Act provided a "hunting license" for environmental groups to stop any project by discovering some obscure species or subspecies in the area affected by the project.

Fears that implementation of the Endangered Species Act of 1973 would bring development to a standstill came to a head in the celebrated Tellico Dam case, in which construction of a dam by the Tennessee Valley Authority (TVA) across the Little Tennessee River threatened the survival of the snail darter, a small fish thought to be found only in the affected stream reach. Environmental groups challenged the completion and operation of the dam as threatening the critical habitat of the snail darter. The case was taken to the U.S. Supreme Court, which ruled in 1978 that the Endangered Species Act required all other objectives to be subordinated to the protection of critical habitat: "One would be hard pressed to find a statutory provision whose terms were any plainer

than those of Section 7 of the Endangered Species Act.... This language admits of no exception" (*TVA v. Hill*, 1978). To bring some balance between economic and preservation objectives, the act was amended again in 1978 to provide the possibility of an exemption from the absolute strictures of the act under some circumstances. However, the procedure for making such tradeoffs was made so cumbersome that it rarely has been used.[2]

Fears that the act was going to be a strong deterrent to economic development have proved—so far—to be greatly exaggerated. This assessment needs careful qualification. For example, it ignores any instances in which a project may have been abandoned at the outset because of potential problems with the Endangered Species Act. In addition, there is no guarantee that such conflicts will never occur, and there is at least one unresolved case—that involving the spotted owl—that could make this judgment obsolete. Protection of this species could bring an end to timber operations in certain old-growth forest areas of the Pacific Northwest, with substantial economic effects.

The Endangered Species Act is now, in 1991, eighteen years old. During those years the number of species listed a endangered and threatened has grown from about 150, on the U.S. Department of the Interior list in 1973, to the current 531. In addition, recovery plans have been approved for 242 species and are in preparation for 42 more ("Box Score of Listings and Plans," 1988). Species may be added to or dropped from the list for more than one reason, and it is difficult to tell from the numbers of listed species whether change represents improvement or retrogression. A species added to the list may have experienced a worsening condition, or it may simply represent successful rulemaking for a species that always had been endangered. Likewise, a species may be dropped from the list either because programs have been so successful that the species is no longer in danger, or because the species has been wiped out. So far, evidently, most additions to the list have been from species that probably were in bad condition all along, and most deletions have resulted from extinctions.

A better, though more elusive, indicator of the effectiveness of the Endangered Species Act would be the number of species whose extinction had been prevented. Certainly there have been some successful efforts to save endangered species, of which the most outstanding probably has been the campaign to pre-

Protection of this owl could bring an end to timber operations in certain old-growth forest areas of the Pacific Northwest, with substantial economic effects.

vent the extinction of the whooping crane. From the low of 13 individuals in 1941, there are now more than 200 whooping cranes in existence. Some 60 are in captivity at the Patuxent Wildlife Research Station in Maryland, but most are in the wild. The Aransas–Wood Buffalo flock now numbers 130 birds, and attempts are under way to establish a second flock to accompany the flock of sandhill cranes that spends its summers at Grays Lake National Wildlife Refuge in Idaho and winters in the Bosque del Apache in New Mexico. So far this second whooping crane flock contains only 13 individuals (Jim Lewis, Fish and Wildlife Service, personal communication, July 19, 1989). The buildup of the first flock and the establishment of the second was the result of active management by researchers at the Patuxent Wildlife Research Station, who are now approaching the goal of the recovery plan to have two independent flocks of 20 breeding pairs each. Efforts to protect the alligator also have been successful, to the point where alligators are now being regarded as a nuisance in parts of Florida and Louisiana. Both states recently instituted a limited hunting season for alligators.

The role played by the Endangered Species Act in the recovery of the whooping crane probably has been minor, because the population of birds at Aransas had already reached 70 by 1970 (U.S. Department of the Interior, Fish and Wildlife Service, 1977). However, the act did play a role. One of the earliest critical habitat designations was made to protect the rest stops used by the whoopers (and sandhill cranes as well) during their spring migration from Aransas to Wood Buffalo. These stops are located on sandbars in the channels of the broad, shallow rivers of the northern Great Plains, including the North Platte, Blue, and Niobrara rivers. Water resource development on these rivers during the preceding fifty years had controlled high flows to the point where the sandbars were no longer being scoured of vegetation, which made them less suitable as stopover habitat for the cranes. The critical habitat designation prevented further water withdrawals from these rivers and saved the remaining sandbars. On the other hand, the alligator recovery is believed to be largely attributable to the Endangered Species Act, because populations showed remarkable improvement only a few years after protection was implemented (Jay Shepherd, Fish and Wildlife Service, personal communication, July 19, 1989). The prohibition on killing alligators and trading in alligator products removed the incentive to hunt them.

The Endangered Species Act has become an important symbol of the commitment to endangered species protection in the United States and is often held up as an example for other countries. On the basis of actual results, however, some authorities have begun to question whether the species-by-species approach of the act is a viable approach to protection of endangered species.

Prospects for Wildlife Resources

With the arrival of the Europeans, a drastic decline in the numbers and variety of North American wildlife began and continued until 1900. Before 1900, wildlife had generally seemed so abundant that its decline or disappearance in a particular area seemed at most a local concern. Moreover, inability to own wildlife resources and thereby to enjoy exclusively the benefits contributed to the lack of a private incentive to manage wildlife resources. At about the turn of the century, growing concern over declining wildlife populations began to become effective, and since 1900 the populations of many bird and mammal game species have staged remarkable recoveries.

Most game species are probably found today in fewer numbers than existed in pre-Columbian times, but many are more numerous today than 80 or 100 years ago. For example, it is estimated that before the arrival of the Europeans 30 million to 40 million pronghorn antelope roamed the plains and the Rocky Mountains. By 1930 antelope numbers had dropped to an estimated 13,000, but have since recovered to a total population of about 1 million. The beaver, once eliminated from all eastern states except Maine and common only in parts of the Rockies and Pacific Northwest, is now common in all states except Hawaii. White-tailed deer have increased in population from about 350,000 in a few states in 1895 to 20 million in forty-eight states. Dramatic increases have also been experienced by bison (from 800 to 6,000) and elk (from 41,000 to 1 million). The wild turkey, found in 1930 in only a few southern states, is now found in forty-three states. Several egret and heron species nearly extinct in 1910 are now common to abundant throughout the United States. Northern fur seals have increased from 215,000 in 1911 to 1.5 million today, and the sea otter is again being found in its historic range off the Pacific Coast from Washington to northern California. Migratory bird populations also have recovered from low levels early in the twentieth century. Such species include the wood duck, the trumpeter swan (from 66 individuals in the 1930s to about 10,000 currently), and the whooping crane (from 14 individuals in 1953 to well over 100 individuals in two flocks today). At least two highly desired species, the beaver and white-tailed deer, may even be more numerous today than ever before.

With nongame species the patterns are less clear, partly because many continue to decline and partly because such species did not attract attention in the past, making it difficult to determine their pre-Columbian populations. Certainly, with only a few exceptions, all wildlife had declined to a low state by the end of the nineteenth century. (The exceptions were those species that seem to prosper in the vicinity of human settlements, such as raccoons.) In the view of many experts, since 1900 many of the nongame species also have experienced a modest recovery, if for no other reason than the provision of habitat to aid game species incidentally helps many nongame species as well.

Looking ahead, the expectations for wildlife populations are mixed, depending on who is making the projection and which species are being examined (see Flather and Hoekstra, 1988, chapter 3). For big and small game mammals, observers generally project future populations to remain stable or to increase in the next several decades, for all regions and for most species examined. Trend projections for waterfowl are more mixed. The North American Waterfowl Plan projects that recent declines in duck populations will be reversed, with populations climbing from 27 million to 36 million by the year 2000, assuming implementation of a habitat acquisition and protection program. However, this is an important condition, and this projection might more properly be considered a goal. Thomas and coauthors (1988, p. 6) offer a somber assessment of the current duck predicament: "When surface water is scarce, the situation for ducks is grim. This situation in 1988 and beyond is grim and reflects the cumulative consequences of years of habitat destruction aggravated by severe and prolonged drought." Thomas and coauthors (1988) imply that the recovery of duck populations is contingent on a return to more typical rainfall patterns, although even then the effects of past population declines would likely persist for some years.

Flather and Hoekstra (1988) also report on a "habitat-based" projection of wildlife populations prepared for the Southeast. Population changes are based on projections of habitat changes, which in turn are projected from assumed changes in land use. These projections are somewhat pessimistic, with a 70-percent decline in the red-cockaded woodpecker and more moderate declines for deer, wild turkey, and trout projected by 2030. These projections are not nearly as dire as those made by Hornaday and Grant and others at the turn of the century. Those earlier projections turned out to be, in effect, calls to action,

Earlier projections of wildlife populations turned out to be, in effect, calls to action, and helped to change the conditions being projected.

and helped to change the conditions being projected. Once wildlife resources were provided with effective protection and enhancement, they were able to recover from severely depleted conditions. This apparent resiliency is a cause for some optimism that wildlife management can be effective in dealing with future population declines, should they occur.

Such optimism is not unbounded, of course. For one thing, it mainly reflects the recovery of terrestrial species, not aquatic or semiaquatic ones. In addition, a number of biologists remain concerned about the long-term effects on native wildlife of the settlement of the continent. These concerns reflect theories of "island biogeography," which posit an equilibrium relationship between habitat size and the number and diversity of species (Wilson and Simberloff, 1969; Diamond, 1975). Such theories are based largely on empirical studies correlating island size with the number and mix of species. Because such empirical studies are ordinarily cross-sectional rather than longitudinal, it is difficult to determine the causal mechanisms involved. (However, the Wilson-Simberloff study observed the repopulation of tiny islands in the Florida Keys following their treatment with biocides.)

In qualitative terms, it is likely that similar relationships obtain for habitat "islands" on land. In particular, a loss of wildlife species may result from forest "fragmentation" when forest habitat is converted to other land uses. Whether such species loss would accompany forest fragmentation depends on the relationship between habitat size and species number. Where smaller regions tend to have fewer species simply because they are less diverse, perhaps fragmentation would not reduce the number of species. But to the extent that size itself contributes to the number of species—for example, by supporting a larger population less susceptible to catastrophe—forest fragmentation will reduce species number. Some evidence has emerged regarding the adverse effects of forest fragmentation on small mammals (Thomas and coauthors, 1988). In addition, declines in the number and diversity of forest songbirds has been linked to the fragmentation of forests and, in particular, to the exposure of these interior forest species to predators and competitors found on the forest edge. Many of these species are also neotropical migrants, spending their winters in Central and South America; they are also being put at risk by tropical deforestation.

Emerging global environmental problems, particularly those related to possible changes in climate, may also affect North American wildlife. It has been predicted that over the next century or so increasing concentrations of carbon dioxide and other "greenhouse gases" in the atmosphere may cause a global temperature increase of a magnitude comparable with the difference between current and Ice Age temperatures. Higher temperatures also would change precipitation patterns; some areas would become much drier than they are now, and others might become wetter. In general, global warming would presumably shift climate zones northward.

Although nearly all scientists agree that continuing increases in carbon dioxide concentrations in the atmosphere would eventually cause global warming, there is considerable disagreement about the magnitude and timing of the warming trend. If global warming does occur, and especially if it occurs rapidly, serious consequences will ensue for both human and wildlife populations ("No Escape," 1988; "How Fast Can Trees Migrate," 1989). Wildlife's difficulties in adapting to climate change will be exacerbated by forest fragmentation, because the isolation of islands will not permit affected species an easy path of retreat. In addition, the current network of wildlife refuges could be of dubious value if changes in climate render them unable to support their current mix of species.

One of the most interesting of current developments in wildlife policy is the search for practical mechanisms that compensate landowners for the enjoyment by others of wildlife on their property.

Climate-induced changes in habitat are surrounded by great uncertainty. Less uncertain is the likelihood that the demand for wildlife-related services, especially recreation, will continue to increase, at least in the near term. The fastest growing part of wildlife-related recreation will probably continue to be nonconsumptive use, such as birdwatching or nature study. Nonconsumptive wildlife use is growing particularly fast around the home, where participation is reported to have increased by one-third between 1980 and 1985. The probable increase in demand for wildlife services will in all likelihood not be matched by expanded reservation of public land for wildlife habitat. Therefore the future of wildlife resource use—both the provision of suitable wildlife habitat and public access to wildlife resources—depends to a considerable extent on the status of wildlife on privately owned land.

There is nothing new in the importance of private land to wildlife. Most rural land, especially east of the Rockies, is privately owned—by farmers, railroads, or large wood-product companies. In the past the inability of wildlife to "pay its own way" induced landowners to disregard consequences to wildlife in making land development decisions. It was not that these activities were necessarily unfavorable to all wildlife; the wildlife recoveries of the past century would not have been possible otherwise. However, certain activities were highly destructive to wildlife populations, most notably the conversion of wetlands. Wetlands conversion continues, and continues to have an adverse effect.

A more recent development in the relationship between wildlife and private land is the effort to maintain public access to the land for the purpose of enjoying wildlife. Because allowing access to hunters seldom provided any income to the farmer and occasionally imposed costs, it is surprising that so much free access was provided in the past. The problem of access has been attributed largely to damage from users and also to the concern of landowners over increased exposure to liability losses in this litigious age.

One of the most interesting of current developments in wildlife policy is the search for practical mechanisms that compensate landowners for the enjoyment by others of wildlife on their property. If successful, such mechanisms would provide landowners with an incentive both to provide wildlife habitat on their property and to allow others access to it. These measures could involve the direct payment by users to landowners for access, or payments from government units to landowners in exchange for adopting measures to enhance habitat and make it available to others. The Farm Act of 1985, for example, contains several provisions that may indirectly benefit wildlife. The most important of these is the Conservation Reserve, designed to remove the most erodible land from crop production. If successful, the Conservation Reserve is projected eventually to return 40 million to 45 million acres of vulnerable cropland to grassland and forest. Additional wildlife benefits may result from the "sodbuster" and "swampbuster" provisions (see chapter 5), which deny agricultural subsidies to farms that convert wetlands and highly erodible land to croplands.

In addition, nearly half the states now have programs to encourage wildlife habitat and public access to it on private land. State initiatives run the gamut from liability limitations to purchase of development rights to direct cash subsidies. Despite the enormous variety, these programs all have one thing in common: they attempt to give private landowners an incentive to provide wildlife services. Whether the incentives provided are appropriate to the purpose or sufficient to achieve it is still to be determined.

These state provisions might best be regarded as experiments in wildlife policy. If successful, they offer the prospect of allowing landowners to treat wildlife resources comparably with other products of the land. Private incentives may be the best hope of simultaneously protecting wildlife habitat while also preserving public access to wildlife resources.

Notes

The outstanding research assistance of Caroline Harnett and Sari Radin is gratefully acknowledged.

1. If the actual trends in bird populations were stable, then the expected number of statistically significant observations of increasing trends, on the basis of chance alone, is 25 (at a 5-percent level of significance). The standard deviation on the number of increasing trends is about 5.1. Likewise, another 25 in expectation would show a significant decreasing trend, with standard deviation also of 5.1. Because the number of observations of significantly increasing (decreasing) trends is 8 (4) standard deviations more than what would have been observed by chance, it can be concluded that there truly are some species enjoying increasing trends, and some suffering decreasing ones.

2. The 1978 amendments mandated use of this procedure (which involved review of the case by an Endangered Species Committee of high-ranking officials of the federal government and the governments of the states involved) in two cases, one of which was the Tellico Dam case. In this case the committee ruled against allowing an exemption, largely on the basis of a benefit-cost analysis that could not find an economic justification for the dam's completion even though most of the costs were already incurred. Congress subsequently overrode this decision by enacting legislation authorizing the construction of the Tellico Dam specifically. The final chapter of the Tellico story came several years later, when snail darter populations were found on stream reaches other than that affected by the Tellico Dam.

Appendix 6

Table 6-A1. Acquisitions and Restorations Under the Pittman-Robertson Act, by State

State	Land acquisition	Principal species restorations
Alabama	32,000 acres acquired	White-tailed deer Wild turkey
Alaska		Sea otter Musk-ox
Arizona		Deer Quail
Arkansas	300,000 acres acquired	White-tailed deer Eastern wild turkey
California	54,200 acres acquired	Tule elk Big horn sheep Golden eagle Spotted owl Sandhill crane
Colorado		Sage grouse Big horn sheep Deer Elk
Connecticut	9,550 acres acquired	Deer Wild turkey
Delaware	35,000 acres acquired (50% of Delaware shoreline)	Wild turkey
Florida	112,000 acres acquired (maybe more)	Dove White-tailed deer
Georgia		Deer Wild turkey
Hawaii	1,003,168 public hunting acres added partly as a result of the act; 80,000 acres managed	Big game and game birds introduced; nene and koloa studies funded
Idaho	55,893 acres acquired	Mountain goat Black bear
Illinois	10,877 acres purchased; 150,000 acres set aside	Wood duck White-tailed deer Wild turkey Giant Canada goose
Indiana	At least 55,000 acres acquired	White-tailed deer
Iowa	42,146 acres acquired	Canada goose Wild turkey
Kansas	57,000 acres purchased; 175,000 acres managed	Deer Antelope Canada goose Wild turkey
Kentucky	60,000 acres acquired; 200,000 acres managed	Deer Turkey
Louisiana	1,080,915 acres managed	Dove Deer Wild turkey
Maine	500,000 acres (some acquired, some managed)	Black bear Beaver Wild turkey Waterfowl research
Maryland		White-tailed deer Wild turkey

(continued)

Table 6-A1. *(continued)*

State	Land acquisition	Principal species restorations
Massachusetts		White-tailed deer Wild turkey Black bear
Michigan	300,000 acres acquired	Land restoration priority
Minnesota	528,000 acres acquired in large part with act funds	Giant Canada goose Wild turkey
Mississippi	36,427 acres acquired	White-tailed deer
Missouri	105,000 acres acquired	Wild turkey White-tailed deer
Montana	192,307 acres bought and leased	Deer Antelope Gray partridge studies
Nebraska	33,400 acres acquired	Wild turkey Pronghorn antelope Canada goose
Nevada	267,874 acres bought or leased	Chukar and gray partridge Pronghorn antelope Mule deer
New Hampshire	375 acres preserved	Beaver management
New Jersey	21,685 acres acquired	Deer Wild turkey
New Mexico	Some acreage	Antelope Elk Big horn sheep Ibex, oryx, and barbary sheep introduced
New York	32,807 acres acquired	Deer Wild turkey
North Carolina	50,000 acres acquired	Deer Wild turkey
North Dakota	45,000 acres acquired	Canada goose Big horn sheep
Ohio	57,820 acres acquired	Canada goose Wild turkey White-tailed deer Beaver
Oklahoma	74, 250 acres acquired	Deer Wild turkey
Oregon	114,000 acres acquired	Beaver Big horn sheep Sea otter
Pennsylvania	176,934 acres acquired	White-tailed deer Wild turkey Woodcock Snowshoe hare
Rhode Island	At least 8,300 acres acquired	Wild turkey
South Carolina	Some acreage acquired	Dove Wild turkey Deer
South Dakota	154,000 acres managed	Canada goose Wild turkey
Tennessee	169,000 acres acquired	Wild turkey Deer

(continued)

Table 6-A1. *(continued)*

State	Land acquisition	Principal species restorations
Texas	180,127 acres acquired	White-tailed deer Wild turkey Pronghorn antelope
Utah	250,000 acres acquired	Wild turkey Big horn sheep White-tailed ptarmigan
Vermont	92,000 acres mostly purchased with act funds	Wild turkey
Virginia	103,193 acres acquired	Deer Wild turkey Bald eagle
Washington	154,669 acres acquired, in part with act funds	Waterfowl Big game Game birds
West Virginia	Some acreage acquired	Wild turkey Deer Canada goose Fisher
Wisconsin	450,000 acres acquired and developed	Canada goose White-tailed deer
Wyoming	100,000 acres acquired	Antelope Elk Big horn sheep

Source: Kallman (1987).
Note: Empty cells indicate lack of data.

References

Balenger, Dian Olson. 1988. *Managing American Wildlife: A History of the International Association of Fish and Wildlife Agencies*. Amherst, Mass.: University of Massachusetts Press.

Bean, Michael J. 1983. *The Evolution of National Wildlife Law*. New York: Praeger.

Dehnke, Bob. 1980. "The Impacts of Habitat Alterations on the Endangered and Threatened Fishes of the Upper Colorado River Basin." In *Energy Development in the Southwest: Problems of Water, Fish and Wildlife in the Upper Colorado River Basin*, edited by W. O. Spofford, Jr., A. L. Parker, and A. V. Kneese. Washington, D.C.: Resources for the Future.

"Box Score of Listings and Plans." 1988. *Endangered Species Technical Bulletin* 13, no.11–12:12.

Braudel, Fernand. 1981. *The Structures of Everyday Life*. Translated by Sian Reynolds. New York: Harper and Row.

Burger, George V. 1978. "Agriculture and Wildlife." In *Wildlife and America*, edited by Howard P. Brokaw. Washington, D.C.: GPO.

Carson, Rachel. 1962. *Silent Spring*. Boston: Houghton Mifflin.

Chapman, D. W. 1986. "Salmon and Steelhead Abundance in the Columbia River in the Nineteenth Century." *Transactions of the American Fisheries Society* 115:662–670.

Clawson, Marion, and Carlton S. Van Doren, eds. 1984. *Statistics on Outdoor Recreation*. Washington D.C.: Resources for the Future.

Courtenay, Walter R. 1978. "The Introduction of Exotic Organisms." In *Wildlife and America*, edited by Howard P. Brokaw. Washington, D.C.: GPO.

Dahlgren, Robert B. 1987. "The Ring-necked Pheasant." In *Restoring America's Wildlife*, edited by Harmon Kallman. Washington D.C.: U.S. Department of the Interior, Fish and Wildlife Service.

Dale, Edward E. 1930. *The Range Cattle Industry*. Norman, Okla.: University of Oklahoma Press.

Degler, Carl. 1970. *Out of Our Past: The Forces That Shaped Modern America*. New York: Harper and Row.

Diamond, Jared. 1975. "The Island Dilemma: Lessons of Modern Biogeographic Studies for the Design of Natural Reserves." *Biological Conservation* 7 (February):129–146.

Doane, C. C., and M. L. McManus. 1981. *The Gypsy Moth: Research Toward Integrated Pest Management*. Technical Bulletin no. 1584. Washington, D.C.: U.S. Department of Agriculture, Forest Service.

Evans, David L. 1982. *Status Report on Twelve Raptors*. Special Scientific Report—Wildlife, no. 238, U.S. Department of the Interior, Fish and Wildlife Service. Washington, D.C.

Farb, Peter. 1978. *Man's Rise to Civilization: The Cultural Ascent of the Indians of North America*. New York: E. P. Dutton.

Flather, Curtis H., and Thomas W. Hoekstra. 1988. *An Analysis of the Wildlife and Fish Situation in the United States: 1989–2040*. Washington, D.C.: U. S. Department of Agriculture, Forest Service.

Foresta, Ronald. 1984. *America's National Parks and Their Keepers*. Washington, D.C.: Resources for the Future.

Haveman, Robert. 1965. *Water Resource Investment and the Public Interest*. Nashville, Tenn.: Vanderbilt University Press.

"How Fast Can Trees Migrate?" 1989. *Science* 243 (February):735–737.

Innis, H. A. 1970. *The Fur Trade in Canada*. Toronto, Ontario: Toronto University Press.

Johnson, Paul. 1974. *A History of the English People*. New York: Harper and Row.

Kallman, Harmon, ed. 1987. *Restoring America's Wildlife*. Washington, D.C.: U. S. Department of the Interior, Fish and Wildlife Service.

Kimball, T. L., and R. E. Johnson. 1978. "The Richness of American Wildlife." In *Wildlife and America*, edited by Howard P. Brokaw. Washington, D.C.: GPO.

Lassiter, Roy L. 1985. "Access to and Management of the Wildlife Resources on Large Private Timberland Holdings in the Southeastern United States." Monograph Series no. 1, Tennessee Technological University, College of Business Administration. Cookeville, Tenn.

Lewis, John B. 1987. "Success Story: Wild Turkey." In *Restoring America's Wildlife*, edited by Harmon Kallman. Washington, D.C.: U. S. Department of the Interior, Fish and Wildlife Service.

"Listing Protection Proposed for Seven Species: Two Florida Beach Mice." 1988. In *Endangered Species Technical Bulletin* 13, no. 8:1,6. Washington, D.C.: U. S. Fish and Wildlife Service.

Matthiessen, Peter. 1987. *Wildlife in America*. New York: Viking Press.

Merk, Frederick. 1978. *A History of the Westward Movement*. New York: Alfred Knopf.

Molles, Manuel. 1980. "The Impacts of Habitat Alterations and Introduced Species on the Native Fishes of the Upper Colorado River Basin." In *Energy Development in the Southwest*, vol. 1, edited by Walter O. Spofford, Jr., A. L. Parker, and A. V. Kneese. Research Paper R-18. Washington, D.C.: Resources for the Future.

Montana Department of Fish, Wildlife and Parks. 1987. "Compensation to Landowners for Recreational Access: A Survey of All State Programs." Draft.

National Research Council. 1982. *Impact of Emerging Agricultural Trends on Fish and Wildlife Habitat*. Washington, D.C.: National Academy Press.

"No Escape from the Global Greenhouse." 1988. *New Scientist* (November 12):38–43.

Northwest Power Planning Council. 1986. "Compilation of

Information on Salmon and Steelhead Losses in the Columbia River Basin."

Opler, Paul A. 1971. "The Parade of Passing Species: A Survey of Extinction in the U.S." *The Science Teacher* 44 (January).

Outdoor Recreation Resources Review Commission. 1962. *ORRRC Study Report 6: Hunting in the United States—Its Present and Future Role*. Washington, D.C.: GPO.

Peterle, Tony J. 1987. "Substituting Facts for Myths." In *Restoring America's Wildlife*, edited by Harmon Kallman. Washington, D.C.: U. S. Department of the Interior, Fish and Wildlife Service.

Pinchot, Gifford. 1947. *Breaking New Ground*. New York: Harcourt, Brace and Co.

Poole, Daniel A., and James B. Trefethen. 1978. "Maintenance of Wildlife Populations." In *Wildlife and America*, edited by Howard P. Brokaw. Washington, D.C.: GPO.

Rieger, John F. 1986. *American Sportsmen and the Origins of Conservation*. Norman, Okla.: Oklahoma University Press.

Robbins, Roy M. 1942. *Our Landed Heritage*. Princeton, N.J.: Princeton University Press.

Smith, Frank E. 1971. *Conservation in the United States: A Documentary History*. 5 vols. New York: Chelsea House Publishers.

Stankey, George H. 1989. "Beyond the Campfire's Light: Historical Roots of the Wilderness Concept." *Natural Resources Journal* 29 (Winter):9–24.

Thomas, J. W., J. Verner, L. R. Jahn, R. D. Sparrowe, D. E. Toweill, M. Bender, and T. M. Quigley. 1988. "Status and Trends of America's Major Renewable Resources—Wildlife." U. S. Department of Agriculture, Forest Service. Typescript.

Thoreau, Henry David. 1947. *The Portable Thoreau*. New York: Viking Press.

Tiner, Ralph W. 1984. *Wetlands of the United States: Current Status and Recent Trends*. Washington, D.C.: U.S. Department of the Interior, Fish and Wildlife Service.

U.S. Council on Environmental Quality. 1973. *Fourth Annual Report*. Washington, D.C.: GPO.

U.S. Department of Agriculture, Forest Service. 1985. *Gypsy Moth Suppression and Eradication Projects: Final Environmental Impact Statement*. Washington, D.C.: GPO.

U.S. Department of Commerce, Bureau of the Census. 1960. *Historical Statistics of the United States, Colonial Times to 1957*. Washington, D.C.: GPO.

U.S. Department of the Interior. 1980. "Annual Report of Lands Under Control of the U.S. Fish and Wildlife Service as of September 30, 1980 and Addendum—December 2, 1980." Washington, D.C.

————. 1988. "The Impact of Federal Programs on Wetlands," vol. 1: "The Lower Mississippi Alluvial Plain and the Prairie Pothole Region." Report to Congress.

————. 1990. "Annual Report of Lands Under Control of the U.S. Fish and Wildlife Service as of September 30, 1990." Washington, D.C.

U.S. Department of the Interior, Fish and Wildlife Service. 1977. "Whooping Crane Recovery Plan Draft."

————, Fish and Wildlife Service. 1982. *1980 National Survey of Fishing, Hunting and Wildlife-Associated Recreation*. Washington, D.C.: GPO.

————, Fish and Wildlife Service. 1988. *1985 National Survey of Fishing, Hunting and Wildlife-Associated Recreation*. Washington, D.C.: GPO.

————, Fish and Wildlife Service. Various years, 1973–1990. *Waterfowl Status Report*. Washington, D.C.

Vogt, William. 1948. "North American Animals Threatened with Extinction." In *Transactions of the Thirteenth North American Wildlife Conference*, 106–112.

Weinberg, Susan. 1989. "The Once and Future Ferret." *Zoogoer* 18 (January/February):4–7.

Wells, LaRue, and A. L. McLain. 1973. "Lake Michigan: Man's Effects on Native Fish Stocks and Other Biota." Technical Report no. 20. Ann Arbor, Mich.: Great Lakes Fishery Commission.

Williamson, Lonnie L. 1987. "Evolution of a Landmark Law." In *Restoring America's Wildlife*, edited by Harmon Kallman. Washington, D.C.: U.S. Department of the Interior, Fish and Wildlife Service.

Wilson, E. O., and D. S. Simberloff. 1969. "Experimental Defaunation of Islands: Defaunation and Monitoring Techniques." *Ecology* 50 (Spring):267–278.

7

The Growing Role of Outdoor Recreation

Marion Clawson and Winston Harrington

The subject of this chapter is not a particular resource, but a category of uses that cuts across several different resources. Although the activities of outdoor recreation are distinguished more by their enormous variety than by their similarities, one characteristic common to nearly all forms of outdoor recreation is the use of large amounts of land or water. In urban areas, the demand for land for outdoor recreation conflicts with the use of land for housing and commercial or industrial development. In rural areas, the conflict is with the use of land for production of agricultural and other natural resource commodities. In the course of U.S. history, outdoor recreation has progressed from being an unimportant, almost nonexistent user of natural resources to its current role as one of the most important users. As its role has grown, so has the scope of conflict with other natural resource uses. This chapter traces that change by describing trends in recreation use and by examining important influences on those trends.

From the Colonial Period to 1870: Little Outdoor Recreation Use

Recreational Activities

For 250 years after European settlement began, Americans were rural and agricultural to a degree that is almost impossible to comprehend today. In 1870 the population was still predominantly rural, with 72 percent of the nearly 37 million total population living in rural areas. "Rural" is defined by the U.S. Bureau of the Census as including people in small towns and villages with a population of 2,500 or less, as well as people living in open country. Approximately one-fourth of the total population lived on farms in 1870 (U.S. Department of Commerce, Bureau of the Census, 1975).

During colonial and early national times, most people—even professionals such as lawyers and doctors, as well as tradespeople—lived on farms or carried on an agricultural operation. They not only grew most of their own food, but harvested timber for fuel and for building material, harvested game for sport and food, produced hides for shoe leather, and produced wool for clothing. Most people lived close to the land, whether on a farm or in a small village, and necessarily spent a great deal of time outdoors.

Not only were these people rural and agricultural, but the range of their activities was severely constrained to local areas. Roads were typically mere trails, ungraded and unimproved, impossibly muddy and bog-prone in wet weather and dusty in dry weather. When it was necessary to travel beyond ordinary walking distance, travel by water or on horseback was the most practical and most common means of transportation. There was some trade in essential items that could not be produced locally; but that trade was small even in terms of the limited consumption standards of the time.

Under these circumstances, there was little time, money, or opportunity for outdoor recreation as people currently know the activity. Instead, most human activity had to be directed to the essentials of existence. Attitudes toward and practices of outdoor recreation varied in different parts of the colonies and the early nation. In New England, the Puritans were a humorless and God-fearing lot; to them outdoor recreation was frivolous and childish. They especially frowned upon outdoor recreation on Sunday. In the Middle Atlantic states, Dutch and German settlers were more relaxed about the matter and often engaged in a number of innocent pastimes (such as picnics) that they had brought with them from Europe. In the South, the plantation aristocracy made much of recreation for themselves, but did not necessarily extend such recreation to workers or slaves. On the frontier, many people engaged in a type of lawlessness that was recreation for them. In general, there was some outdoor recreation in all areas and at all times, and it would be a mistake to assume that the desire for recreation did not exist and did not find some outlets.

Recreational activities often involved fishing and hunting, much of which was a utilitarian search for food rather than a sport. However, an extensive fly-fishing community existed throughout the nineteenth century and earlier (Schullery, 1987). In addition, people engaged in wanton slaughter of animals, sometimes merely to see who could kill the most on any day or occasion. Even Native Americans—often good conservationists as far as game was concerned—killed large numbers of buffalo, partly for meat but frequently for hides. Another activity was the nearly ubiquitous horse racing, often under relatively informal circumstances. With the heavy dependence on horses characteristic of those times, high premiums were placed on good horses. In the northern areas, people engaged in skating on natural ice on ponds and lakes. Moreover, modern baseball is generally considered to have begun in 1839 and to have spread widely in the following years; it was an active recreation during the Civil War.

These activities were not restricted to particular locations. During the nineteenth century, other opportunities for recreation arose when several areas of outstanding amenity value became tourist attractions and resorts. Foremost among them was Niagara Falls, which became a necessary stop for wealthy European visitors to America. Other important tourist sites of the period were Hot Springs, Arkansas, which became a famous spa, and the Palisades of the Hudson River. In addition, several seaside communities became known as resort towns, including Cape May and Atlantic City in New Jersey and, somewhat later, Newport, Rhode Island. These early developments in tourism were facilitated by the rapid development of railroads after 1840. Atlantic City even became the eastern terminus of the Camden and Atlantic railroad in 1854, following which it soon became the nation's leading seaside resort.

Public Provision of Facilities for Recreation

From the earliest days of the colonial period, permanent reservations were made of public land that would later become parks. These reservations were in villages and towns. Every New England town had a village green; most of these derived from a requirement established by the Massachusetts Bay Colony about 1650 that a large tract be reserved for a Puritan meeting house (originally this tract was about 50 acres, but most eventually dwindled to a much smaller area). The Boston Common, established in 1634, was one of the few such urban open spaces that was originally a common pasturage. These open spaces served numerous functions, but among them were various recreational activities. In the stories of Washington Irving, for example, Rip Van Winkle bowls on the village green. Open space was also provided for occasionally by design. Several cities established before 1800, including Philadelphia (in 1682), Savannah (in 1733), and Washington (in 1791) made generous provision for parks and open space.

In the second half of the nineteenth century efforts to establish urban parks became a minor social movement. The establishment of many parks during this period was attributable largely to the efforts and influence of Frederick Law Olmsted, the noted landscape architect. The most famous park designed (in part) by Olmsted was Manhattan's Central Park, originally authorized in 1853. In the ensuing half-century, Olmsted helped to plan nearly forty city parks, including Prospect Park in Brooklyn, New York, and Golden Gate Park in San Francisco (Roper, 1973). Except for these local efforts to provide open space, there was little government activity before 1870 in what would be called outdoor recreation today. State legislatures gave almost no attention to any aspect of parks or outdoor recreation, from the supply of such areas to management and safety measures.

The federal government paid enormous attention (for that period) to the problems and opportunities of public lands, but this attention did not include any systematic consideration of outdoor recreation. The nation's first concern was to acquire the central part of the North American continent, by measures such as the Louisiana Purchase, the war with Mexico, the treaty with Great Britain, and the annexation of Texas. Concern then shifted to the disposal of land, through myriad laws and arrangements, to private people and corporations (Clawson and Held, 1957; Clawson, 1983; Culhane, 1981). Indeed, next to slavery and tariffs, the acquisition, management, and disposition of public land probably constituted the most important and contentious national issue between 1787 and 1870.

Outdoor recreation, in the modern sense of that term, was not a concern of the federal government. However, the Northwest Ordinance of 1785 provided for a reservation of public land in every township for a school; this land also was available for recreation. Even today, a substantial part of local recreation is

carried on in the neighborhood schoolyard. In addition, on a small scale the federal government reserved some public land for purposes including recreation. It withdrew about 1,000 acres at Hot Springs, Arkansas, from disposal in 1832. Despite its use as a tourist attraction, Hot Springs did not become a national park until 1921. In 1864, the area that eventually became Yosemite National Park was granted by the federal government to the state of California "for public use, resort, and recreation"—possibly the first appearance of the concept of recreation in federal land policy.

Wilderness Attitudes

Most people in the decades before 1870 were ambivalent about wilderness areas (Nash, 1967). On the one hand, there was much romancing about the beauty and the naturalness of the wild land of the frontier and beyond. Several painters were much attracted to natural scenes, especially in New England and the Middle Atlantic states. Moreover, many explorers traveled unknown wild land; most of them had economic motives, as did fur trappers. However, there was also an element of adventure and, in modern terms, recreational motivation. On the other hand, most people also feared the wilderness. To pioneers and settlers along the frontier, Native Americans who emerged from bordering wilderness were often seen as a threat, and sometimes there was killing and looting. Most people were more motivated to clear the forest and to convert the wilderness to farms than they were to preserve the natural conditions. Indeed, people were little interested in or concerned about preserving wilderness areas and conditions—the wilderness was deemed so extensive that it seemed incomprehensible that any effort should be directed to preserving it.

These decades witnessed great conversion of the virgin natural forests to cropland and the destruction of much wildlife (see chapters 3, 4, and 6), but outdoor recreation itself was not a significant adverse environmental force, mostly because there was so little of it. By the same token, provision of parks and wilderness areas was not a significant positive force in environmental protection. Both adverse and protective influences of outdoor recreation and wilderness preservation came in the following decades.

The Beginnings of Conservation: 1870–1920

The fifty years between 1870 and 1920 marked the beginnings of the modern conservation movement. The term "conservation" entered into popular usage around the turn of the twentieth century, introduced primarily in the speeches of President Theodore Roosevelt and of Chief Forester Gifford Pinchot (Pinchot, 1947). As with many a word or phrase entering into popular usage, its meaning shortly deteriorated to nothing or to everything—what the user meant was not always what the hearer understood. However, then as now the force of a popular slogan was not to be underestimated. President William Taft, who succeeded Roosevelt, is reputed to have said that he was for conservation, whatever that was.

These were also the years of the rise of the conservation ethic and of concern for efficiency, especially in government but also in private business (Hays, 1959). Leaders of the conservation movement ex-

The term "conservation" entered into popular usage around the turn of the twentieth century, introduced primarily in the speeches of President Theodore Roosevelt and of Chief Forester Gifford Pinchot.

tolled the virtues of a civil service isolated from politics, of a managerial system of city government, and of public ownership of utilities and local transport services. The direct effects of these trends toward more professional and responsible government upon outdoor recreation and wilderness resources were limited at the time. In later years, this influence was considerable.

This period saw the emergence of numerous government agencies—both federal and state—specifically concerned with natural resources. Many of these agencies eventually had important recreational resource responsibilities. Thus, the U.S. Fisheries Commission was created in 1871, and the Bureau of Biological Survey—forerunner of the Fish and Wildlife Service—was established in the U.S. Department of Agriculture (USDA) in 1885. During the 1870s nearly every state established its own fisheries commission; by the turn of the century most states had wildlife and game protection agencies as well. The National Park Service was established in 1916 to look after the fledgling national park system.

Moreover, numerous private environmental and resource organizations also were created. Among the well-known private organizations to be established between 1870 and 1920 were the American Forestry Association (1875); the Appalachian Mountain Club (1876); the Boone and Crockett Club (1887); the Sierra Club (1892); the National Audubon Society (1905); the National Recreation and Park Association (initially known as the National Recreation Association) (1908); the American Camping Association (1910); the Boy Scouts of America (1910); the Girl Scouts of America (1912); and the National Parks and Conservation Association (1919). Nonetheless, before World War I there were no more than fifty private national "conservation" organizations, taking that term in the broadest sense. Many of these organizations were influential at that time, but primarily through education and exhortation. Some of them were also actively acquiring land of outstanding beauty or historical interest. The trustees of Reservations, established in Massachusetts in 1891, founded the nation's first private land trust organization (Task Force on Outdoor Recreation Resources, 1988). It served as a model for similar preservation organizations both in the United States and abroad. However, some of the principal activities now associated with preservation organizations—political activism and litigation—lay far ahead.

Public Land/Reservations

One of the most obvious and most easily quantified changes of these years was the shift in national policy for public land, from the strong emphasis on acquisition and disposal to a new focus on reservation and custodial management (Clawson, 1983; Clawson and Held, 1957; Culhane, 1981). Although the shift was most noticeable at the federal level, the states also made important set-asides. In 1885, New York established the Niagara State Reservation at Niagara Falls, as well as the Adirondack and Catskill state parks. State parks also were established before the turn of the century in Massachusetts, Minnesota, and California, and New Jersey and New York jointly established the Palisades Interstate Park in 1895 (Task Force on Outdoor Recreation Resources, 1988).

At the federal level, an act of Congress in 1872 established Yellowstone National Park—the first area designated as a national park not only in the United States but in the world, and often described as the

beginning of the national park movement. The area was set aside, at the urging of a few influential easterners, in large part because there were no settlers and no mining interests within it and because it was remote from railroads and urban areas (Ise, 1961). Even so, its advocates had to promise that it would never cost any federal funds—concessionaires would pay fees and the user public would defray all the costs. To back up this point, Congress required the first superintendent to serve without pay for at least five years. Later, army units were stationed within the park in a largely vain attempt to reduce poaching of game.

Although the establishment of Yellowstone National Park was indeed an event of great—largely future—significance, its founding certainly did not represent a strong popular commitment to national parks, nor did it represent a consistent settled policy. Other national parks were established in the thirty to forty years that followed, including Yosemite National Park (Clawson and Van Doren, 1984). Lacking funds and expertise, California relinquished its claims to Yosemite in 1890, and a national park, essentially the size of the present Yosemite park, was established there in the same year. However, it was not until 1916 that Congress passed an act for the management of national parks (Dana, 1956) and a system of national parks was conceived.

The first nonmilitary system of permanent federal land ownership was initiated in 1891 with the passage of the Forest Reserve Act (Dana, 1956; see also chapters 3 and 4). Under that act, the federal government made substantial withdrawals of previously open public domain; the system reached about its present total area by 1910, although considerable adjustments in boundaries have followed since then. More important than the withdrawals was that Gifford Pinchot was soon able to create his own empire by transferring these reserves from the Department of the Interior to the Department of Agriculture, and to get himself named as the first chief forester of the newly created Forest Service. Even his admirers conceded that Pinchot was controversial and tried hard and successfully to be so; likewise, his critics conceded that he brought to public agency operations a level of honesty, competence, and dedication rare for its day and still outstanding. He also introduced the idea of decentralized federal agency operations.

Policy conflict also emerged from 1870 to 1920— and continues today. The conflict was between the use and the preservation of land areas and associated

> *Policy conflict also emerged from 1870 to 1920— and continues today. The conflict was between the use and the preservation of land areas and associated natural characteristics.*

natural characteristics, and was epitomized by an ongoing clash between two outstanding personalities: Gifford Pinchot and John Muir. Pinchot believed in use; if asked, he probably would have included active outdoor recreation as a use, although that phrase does not figure prominently in his writings. John Muir had done much to dramatize the glories of western scenery to eastern readers (Muir, 1976). Muir believed in preservation, not in commercial use. Muir was opposed to mass outdoor recreation because he believed it would damage the natural qualities of the areas he thought should be preserved.

The tension between use and preservation also affected the National Park Service, established in 1916 to administer the growing number of national parks, and led to ambivalence in the very mission of the organization. Was the Park Service simply to be a custodian of the great natural wonders such as the Grand Canyon and Yellowstone? Or was it to be the federal government's flagship agency in the promotion and provision of recreation on federal land? Throughout the history of the Park Service there has been a shifting emphasis between these two largely conflicting goals.

Recreational Use of Federal Lands

The foregoing changes in national policy toward the federal land became immensely important for all uses of the newly reserved federal holdings, outdoor recreation included, but largely after 1920. The direct effects of land policy on recreational use during the 1870–1920 period were small. The dedicated areas had always been open to the public for recreation, especially hunting, albeit lacking in facilities for the comfort or convenience of the users. The earliest efforts to "market" visits to the new national parks were made by the railroads, which affiliated with hotels at Yellowstone (Old Faithful Inn) and the Grand Canyon (El Tovar).

Total attendance at all national parks was only 200,000 in 1910 and did not reach 1 million visits until 1921 (see appendix 7). Although reported national park visits start from a low base, the rate of growth in the number of visitors was quite rapid, averaging 16 percent per year between 1910 and 1920. (Apparently only the national parks collected visitor data before 1920; the Forest Service did not collect data on numbers of recreational visits until 1924.) Further, attendance at national parks did not decrease as a result of World War I, and may even have increased at that time. This is in sharp contrast to the severe reductions in the use during World War II. Although U.S. participation in World War I was militarily significant, it did not intrude on the lives of ordinary people to the extent that World War II did. Steven Mather, the first director of the National Park Service, prevailed upon railroads and travel agencies to advertise the attractions of the western national parks during World War I when travel to Europe was cut off. Although visits were on a rising trend in any event, these efforts may have increased national park attendance somewhat above what it otherwise would have been.

Participation in Outdoor Recreation

The outdoor recreational activities evident in the period before 1870 continued until 1920. People still engaged in much fishing and hunting—again, partly for meat but partly for recreation. They continued to indiscriminately slaughter animals (see chapter 6), nearly wiping out the buffalo, in part because white hunters followed the building of the transcontinental railroads in search of buffalo hides. Even Theodore Roosevelt, later accepted as a great conservationist, slaughtered animals and birds in the northern Great Plains in the late 1880s in ways that today would be condemned severely (Morris, 1979). He was not alone. Game laws were largely nonexistent or were not fully enforced. Uncontrolled hunting reduced game numbers in many areas until hunting success was greatly reduced. Game management was in its infancy.

The outdoor recreation that existed took place close to home, although technology was about to change that situation. By 1920 there were about 8 million automobiles registered in the United States. With the growing importance of the automobile came improvement in roads. The Bureau of Public Roads was established as a federal agency during the latter part of the period—but within the U.S. Department of Agriculture, since a major concern was the development of farm-to-market roads. Nonetheless, at that time both cars and roads were primitive by modern standards, and a trip by car to a faraway recreation site such as a national park or a national forest was likely to be a major adventure. The larger influence

of the automobile on outdoor recreation was to be manifested later.

One particularly interesting technological innovation that directly affected use of the outdoors was the bicycle, developed as a practical and comfortable means of travel for relatively short distances. Bicycle manufacturing boomed around 1900, but fell off sharply before World War I (Clawson and Van Doren, 1984). The advent of the automobile both diverted the attention (and money) of bicycle users and took away from the bicyclist a relatively safe use of country roads.

Overall, however, no major technological changes involving outdoor recreation occurred between 1870 and 1920. Most parks were still local, and there were comparatively few of them. Most of the states did not provide parks or recreation areas for their citizens. The larger cities did provide some parks, but there were fewer than 5,000 of these as late as 1926 (Clawson and Van Doren, 1984). Some smaller cities had parks, but many had none. Sports continued as a recreational activity, especially at schools. These decades did not see the great development of outdoor recreation demand or resources that would be evident in later decades.

This also was a period of no activity for the preservation of wilderness. The very idea of closing some wilderness areas to development to retain them in a natural condition would come later. Nevertheless, some adventurers, trappers, and miners used the wilderness

One particularly interesting technological innovation that directly affected use of the outdoors was the bicycle, developed as a practical and comfortable means of travel for relatively short distances.

for recreational purposes. Mountain climbing as a recreational activity had begun in the Northeast and in Colorado (Chapin, 1987). The entire United States had been explored by 1920, and wilderness areas were at least somewhat known even if not heavily visited. Overall, these were beginning years. Accomplishments were important at the time, but the period is more significant for what started then and proved fruitful later than for actual accomplishments.

An Expanding Federal Role: The Interwar and War Years, 1920–1945

It was during the years 1920 to 1945 that recreation became firmly established as a legitimate and valuable service provided by state and federal governments (having long been so accepted by local governments). The expanded role of the federal government in everyday life (after 1932) influenced this situation. However, even before the New Deal, the Park Service, under the energetic leadership of Steven T. Mather and Horace M. Albright, had begun greatly to expand the scope of its activities and holdings. Largely on land acquired by gift, new national parks were added in the East, including Acadia (in 1919), Great Smoky Mountains (in 1931), and Shenandoah (in 1935). The two most-visited national parks in 1941 were Great Smoky Mountains and Shenandoah.

In a way, the expansion of the Park Service offered a solution to the preservation-or-use dilemma. The growing demand for recreational services could be met on these expanded holdings, which would allow the Park Service to manage sensitive areas in the national parks for preservation. The responsibilities of the Park Service were greatly increased in 1933 when, by executive order, administration of the national monuments was transferred from the Forest Service, and fifty national historic sites were established and put under Park Service management. Among those sites were the great Civil War battlefields, which previously had been managed by the army. The growth of additional responsibilities of the Park Service was so rapid that by 1935 fewer than half the visits to units administered by the National Park Service were to the national parks (see appendix 7).

Mather and Albright also were instrumental in the rapid development of state park systems during the 1920s and 1930s. The existence of state parks in closer proximity to centers of population would ease the conflict between preservation and use at the national parks. At Mather's urging, a national conference of state parks was held in 1921; this meeting led to the establishment of a permanent institution called the National Conference of State Parks. This quarter century also was marked by three external events or situations of major importance to outdoor recreation: the growing availability of the automobile as a major means of transportation for most citizens, the Great Depression, and World War II.

The Automobile

Between 1920 and 1941, the number of private automobiles in the United States increased from fewer than 8 automobiles per 100 people to 22, or nearly three times as many, against a 25-percent increase in total population (U.S. Department of Commerce, Bureau of the Census, 1975). Automobile manufacturers also were experimenting with different features during these years, and millions of persons were eager to buy the results. However, cars lacked many of the conveniences and amenities they possess today. No car had a fully automatic transmission, power brakes, power steering, or air conditioning; only toward the end of this period did cars typically have glove compartments, trunks (which were usually small), and heaters. Self-starters were introduced generally about the beginning of this period, but most cars came with cranks, especially useful when batteries were not powerful enough to start cars in cold weather. Although millions of families could not afford a car, a few families had two or more.

The improvement of roads kept up with the improvement and multiplication of cars. Better roads made car ownership more practical and more enjoyable; more cars made improved roads a necessity. Dirt roads were first graded, then graveled, and later paved. The best and most heavily traveled paved roads still had only two lanes, one in each direction. Eventually, a vast network of all-weather roads led into most parts of the nation. Recreationists could more readily and

more quickly go from homes to some outdoor recreation spot, such as a national forest or national park.

People responded to these improved cars and roads by traveling by car much more. In 1920, the per capita mileage of automobile travel was 1,450; by 1941, it was 4,300 (Clawson, Held, and Stoddard, 1960). Only part of this increased car travel was for outdoor recreation, of course. Not only were vacation trips to national parks and national forests now possible for millions of people, but the car enabled the family to have a weekend picnic in some nearby park and the businessperson to have a round of golf after work. In those days, the family would go for a drive, simply for pleasure even though it was over roads traveled many times before. The substantial increase in recreation participation was attributable largely to improved transportation, although higher real incomes and more leisure time, some of it as paid vacations, also played major roles.

The Great Depression

The Great Depression was perhaps the most traumatic peacetime experience of the United States. Millions of people were unemployed; unemployment compensation, federal relief, or other measures for the relief of millions of people in desperate straits did not become available until initiation of the New Deal programs beginning in 1933. One of the early New Deal measures was the creation of the Civilian Conservation Corps (CCC). Many thousands of young men were recruited (generally in cities) and placed in camps of 100 to 150 men each; most camps were in rural and sometimes in rather isolated areas. Their efforts were shortly supplemented by the Works Progress Administration and the Public Works Administration, which employed somewhat older workers who continued to live in their home communities. The purchase of submarginal farmland, much of which became local parks and wildlife refuges, also supplemented these employment measures. States and local areas were encouraged to acquire or to develop land for parks.

The result of this substantial pool of labor, free to the local area but requiring outlays from the U.S. Department of the Treasury, was the construction of and improvement of a great many parks. In 1935, 884 CCC camps had been erected in state parks and forests and another 862 in national parks and forests (Task Force on Outdoor Recreation Resources, 1988). Thousands of miles of roads were built to make areas accessible. Small dams with fixed overflow structures formed the basis of attractive artificial lakes, which, after the shorelines became stabilized, were nearly indistinguishable from natural lakes. Sanitary facilities—typically pit toilets and simple structures—were constructed. Picnic tables and fireplaces were built. In the few years from the beginning of the New Deal until World War II, U.S. park and recreation facilities underwent a major transition. The CCC program demonstrated that otherwise unemployed labor could be used effectively to create parks and other needed public improvements.

World War II

World War II was a more traumatic experience for the United States than World War I because it lasted longer, it involved millions of men and women in the armed services and in the manufacture of war machines and materials, and civilians were far more affected in their daily lives. New cars were unobtainable by the average citizen (farmers were an exception); because some older cars could no longer be repaired, the total number of cars registered declined by about 10 percent. Gasoline and tires were rationed, and few families were willing to use their limited tires and gas for outdoor recreation. Not only did the war virtually eliminate the lingering unemployment of the depression, but the work week was incresed from the typical 5-day, 40-hour week to one of 48 hours and 6 days—even longer for some people. People experienced much social pressure to stay on the job and not take vacations.

The consequences of these wartime measures on outdoor recreation were twofold: first, attendance at national parks and national forests declined by two-thirds; second, maintenance of all recreation areas was postponed, with consequent deterioration of facilities and structures. The full consequences of this deterioration were felt in the years after the war. A few national parks—Yosemite, for instance—were used as training areas for wilderness or wild area warfare.

Recreation Participation

For the quarter-century as a whole, attendance at national parks and national forests (and probably at

The result of this substantial pool of labor, free to the local area but requiring outlays from the U.S. Department of the Treasury, was the construction of and improvement of a great many parks.

Table 7-1. Rates of Growth in Visits to the National Parks and Forests (annual percentage change)

Period	National park system			National forests			State parks total	Total population
	National parks	Other	Total	Improved areas	Other	Total		
1910–1921	14.6							1.5
1921–1931	11.6			7.7[a]	8.0[a]	7.8[a]		1.3
1931–1941	9.8	34.6	18.0	5.8	12.5	8.1		0.7
1941 1945	−15.9	−14.2	−14.8	−18.5	−9.5	−14.4	−6.7[b]	1.2
1946–1961	7.7	10.1	9.2	9.6	19.2	11.5	7.2	1.7
1961–1971	5.4	9.6	8.4	6.4	5.1	5.6	6.3[c]	1.2
1971–1981	2.5	5.7	5.0	2.0	3.3	2.8	2.3[d]	1.0
1981–1986	2.0	2.0	2.0	−0.3	−0.9	−0.7	1.8	1.0

Note: Empty cells indicate that data are not available.
[a] 1924–1931.
[b] 1942–1945.
[c] 1961–1970.
[d] 1970–1981.

state parks as well, though accurate and detailed data are unavailable) increased rapidly (table 7-1). At the national parks, annual attendance increases during the 1920s averaged more than 11 percent per year. The more Americans visited these areas, apparently, the more they wanted to do so. Despite the depression, the rate of increase was almost as fast during the 1930s (10 percent). Attendance did decline briefly during the worst depression years, but not by much. In the national forests, data on recreation were not collected until 1924; after that, the data showed greater numbers of recreational users than at the national parks. However, the growth rate was somewhat slower, at 7.7 percent per year for the period between 1924 and 1931. In 1940, the Park Service and the Forest Service reported almost equal numbers of recreational users.

The combination of better cars and better roads, modestly improved real incomes (at least of employed people), and greater leisure time (much of it paid vacation or weekend leisure available as part of the employment terms) all combined to increase the use of the relatively remote outdoor recreation areas at national parks and forests. However, the rate of increase was even greater at the units of the national park system closer to population centers. Between 1930 and 1940, the attendance at these units increased from a scant half million to nearly 10 million, an average annual growth rate of 29 percent. Certainly, some of this increase is spurious, because part of it represented established use at sites that were transferred to the Park Service from the Forest Service

or the army. Still, a major part of the increase represents the aggressive marketing of these areas by the Park Service, the opening of new areas such as Lake Mead, and the growing interest in outdoor recreation facilities close to home.

No reliable data are available on use or attendance at city and other local parks. Indeed, then as now many of those parks were open to any visitors and frequently had no supervisory employees present; thus it is nearly impossible to obtain attendance data. However, cities and counties as a whole increased their expenditures for outdoor recreation and increased the number and variety of facilities. Total reported acreage of city and county parks (as reported annually by the National Recreation Association) increased from 316,000 to 641,000 between 1925 and 1940 (Clawson and Van Doren, 1984). Because additions to local park supply are clearly a local government response to growth in population and perceived recreation demand, the increase in park acreage was a clear indication that attendance and use of these areas also increased.

The familiar activities of outdoor recreation continued during this quarter century. They included fishing, hunting, camping, picnicking, hiking, canoeing and boating, and a host of sports activities. For some new activities or some old activities, the scale of participation increased; snow skiing, for example, although long known, developed greatly during these years. However, development of new technology for outdoor recreation was slow during this period, especially when compared with the years after World War II.

Recreational use of the national parks and national forests and state parks fell dramatically during the war years. In the national parks, the attendance in 1943 was barely a quarter of the 1941 attendance. The decline was almost as severe at other units of the national park system and at improved areas of the national forests. Within a year after the end of the war, however, attendance was back to prewar levels.

The Role of Publications

One reliable measure of the importance of any activity or social development is the publication of books about it. When a publishing house brings out a book on any subject, it is because, among other factors, it believes there is a market for such a book. The book itself helps to stimulate public interest in the subject. Most serious books are under development or writing by their authors for several years before publication. For this reason, the books in this quarter of a century and in the decade or so after the war may be considered together; many of the books published after World War II might have been published earlier, had there been no war.

Among books published during this period that were related to recreation, some were sociological, focusing mostly on leisure and play (see Barnes, 1942; Brightbill, 1961; Dulles, 1940; Gulick, 1920; Neumeyer and Neumeyer, 1958; Pack, 1934; Romney, 1945; Sapora and Mitchell, 1961; and Steiner, 1933). Each of the works cited describes the amount and kinds of leisure engaged in, how people used it, and why people of all ages wanted to play. Other books published at that time included nature-glorifying works, especially about the national parks but also about other kinds of areas (see Butcher, 1951; National Geographic Society, 1959; Tilden, 1951, 1962). Each of these works cited is heavily and beautifully illustrated. Still other books published at the time focused on administrative or managerial matters, and were concerned with telling citizens, officials, and park managers how to manage parks, playgrounds, and recreation areas (see Butler, 1959; Meyer and Brightbill, 1956).

Some of these books include consideration of the costs of supplying outdoor recreational opportunities

in various areas. All assert the value of outdoor recreation, but none attempts a quantitative monetary measure of such value—indeed, many deny that such values could be estimated. None is the kind of economic demand analysis that would become so common in later years (see Brown, Singh, and Castle, 1964; Clawson, 1959; Cordell and Hendee, 1982; Outdoor Recreation Resources Review Commission, 1962c; and Wood, 1985). However, these books were highly influential in their time, both in stimulating the establishment of parks and recreation areas and in guiding their management. Among the authors of these books, Butler in particular had an influence far greater and more pervasive than the three editions of his book might suggest. Employed by the National Recreation Association (now the National Recreation and Park Association), he traveled frequently around the country, consulting with local park officials and offering advice and criticisms in a way that greatly influenced the management of these areas and facilities.

People today who are critical of the Forest Service, either for its reluctance to recommend more wilderness or for its alleged foot-dragging in administration, tend to overlook the important originating role that the agency had played.

The Wilderness Concept

In the early 1920s, formally established wilderness areas were first created. Two U.S. Forest Service professional employees, Aldo Leopold in New Mexico and Arthur Carhart in Colorado, persistently urged that some parts of the national forest system be withheld from commercial development and be retained in as near a natural state as possible (*Idaho Law Review*, 1980). In 1924 the chief forester formally established a wilderness area in the Gila National Forest in the Southwest, the first so designated. The idea of withholding some areas from development was by no means universally accepted within a Forest Service imbued by Pinchot's dedication to use. However, additional areas were added throughout the 1920–1945 period. Robert Marshall, a noted outdoorsman of the day, joined the Forest Service for a time and was influential in the withdrawal of other areas and in the promulgation of rules for their management. This early establishment of wilderness areas was by order of the chief forester or the secretary of agriculture, without specific congressional action. The withdrawals were legal enough, but they were not legislatively required or supported. People today who are critical of the Forest Service, either for its reluctance to recommend more wilderness or for its alleged foot-dragging in administration, tend to overlook the important originating role that the agency had played (Brower, 1960).

Leopold had envisaged rather large areas, so that the center would not be influenced by conditions and uses around the edges. He proposed that areas be large enough to require two days of travel by pack train to reach the center, from any entry point. Marshall also favored large areas, preferably 300,000 acres, but he recognized that such large areas might be forced to accept some moderate intrusion of nonconforming uses (Dana and Fairfax, 1980). At first, and for many years, the Forest Service held to a definition that a wilderness area should include at least 100,000 acres. Later, as it became apparent that some attractive areas were not this large, a category of "wild" area was established, which could be as small as 5,000 acres. The Forest Service also established primitive and roadless areas, which were similar in the absence of economic development. However, in those days there was no thinking, as far as can be determined, that areas smaller than 5,000 acres should be recognized; modern wildernesses established by congressional action can be—and some are—much smaller; one (an island off the Florida coast) is no more than 3 acres in size.

Under this system, about 15 million acres of national forest were withdrawn from commercial development before 1942. Most of the acreage was classified as "primitive," about 10 percent was "wilderness," and smaller acreages were "roadless" and "wild" (Clawson and Van Doren, 1984). The Forest Service and later the secretary of agriculture issued various regulations concerning their withdrawal and use; these regulations often were the center of controversy at the time, but have now been superseded by legislation—the Wilderness Act of 1964 and the Eastern Wilderness Act of 1974.

A cynic or a critic might say, with at least some credibility, that the Forest Service's actions were influenced as much by its rivalry with, and its fear of, the National Park Service, as they were by a genuine conviction that such withdrawal from development was good natural resource management. Most of the national parks had been located at least in part within national forest areas before their establishment as parks. The National Park Service and it supporters were eagerly seeking the expansion of the national park system in ways that were natural enough but that reduced the area of the national forest system. Some expansion led to emotional public quarrels—the expansion of Olympic National Park, for instance. At least some people in the Forest Service and some of its supporters thought that, by establishing wilderness areas, they could divert the pressure for national park expansion.

During this quarter-century, two major conservation organizations, each well known and active today, were created: the Wilderness Society and the National Wildlife Federation. The Wilderness Society was created under the stimulus of Robert Marshall; it was relatively small in membership and in staff during these years, but has greatly expanded since World War II. The National Wildlife Federation was, as its name suggests, a federation of a number of small, struggling, and not-too-effective organizations. At least some of the stimulus for its formation came from Ding Darling, the noted cartoonist who was also for a time head of the Bureau of Biological Survey in the New Deal federal government.

A great deal of legislation was passed during this quarter-century, especially during the New Deal period, that was important for wildlife, forestry, and grazing (see chapters 3, 4, and 6). Although much of this legislation had some indirect and perhaps remote effect on outdoor recreation, there was almost no federal legislation directed at outdoor recreation; the period of federal legislative activism came later.

Rapid Growth: 1945–1970

Following World War II, some 10 million men and women were demobilized from the armed forces. They, and the civilian population who had stayed home, faced rather serious shortages of clothing, automobiles, household appliances, and housing. However, those shortages were soon overcome as a result of a booming economy. Of far more lasting consequence and more importance for outdoor recreation was the "baby boom" that ensued. Every experienced demographer had realized that when the men and women were released from military service, marriages and birth rates would increase, because marriages and births had been postponed during the war. What had not been foreseen was the long continuance of the high birth rates well into the 1960s. As many as 20 million "extra" births, above the normal trend line of total births, occurred. The 1945–1970 period was a time of demographic development of great social, economic, and political importance; it also has had, and will continue to have, its effect upon outdoor recreation, because many kinds of outdoor recreation are very much age-conditioned.

With the revival of the economy came generally higher real incomes per capita, far more opportunities for travel, and increased leisure, especially in the form of paid vacations. All of this directly affected outdoor recreation. The quarter-century also saw the formation of several major conservation organizations with concern for outdoor recreation. The Conservation Foundation was established in 1948, the Sport Fishing Institute in 1949, The Nature Conservancy in 1951, and Trout Unlimited in 1959. Moreover, although total recreation attendance at national parks and national forests fell by two-thirds during the war, in 1946 attendance at each system almost precisely regained the prewar level—and this despite the frequently poor condition of aged autos and neglected roads (Clawson and Van Doren, 1984). From then on, during this quarter-century, attendance at these and other federal areas and at state parks resumed its upward march.

One legacy of the New Deal was the enormous expansion of federally financed water resource development in the United States. These impoundments created major new recreation opportunities (see chapter 2). Three federal agencies were the principal dam builders: the Tennessee Valley Authority (TVA); the Bureau of Reclamation (BR); and the U.S. Army Corps of Engineers (COE). Throughout the 1950s and 1960s, the recreational use of reservoirs built and operated by these agencies increased rapidly. By 1960, the Corps of Engineers had become the leading federal agency providing recreational opportunities at water project sites, in terms of recreation days provided. Recreational use of Bureau of Land Management land and of national wildlife refuges also increased during these years.

Attendance at National Park Service facilities grew rapidly during the 1946–1970 period but not quite as fast as before the war. Between 1946 and 1961, attendance at the national parks increased an average of 7.7 percent per year (table 7-1). At other units of the national park system, the rate of increase was 10 percent. During this same period, use of the recreational units of the national forests grew somewhat

The rapid increase in attendance at parks and other outdoor areas of all kinds soon overran the generally wartime-neglected facilities—roads, sanitary facilities and other structures, and picnic and camping facilities.

Table 7-2. Size of State Parks and Attendance at State Parks, 1941–1981

Year	Acres (thousands)	Attendance per year (millions)	Attendance per acre per year
1941	4,260[a]	70[b,c]	16.4
1946	4,655[a]	93[c]	20.0
1950	4,657[d]	114[e]	24.5
1954	5,077[a]	166[a]	32.7
1962	5,757	290	50.4
1967	7,068	378	53.5
1970	8,282	471	56.9
1975	9,505	549	57.8
1979	10,773[f]	601[g]	55.8
1981	10,973	618	56.3

Source: Clawson and Van Doren (1984), pp. 63, 72, 328, 333.
[a]47 states reporting.
[b]1942.
[c]38 states reporting.
[d]48 states reporting.
[e]40 states reporting.
[f]In 1979, New York stopped reporting the Adirondack Forest as recreational land. To make the data in this table consistent with earlier data, 2 million acres were added in this and subsequent years.
[g]1978.

faster, at an average rate of 11.5 percent per year. Attendance at state parks also grew rapidly, averaging 10 percent per year.

The rapid increase in attendance at parks and other outdoor areas of all kinds soon overran the generally wartime-neglected facilities—roads, sanitary facilities and other structures, and picnic and camping facilities. In the postwar period, there was no CCC to rebuild and generally to rescue burdened park administrators. Many public recreation agencies felt overwhelmed. The strain on the national parks and national forests was not so much a result of pure density—persons per acre—as it was of a lack of facilities such as campsites, picnic tables, and latrines. Moveover, the increased strain on recreation at state parks is evident from the acreage data. Although attendance at state parks was growing at a steady clip of 10 percent per year, the acreage of state parks was growing much more slowly, from 4.7 million acres in 1946 to 5.1 million in 1954 and 5.8 million in 1962 (table 7-2). Participation density increased from 16 people to 50 people per acre per year.

The major public agencies providing opportunities for outdoor recreation reacted in various ways to this flood of visitors. In 1956, the National Park Service undertook its "Mission 66," a long-range plan for the national parks to be carried out if possible by 1966, the fiftieth anniversary of the creation of the national park system (Everhart, 1972). The Forest Service in 1957 undertook "Operation Outdoors," a generally similar planning exercise (U.S. Department of Agriculture, Forest Service, 1957). Each of these planning exercises called for much larger appropriations for outdoor recreation—calls that to a considerable degree were heeded in the federal appropriation process. A number of states floated major bond issues for state and local parks. To win political support for these bond issues, most of them provided that a major part of the funds so raised would be available to counties and cities for park purposes. Nearly $3 billion was approved in such bond issues—a sum that, in 1991 dollars, would be $10 billion or more. The acreage of state park systems expanded rapidly between 1962 and 1970, growing from 5.8 million to 8.3 million acres (table 7-2).

Overall, at the federal level, the land and water areas were relatively fixed in extent. It was the addition of other components, such as roads, campsites, and toilet facilities, that increased the recreation capacity of these fixed sites. Perhaps no more dramatic example of the role of knowledge, entrepreneurship, labor, and capital in the provision of natural resources could be found than these moves to increase outdoor recreation capacity.

While these capacity additions were being made, recreation use continued to grow, but at a slower rate than before. Between 1961 and 1971 attendance at the national parks grew by 5.4 percent, down from 7.7 percent in the 1946–1961 period (table 7-1). Somewhat faster was the growth in attendance at the entire national park system, which grew by 8.4 percent from 1961–1971, down from 9.2 percent. Recreation attendance at units of the Forest Service grew by 5.6 percent, half the 11-percent rate experienced during the 1946–1961 interval (table 7-1). At state parks, the increase in participation slowed from 10 percent per year to 6.3 percent per year (table 7-2). At this rate of increase, states were able to add acreage to keep up with the continuing though slowing growth of recreation at state parks. Throughout the 1960s and into the 1970s, additions of land kept participation density at state parks around 50 per acre per year (table 7-2).

Recreation at privately owned recreation sites most likely increased rapidly during the 1945–1970 period as well, but data are much more difficult to find. One

sport in which significant growth did occur, especially after 1955, was golf. Between 1945 and 1955, the number of golf courses did not increase, but participation did, at about 3.5 percent annually. From 1955 to 1971 a relatively rapid expansion in the number of golf courses occurred, at nearly 5 percent annually; more of these were public courses than private. With the increased number of courses, the golfing population expanded rapidly, at more than 10 percent per year. The expansion in the number of golfers was more rapid than the expansion in the number of courses, indicating some increase in usage and perhaps in crowding. Skiing participation also increased rapidly. Skiing opportunities were offered jointly by the public and private sectors, with private operators taking out long-term leases on federal land, especially in the West.

The Outdoor Recreation Resources Review Commission

Mission 66, Operation Outdoors, and the planning studies that underlay the state bond issues were influential and, given the data and the methods of analysis then available, quite competent professional analyses. However, each at best was concerned with a specific situation. A number of conservation leaders were concerned that a more comprehensive view of the use of natural resources for outdoor recreation should be taken. According to Foresta (1984), there was widespread dissatisfaction with the failure of the Park Service to undertake this challenge, and many felt that a special commission was needed to carry out a comprehensive study of recreation facilities and the rapidly expanding demands being placed on them. Conservationists were successful in 1958 in getting an act passed by the Congress that established the Outdoor Recreation Resources Review Commission (ORRRC)(Outdoor Recreation Resources Review Commission, 1962b). The commission consisted of eight congressional members, two from each party in the House and in the Senate, and seven private citizens appointed by the president, one of whom (Laurance S. Rockefeller) was named chair.

The legislation had been carefully designed to ensure that the focus would be on natural resources, that the congressional members would come from the committees on Interior and Insular Affairs in the House and in the Senate, to ensure that those members had knowledge of natural resources, and to forestall and shunt aside any criticism that outdoor recreation was not a proper activity for federal concern. Joseph W. Penfold, conservation director of the Izaak Walton League, played a particularly important role in devising the legislation and in getting it passed, and became a member of the ORRRC. Beginning in 1958, the commission and its staff issued a number of specific studies, later supplemented by studies by people and organizations outside of its staff. Following publication of the commission report in January 1962, 27 ORRRC study reports were published. Although the ORRRC report and the study reports were influential in their day, they have been superseded by later studies and by events.

One of the major concerns of the ORRRC was the apparent lack of a coherent federal policy with respect to outdoor recreation, especially on federally owned land. As the commission noted, "by 1960 it was too late for the Federal Government to decide whether it should be, or wanted to be, in the recreation business. It was already in it" (Outdoor Recreation Resources Review Commission, 1962a). The commission observed that numerous federal agencies provided recreational opportunity as an incidental matter, but for none was it a primary or even official responsibility. In particular, the Park Service had never

> *One of the major concerns of the ORRRC was the apparent lack of a coherent federal policy with respect to outdoor recreation, especially on federally owned land.*

really solved the preservation-or-use dilemma, which had become acute with the steady growth of the postwar period (although in percentage terms the growth rate of visits to the national parks had slowed down after the war, and in absolute terms the number of visitors tripled between 1946 and 1970).

Far beyond the influence of its reports, the ORRRC had several major consequences for outdoor recreation in the United States. First, it clearly elevated outdoor recreation to a national issue, and one properly deserving of federal as well as state and local attention. Second, it led directly to the establishment of the Bureau of Outdoor Recreation to coordinate federal recreation activities and to serve as a channel for directing federal aid to the states. Foresta (1984) suggested that the new agency was created because the Park Service had failed to provide this function. At the time, the Bureau of Outdoor Recreation was regarded as a natural rival of the Park Service: "To ensure against undue influence by the Park Service, a Forest Service Administrator was selected to head the new bureau. He in turn was careful not to go to the Park Service when filling the new bureau's top positions" (Foresta, 1984, p. 64). In any event, the bureau later had its name changed to The Heritage Conservation and Recreation Service; still later (after the period under consideration here), it was severely reduced in size and funds, and merged into the National Park Service.

However, for some years, the bureau did serve as an information clearinghouse for federal activities in outdoor recreation, including data collection. It was the bureau that coordinated the implementation of one of the major technical recommendations of the ORRRC, namely, that recreation participation data be reported consistently across all federal agencies in terms of visitor days (12 hours of visitor use). Calculation in terms of visitor days sheds a different light on the amount of recreation supplied by the various federal agencies. In particular, the National Park Service experiences about the same number of visitors at its sites each year as the Forest Service. In terms of visitor days, however, Park Service visitation is only about one-third of the Forest Service visitation.

The bureau also was responsible for coordinating federal land acquisitions under the newly established Land and Water Conservation Fund. Establishment of this fund was a third major consequence of the ORRRC. Its funding sources consisted of proceeds from taxes on recreation goods, fees collected at some public recreation areas, and receipts from some offshore mineral leases. Part of those funds went to federal agencies such as the Forest Service and the National Park Service (and others) to acquire land or to make improvements, but not for current operations. Another part went to states, which in turn generally parcelled out some of the money to local governments. The use of funds going to states was likewise limited to land acquisition and facility construction or improvement. The funds could not be used for annual operating purposes. In addition, the federal allocations to the states had to be matched to some degree by local funds. Some $5.5 billion were disbursed under this fund (Stevens, 1983), of which the federal portion was $2.4 billion (Clawson and Van Doren, 1984). In terms of 1988 dollars, this sum would be three times larger or more. Between 1960 and about 1975, the Land and Water Conservation Fund was extremely important in stimulating expenditure of public funds for the provision of outdoor recreation opportunity. Later, appropriations from the fund were greatly reduced.

Legislation

The legislative and judicial activism on resource and environmental matters that so characterizes the United States today really began only in 1970. However, some federal legislation enacted between 1945 and 1970 had important direct effects on outdoor recreation and wilderness. In 1960, the Multiple-Use,

The legislative and judicial activism on resource and environmental matters that so characterizes the United States today really began only in 1970.

Sustained-Yield Act provided a solid legal base for the kind of multiple-use management the Forest Service had been carrying out on the national forests (Dana and Fairfax, 1980). For the first time, there was specific and direct legal authorization for outdoor recreation and for protection of wildlife, including fish, on national forestland. Previously, such authority was limited to annual appropriation acts, which often provided funds explicitly for recreation and wildlife management. The Multiple-Use, Sustained-Yield Act of 1960 was somewhat vague, which is one reason Congress could accept it. It provided little specific guidance to the Forest Service. However, it did provide a rallying cry for those people and groups who wanted the Forest Service to manage certain areas of national forests more in the way the groups wanted.

The Wilderness Act was passed in 1964, after years of effort by wilderness supporters. This act was defended by its supporters in and outside of Congress as simply giving legislative protection to the approximately 14 million acres already in wilderness and related kinds of areas by Forest Service administrative action. Any extension of wilderness to additional areas was specifically denied in the House and in the Senate by the sponsors of the legislation. At the time, this commitment helped in some degree to mute the opposition of those groups opposed to wilderness; however, it has long since been repudiated because Congress has authorized extension into other areas and because the courts have de facto extended most of the powers of the act to additional large areas under study for possible wilderness use. Four years later, the Wild and Scenic Rivers Act of 1968 established a

national system of rivers that were to be kept from commercial development, including dam construction. In addition, the National Trail System Act of 1968 sought to create a national system of hiking trails.

Federal Appropriations for Outdoor Recreation

The years 1945 to 1970 were marked by some significant changes in federal appropriations for outdoor recreation—and it is money that translates general ideas into specifics. In 1959, the Minute Man Historical Park Act authorized the first-ever appropriation of federal funds to buy land for establishment of a new unit in the national park system. Previously, national parks and monuments had been created out of public domain, including that within national forests, or from land that had been purchased by private funds and donated to the federal government. Although there had always been strong opposition to the expenditure of federal funds to create new parks, the significance of this apparent policy shift did not attract much attention at the time.

In 1961 larger sums were authorized to create the Cape Cod National Seashore, and this action did at-

tract a good deal of popular attention. In 1968, the Redwood National Park Act authorized the expenditure of federal funds for land acquistion, in what has become the most expensive national park acquisition to date. Since then a large number of additional areas have been authorized. Congress has been generous, relatively speaking, in park authorization, but together with the administration, it has been miserly in providing funds to carry out the authorized extensions. By 1980, nearly $3 billion of unfunded authorizations of park acquistitions had accumulated.

In 1964 the Bureau of Land Management received its first appropriation for general recreation purposes. Its lands had always been open to hunting, and streams through its lands open to fishing, both under the jurisdiction of state laws. However, other recreation on its lands generally had been limited, in part because nearby national forests typically had trees and water that BLM lands usually lacked. By 1970, however, outdoor recreation in winter months on BLM land in the southeastern California deserts had become an active, and often highly damaging, form of outdoor recreation use.

In all of these and other ways, the federal government moved substantially into the field of outdoor recreation in the quarter-century following World War II.

Environmental Activism: 1970 to the Present

Awareness of and concern for environmental quality became an important element of the social and political climate in 1970. To list merely the important environmental events in the 1970s, with no more than three or four lines to describe each, took eleven book pages (Dana and Fairfax, 1980), and the 1980s likely will take as much space. In regard to public land in particular, these years have been called "the era of consultation and confrontation" (Clawson, 1983) or the "era of extensive preservation" (Culhane, 1981). By almost any standard, the period since 1970 has differed greatly from the preceding quarter-century.

This period of environmental activism began with the signing of the National Environmental Policy Act of 1969 on January 1, 1970. The signing of this act was followed by Earth Day in April, celebrated across the nation and especially in the schools. It manifested a great popular support for environmental measures. The act was concerned primarily with environmental matters rather than outdoor recreation, but it has provided a political framework for many government decisions and private actions. One feature of the act, substantially broadened later by court decisions, was the requirement for an environmental impact statement to support every government action that had,

or was alleged to have, significant effect on the environment. The requirement to produce an acceptable environmental impact assessment frequently has been the tool used by environmentalists to bring about actions more in conformity with their perceptions and preferences. The increase in environmental activism is associated with the establishment of several environmental groups, such as the Environmental Defense Fund (in 1967), Friends of the Earth (in 1968), and the Natural Resources Defense Council (in 1970). These groups are characterized by a more confrontational style in pursuit of their objectives than many of the older conservation organizations.

As in other areas of American life, this contentiousness, together with the enormous expansion in legislation, led to much greater use of litigation in settling political differences. Numerous court actions and decisions in this period affected outdoor recreation (Dana and Fairfax, 1980). The new organizations, together with the established Sierra Club, the Izaak Walton League, and other national and regional conservation organizations, brought suits to prevent actions of which they disapproved, such as clearcutting timber or building resorts in highly attractive areas. Even more "conservative" organizations, such as the National Wildlife Federation, became more activist and willing to use the courts and the voluminous environmental legislation enacted during this period to prevent what they regarded as environmentally harmful development. The National Wildlife Federation, for example, was a major player in the Grayrocks Dam case, in which the construction of a power plant was opposed because the increase in water withdrawals would adversely affect whooping crane migratory habitat on the Platte River in Nebraska.

Recreation Participation

The environmental movement reinforced, and was reinforced by , the continued increase in recreational activity. Yet even though attendance at units of the national park system, at national forests, at other federal areas, and at state and local parks continued to increase after 1970, it did so at a much slower rate than in earlier decades. At the national parks, the growth rate in visits was only 2.5 percent during the 1970s. At the other units of the national park system, the rate of increase was a much larger 5.7 percent, reflecting the growing popularity of the more accessible national recreation areas, which tend to be located in urban areas (for example, Golden Gate National Recreation Area in San Francisco, Gateway Regional National Recreation Area in New York City, Jean Lafitte National Recreation Area in New Orleans, and Cuyahoga National Recreation Area in Cleveland). The growth rate of visits to national forests was only 2 percent in improved areas during the 1970s, but a rather larger 3.3 percent in the less developed areas of the national forest system (table 7-1). Evidently, growth was greatest where there was demand for experiences in unimproved areas of the national forests.

The slowdown was evident as well in the state parks, where growth in visitation dropped to 2.3 percent per year, and also in recreation sites managed by other federal agencies. Even the Corps of Engineers sites, which had experienced such rapid growth in the 1950s and 1960s, experienced a slowdown. The number of visits to COE recreation sites increased by 16 percent in the 1950s, 9 percent in the 1960s, but only 5 percent in the 1970s. Part of the decrease reflected a slowdown in the completion of dams, in part brought on by the objections of participants in the environmental movement.

The decline in the growth rate of recreation participation was even more pronounced when measured in terms of visitor days rather than visits. Total visitor days at all federal recreation sites peaked in 1976 and have since declined slightly (Task Force on Outdoor Recreation Resources, 1988). The discrepancy between the visit trends and the visitor-day trends is accounted for by the tendency for participants to engage in recreation outings of shorter duration. Between 1977 and 1986, the share of visits to National Park Service or National Forest Service sites of less than four hours' duration increased from 14 percent to 30 percent of all visits (Task Force on Outdoor Recreation Resources, 1988).

Rapid growth in use has been experienced since 1970, at a rate not anticipated in the ORRRC report, at private areas and facilities for outdoor recreation. Snow skiing, golf, tennis, and other sports for which there are some data all gained rapid growth in this period (Clawson and Van Doren, 1984), although, as in the public sector, the rate of growth overall may have slowed compared with that of the 1945–1970 period. From 1967 to 1982 growth in the number of golfers and number of courses was slower than it had been during earlier periods. However, since 1981 the number of golf courses has increased dramatically.

The environmental movement reinforced, and was reinforced by, the continued increase in recreational activity.

Overall, the most recent decade has seen a profound change in the direction of public outdoor recreation. This change is most noticeable in the slowdown in growth in the per-capita visits to national parks and forests, except for some units of the national park system near major urban areas. The slowdown is now more than a decade old and can no longer be easily dismissed as a fluke or an anomaly.

Other important and related changes in recreation behavior have been observed. For example, leisure activity reportedly has declined sharply. A survey of leisure activity conducted for the President's Commission on Americans Outdoors revealed that between 1973 and 1984 average leisure declined from 26 to 18 hours per week. Although this change was not accompanied by a decline in reported outdoor recreation activities, there was an apparent shift to recreation close to home and a shift to visits of shorter duration at federal recreation sites. This momentous change in recreation activity is probably the result of demographic changes in the population, the most important of which most likely has been the aging of the U.S. population. The mix of outdoor recreation activities probably also has been affected by the changing employment status of women. The growth of women's participation in the labor force since 1965 accounts for a major portion of the decline in reported leisure. Moreover, the increase in the number of working women probably contributes to the shorter duration of recreation visits and the preference for recreation activities close to home. Couples with two wage earners have more difficulty arranging for lengthy vacations at national parks.

This shift in recreation participation has coincided with the rise in interest and participation in physical

fitness activities. Although time series data on numbers of people running or jogging are unavailable, it is generally believed that the number of people engaged in these activities has risen greatly in recent years. It is known that the use of bicycles—a kindred activity—as well as the number of bicycles in use, has expanded greatly since 1966, especially among adults. Between 1965 and 1973, annual sales of bicycles tripled from 5 million to 15 million, declining to about 10 million by 1980 (Clawson and Van Doren, 1984). Both jogging and bicycling are activities that people generally engage in close to home and that do not require specialized recreation facilities or large unimproved land areas. Indeed, both can make use of city streets and country roads in addition to hiking or biking trails.

Local governments have always been important providers of recreational opportunities, but estimates of the use of local recreation sites are notoriously difficult to produce. Consider how nearly impossible it is to estimate usage at a neighborhood park. However, Ken Cordell of the U.S. Forest Service Southeast Experiment Station recently estimated that the federal sites provide only about 13 percent of the total activity time, and that more than 50 percent occurs at local recreational facilities (Cordell, 1989). State-

and privately owned lands provide the remainder. Naturally, the proportion of the federal government's contribution is much higher for certain types of activities (such as back-country camping or hiking) and much lower for others (such as ball games).

Technological Improvements

The 1960s to some extent and the period since 1970 to a much greater extent have been marked by many new technological developments in outdoor recreation. More powerful outboard motors were developed, which made motorboating more attractive and also permitted water skiing. (Until boats could attain a critical speed, water skiing had been impossible.) Dune buggies and other off-road vehicles were used recreationally in many areas that previously had been inaccessible except by walking or on horseback; this, in turn, led to environmental degradation of some of these areas. Development of scuba diving and snorkeling equipment opened up underwater areas. Hang gliding enlisted the participation of adventurists and increased demand for areas adjacent to cliffs or steep hills. Not all such technological developments caught on, however. Snowmobiles, developed in the late

1960s, had annual sales of 405,000 units by 1970; annual sales in 1982–1984 averaged only 57,000.

Major improvements also were made in some of the old standbys of outdoor recreation—tents, sleeping bags, cooking utensils, clothing, and foods, especially for backpacking. For example, the replacement of canvas by lightweight fabrics and the development of dome tents and other new designs made it possible to have roomy but nonetheless lightweight tents.

Recreation Planning

The Bureau of Outdoor Recreation Act, passed in 1963, established the bureau and directed that the bureau prepare a "comprehensive nationwide outdoor recreation plan" within five years and that the plan should be revised and updated every five years thereafter (U.S. Congress, 1974). The initial plan was prepared, two years late and at a cost of $7 million, and transmitted by Secretary of the Interior Walter J. Hickel to President Richard M. Nixon in July 1970. The report was never released by the White House and never transmitted officially to Congress. No official reason was ever given for its attempted suppression, but rumor suggests that the report was too rich for the blood of the Bureau of the Budget. Although the plan did not include specific sums for recommended appropriations, it clearly envisaged a far larger and more expensive role for the federal government, especially in the cities, than many people thought appropriate.

By September 1974, Senator Henry M. Jackson, chair of the Senate Committee on Interior and Insular Affairs and a member of the ORRRC, managed to pry loose from the Department of the Interior and to publish the suppressed report as *The Recreation Imperative* (U.S. Congress, 1974). The report is long and full of charts and photos. Written in colorful language, it glorifies outdoor recreation and the role of the Bureau of Outdoor Recreation, while largely ignoring efforts and studies by others. Judged as a professional document, the report was not too bad if one chooses to push hard for a larger federal role in local outdoor recreation. A revised and toned-down report was prepared and transmitted to Congress in December 1973 as *Outdoor Recreation: A Legacy for America* (U.S. Department of the Interior, Bureau of Outdoor Recreation, 1973). Although less strident, this report, now called the second nationwide plan, did not deviate greatly from the first report, except

for a reduced emphasis on the role of the federal government.

In 1979, the Heritage Conservation and Recreation Service submitted the *Third Nationwide Outdoor Recreation Plan* to the secretary of the interior (U.S. Department of the Interior, Heritage Conservation and Recreation Service, 1979). Underlying this third report were two comprehensive surveys: one on outdoor recreation participation nationally, and another on urban outdoor recreation (U.S. Department of the Interior, Heritage Conservation and Recreation Service, 1978). In the words of the third plan, "This plan is different from prior efforts in that it sought broad public participation both in the preliminary issue identification phase and in the shaping of recommendations for decisions" (p. 2).

These three comprehensive reports resemble each other and each resembles the ORRRC report. Each considers recreation demand, based in part on population and economic factors and in part on participation rates by defined segments of the population. Moreover, each considers land and water areas available for outdoor recreation, noting the relatively larger areas in the West than in the East. The reports do discuss the role of governments at various levels. The third plan especially calls for better data and for more research. However, there is little mention of the slowing of recreation visitation, especially to federal recreation sites, a trend that had become quite noticeable by 1979, if not earlier. Each report discussed policy issues somewhat, but the discussion typically was muted and carefully avoided the most difficult and thorny policy issue of all: Who is going to pay the bill?

The Commission on Americans Outdoors

When Ronald Reagan assumed office in January 1981, his administration began to cut back substantially on federal funds for outdoor recreation. The government still made payments into the Land and Water Conservation Fund, in accordance with legislation, but appropriations out of the fund lagged greatly. As a result, a surplus accumulated in this fund. The existence of this unappropriated surplus greatly irked recreation and conservation leaders, especially because it developed at a time when funds for outdoor recreation management were insufficient to meet the aspirations of such leaders. The Reagan administration also cut back funds for acquisition of private inholdings in national parks and other federal areas. More-over, it abolished the Heritage Conservation and Recreation Service, transferred its functions to the National Park Service, cut back its funds and person-nel, and greatly reduced the federal effort in outdoor recreation.

A general feeling that outdoor recreation was being reduced by the federal government led several con-servation and recreation leaders to consider a differ-ent approach. After some informal discussions, a self-selected group was established, with Laurance Rocke-feller as honorary chairman and Henry Diamond, who had been employed by the ORRRC, as operating chair-man (Outdoor Recreation Policy Review Group, 1983). The group solicited statements from specialists in out-door recreation and published a report. The group considered changes since the 1962 ORRRC report and recommended that a new commission be autho-rized by Congress to reconsider and update the ORRRC report. Although this recommendation was accepted by the Department of the Interior and by the presi-dent and a proposal was made to Congress, action was stalled primarily by members of Congress who were opposed to giving President Reagan the power to appoint civilian members to a new commission. Nevertheless, a President's Commission on Americans Outdoors (PCAO) was appointed by Executive Order (President's Commission on Americans Outdoors, 1987).

The President's Commission on Americans Out-doors in the 1980s was in some respects similar to the ORRRC and in other ways quite different. For example, the ORRRC had a larger budget and more time to prepare its report (four years compared with one year). In addition, the PCAO held conferences, public hearings, and symposia around the country, enlisting the attendance and participation of literally thousands of people, whereas the ORRRC worked almost exclusively with its own staff, its formal con-sultants, and its contractors. Some of this difference in method of operation may have reflected the per-sonalities of the respective chairs, but in considerable part it also reflected the much greater emphasis on public participation than was true around 1960.

In many respects, the PCAO report was conven-tional: it included a review of demand for recreation, including such demand factors as population, income, race, and leisure; a review of areas available for out-door recreation, but with more emphasis on private areas than there was in earlier reports; discussion of

the roles of governments at various levels; and an especially strong and cogent argument for better data and more research. A number of technical reports were commissioned from experts on outdoor rec-reation, and their findings were included in the final report. A special feature of the PCAO was the exten-sive and highly competent literature review. In the 1958–1962 period of ORRRC activity, there was not much literature to review; in the 1980s there was a great deal.

Nonetheless, the PCAO report displayed an exhor-tatory rather than analytical orientation, probably the result of the PCAO's strategy of relying heavily on public participation. As is often the case, the public meetings held by the PCAO tended to bring out ad-vocates of more public outdoor recreation rather than a representative cross-section of public opinion. In-deed, the PCAO saw increased advocacy as a weapon for assuring the future adequacy of recreation re-sources and opportunities: "The best way to assure that Americans will have adequate outdoor recreation opportunities is through a prairie fire of concern and investment, community by community" (President's Commission on Americans Outdoors, 1987).

The declining growth in use of the federal recre-ation areas was acknowledged but did not receive prominent attention in the report. In fact, the idea that the pressure on recreation resources was easing was soundly rejected: "While this [decline in growth rate] might be taken as a sign that demand and rec-reation supply are approaching balance, that is em-phatically not the case. Increasing interest in outdoor recreation opportunities close to home, where avail-able resources and facilities are perceived as crowded already, especially on weekends, complicates the problem" (President's Commission on Americans Outdoors, 1987, p. 23).

The PCAO's recommendations for funding sources to increase local recreational opportunities were in some ways conventional. As others had been doing for some time, it recommended greater reliance on recreation participants themselves through higher en-try fees and equipment taxes resembling the Pittman-Robertson funding mechanism (see chapter 6). If im-plemented, this recommendation would amount to an important shift in the funding of public outdoor recreation, which generally has involved substantial payments out of general public revenues. In 1982, the expenditures per capita were about equal for the federal government and for all state governments; but combined, they were less than half of the amounts spent by county and city governments. User charges raised nearly one-quarter of the operating costs for state parks and recreation areas and about one-sixth for local areas, but much less for federal areas. Because so many federal areas are available without charge, the average user charge for federal areas was only 39 cents per visitor day in 1983. The funds raised by such entry fees are not earmarked for recreation but go into the general fund; this may account for the historic lack of interest in recreation entry fees on the part of park managers. However, the PCAO was emphatic that such revenues should be dedicated to recreation uses. The PCAO also recognized the importance of private providers of recreational opportunities and recommended the investigation of more effective incentives for private recreation supply. Special attention was sought for the problem of increased landowner liability, which was seen to be a particular barrier to greater use of private land for recreation.

Where the PCAO broke new ground and entered a highly controversial policy field was in its recommendations for $1 billion or more in annual federal appropriations and for the creation of an outdoor recreation trust fund, into which not only funds from the Land and Water Conservation Fund would flow but also other federal appropriations. Out of this trust fund expenditures could be made by government employees without going through the appropriation process. These funds then would be made available to local and state agencies, perhaps on a matching basis, for expansion of recreational facilities locally. The PCAO and supporters of these provisions were anxious to establish a reliable and dependable source of funds annually, free from the control of both Congress and the Office of Management and Budget.

It is precisely this freedom from control that leads many people, in Congress and outside Congress, to strongly oppose the creation of such a fund. Increased appropriations in this time of budget stringency are also hard to secure. Bills to implement the PCAO recommendations were introduced but had yet to be approved in either House or Senate by the end of 1990; if approved, they would likely face a presidential veto. Nevertheless, this part of the PCAO report has been strongly endorsed and pushed by a coalition of many organizations interested in outdoor recreation, with scarcely a mention of the major role of local government emphasized by the PCAO.

The Domestic Policy Council of the Reagan administration, after reviewing the PCAO report, decided to produce still another report, and to that end assembled a task force of officials from federal agencies concerned with recreation, including the Department of the Interior, the Corps of Engineers, the Council on Environmental Quality, the Department of Agriculture, and the Environmental Protection Agency (Task Force on Outdoor Recreation Resources, 1988). The report by this task force drew heavily on the studies commissioned by the PCAO, but differed from that report in tone and in that it was more analytical in its approach. Where the PCAO report conveyed a sense of urgency and a concern about deterioration, the task force report was congratulatory about what were seen as the superior accomplishments of the Reagan administration. This substantial difference in tone has perhaps obscured the extent to which the two studies reached similar conclusions. In view of the slowing growth in use of federal facilities, the task force apparently saw the main federal issue as being the improvement of coordination among federal agencies, especially at adjacent national forest and national park units, rather than the expansion of recreation supply. The task force report also came out strongly in favor of a greater reliance on fees at federal recreation sites. Such fees were promoted as rationing devices, as revenue raisers, and as a means of encouraging private provision of recreation opportunity, by eliminating "unfair competition." In addition, the task force report pointed out that fees at federal campsites did rise substantially between 1980 and 1983: 70 percent at the national parks, 55 percent at the national forests, and 39 percent at Corps of Engineers sites (during a period when the cost of living increased by 19 percent).

Like the PCAO, the task force placed special emphasis on the importance of local organizations, and the report supported those recommendations made by the PCAO for the encouragement of local and private provision of recreational opportunities. However, the task force parted company with the PCAO on the issue of funding; there is no mention whatsoever of the $1 billion annual appropriations and the trust fund. Both of these positions were consistent with the political philosophy of the Reagan administration.

Wilderness Areas Since 1970

Wilderness areas expanded greatly after 1970. Actual extensions could be made only by acts of Congress, and these were frequently slow in coming because of opposition from other public land users. However, large areas were considered or under study by the agencies, and the courts ruled that these could not be used in any way that would jeopardize their wilderness character should they later be established as wilderness areas. Thus commercial developments were prohibited in these wilderness study areas, even if the restrictions lacked the permanence of congressional authorization. Popular support for wilderness grew rapidly and strongly, even among people who never had used and never expected to use any wilderness area. Moreover, popular concepts of wilderness changed: many attractive but heavily used areas that Leopold would have scorned as wilderness came to be called just that.

The acreage set aside for wilderness by executive order or by legislation has increased greatly, especially in the past fifteen years. The first wilderness area in national forests was established in 1924, by order of the chief forester. Revised regulations involving orders by the secretary of agriculture became effective in 1930. The early areas considered for wilderness designation in the national forests were ca-

tegorized as "primitive," "wilderness," "wild," or "roadless." By far, the greatest area was in the "primitive" category. From 1930 to 1974, the acreage of land in these four categories in national forests varied around 14 million acres, increasing slightly as new areas were added and decreasing slightly as some areas were excluded, and in no year reaching 15 million acres. With the passage of the Wilderness Act of 1964, nearly all these areas were included in the wilderness system and were designated as "wilderness." After 1974, wilderness area in the national forests increased rapidly, more than doubling by 1984.

The acreage of wilderness area outside of the national forests also increased rapidly as a result of the 1964 act. Some of the newly designated areas, as in national parks, had always enjoyed a considerable degree of protection from commercial development, but their designation under law gave them added protection. By the end of 1988, more than 90 million acres had formally been designated by law as wilderness (table 7-3). This is an area nearly equal to that of the state of California, and well over twice the area of Iowa. Almost two-thirds of the total was in Alaska, with the rest in the lower forty-eight states. In Alaska, the national park system had by the far the largest area, followed by the U.S. Fish and Wildlife Service, with only 10 percent in national forests. In the lower forty-eight states, more than three-fourths of the total area of designated wilderness was in national forest, with lesser acreages in the national park system. Some of the areas were in the East and, in past decades, had been developed by timber harvest or farming, but the land generally had reverted to trees and something of the original wilderness character had been restored.

In addition to areas designated by law as wilderness, large areas also have been under study or are included in legislative proposals not yet approved. Some of these areas ultimately will be legislatively designated as wilderness, but some will not, in part because of opposition to wilderness extension and demands for other uses. From the point of view of commercial interests, the areas under study are seen as de facto wilderness; from the point of view of the wilderness advocates, they are not firmly protected as wilderness.

The ultimate extent of the National Wilderness Preservation System depends on standards accepted for degree of human intrusion and for minimum acreage per area. The original Forest Service standard of 100,000

Table 7-3. Designated Wilderness Areas, the Lower Forty-eight States and Alaska, by Agency, Late 1988

Agency	Units	Millions of acres	Percentage of total
National Wilderness Preservation System			
Forest Service	354	32.5	36
National Park Service	41	38.5	42
Fish and Wildlife Service	71	19.3	21
Bureau of Land Management	25	.5	1
Total	491	90.8	100
National Wilderness Preservation System, excluding Alaska			
Forest Service	340	27.1	79
National Park Service	33	6.1	18
Fish and Wildlife Service	50	.7	2
Bureau of Land Management	25	.5	1
Subtotal	448	34.4	100
National Wilderness Preservation System in Alaska			
Forest Service	14	5.5	10
National Park Service	8	32.4	57
Fish and Wildlife Service	21	18.7	33
Subtotal	43	56.5	100

Source: U.S. Forest Service data.

Note: Acreage reported in table 7-3 excludes millions of acres of land in the national parks that meet the criteria of wilderness but have not been so designated by the Park Service. Acreage totals may not add because of rounding.

acres per unit has long since been abandoned. Some observers believe that standards of naturalness or of minimum human intrusion also have been changed. Sooner or later expansion of the National Wilderness Preservation System will end because all acceptable areas will have been included. Some supporters of wilderness have argued that land can be taken out of the wilderness designation if the need for its other products so demands, but the likelihood of this on any substantial scale seems minimal. However, redesignation based on recreational demand may be possible. The intensive use of some areas of wilderness may suggest that they be given a primitive or even less stringent classification so that they can be managed in a manner consistent with their use. However, such reclassification would require congressional sanction, a formidable obstacle.

The designation, by executive order or by legislation, of some tract of land as "wilderness" did not actually create wilderness. The areas had always had a wilderness character. That some large area (ex-

ceeding 5,000 acres) was roadless in the later twentieth century was ample evidence that little or no commercial development had occurred within the area and that the prospects for such development were poor. Most of the current wilderness areas had been open to prospecting and mineral development, grazing domestic livestock, and commercial hunting and trapping since the days of earliest exploration of the West. It may be reasonably assumed that all present wilderness areas had been combed over thoroughly, with methods then available, for their possible mineral value and that no promising deposits had been found. This does not mean, of course, that modern exploration methods may not find valuable minerals where the early prospectors could not. Most of these areas, at one time or another, had been available for timber harvest but were not harvested because they could not compete with other national forest sites that had greater accessibility or lower harvesting costs. All the areas, at one time or another, had been open for grazing, and some wilderness areas have continued to be available for grazing of domestic livestock. What the designation by executive order or by legislation did accomplish was to preclude *future* commercial development of these areas—to preserve as much of their natural wilderness character as still existed at the date of designation. Following passage of the Wild and Scenic Rivers Act of 1968, the mileage

of rivers and streams so designated rose rapidly. Again the legislation did not create such rivers; the rivers existed, and the legislation gave legal authority to efforts to maintain their wild and scenic character and limit their use for other purposes.

Have outdoor recreation and wilderness designation acted to increase or to reduce the extent or the quality of wilderness lands? On the one hand, setting land and water areas aside for these purposes has precluded commercial development for mining, oil development, timber harvest, and other commercial uses, and to this extent it can be argued that wilderness has been maintained, and even enhanced. By definition commercial development destroys wilderness; whether it also reduces environmental quality depends on the character and scale of the development as well as one's definition of the "environmental quality." Some, but not all, commercial development does indeed reduce environmental quality by any definition, sometimes drastically so, as with an open pit mine.

On the other hand, establishing areas for outdoor recreation, such as campgrounds, surely also reduces the "naturalness" of the areas directly involved. This may be true to some extent even for an area designated as wilderness, because such designation may well increase its use and thereby reduce its natural wilderness character. For many users of wilderness, the degree of use may itself be perceived as a degradation of environmental quality, even in the absence of noticeable physical effects. Indeed, surveys of wilderness users frequently have shown that one of the major factors affecting the quality of the experience is the number of other groups encountered

Establishing areas for outdoor recreation, such as campgrounds, surely also reduces the "naturalness" of the areas directly involved.

(Krutilla, 1972). Thus the impacts of outdoor recreation, including wilderness use, may be more psychological than physical. Moreover, they may be more apparent and greater to the environmental purist or elitist than they are to the ordinary recreationist. Of course, these considerations hardly apply to areas developed for more intensive recreational use, where recreation participants expect to find other users and where the construction of facilities such as latrines and electrical hookups are regarded by many as environmental improvements.

Future Use and Management Issues

During the twentieth century, the role of outdoor recreation in the United States has expanded vastly. Visits to the national park system and the national forests have shown a sustained and, indeed, dramatic upward sweep, from fewer than 250,000 visits in 1910 to more than 300 million visits currently. Comparable growth has been experienced at the state parks since 1940, when the first reliable aggregate data became available. Few economic or social trends show such a rapid and persistent upward trend as do these visits. These figures refer only to public outdoor recreation. Data on similar trends in recreational use of privately owned land are unavailable, but the growth of such use is likely to have been equally rapid and continuous.

Although the rate of growth in recreation has been remarkable, it is nonetheless true that the growth rate in every decade since 1900 has not been quite as fast as the one before. That is, the rate of increase has consistently declined, but the use itself has not. Since the 1980s, visits to the national park system have not been expanding any faster than the rate of population growth. Most of the growth in visits to the national park system has been in the nonnational park units, especially the urban parks. Essentially the same pattern is evident at other major aggregations of recreation sites, including the national forests and (collectively) the state parks. Although data on estimated trends on use of local recreation facilities are unavailable, some evidence suggests that local areas have not experienced this slowdown in use. This evidence includes the rising importance of bicycling, jogging, and other fitness activities in the past two decades. Currently, according to the best available (but still not very good) data, more than half of all recreation visits are to local parks and other sites maintained by local governments. State parks and private land each provide about 15 to 20 percent. Only about 13 percent of visits are to federal land.

Despite this record of sustained growth, ample capacity exists in the United States to meet any reasonable expectations of future outdoor recreation demand, if the costs are acceptable. The area of land now dedicated to outdoor recreation is not large compared with the area devoted to residences or commercial activities in urban locations or to the area given over to farming and forestry in rural regions. However, in rural regions especially, the land available for recreation jointly with other land uses is truly vast. Much of this land is federally owned, especially in the West, but private farmland and timberland also provide considerable recreational opportunities. This is not to say that conflicts do not exist and will not arise—a look at the past dispels any illusions on that score. The costs may seem high, especially in times of tight governmental budgets, but the physical possibilities are ample.

The recent fundamental changes in patterns of recreational use has prompted a reassessment of important issues of recreation policy: Who is to provide opportunities for recreation, who should pay, and in particular what is the federal role? The recent reports of the President's Commission on Americans Outdoors and the task force on Outdoor Recreation Resources and Opportunities can be viewed as initial efforts to discuss these issues, especially the federal role. This reassessment could be as significant as the ORRRC assessment was a generation ago. To be successful, however, the assessment must show a better understanding of the causes of the relative shift away from recreational use of federal and state areas.

The cause of this relative shift away from the use of federal and state areas is not well understood. There are several potential explanations, not mutually exclusive. One is that people have shifted their outdoor recreation to other kinds of areas, notably to private facilities developed during these years. If data on use of private areas suitable for the same kinds of outdoor recreation were available, some measure of the shift might be possible. Moreover, people have shifted their recreation from outdoors to indoors, notably to tele-

vision, where they can watch sports and cultural events at home. Closely similar to this is a shift toward outdoor recreation closer to home—jogging and running, golf, and tennis.

Another view is that popular federal and state outdoor recreation areas have become so crowded, so dirty, so deteriorated, and so unattractive that more and more people have reduced their use of these areas. Although this situation may seem paradoxical, it is nonetheless true that budget cuts during the early 1980s did force closings or the shortening of seasons or daily hours at some federal sites and also may have reduced the attractiveness of some sites. On the other hand, the sites experiencing the greatest slowdown in growth tend to be the remote, uncrowded sites. Possibly of more significance than congestion at recreation sites is the greater difficulty in getting to the sites. The past growth in recreation use at federal sites has closely tracked the decrease in the real price of travel; the only time when recreation use fell substantially was during World War II, when travel was severely curtailed. Since the early 1970s, travel times on rural interstates apparently have increased, in part because of increased congestion and, for most of the period, the 55-mile-per-hour speed limit.

In addition, some demographic and social factors have worked against outdoor recreation in more distant areas. The greater participation of women in the labor force has meant that the coordination of vacations necessary for a family trip to a distant national park or national forest may impose a problem. In addition, the population is aging, and an aging population demands less outdoor recreation. Finally, it is likely that Americans as a whole, with their tastes and incomes determined by social and economic factors, have approximately reached satiety in recent years for the kinds and locations of outdoor recreation and the seasons of use provided by the federal and state systems. As a group, they seem to have all of this kind of recreation they want, and further increases in per capita recreation attendance will be small or nonexistent. For a long time, park managers and recreation specialists believed that usage of such areas would continue to grow at more or less past rates. The likelihood of ultimate satiety was recognized, but the time of its arrival was considered uncertain (Clawson and Knetsch, 1966). It now appears that the old assumption about continued growth is wrong and probably will not apply in the future.

A better grasp of the relative importance of these reasons (and perhaps others) for the decline is essential in determining the appropriate policy or management response. If the principal cause of the leveling out of visits is satiety, for example, then the management implications are much different from what they would be if the principal reason is dirty or crowded

It now appears that the old assumption about continued growth is wrong and probably will not apply in the future.

sites. Whatever the explanation, the unmistakable relative shift away from federal and state recreation areas is of fundamental importance for future management of such areas, and it is of fundamental policy importance as well.

About twenty-five years ago, Clawson and Knetsch (1966) categorized recreation sites as either resource-based or user-based. Resource-based sites offer unique or low-density recreational opportunities, such as wilderness, natural wonders, or important historical sites. These sites produce recreation experiences of unusually high value for which there are no substitutes. The opportunities at user-based sites, in contrast, are common and support activities such as playground use, competitive sports, and swimming that do not depend on unusual site characteristics. Of course, both user-based and resource-based sites are pure types, endpoints on a scale of site substitutability. It is nonetheless a useful way of thinking about the qualities of recreation sites, especially when considering the role of various levels of government in providing opportunities for recreation.

Local governments remain the most important provider in terms of visitation, mainly supporting user-based recreational activities. The federal government is the most important provider of resource-based recreation opportunity. State recreation sites typically fall somewhere between these two extremes. Private-sector provision of recreation can run the gamut from user-based to resource-based, especially if one is willing to call theme parks and ski areas resource-based recreation.

There is a certain economic rationale to the federal provision of resource-based recreation; the proper role of the federal government in outdoor recreation, most observers agree, should be limited to those sites of national interest, such as the "crown jewels" of the national park system and the more important wilderness areas. Truly, residents of the eastern United States have a legitimate interest in matters concerning areas such as Yellowstone or the Grand Canyon. However, numerous federal recreation areas are scarcely distinguishable in their function and attractiveness from state or local sites. The provision of wilderness (meaning areas closed by law to commercial development) is by a public, usually federal, agency. However, private nonprofit organizations such as The Nature Conservancy have for many years been purchasing scenic and ecologically valuable land, some of which it has turned over to the federal government to manage and some which it continues to manage itself. Such land probably is as protected from commercial development as any federal wilderness.

Both the PCAO and the task force of the Domestic Policy Council advocate decentralization of responsibility in the provision of recreation. If the growth in recreation demand is now primarily local, as recent trends suggest, then the best way to meet the demand is through local providers—that is, local government and private landowners. That, at any rate, is the message of the reports of these groups; although the message is more explicit in the task force report. These sentiments, however, apply mainly to increments to recreation capacity. Undoubtedly the federal government will continue to play a major role in the provision of opportunities for outdoor recreation. Nonetheless, neither the PCAO nor the task force envisions major additions to the federal recreation estate.

One special aspect of the growing interest in decentralization is the effect government actions have on private suppliers of outdoor recreation—a problem especially that concerned the task force. It would be desirable to have a greater role for private people and organizations in the supply of outdoor recreational opportunities. Some states have passed laws relieving private property owners of legal liability to recreationists if no fee or charge is made. Although this may help to reduce liability in some instances, it removes any financial incentive for resource owners to provide or allow outdoor recreation on their properties. Having low entrance fees or none at all for public areas and public facilities results in difficult competition for private parties trying to make a profit from the provision of similar opportunities. Rhetoric about the desirability of increased private provision of outdoor recreational opportunities is often negated by specific managerial decisions about public areas.

Judging from the growing number of states resorting to subsidization of private landowners to preserve wildlife habitat or allow recreational use, it appears that wildlife authorities generally regard subsidization as effective. However, even in those instances where the subsidy appears to be successful, it is often difficult to determine whether landowners are engaging in the desired behavior because of the subsidy. Perhaps such actions would have been undertaken regardless of the subsidy.

Although interested parties seem to agree that future additions to recreation capacity will be locally owned and operated, that does not necessarily mean they will be locally financed. It is on this issue that the PCAO and the task force of the Domestic Policy Council disagree. The PCAO came out strongly for federal funding, calling for the creation of a trust fund—expansion of the Land and Water Conservation Fund—that would provide $1 billion in grants per year. This fund, furthermore, would be insulated from the vagaries of the budget process. It would be used to make grants to the states and localities, perhaps on a matching basis, to expand recreation facilities. Legislation to expand the Land and Water Conservation Fund in this fashion has now been introduced in Congress, but not yet acted upon (Siehl, 1988). In contrast, the task force took the position that the funding, like operation, should be left to the local authorities as well.

These issues are unlikely to be resolved until a better understanding is obtained of the recent leveling out of recreation use of federal sites—especially its causes and whether it is likely to continue. Such an understanding will require research and, quite possibly, time so that more data can be collected. Regardless of whether future demand remains stagnant or resumes its historical climb, recreation will remain one of the most important and valuable uses of renewable resources.

Notes

We would like to thank Sarah Bales and Sari Radin for their outstanding research assistance.

Appendix 7

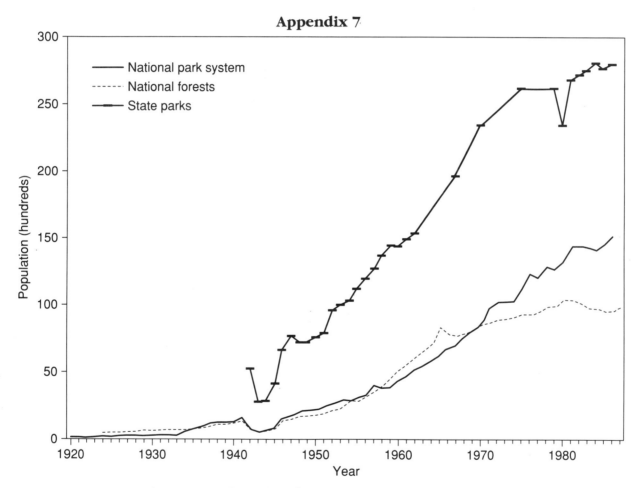

Figure 7–A1. Visits to outdoor recreation areas, 1920 to 1987

References

Barnes, Harry Elmer. 1942. *Social Institutions*. New York: Prentice-Hall.

Brightbill, C. K. 1961. *Man and Leisure: A Philosophy of Recreation*. New York: Prentice Hall.

Brower, David, ed. 1960. *The Meaning of Wilderness to Science*. San Francisco: Sierra Club.

Brown, William G., Ajmer Singh, and Emery N. Castle. 1964. *An Economic Evaluation of the Oregon Salmon and Steelhead Sport Fishery*. Technical bulletin no. 78. Corvallis, Oreg.: Agricultural Experiment Station, Oregon State University.

Butcher, Devereux. 1951. *Exploring Our National Parks and Monuments*. Washington, D.C.: National Parks Association.

Butler, George D. 1959. *Introduction to Community Recreation*. 3d ed. New York: McGraw-Hill Book Co.

Chapin, Frederick. 1987. *Mountaineering in Colorado—The Peaks about Estes Park*. Lincoln, Nebr.: University of Nebraska Press (originally published in 1889 by the Appalachian Mountain Club).

Clawson, Marion. 1959. "Methods of Measuring Demand for and Value of Outdoor Recreation," Reprint no. 10. Washington, D.C.: Resources for the Future.

————. 1983. *The Federal Lands Revisited*. Washington, D.C.: Resources for the Future.

Clawson, Marion, and R. Burnell Held. 1957. *The Federal Lands—Their Use and Management*. Baltimore, Md.: The Johns Hopkins University Press for Resources for the Future.

Clawson, Marion, R. Burnell Held, and Charles H. Stoddard. 1960. *Land for the Future*. Baltimore, Md.: The Johns Hopkins University Press for Resources for the Future.

Clawson, Marion, and Jack L. Knetsch. 1966. *Economics of Outdoor Recreation*. Baltimore, Md.: The Johns Hopkins University Press for Resources for the Future.

Clawson, Marion, and Carlton Van Doren, eds. 1984. *Statistics on Outdoor Recreation, 1984*. Washington, D.C.: Resources for the Future.

Cordell, H. Ken. 1989. "A Methodology for Assessing Outdoor Recreation Demand and Supply Trends in the United States." Mimeographed.

Cordell, H. Ken, and John C. Hendee. 1982. *Renewable Resources Recreation in the United States: Supply, Demand, and Critical Policy Issues*. Washington, D.C.: American Forestry Association.

Culhane, Paul J. 1981. *Public Lands Politics—Interest Group Influence on the Forest Service and the Bureau of Land Management*. Baltimore, Md.: The Johns Hopkins University Press for Resources for the Future.

Dana, Samuel Trask. 1956. *Forest and Range Policy—Its Development in the United States*. New York: McGraw-Hill Book Co.

Dana, Samuel Trask, and Sally K. Fairfax. 1980. *Forest and Range Policy—Its Development in the United States*. 2d ed. New York: McGraw-Hill Book Co.

Dulles, Foster Rhea. 1940. *America Learns to Play*. New York: D. Appleton-Century.

Everhart, William C. 1972. *The National Park Service*. New York: Praeger Publishers.

Foresta, Ronald A. 1984. *America's National Parks and Their Keepers*. Washington, D.C.: Resources for the Future.

Gulick, Luther Halsey. 1920. *A Philosophy of Play*. New York: Charles Scribner's Sons.

Hays, Samuel P. 1959. *Conservation and the Gospel of Efficiency—The Progressive Conservation Movement 1890–1920*. Cambridge, Mass.: Harvard University Press.

Idaho Law Review. 1980. Vol. 16, no. 3 (Summer). This issue has nine articles on wilderness. All are informative, some on attitudes of supporters as well as upon wilderness areas and laws. The article by Stephen H. Spurr is particularly informative.

Ise, John. 1961. *Our National Park Policy: A Critical History*. Baltimore, Md.: The Johns Hopkins University Press for Resources for the Future.

Krutilla, John V., ed. 1972. *Natural Environments: Studies in Theoretical and Applied Analysis*. Baltimore, Md.: The Johns Hopkins University Press for Resources for the Future.

Meyer, Harold D., and Charles K. Brightbill. 1956. *Community Recreation—A Guide to Its Organization*. 2d ed. Boston: D. C. Heath & Co.

Morris, Edmund. 1979. *The Rise of Theodore Roosevelt*. New York: Coward, McCann & Geoghegan.

Muir, John, ed. 1976. *West of the Rocky Mountains*. Philadelphia, Pa.: Running Press.

Nash, Roderick. 1967. *Wilderness and the American Mind*. New Haven, Conn.: Yale University Press.

National Geographic Society. 1959. *America's Wonderlands: The National Parks*. Washington, D.C.: National Geographic Society.

Neumeyer, Martin H., and Esther Neumeyer. 1958. *Leisure and Recreation*. New York: A. S. Barnes and Co.

Outdoor Recreation Policy Review Group. 1983. *Outdoor Recreation for America, 1983*. Washington, D.C.: Resources for the Future.

Outdoor Recreation Resources Review Commission. 1962a. *Federal Agencies and Outdoor Recreation*. Study report no. 13. Washington, D.C.: GPO.

————. 1962b. *Outdoor Recreation for America*. Washington, D.C.: GPO.

————. 1962c. *Prospective Demand for Outdoor Recreation*. Study report no. 26. Washington, D.C.: GPO.

Pack, Arthur N. 1934. *The Challenge of Leisure*. New York: Macmillan Co.

Pinchot, Gifford. 1947. *Breaking New Ground*. New York: Harcourt, Brace and Co.

President's Commission on Americans Outdoors. 1987. *The Report*. Four vols.: *Case Studies, Study Papers*, and *Reports*, and *A Literature Review*. Washington, D.C.: GPO.

Romney, G. Ott. 1945. *Off the Job Living—A Modern Concept of Recreation and Its Place in the Postwar World*. New York: A.S. Barnes and Co.

Roper, Laura Wood. 1973. *FLO—A Biography of Frederick Law Olmsted*. Baltimore, Md.: The Johns Hopkins University Press.

Sapora, Allen V., and Elmer D. Mitchell. 1961. *The Theory of Play and Recreation*. New York: Ronald Press.

Schullery, Paul. 1987. *American Fly Fishing—A History*. New York: American Museum of Fly Fishing.

Siehl, George H. 1988. "Developments in Outdoor Recreation Policy Since 1970." In *Outdoor Recreation Benchmark 1988: Proceedings of the National Outdoor Recreation Forum*, edited by Alan H. Watson, 10–21. Tampa, Fl.

Steiner, Jesse Frederick. 1933. *American at Play*. New York: McGraw-Hill Book Co.

Stevens, Lawrence N. 1983. "ORRRC Revisited." In *Outdoor Recreation for America, 1983*, Appendix B, issued by the Outdoor Recreation Policy Review Group. Washington, D.C.: Resources for the Future.

Task Force on Outdoor Recreation Resources and Opportunities. 1988. *Outdoor Recreation in a Nation of Communities*. A report to the Domestic Policy Council. Washington, D.C.: GPO.

Tilden, Freeman. 1951. *The National Parks: What They Mean to You and Me*. New York: Alfred A. Knopf.

————. 1962 *The State Parks: Their Meaning in American Life*. New York: Alfred A. Knopf.

U.S. Congress. Senate. Committee on Interior and Insular Affairs. 1974. *The Recreation Imperative—A Draft of the Nationwide Outdoor Recreation Plan Prepared by the Department of the Interior*. 93 Cong., 2 sess. Committee Print.

U.S. Department of Agriculture, Forest Service. 1957. *Operation Outdoors—Part I, National Forest Recreation*. Washington, D.C.

————. 1988. *An Analysis of the Outdoor Recreation and Wilderness Situation in the United States: 1988–2040*. Washington, D.C.

U.S. Department of Commerce, Bureau of the Census. 1975. *Historical Statistics of the United States, Colonial Times to 1970*. Washington, D.C.: GPO.

U.S. Department of the Interior, Bureau of Outdoor Recreation. 1973. *Outdoor Recreation: A Legacy for America*. Washington, D.C.: GPO.

U.S. Department of Interior, Heritage Conservation and Recreation Service. 1979. *The Third Nationwide Outdoor Recreation Plan: The Executive Report and the Assessment*. Washington, D.C.: GPO.

U.S. Department of the Interior, Heritage Conservation and Recreation Service, and National Park Service. 1978. *National Recreation Urban Recreation Study*. Washington, D.C.: GPO.

Wood, Jim. 1985. *Proceedings of the 1985 National Outdoor Recreation Trends Symposium II*. Vol. 1: *General Sessions*; vol. 2: *Concurrent Sessions*. Clemson, S.C.: Clemson University, Department of Parks, Recreation and Tourist Management.

About the authors

Marion Clawson is a senior fellow emeritus at Resources for the Future, and a former director of the Bureau of Land Management of the U.S. Department of the Interior. With RFF since 1955, he has been director of RFF's land-use management studies, acting president of RFF, and vice president of RFF. He is the author of the RFF book *The Federal Lands Revisited* and coauthor of *Statistics on Outdoor Recreation*.

Pierre R. Crosson is a senior fellow in the Energy and Natural Resources Division at Resources for the Future. With RFF since 1965, he was formerly an economist with the Bank of America, the Tennessee Valley Authority, and the U.S. Bureau of Mines. He is coauthor of the RFF book *Productivity Effects of Cropland Erosion in the United States*.

Kenneth D. Frederick is a senior fellow in the Energy and Natural Resources Division at Resources for the Future. With RFF since 1971, he was director of RFF's former Renewable Resources Division, an economist with the U.S. Agency for International Development, and an assistant professor of economics at the California Institute of Technology. He is the author of the RFF book *Water for Western Agriculture*, and the editor of *Scarce Water and Institutional Change*. He is a member of the Water Science and Technology Board of the National Research Council.

B. Delworth Gardner is professor of economics at Brigham Young University. He has been professor of agricultural economics and director of the Giannini Foundation at the University of California, professor and head of the Department of Economics at Utah State University, and a visiting scholar at Resources for the Future. He has chaired the Committee on Rangeland Management for the Board of Agriculture of the National Academy of Sciences, and has published widely in the areas of range, water, and agricultural economics.

Winston Harrington is a senior fellow in the Quality of the Environment Division at Resources for the Future. During the 1990–1991 academic year he was visiting professor of economics at the University of California at Santa Barbara. With RFF since 1980, he is coauthor of the RFF books *Enforcing Pollution Control Laws, Measuring Recreation Supply*, and *Economics and Episodic Disease: The Benefits of Preventing a Giardiasis Outbreak*.

Roger A. Sedjo is a senior fellow in the Energy and Natural Resources Division at Resources for the Future. With RFF since 1977, he is director of RFF's Forest Economics and Policy Program, and a former economist with the U.S. Agency for International Development. He is coauthor of the RFF book *The Long-Term Adequacy of World Timber Supply*, and author of *Investments in Forestry, Land Use and Public Policy* (Westview Press) and *Global Forests: Issues for Six Billion People* (McGraw-Hill).

PHOTO CREDITS

Photos not credited here are credited on the page on which the photo appears.

Forest Service Collection, USDA/NAL: photos on pages 3, 6, 9, 16, 22, 29, 30, 32, 36, 38, 83, 86, 89, 93, 97, 98, 101, 104, 110, 122, 133, 136, 139, 141, 156, 160, 168, 178, 181, 192, 211, 218, 225, 227, 229, 233, 239, 268.

National Park Service: photos on pages 11, 28, 42, 59, 65, 69, 222, 253, 255, 257, 260, 264, 267, 270, 273, 277.

U.S. Department of Agriculture: photos on pages 50, 127, 131, 195, 197, 199, 210, 221, 224, and facing page 1.

Index